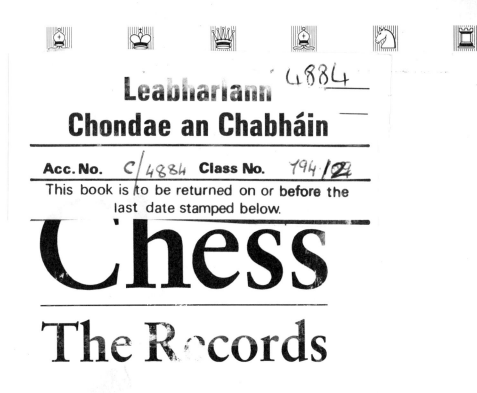

Leabharlann
Chondae an Chabháin

4884

Acc. No. C/4884 Class No. 794/2

This book is to be returned on or before the
last date stamped below.

Chess

The Records

Ken Whyld

Cavan County Library
Withdrawn Stock

D0308905

GUINNESS BOOKS

leabaid ṁid
ċonnḋaé ċaḃain

Acc. No. C 4884
Class No. 794.12
Invoice No. 145
Received ₤ 7.95

EDITOR: Honor Head
DESIGN AND LAYOUT: Michael Morey

© Ken Whyld and Guinness Superlatives Ltd, 1986

Published in Great Britain by Guinness Superlatives Ltd,
33 London Road, Enfield, Middlesex

All rights reserved. No part of this publication may be reproduced,
stored in a retrieval system, or transmitted in any form or by any means,
electronic, mechanical, photocopying, recording or otherwise, without
prior permission in writing of the publisher.

Type set in Sabon
by DP Press Ltd., Sevenoaks, Kent
Printed and bound in Great Britain by
R. J. Acford Ltd, Chichester, Sussex

'Guinness' is a registered trade mark of Guinness Publishing Ltd

British Library Cataloguing in Publication Data
Whyld, Kenneth
Guinness chess, the records.
1. Chess—Records
I. Title
794.1'09   GV1318
ISBN 0−85112−455−0 Pbk

Ken Whyld was the editor of *Chess Students' Quarterly* in the early 1950s and from 1955 – 63, *Chess Reader*, in which he reviewed more than 500 chess books. He has written seven tournament books and one match book. With J. Gilchrist he wrote a three-volume anthology of Lasker's games, and with David Hooper *The Oxford Companion to Chess*. For the book *World Chess Champions* he wrote the chapters on Lasker and Smyslov. In his playing days he was champion of his county many times and played in the British Championship as well as international tournaments.

Withdrawn Stock
Cavan County Library

Introduction

Chess – The Records breaks new ground. The vast increase in chess activity over the last ten or so years has made it even harder to find the kind of information which is packed into this volume.

The main focus is on champions at all levels, as by doing this rather than looking only at the world's best players, a global picture emerges. Perhaps winning some titles demands less skill than finishing last in the USSR championship (by needing to qualify to play in it), but even so it is at the time the ultimate achievement open to the winner.

Biographical details are given for all players in the championship lists or in a leading position in one of the featured tournaments. For the foremost players of the last century-and-a-half a deeper study is given.

There are no chess events barred to women on sex grounds, but a number exclude men. Some women avoid the latter kind, so women's championships may not contain the strongest eligible players.

The author's thanks are due to Bernard Cafferty, Pat Constant, Carl-Eric Erlandsson, Martyn Griffiths, David Hooper, Craig Pritchett, Leonard Reitstein, Rob Verhoeven, and Jim Walsh. Above all the co-operation of one person made the comprehensiveness of this book possible. About twenty years ago Jeremy Gaige of Philadelphia found that chess archives were virtually non-existent. Since then he has devoted his life to rectifying the situation. He now has details of more than 10,000 tournaments and 20,000 chess personalia and is an indispensable resource.

CONTENTS

Glossary *6*

Milestones *7*

World Championships *11*

Individual *12*/Candidates *15*/Women *22*/Junior & Junior Women *25*/Amateur *28*/
Under-16 *28*/World Team *28*/Olympiad *29*/Women's Olympiad *32*/Youth Team *34*/
Correspondence *34*/Telex Olympiad *34*/Blind *34*/Oscar *35*/Problems *35*/
Computer *35*

International Tournaments *37*

International Tournaments *37*/USSR v Rest of World *80*/EEC Team Championship
81/European Cup *81*/European Team Championship *81*/European Junior
Championship *82*/Commonwealth Championship *82*/Nordic Championship *83*/
Mitropa Cup *84*/Balkaniad *84*/Clare Benedict Tournaments *84*/Asian
Championships *84*/Cable Matches *84*

National & City Championships *87*

Argentine *87*/Australian *88*/Austrian *88*/Brazilian *89*/British *89*/Bulgarian *94*/
Canadian *95*/Chilean *96*/Cuban *96*/Czechoslovakian *96*/Danish *97*/Estonian *98*/
Finnish *98*/French *99*/Pre-War German *99*/West German *101*/East German *101*/
Hungarian *102*/Icelandic *102*/Irish *103*/Israeli *104*/Italian *104*/Latvian *104*/
Leningrad *105*/London *105*/Moscow *106*/Netherlands *107*/New Zealand *108*/
Norwegian *108*/Polish *110*/Romanian *110*/Scottish *111*/South African *114*/Spanish
114/Swedish *115*/Swiss *116*/USA *117*/USSR *117*/Welsh *121*/Yugoslav *121*

The Records *123*

The Players *128*

Clash of Kings

France v GB, 1834 *21*/France v GB, 1843 *26*/Morphy *36*/Steinitz & Zukertort *53*/
Lasker & Tarrasch *67*/Capablanca *100*/Alekhine & Euwe *109*/Botvinnik
& Smyslov *120*/Tal *137*/Petrosyan & Korchnoi *145*/Fischer & Spassky *153*/
Karpov & Kasparov *165*

Index *172*

GLOSSARY

Explanation of terms and abbreviations

All-play-all (**or a-p-a**) a tournament in which every player meets every other player (see also Swiss and Knock-out).

Candidate One who qualifies to compete in an event to find a Challenger.

Challenger One who plays against a world champion for the title.

Elo, or **Elo rating** An estimate of playing skill based on performance over a sufficient number of games. It is named after Professor Elo, who provided the statistical basis. Twice a year FIDE issues a list of Elo ratings for the leading players.

FIDE Acronym for *Fédération internationale des échecs*, the body that co-ordinates international chess.

Fifty-move rule If fifty moves by both players have elapsed without a capture or a pawn move the player whose turn it is may claim a draw (there are a few exceptions). For calculating theoretical records, such as the longest possible game, it is assumed that such a claim would always be made. See also Repetition.

Knock-out As in other games and sports. Often based on more than one game. See also All-play-all and Swiss.

Rating, see **Elo.**

Repetition If the same position arises for the third time, with the same player to move, that player may claim a draw. The other player must claim before making the move that will create repetition. For record purposes it is assumed that such a claim must be made if valid. See Fifty-move rule.

Swiss, or **Swiss system** A way of enabling large numbers to play in short tournaments with the advantage, lacking in a knock-out, that everyone has a full programme. Players with like scores meet, provided they have not played each other before. There are many refinements to meet various needs, such as balancing the number of times a player has black or white men for example. The Swiss system finds the best and worst, the ones in the middle being only crudely ordered because of the vagaries of pairing. The same number of rounds are needed as in a knock-out to find with accuracy the best performer, and roughly two further rounds for each extra place.

Milestones

An idea of the way chess has developed can be formed from these key dates and facts.

AD 600 The first positive reference to chess (in a Persian romance). Nobody knows who invented the game, but it is believed to have come from the Punjab in the 6th century. The first form of chess has some differences from today's. The most striking are the lack of queen and bishop in the early game. Instead there were the fers, which was moved only to its nearest diagonal square, and the alfil, which was moved only to its next but one square diagonally.

800 The Moors brought chess to Spain. At about the same time the game reached Sicily, along with the Islamic invaders.

1000 Chess widespread in Europe. It reached Russia from Byzantium in the south and with Viking invaders from the north.

1300 The earliest writings were by monks who found in the game suitable material for allegorical sermons. We know from courtly literature that chess was as popular with knights and their ladies as it was with the clergy. It may well have had a popular following also. Some travelling entertainers included trick problems in their repertoires. They would set up a position and wager on its outcome, giving the punter the choice of side but taking first move. Naturally these positions could always be won by the side moving first.

1475 The queen and bishop were introduced. For some time both versions of chess – 'old' and 'mad queen' – existed side by side, but the dynamism of the new game soon won. However it was to be another four centuries before the rules were standardized in all details, castling and pawn promotion being the most troublesome.

1495 The first practical chess book printed (in Spain). The last known copy was destroyed in 1811. Another, by Lucena, published two years later, still survives in a handful of copies. Since then a further 20 000 titles have been printed (more than for any other game).

1600 Appearance of professional players who made their living by playing for stakes and writing manuscripts for rich patrons.

1700 Among the idle rich playing cards had taken the place of chess, and never again was it to be a popular game among the aristocracy. Coffee houses became the centre of chess activity and professionals played there for small sums. One who scraped such a living was Abraham de Moivre, a great mathematician but mediocre player.

1747 In London the Frenchman, Philidor, played a match against the Syrian, Stamma, who was to count drawn games as wins. Philidor won 8 – 2, and one of those two was a draw. Philidor, an operatic composer, was regarded as the best player in the world at that time, but he never met the leading Italians.

Engraving of Philidor.

1749 Philidor's book *L'analyze des échecs* published. The most important work to date, it was republished in various forms more than 100 times.

1769 The Turk appeared in Vienna. This apparent

The oldest chess photograph (1846), this also fetched the highest price for a 19th-century photograph (100,000 deutsch Marks). It was taken by Fox Talbot in the studio of Claudet (on the left). (Lacock Abbey Collection)

automaton chess-player baffled and delighted onlookers for 70 years. It was the first great cabinet illusion and contained a full-grown man.

1780s Atwood systematically recorded the moves of games as they were played. He was the first to do this successfully. Caze, trying this a century earlier, found that the players objected.

1783 Philidor gave the first of his displays playing three games simultaneously without sight of the board. Wrongly thought to be unprecedented, the achievement was attested by a notary. Today hundreds of players could match that number, and thousands can play through a single game without sight of the board.

1795 Philidor died. Perhaps Verdoni, Sarratt and Deschapelles were the strongest players over the next 30 years.

1804 The first documented game played by regular post. It was between players in Breda and The Hague.

1811 Third edition of Allgaier's book (in German) (first edition appeared in 1795) giving openings in tabular form, for the first time anywhere.

1813 First newspaper chess column, in *Liverpool Mercury*.

1824 – 8 Correspondence match between London and Edinburgh. Edinburgh won 2 games and lost 1, the remaining 2 being drawn. The London players sulked when they were not allowed to take back a hasty move. The games were reported in newspapers and followed by the public with great interest.

1834 McDonnell and Bourdonnais played six matches in London, a total of 85 highly acclaimed games. Chess fever spread.

1836 The first chess magazine, *Le Palamède*, launched by Bourdonnais in France.

1840 Penny post led to a boom in postal chess.

1841 Formation of first regional union, the Yorkshire Chess Association. The rush of railway building made away matches feasible. Staunton brought out *Chess Player's Chronicle* in London.

1843 St Amant-Staunton match in Paris. After his win (11 to 6, with 4 draws) many of Staunton's admirers considered him the world's best but others attached less importance to it.

1843 – 5 The defeat of Paris in a correspondence match against Budapest signalled the end of France's world supremacy. London took the lead.

1844 First electric telegraph match, between Washington, DC, and Baltimore.

1845 First American chess column in *The Spirit of the Times*. The 'Indian' problem, published in *CPC*, heralded the emergence of composition as an art form independent of the game.

1846 *Deutsche Schachzeitung*, the oldest magazine still in existence. It did not appear 1945 – 9. In America two magazines, *Chess Palladium & Mathematical Sphinx*, and *American Chess Monthly*, came out, both short-lived.

1849 First fully-documented tournament. Played in London, it was won by noted historian Henry Thomas Buckle.

1851 During the Great Exhibition in London the world's first international tournament took place, largely due to Staunton's efforts. He played indifferently and the German school teacher Anderssen won, being regarded as the leading player as a result.

1857 The Chess Association formed, the first national body in Great Britain.

1857 – 8 Morphy appeared and in six months played 51 competitive games against first class opposition establishing himself as undisputed top of the chess world. His modest demeanour, not always found in great players, endeared him to all. Chess fever broke out. Then Morphy withdrew from the

Anderssen.

chess world, never to play again in public.

1859 First Russian magazine, *Shakhmatny Listok*.

1861 Anderssen-Kolisch match the first with timed moves (by sandglass). Liverpool-Dublin match the first by submarine cable.

1866 Anderssen-Steinitz match the first with moves timed by mechanical clocks.

1871 First county match in England (Yorkshire-Lancashire).

1876 At New York tournament the brilliancy prize was introduced.

1877 German national body (*DSB*) formed. Taking over from England, Germany became the leading nation around this time, and remained so for about half a century.

1878 First match by telephone, in Derbyshire.

1881 *British Chess Magazine* began, the oldest existing magazine to have appeared without a break.

1884 The Scottish Chess Association founded and,

like another product of that country, is 'still going strong'. Morphy died.

1886 Steinitz beat Zukertort ($+10=5-5$) in what was accepted, for the first time, as a world championship match.

1887 London Chess League formed (then named Metropolitan Chess Club Competition).

1892 Southern Counties Chess Union.

1894 Lasker beat Steinitz to become world champion, but Tarrasch, with a string of tournament successes, was thought by many to be the better player. Time provided the answer.

1897 Midland Counties Chess Union.

1899 Northern Counties Chess Union.

1902 First radio match, between ships in the Atlantic.

1904 British Chess Federation founded. It co-ordinates chess in England, but not Scotland, nor, since 1971, Wales.

1908 At last the Lasker-Tarrasch match for the world championship, but the holder won easily enough ($+8=5-3$).

1918 British Chess Problem Society.

1921 Young, popular, Capablanca won the world championship from aging, out-of-favour, Lasker.

1924 Formation of world chess body, FIDE (*Fédération internationale des échecs*).

1927 On his first defence of the title the invincible Capablanca lost to Alekhine. FIDE ran the first world championship for national teams of four, later to be known as chess Olympiads, and a women's competition for world championship.

1928 International association for correspondence chess, IFSB (*Internationaler Fernschach Bund*).

1935 Over-confident Alekhine shocked by loss of title to Euwe. However he had thoughtfully included a return-match clause.

1937 A more sober approach by Alekhine brought back the title. In Edinburgh the Belgian (later American) player Koltanowski played 34 games at the same time, blindfold. He won 24 and drew the other ten. More recent claims for greater numbers have not been fully convincing.

1945 USA-USSR radio match on 3 September the first international sporting event of any kind after the end of the war.

1946 Alekhine died giving FIDE the opportunity to seize control of the world title.

1947 West of England Chess Union.

1948 Uniquely, a tournament for the world

championship. The winner, Botvinnik, inaugurated a 24-year spell of Soviet domination which tended to kill popular interest.

1950 Titles introduced by FIDE – International Grandmaster (IGM, or more often GM), and International Master (IM).

1950 – 3 First world championship by correspondence (final).

1951 World junior championship, for under-20s.

1952 Liverpool hosted the first international tournament for students. Subsequently it became a team event, and in 1978 it was renamed World Youth Team Championship (for under-26s).

1953 Titles of Grandmaster of Correspondence Chess and International Master of Correspondence Chess instituted, based on results of the first championship.

1954 Welsh Chess Union.

1957 Women's Olympiad. European team championship.

1958 A computer played chess.

1959 Title of International Master for Chess Composition.

1967 Chess Oscar.

1971 European junior championship.

1972 Fischer won world championship from current Soviet holder Spassky (now a French citizen). The combination of brilliant chess and prima donna theatre seized world attention. Another outbreak of chess fever. Title of Grandmaster for Chess Composition first awarded.

1975 The American genius Fischer dismayed the chess world, east and west, by not defending his title. He has not played seriously since then.

1976 Chess playing computer for home use.

1977 World cadet championship for under-17s (after 1980, under-16s). Telechess Olympiad.

1978 Title introduced, below IM, of FIDE Master (FM).

1982 World under-20 championship for women.

1983 East Anglian Chess Union.

1985 World team tournament (in addition to Olympiads). Computerized championship in Britain for primary school players, using computer terminals and Ceefax. For the first time a match for the world championship abandoned. In the replay Kasparov defeated Karpov to become the youngest-ever champion.

1986 World championship played in England for first time.

Cruikshank's satirical cartoon 'Game of Chess' (1819). (Author)

World Championships

Before the title of World Champion came into use various players, notably Philidor, Bourdonnais, Staunton and Anderssen, were thought to be the strongest of their day, but only in the case of Morphy, and that for a brief period, was there unanimity. After defeating Anderssen in 1866 Steinitz gradually overcame all of his rivals, at the same time creating modern chess. He changed it from a game to a science.

After Morphy's death in 1884 it was possible to run a world championship match without anyone denying the winner's claim to the title, and this happened in 1886.

Although almost every national championship is fought afresh each year the world title can be won only by defeating the holder in a match. Until FIDE assumed control of the event there was no fixed cycle of competition and the holder could choose his own challenger, or ignore all of them. To some extent popular opinion ensured that worthy candidates were able to command the necessary financial support.

At one time there was pressure for a world title based on tournament results. Currently there is interest in the idea of a world grand prix title based on results in previously nominated tournaments. Until FIDE took control of the world championship title in 1948 the question of determining who should be able to challenge the reigning champion to a title match was largely determined by the ability to find financial backers.

Under FIDE a cycle of three-yearly eliminating contests was introduced, throwing forward a number of candidates from whom the challenger

was to come. For the first five cycles the candidates met in a tournament, with a play-off if needed. Because there were so many Soviet candidates it was suggested that they could help each other by blocking out dangerous aliens, and so for the next seven cycles the candidates met in a series of knock-out matches to determine the challenger. From 1985 the system was changed to a two-yearly cycle ending with a tournament for candidates from which the leading four play a series of knock-out matches.

World Championship totals

	Matches	Games	W	D	L	%
Lasker	7	102	45	42	15	64.7
Fischer	1	21	7	11	3	59.5
Alekhine	5	140	43	73	24	56.8
Reshevsky	1	20	6	9	5	52.5
Keres	1	20	8	5	7	52.5
Karpov	4	122	20	87	15	52.0
Smyslov	4	89	24	44	21	51.7
Petrosyan	3	69	13	45	11	51.4
Botvinnik	8	177	46	90	41	51.4
Capablanca	2	48	7	35	6	51.0
Bronstein	1	24	5	14	5	50.0
Kasparov	2	72	8	56	8	50.0
Schlechter	1	10	1	8	1	50.0
Steinitz	6	115	43	29	43	50.0
Tal	2	40	11	17	12	48.8
Spassky	3	68	12	41	15	47.8
Korchnoi	2	50	7	31	12	45.0
Gunsberg	1	19	4	9	6	44.7
Chigorin	2	40	14	6	20	42.5
Bogoljubow	2	51	8	24	19	39.2
Euwe	3	75	14	30	31	38.7
Zukertort	1	20	5	5	10	37.5
Tarrasch	1	16	3	5	8	34.4
Marshall	1	15	0	7	8	23.3
Janowsky	1	11	0	3	8	13.6

These figures include the 1948 match-tournament.

Chigorin.

Individual World Championship Matches

11 January – 29 March 1886 *New York, St Louis and New Orleans*

Steinitz
1 0 0 0 0 1 1 ½ 1 ½ 1 1 0 ½ ½ 1 ½ 1 1 1 **12½**
Zukertort
0 1 1 1 1 0 0 ½ 0 ½ 0 0 1 ½ ½ 0 ½ 0 0 0 **7½**

20 January–4 February 1889 *Havana*

Steinitz
0 1 0 1 1 0 0 1 1 1 0 1 0 1 1 1 ½ **10½**
Chigorin
1 0 1 0 0 1 1 0 0 0 1 0 1 0 0 0 ½ **6½**

9 December 1890–22 January 1891 *New York*

Steinitz
½ 1 ½ 0 0 1 1 ½ ½ 1 ½ 0 1 ½ ½ 0 ½ 1 ½ **10½**
Gunsberg
½ 0 ½ 1 1 0 0 ½ ½ 0 ½ 1 0 ½ ½ 1 ½ 0 ½ **8½**

2 January–28 February 1892 *Havana*

Steinitz
0 ½ ½ 1 ½ 1 0 0 ½ 0 1 0 1 1 0 1 0 1 0 1 ½ 1 1
12½
Chigorin
1 ½ ½ 0 ½ 0 1 1 ½ 1 0 1 0 0 1 0 1 0 1 0 ½ 0 0
10½

15 March–26 May 1894 *New York, Philadelphia and Montreal*

Steinitz
0 1 0 1 ½ ½ 0 0 0 0 0 ½ 1 1 0 0 1 ½ 0 **7**
Lasker
1 0 1 0 ½ ½ 1 1 1 1 1 ½ 0 0 1 1 0 ½ 1 **12**

7 November 1896–14 January 1897 *Moscow*

Lasker
1 1 1 1 ½ 1 ½ ½ ½ 1 1 0 0 1 ½ 1 1 **12½**
Steinitz
0 0 0 0 ½ 0 ½ ½ ½ 0 0 1 1 0 ½ 0 0 **4½**

26 January–8 April 1907 *New York, Philadelphia, Memphis, Chicago and Baltimore*

Lasker
1 1 1 ½ ½ ½ ½ 1 ½ ½ ½ 1 1 1 1 **11½**
Marshall
0 0 0 ½ ½ ½ ½ 0 ½ ½ ½ 0 0 0 0 **3½**

17 August–30 September 1908 *Düsseldorf and Munich*

Lasker
1 1 0 1 1 ½ 1 ½ ½ 0 1 0 1 ½ ½ 1 **10½**
Tarrasch
0 0 1 0 0 ½ 0 ½ ½ 1 0 1 0 ½ ½ 0 **5½**

7 January–10 February 1910 *Vienna and Berlin*

Lasker
½ ½ ½ ½ 0 ½ ½ ½ ½ 1 5
Schlechter
½ ½ ½ ½ 1 ½ ½ ½ ½ 0 5

8 November–8 December 1910 *Berlin*

Lasker
1 ½ ½ 1 1 ½ 1 1 1 1 1 **9½**
Janowsky
0 ½ ½ 0 0 ½ 0 0 0 0 0 **1½**

15 March – 28 April 1921 *Havana*

Lasker
$\frac{1}{2}$ $\frac{1}{2}$ $\frac{1}{2}$ $\frac{1}{2}$ 0 $\frac{1}{2}$ $\frac{1}{2}$ $\frac{1}{2}$ $\frac{1}{2}$ 0 0 $\frac{1}{2}$ $\frac{1}{2}$ 0 5

Capablanca
$\frac{1}{2}$ $\frac{1}{2}$ $\frac{1}{2}$ $\frac{1}{2}$ 1 $\frac{1}{2}$ $\frac{1}{2}$ $\frac{1}{2}$ $\frac{1}{2}$ 1 1 $\frac{1}{2}$ $\frac{1}{2}$ 1 9

16 September – 29 November 1927 *Buenos Aires*

Capablanca
0 $\frac{1}{2}$ 1 $\frac{1}{2}$ $\frac{1}{2}$ $\frac{1}{2}$ 1 $\frac{1}{2}$ $\frac{1}{2}$ 0 0 $\frac{1}{2}$ $\frac{1}{2}$ $\frac{1}{2}$ $\frac{1}{2}$ $\frac{1}{2}$ $\frac{1}{2}$ $\frac{1}{2}$ $\frac{1}{2}$ 0 $\frac{1}{2}$ $\frac{1}{2}$ $\frac{1}{2}$ $\frac{1}{2}$ $\frac{1}{2}$ $\frac{1}{2}$ 1 1 $\frac{1}{2}$ $\frac{1}{2}$ 0 $\frac{1}{2}$ 0 15$\frac{1}{2}$

Alekhine
1 $\frac{1}{2}$ 0 $\frac{1}{2}$ $\frac{1}{2}$ $\frac{1}{2}$ 0 $\frac{1}{2}$ $\frac{1}{2}$ 1 1 $\frac{1}{2}$ $\frac{1}{2}$ $\frac{1}{2}$ $\frac{1}{2}$ $\frac{1}{2}$ $\frac{1}{2}$ $\frac{1}{2}$ $\frac{1}{2}$ 1 $\frac{1}{2}$ $\frac{1}{2}$ $\frac{1}{2}$ $\frac{1}{2}$ $\frac{1}{2}$ $\frac{1}{2}$ 0 $\frac{1}{2}$ $\frac{1}{2}$ 1 $\frac{1}{2}$ 1 18$\frac{1}{2}$

6 September – 12 November 1929 *Germany and Holland*

Alekhine
1 $\frac{1}{2}$ $\frac{1}{2}$ 0 1 0 1 1 $\frac{1}{2}$ 1 $\frac{1}{2}$ 1 0 0 $\frac{1}{2}$ 1 1 0 1 $\frac{1}{2}$ 1 1 $\frac{1}{2}$ $\frac{1}{2}$ $\frac{1}{2}$ 15$\frac{1}{2}$

Bogoljubow
0 $\frac{1}{2}$ $\frac{1}{2}$ 1 0 1 0 0 $\frac{1}{2}$ 0 $\frac{1}{2}$ 0 1 1 $\frac{1}{2}$ 0 0 1 0 $\frac{1}{2}$ 0 0 $\frac{1}{2}$ $\frac{1}{2}$ $\frac{1}{2}$ 9$\frac{1}{2}$

1 April – 14 June 1934 *Germany*

Alekhine
$\frac{1}{2}$ 1 $\frac{1}{2}$ 1 $\frac{1}{2}$ $\frac{1}{2}$ $\frac{1}{2}$ $\frac{1}{2}$ 1 0 1 $\frac{1}{2}$ $\frac{1}{2}$ $\frac{1}{2}$ $\frac{1}{2}$ 1 1 $\frac{1}{2}$ $\frac{1}{2}$ $\frac{1}{2}$ 1 $\frac{1}{2}$ 0 0 1 $\frac{1}{2}$ 15$\frac{1}{2}$

Bogoljubow
$\frac{1}{2}$ 0 $\frac{1}{2}$ 0 $\frac{1}{2}$ $\frac{1}{2}$ $\frac{1}{2}$ $\frac{1}{2}$ 0 1 0 $\frac{1}{2}$ $\frac{1}{2}$ $\frac{1}{2}$ $\frac{1}{2}$ 0 0 $\frac{1}{2}$ $\frac{1}{2}$ $\frac{1}{2}$ 0 $\frac{1}{2}$ 1 1 0 $\frac{1}{2}$ 10$\frac{1}{2}$

3 October – 15 December 1935 *Holland*

Alekhine
1 0 1 1 $\frac{1}{2}$ $\frac{1}{2}$ 1 0 1 0 $\frac{1}{2}$ 0 $\frac{1}{2}$ 0 $\frac{1}{2}$ 1 $\frac{1}{2}$ $\frac{1}{2}$ 1 0 0 $\frac{1}{2}$ $\frac{1}{2}$ $\frac{1}{2}$ 0 0 1 $\frac{1}{2}$ $\frac{1}{2}$ $\frac{1}{2}$ 14$\frac{1}{2}$

Euwe
0 1 0 0 $\frac{1}{2}$ $\frac{1}{2}$ 0 1 0 1 $\frac{1}{2}$ 1 $\frac{1}{2}$ 1 $\frac{1}{2}$ 1 0 $\frac{1}{2}$ $\frac{1}{2}$ 0 1 1 $\frac{1}{2}$ $\frac{1}{2}$ $\frac{1}{2}$ 1 1 0 $\frac{1}{2}$ $\frac{1}{2}$ $\frac{1}{2}$ 15$\frac{1}{2}$

5 October – 16 December 1937 *Holland*

Euwe
1 0 $\frac{1}{2}$ $\frac{1}{2}$ 1 0 0 0 $\frac{1}{2}$ 0 $\frac{1}{2}$ $\frac{1}{2}$ 1 0 $\frac{1}{2}$ $\frac{1}{2}$ 1 1 $\frac{1}{2}$ $\frac{1}{2}$ 1 0 0 $\frac{1}{2}$ 0 0 9$\frac{1}{2}$

Alekhine
0 1 $\frac{1}{2}$ $\frac{1}{2}$ 0 1 1 1 $\frac{1}{2}$ 1 $\frac{1}{2}$ $\frac{1}{2}$ 0 1 $\frac{1}{2}$ $\frac{1}{2}$ 0 0 $\frac{1}{2}$ $\frac{1}{2}$ 0 1 1 $\frac{1}{2}$ 1 1 15$\frac{1}{2}$

15 March – 11 May 1951 *Moscow*

Botvinnik
$\frac{1}{2}$ $\frac{1}{2}$ $\frac{1}{2}$ $\frac{1}{2}$ 0 1 1 $\frac{1}{2}$ $\frac{1}{2}$ $\frac{1}{2}$ 0 1 $\frac{1}{2}$ $\frac{1}{2}$ $\frac{1}{2}$ $\frac{1}{2}$ 0 $\frac{1}{2}$ 1 $\frac{1}{2}$ 0 0 1 $\frac{1}{2}$ 12

Bronstein
$\frac{1}{2}$ $\frac{1}{2}$ $\frac{1}{2}$ $\frac{1}{2}$ 1 0 0 $\frac{1}{2}$ $\frac{1}{2}$ $\frac{1}{2}$ 1 0 $\frac{1}{2}$ $\frac{1}{2}$ $\frac{1}{2}$ $\frac{1}{2}$ 1 $\frac{1}{2}$ 0 $\frac{1}{2}$ 1 1 0 $\frac{1}{2}$ 12

16 March – 13 May 1954 *Moscow*

Botvinnik
1 1 $\frac{1}{2}$ 1 $\frac{1}{2}$ $\frac{1}{2}$ 0 $\frac{1}{2}$ 0 0 0 1 1 0 1 1 $\frac{1}{2}$ $\frac{1}{2}$ $\frac{1}{2}$ 0 $\frac{1}{2}$ $\frac{1}{2}$ 0 $\frac{1}{2}$ 12

Smyslov
0 0 $\frac{1}{2}$ 0 $\frac{1}{2}$ $\frac{1}{2}$ 1 $\frac{1}{2}$ 1 1 1 0 0 1 0 0 $\frac{1}{2}$ $\frac{1}{2}$ $\frac{1}{2}$ 1 $\frac{1}{2}$ $\frac{1}{2}$ 1 $\frac{1}{2}$ 12

5 March – 27 April 1957 *Moscow*

Botvinnik
0 $\frac{1}{2}$ $\frac{1}{2}$ 1 1 0 $\frac{1}{2}$ 0 $\frac{1}{2}$ $\frac{1}{2}$ $\frac{1}{2}$ 0 1 $\frac{1}{2}$ $\frac{1}{2}$ $\frac{1}{2}$ 0 $\frac{1}{2}$ $\frac{1}{2}$ 0 $\frac{1}{2}$ $\frac{1}{2}$ 9$\frac{1}{2}$

Smyslov
1 $\frac{1}{2}$ $\frac{1}{2}$ 0 0 1 $\frac{1}{2}$ 1 $\frac{1}{2}$ $\frac{1}{2}$ $\frac{1}{2}$ $\frac{1}{2}$ 1 0 $\frac{1}{2}$ $\frac{1}{2}$ $\frac{1}{2}$ 1 $\frac{1}{2}$ 1 $\frac{1}{2}$ $\frac{1}{2}$ 12$\frac{1}{2}$

4 March – 9 May 1958 *Moscow*

Smyslov
0 0 0 $\frac{1}{2}$ 1 0 $\frac{1}{2}$ $\frac{1}{2}$ $\frac{1}{2}$ $\frac{1}{2}$ 1 0 $\frac{1}{2}$ 0 1 $\frac{1}{2}$ $\frac{1}{2}$ 0 1 $\frac{1}{2}$ $\frac{1}{2}$ 1 $\frac{1}{2}$ 10$\frac{1}{2}$

Botvinnik
1 1 1 $\frac{1}{2}$ 0 1 $\frac{1}{2}$ $\frac{1}{2}$ $\frac{1}{2}$ $\frac{1}{2}$ 0 1 $\frac{1}{2}$ 1 0 $\frac{1}{2}$ $\frac{1}{2}$ 1 0 $\frac{1}{2}$ $\frac{1}{2}$ 0 $\frac{1}{2}$ 12$\frac{1}{2}$

2 April – 16 May 1948 *The Hague and Moscow* *

		Botvinnik	Smyslov	Keres	Reshevsky	Euwe	
1	Botvinnik	♛	$\frac{1}{2}$ $\frac{1}{2}$ 1 $\frac{1}{2}$ $\frac{1}{2}$	11110	1 $\frac{1}{2}$ 011	1 $\frac{1}{2}$ 1 $\frac{1}{2}$ $\frac{1}{2}$	14
2	Smyslov	$\frac{1}{2}$ $\frac{1}{2}$ 0 $\frac{1}{2}$ $\frac{1}{2}$	♛	00 $\frac{1}{2}$ 1 $\frac{1}{2}$	$\frac{1}{2}$ $\frac{1}{2}$ 1 1 $\frac{1}{2}$	11011	11
3	Keres	00001	11 $\frac{1}{2}$ 0 $\frac{1}{2}$	♛	0 $\frac{1}{2}$ 10 $\frac{1}{2}$	1 $\frac{1}{2}$ 111	10$\frac{1}{2}$
4	Reshevsky	0 $\frac{1}{2}$ 100	$\frac{1}{2}$ $\frac{1}{2}$ 0 $\frac{1}{2}$ $\frac{1}{2}$	1 $\frac{1}{2}$ 01 $\frac{1}{2}$	♛	1 $\frac{1}{2}$ 11	10$\frac{1}{2}$
5	Euwe	0 $\frac{1}{2}$ 0 $\frac{1}{2}$ $\frac{1}{2}$	00100	0 $\frac{1}{2}$ 000	0 $\frac{1}{2}$ $\frac{1}{2}$ 00	♛	4

* A match-tournament to find a successor to Alekhine who died in 1946.

15 March–7 May 1960 *Moscow*

Botvinnik
0 ½ ½ ½ ½ 0 0 1 1 ½ 0 ½ ½ ½ ½ ½ 0 ½ 0 ½ ½ **8½**
Tal
1 ½ ½ ½ ½ 1 1 0 0 ½ 1 ½ ½ ½ ½ ½ 1 ½ 1 ½ ½ **12½**

15 March–12 May 1961 *Moscow*

Tal
0 1 0 ½ ½ ½ 0 1 0 0 0 1 0 ½ 0 ½ 1 0 1 ½ 0 **8**
Botvinnik
1 0 1 ½ ½ ½ 1 0 1 1 1 0 1 ½ 1 ½ 0 1 0 ½ 1 **13**

15 March–22 May 1963 *Moscow*

Botvinnik
1 ½ ½ ½ 0 ½ 0 ½ ½ ½ ½ ½ ½ 1 0 ½ ½ 0 0 ½ ½ ½ **9½**
Petrosyan
0 ½ ½ ½ 1 ½ 1 ½ ½ ½ ½ ½ ½ 0 1 ½ ½ 1 1 ½ ½ ½ **12½**

15 March–29 May 1966 *Moscow*

Petrosyan
½ ½ ½ ½ ½ ½ 1 ½ ½ 1 ½ ½ 0 ½ ½ ½ ½ ½ 0 1 ½ 1 0 ½
12½
Spassky
½ ½ ½ ½ ½ ½ 0 ½ ½ 0 ½ ½ 1 ½ ½ ½ ½ ½ 1 0 ½ 0 1 ½
11½

15 March–25 May 1969 *Moscow*

Petrosyan
1 ½ ½ 0 0 ½ ½ 0 ½ 1 1 ½ ½ ½ ½ ½ 0 ½ 0 1 0 ½ ½
10½
Spassky
0 ½ ½ 1 1 ½ ½ 1 ½ 0 0 ½ ½ ½ ½ ½ 1 ½ 1 0 1 ½ ½
12½

11 July–2 September 1972 *Reykjavik*

Spassky
1 1 0 ½ 0 0 ½ 0 ½ 0 1 ½ 0 ½ ½ ½ ½ ½ ½ ½ 0 **8½**
Fischer
0 0 1 ½ 1 1 ½ 1 ½ 1 0 ½ 1 ½ ½ ½ ½ ½ ½ ½ 1 **12½***

*Fischer lost the second game by default.

18 July–17 October 1978 *Baguio City*

Karpov
½ ½ ½ ½ ½ ½ ½ 1 ½ ½ 0 ½ 1 1 ½ ½ 1 ½ ½ ½ 0 ½ ½ ½
½ ½ 1 0 0 ½ 0 1 **16½**
Korchnoi
½ ½ ½ ½ ½ ½ ½ 0 ½ ½ 1 ½ 0 0 ½ ½ 0 ½ ½ ½ 1 ½ ½ ½
½ ½ 0 1 1 ½ 1 0 **15½**

1 October–20 November 1981 *Merano*

Karpov
1 1 ½ 1 ½ 0 ½ ½ 1 ½ ½ ½ 0 1 ½ ½ ½ 1 **11**
Korchnoi
0 0 ½ 0 ½ 1 ½ ½ 0 ½ ½ ½ 1 0 ½ ½ ½ 0 **7**

10 September 1984–15 February 1985 *Moscow*

Karpov
½ ½ 1 ½ ½ 1 1 ½ 1 ½ ½ ½ ½ ½ ½ ½ ½ ½ ½ ½ ½ ½ ½ ½ ½
½ 1 ½ ½ ½ ½ 0 ½ ½ ½ ½ ½ ½ ½ ½ ½ ½ ½ ½ ½ ½ 0 0 **25**
Kasparov
½ ½ 0 ½ ½ 0 0 ½ 0 ½ ½ ½ ½ ½ ½ ½ ½ ½ ½ ½ ½ ½ ½ ½ ½
½ 0 ½ ½ ½ ½ 1 ½ ½ ½ ½ ½ ½ ½ ½ ½ ½ ½ ½ ½ ½ 1 1 **23**
match abandoned

3 September–9 November 1985 *Moscow*

Karpov
0 ½ ½ 1 1 ½ ½ ½ ½ ½ 0 ½ ½ ½ ½ 0 ½ ½ 0 ½ ½ 1 ½ 0
11
Kasparov
1 ½ ½ 0 0 ½ ½ ½ ½ ½ 1 ½ ½ ½ ½ 1 ½ ½ 1 ½ ½ 0 ½ 1
13

Karpov in London (1984).
(City Syndication Ltd)

Candidates Competitions

Budapest *11 April–18 May 1950*

	1	2	3	4	5	6	7	8	9	10	Total
1 Boleslavsky	♛	½½	1½	½½	½½	1½	½½	11	½1	½1	12
2 Bronstein	½½	♛	01	½1	11	1½	01	½1	½½	1½	12
3 Smyslov	0½	10	♛	½½	1½	½1	01	½½	½1	½½	10
4 Keres	½½	½0	½½	♛	½½	10	1½	½½	½½	½1	9½
5 Najdorf	½½	00	0½	½½	♛	½½	½½	½½	11	½1	9
6 Kotov	0½	0½	½0	01	½½	♛	½1	1½	10	10	8½
7 Stahlberg	½½	10	10	0½	½½	½0	♛	½½	½½	½½	8
8 Flohr	00	½0	½½	½½	½½	0½	½½	♛	½½	01	7
9 Lilienthal	½0	½½	½0	½½	00	01	½½	½½	♛	10	7
10 Szabó	½0	0½	½½	½0	½0	01	½½	10	01	♛	7

Play-off

31 July–27 August 1950 *Moscow*

Bronstein
1 ½ ½ ½ ½ ½ 1 0 ½ ½ 0 ½ ½ 1 7½

Boleslavsky
0 ½ ½ ½ ½ ½ 0 1 ½ ½ 1 ½ ½ 0 6½

Neuhausen & Zurich *28 August–24 October 1953*

	1	2	3	4	5	6	7	8	9	10	11	12	13	14	15	Total
1 Smyslov	♛	½½	11	½1	½½	11	½½	½0	½½	½½	½½	½½	1½	11	1½	18
2 Bronstein	½½	♛	1½	11	½½	½0	½½	½½	1½	½½	½½	01	1½	½½	½½	16
3 Keres	00	0½	♛	½½	½1	½1	½½	½½	½½	0½	11	1½	½1	½½	11	16
4 Reshevsky	½0	00	½½	♛	½½	½½	½½	10	½½	½1	½1	1½	½1	11	1½	16
5 Petrosyan	½½	½½	½0	½½	♛	½½	0½	½½	00	½½	½½	11	½1	1½	11	15
6 Geller	00	½1	½0	½½	½½	♛	11	½0	01	½½	01	1½	½1	01	½½	14½
7 Najdorf	½½	½½	½½	½½	1½	00	♛	1½	1½	½0	½½	½½	½½	0½	11	14½
8 Kotov	½1	½½	½½	01	½½	½1	0½	♛	10	1½	00	10	1½	0½	01	14
9 Taimanov	½½	0½	½½	½½	11	10	0½	01	♛	10	½½	½½	½0	0½	11	14
10 Averbakh	½½	½½	1½	½0	½½	½½	½1	0½	01	♛	½½	½½	0½	11	00	13½
11 Boleslavsky	½½	½½	00	½0	½½	10	½½	11	½½	½½	♛	½0	½½	½1	½½	13½
12 Szabó	½½	10	0½	0½	00	0½	½½	01	½½	½½	½1	♛	1½	½½	1½	13
13 Gligorić	0½	0½	½0	½0	½0	½0	½½	0½	½1	1½	½½	0½	♛	½1	11	12½
14 Euwe	00	½½	½½	00	0½	10	1½	1½	1½	00	½0	½½	½0	♛	1½	11½
15 Stahlberg	0½	½½	00	0½	00	½½	00	10	00	11	½½	0½	00	0½	♛	8

Amsterdam & Leeuwarden *27 March–30 April 1956*

	1	2	3	4	5	6	7	8	9	10	Total
1 Smyslov	♛	½½	½1	11	½½	0½	½½	½1	1½	½1	11½
2 Keres	½½	♛	½1	½½	½½	½½	½½	½0	1½	1½	10
3 Bronstein	½0	½0	♛	½1	1½	½0	½½	1½	½½	½1	9½
4 Geller	00	½½	½0	♛	10	1½	½0	11	½1	1½	9½
5 Petrosyan	½½	½½	0½	01	♛	½½	½½	1½	½½	1½	9½
6 Spassky	1½	½½	½1	0½	½½	♛	0½	½½	½½	½1	9½
7 Szabó	½½	½½	½½	½1	½½	1½	♛	0½	½½	01	9½
8 Filip	½0	½1	0½	00	0½	½½	1½	♛	10	½1	8
9 Panno	0½	0½	½½	½0	½½	½½	½½	01	♛	1½	8
10 Pilnik	½0	0½	½0	0½	0½	½0	10	½0	0½	♛	5

Bled, Zagreb & Belgrade *6 September–31 October 1959*

	1	2	3	4	5	6	7	8	Total
1 Tal	♛	0010	½½½½	01½1	1111	1½11	111½	111½	20
2 Keres	1101	♛	0½½½	1½½0	0101	½½11	1110	1111	18½
3 Petrosyan	½½½½	1½½½	♛	½½0½	11½½	0½½1	100½	½11½	15½
4 Smyslov	10½0	0½½1	½½1½	♛	½½10	0½10	½1½1	½011	15
5 Fischer	0000	1010	00½½	½½01	♛	10½½	01½1	½1½1	12½
6 Gligorić	0½00	½½00	1½½0	1½01	01½½	♛	½½10	½1½½	12½
7 Olafsson	000½	0001	011½	½0½0	10½0	½½01	♛	00½1	10
8 Benko	000½	0000	½00½	½100	½0½0	½0½½	11½0	♛	8

Curacao *2 May–26 June 1962*

	1	2	3	4	5	6	7	8	Total
1 Petrosyan	♛	½½½½	½½½½	½1½½	½½11	½½1½	½11½	11½–	17½
2 Geller	½½½½	♛	½½½½	11½0	½½1½	½½½1	½11½	½11–	17
3 Keres	½½½½	½½½½	♛	0½1½	½½1½	1110	½11½	1½1–	17
4 Fischer	½0½½	00½1	1½0½	♛	010½	01½1	1½1½	½1½–	14
5 Korchnoi	½½00	½½0½	½½0½	101½	♛	½½½0	1111	10½–	13½
6 Benko	½½0½	½½½0	0001	10½0	½½½1	♛	011½	10½–	12
7 Filip	½00½	½00½	½00½	0½0½	0000	100½	♛	01½–	7
8 Tal	00½–	½00–	0½0–	½0½–	01½–	01½–	10½–	♛	7

Due to illness Tal withdrew after playing each competitor three times.

Candidates 1965, Quarter-finals

17–27 April *Moscow*

Geller	1 ½ 1 ½ 1 ½ ½ ½	5½
Smyslov	0 ½ 0 ½ 0 ½ ½ ½	2½

7–23 April *Riga*

Spassky	0 ½ 1 1 1 ½ ½ 0 ½ 1	6
Keres	1 ½ 0 0 0 ½ ½ 1 ½ 0	4

26 June–8 July *Bled*

Tal	½ 1 0 1 ½ ½ 1 1	5½
Portisch	½ 0 1 0 ½ ½ 0 0	2½

27 June–10 July *Bled*

Larsen	1 ½ ½ 1 1 ½ 0 1	5½
Ivkov	0 ½ ½ 0 0 ½ 1 0	2½

Semi-finals

26 May – 9 June

Spassky	½	1	½	½	½	1	½	1	5½
Geller	½	0	½	½	½	0	½	0	2½

23 July – 8 August *Bled*

Tal	0	1	½	½	0	1	½	½	½	1		5½
Larsen	1	0	½	½	1	0	½	½	½	0		4½

Final

1 – 26 November *Tbilisi*

Spassky	½	0	1	½	½	½	½	½	1	1	1	7
Tal	½	1	0	½	½	½	½	½	0	0	0	4

Candidates 1968, Quarter-finals

2 – 18 April *Sukhumi*

Spassky	½	1	½	1	½	1	½	½	5½
Geller	½	0	½	0	½	0	½	½	2½

20 April – 15 May *Belgrade*

Tal	0	½	½	½	½	1	1	½	1	5½
Gligorić	1	½	½	½	½	0	0	½	0	3½

5 – 24 May *Porec*

Larsen	½	1	1	0	½	½	0	½	½	1	5½
Portisch	½	0	0	1	½	½	1	½	½	0	4½

7 – 20 May *Amsterdam*

Korchnoi	½	1	½	1	½	1	½	½	5½
Reshevsky	½	0	½	0	½	0	½	½	2½

Semi-finals

26 June – 15 July *Moscow*

Korchnoi	½	½	½	1	1	0	½	½	½	½	5½
Tal	½	½	½	0	0	1	½	½	½	½	4½

5 – 20 July *Malmo*

Spassky	1	1	1	½	0	½	1	½	5½
Larsen	0	0	0	½	1	½	0	½	2½

Geller ponders his move during a simultaneous display in Budapest in 1983. (Judit Pálffy)

Final

6 – 26 September *Kiev*

Spassky	½	1	½	1	½	0	1	1	½	½	6½
Korchnoi	½	0	½	0	½	1	0	0	½	½	3½

Candidates 1971, Quarter-finals

13 May – 1 June *Las Palmas*

Larsen	1	0	½	1	½	1	½	0	1	5½
Uhlmann	0	1	½	0	½	0	½	1	0	3½

13 – 31 May *Moscow*

Korchnoi	1	½	½	0	1	½	1	1	5½
Geller	0	½	½	1	0	½	0	0	2½

13 – 23 May *Seville*

Petrosyan	½	½	½	½	½	½	1	4
Hübner	½	½	½	½	½	½	0	3

Hübner withdrew from the match because of noise. Petrosyan was rather deaf.

16 May–2 June *Vancouver*

Fischer	6
Taimanov	0

Semi-finals

4–28 July *Moscow*

Petrosyan	½ ½ ½ ½ ½ ½ ½ ½ 1 ½	5½
Korchnoi	½ ½ ½ ½ ½ ½ ½ ½ 0 ½	4½

6–25 July *Denver*

Fischer	6
Larsen	0

Final

30 September–26 October *Buenos Aires*

Fischer	1 0 ½ ½ ½ 1 1 1 1	6½
Petrosyan	0 1 ½ ½ ½ 0 0 0 0	2½

Candidates 1974, Quarter-finals

14–19 January *San Juan*

Spassky	½ ½ 1 1 ½ 1	4½
Byrne, R	½ ½ 0 0 ½ 0	1½

16 January–4 February *Moscow*

Karpov	½ ½ ½ 1 ½ 1 ½ 1	5½
Polugayevsky	½ ½ ½ 0 ½ 0 ½ 0	2½

16 January–13 February *Augusta*

Korchnoi	½ ½ ½ ½ 1 ½ 1 ½ ½ ½ ½ 0 1	7½
Mecking	½ ½ ½ ½ 0 ½ 0 ½ ½ ½ ½ 1 0	5½

18 January–17 February *Palma de Mallorca*

Petrosyan	½ ½ ½ ½ 1 ½ ½ ½ 1 0 ½ 0 1	7
Portisch	½ ½ ½ ½ 0 ½ ½ ½ 0 1 ½ 1 0	6

Semi-finals

12–24 April *Odessa*

Korchnoi	1 ½ 1 0 1	3½
Petrosyan	0 ½ 0 1 0	1½

Polugayevsky. (Reproduced by courtesy of B.T. Batsford)

12 April–10 May *Leningrad*

Karpov	0 ½ 1 ½ ½ 1 ½ ½ 1 ½ 1	7
Spassky	1 ½ 0 ½ ½ 0 ½ ½ 0 ½ 0	4

Final

16 September–22 November *Moscow*

Karpov	½ 1 ½ ½ ½ 1 ½ ½ ½ ½ ½ ½ ½ ½ ½ ½ 1 ½ 0 ½ 0 ½ ½ ½	12½
Korchnoi	½ 0 ½ ½ ½ 0 ½ ½ ½ ½ ½ ½ ½ ½ ½ ½ 0 ½ 1 ½ 1 ½ ½ ½	11½

Fischer did not defend his title and Karpov became world champion by default.

Candidates 1977, Quarter-finals

25 February–27 March *Rotterdam*

Portisch	1 ½ 0 1 ½ 1 0 1 ½ 1	6½
Larsen	0 ½ 1 0 ½ 0 1 0 ½ 0	3½

26 February–3 April *Luzern*

Polugayevsky	½ 1 ½ ½ ½ ½ ½ ½ ½ ½ ½ ½	6½
Mecking	½ 0 ½ ½ ½ ½ ½ ½ ½ ½ ½ ½	5½

27 February–3 April *Il Ciocco*

Korchnoi	½ ½ ½ ½ 0 1 ½ 1 ½ ½ ½ ½	6½
Petrosyan	½ ½ ½ ½ 1 0 ½ 0 ½ ½ ½ ½	5½

28 February–? April *Reykjavik*

Spassky	½ ½ 1 ½ ½ ½ ½ ½ ½ 0 ½ ½ ½ ½ 1 ½	8½
Hort	½ ½ 0 ½ ½ ½ ½ ½ ½ 1 ½ ½ ½ ½ 0 ½	7½

Semi-finals

1 July–6 August *Evian*

Korchnoi	1 1 1 ½ ½ 1 1 0 ½ ½ ½ ½ ½	8½
Polugayevsky	0 0 0 ½ ½ 0 0 1 ½ ½ ½ ½ ½	4½

3 July–19 August *Geneva*

Spassky	½ ½ 0 ½ 1 ½ ½ 0 1 ½ ½ ½ 1 1 ½	8½
Portisch	½ ½ 1 ½ 0 ½ ½ 1 0 ½ ½ ½ 0 0 ½	6½

Final

21 November–13 January 1978 *Belgrade*

Korchnoi	½ 1 1 ½ ½ ½ 1 1 ½ 1 0 0 0 0 ½ ½ 1 1	10½
Spassky	½ 0 0 ½ ½ ½ 0 0 ½ 0 1 1 1 1 ½ ½ 0 0	7½

Candidates 1980, Quarter-finals

8–23 March *Velden*

Korchnoi	½ ½ ½ ½ 1 ½ ½ ½ 1	5½
Petrosyan	½ ½ ½ ½ 0 ½ ½ ½ 0	3½

9 March–April *Alma Ata*

Polugayevsky	1 1 ½ ½ ½ ½ 1 ½	5½
Tal	0 0 ½ ½ ½ ½ 0 ½	2½

14 March–April *Bad Lauterberg*

Hübner	½ ½ 1 ½ 1 0 ½ ½ ½ ½	5½
Adorjan	½ ½ 0 ½ 0 1 ½ ½ ½ ½	4½

March–April *Mexico City*

Portisch	1 ½ ½ ½ ½ ½ ½ ½ 0 ½ ½ ½ ½ ½	7
Spassky	0 ½ ½ ½ ½ ½ ½ ½ 1 ½ ½ ½ ½ ½	7

Portisch was awarded the tie because his won game was with black pieces, Spassky's with white.

Semi-finals

July–August *Buenos Aires*

Korchnoi	½ ½ ½ 1 ½ 0 ½ 1 ½ ½ ½ 0 ½ 1	7½
Polugayevsky	½ ½ ½ 0 ½ 1 ½ 0 ½ ½ ½ 1 ½ 0	6½

August *Abano Terme*

Hübner	½ ½ ½ ½ ½ ½ ½ ½ 1 1 ½	6½
Portisch	½ ½ ½ ½ ½ ½ ½ ½ 0 0 ½	4½

Final

20 December–January 1981 *Merano*

Korchnoi	0 1 ½ 0 ½ ½ 1 1	4½
Hübner	1 0 ½ 1 ½ ½ 0 0	3½

Games 9 and 10 were begun, but Hübner withdrew from the match.

Candidates 1983, Quarter-finals

26 Feb–19 March *Moscow*

Kasparov	½ 1 ½ 0 1 ½ ½ 1 1	6
Belyavsky	½ 0 ½ 1 0 ½ ½ 0 0	3

Has Korchnoi seen a ghost?
(David Fowler)

24 March–20 April *Velden*

Smyslov	½ ½ ½ 1 ½ ½ ½ ½ 0 ½ ½ ½ ½ ½	7
Hübner	½ ½ ½ 0 ½ ½ ½ ½ 1 ½ ½ ½ ½ ½	7

The tie was decided by the spin of a roulette wheel.

25 March–18 April *Bad Kissingen*

Korchnoi	1 ½ 1 1 ½ ½ ½ 0 1	6
Portisch	0 ½ 0 0 ½ ½ ½ 1 0	3

4–26 April *Alicante*

Ribli	½ ½ ½ ½ 1 1 0 ½ ½ 1	6
Torre	½ ½ ½ ½ 0 0 1 ½ ½ 0	4

Semi-finals

21 November–16 December *London*

Kasparov	0 ½ ½ ½ ½ 1 1 ½ 1 ½ 1	7
Korchnoi	1 ½ ½ ½ ½ 0 0 ½ 0 ½ 0	4

22 November–17 December *London*

Smyslov	1 0 ½ ½ 1 ½ 1 ½ ½ ½ ½	6½
Ribli	0 1 ½ ½ 0 ½ 0 ½ ½ ½ ½	4½

Final

10 March–9 April 1984 *Vilnius*

Kasparov	½ ½ 1 1 ½ ½ ½ ½ 1 ½ ½ 1 ½	8½
Smyslov	½ ½ 0 0 ½ ½ ½ ½ 0 ½ ½ 0 ½	4½

Yusupov shows Kasparov how to do it. (Courtesy of B.T. Batsford)

Play-off for 4th place

2–8 December 1985 *Montpellier*

Timman	½ 1 ½ ½ 0 ½	3
Tal	½ 0 ½ ½ 1 ½	3

Timman awarded place on tournament tie-break.

Semi-finals

9–27 January 1986 *Minsk*

Sokolov	½ 1 1 1 ½ ½ ½ 1	6
Vaganyan	½ 0 0 0 ½ ½ ½ 0	2

16 January–3 February 1986 *Tilburg*

Yusupov	0 ½ ½ ½ 1 1 1 ½ 1	6
Timman	1 ½ ½ ½ 0 0 0 ½ 0	3

Montpellier *11 October–3 November 1985*

		1	*2*	*3*	*4*	*5*	*6*	*7*	*8*	*9*	*10*	*11*	*12*	*13*	*14*	*15*	*16*	***Total***
1	Yusupov	♛	0	1	½	½	1	½	½	½	½	½	½	1	½	1	½	9
2	Vaganyan	1	♛	½	0	½	0	½	½	½	½	½	1	½	1	1	1	9
3	Sokolov	0	½	♛	½	½	0	½	1	½	½	½	1	1	1	½	1	9
4	Timman	½	1	½	♛	½	1	½	½	½	1	1	0	½	½	½	0	8½
5	Tal	½	½	½	½	♛	½	½	½	1	0	½	½	1	1	½	½	8½
6	Spassky	0	1	1	0	½	♛	½	½	½	1	½	½	½	½	1	0	8
7	Belyavsky	½	½	½	½	½	½	♛	0	½	½	1	½	½	½	½	1	8
8	Smyslov	½	½	0	½	½	½	1	♛	½	½	½	½	½	½	0	1	7½
9	Chernin	½	½	½	½	0	½	½	½	♛	½	½	½	½	½	½	1	7½
10	Seirawan	½	½	½	0	1	0	½	½	½	♛	1	½	½	0	½	½	7
11	Short	½	½	½	0	½	½	0	½	½	0	♛	1	1	½	½	½	7
12	Portisch	½	0	0	1	½	½	½	½	½	½	0	♛	0	1	½	1	7
13	Ribli	0	½	0	½	0	½	½	½	½	½	0	1	♛	½	1	½	6½
14	Korchnoi	½	0	0	½	0	½	½	½	½	1	½	0	½	♛	1	½	6½
15	Nogueiras	0	0	½	½	½	0	½	1	½	½	½	½	0	0	♛	1	6
16	Spraggett	½	0	0	1	½	1	0	0	0	½	½	0	½	½	0	♛	5

France v GB, 1834

The public's appetite for chess was whetted by the correspondence match between London and Edinburgh, 1824 – 8. The mood was right in 1834 when four men collaborated to create a lasting monument to their age.

The main actors were Louis Charles de la Bourdonnais and Alexander McDonnell who contested a series of six matches, a total of 85 games, over a period of four months. They would hardly have been immortalized were it not for the diligence, imagination and flair of a pair of Walkers, and we look at their part first.

William Greenwood Walker (c.1760 – c.1840) greatly admired the genius of McDonnell and sat breathlessly by his side recording all the moves of all the games of this classic encounter. At that time players did not write down their moves, and without Walker keeping the game scores the matches might well have been dismissed by history.

The other Walker was less pedestrian. George Walker (13 March 1803 – 23 April 1879) created great interest in the game amongst the population at large and at the same time irritated the more desiccated experts by his cheerful inaccuracies. He wrote a lively chess column in a colourful newspaper *Bell's Life in London* which specialized in gossip and sport in a vivid style and although his column did not begin until after the great encounter, it is the surviving evidence of the kind of total enthusiasm with which he invested such an occasion. Without him the contest would not have attracted the vast crowds that thronged around the players, and even between them as there were no barriers to restrain the spectators!

Louis Charles de la Bourdonnais was born in 1797 on what is now Réunion Island where his grandfather had been Governor. He became addicted to chess while at school in Paris and soon became probably the strongest player anywhere in the world. Early in the 1830s he lost his considerable fortune in land speculation and was forced to earn his living at chess, which led to his famous meeting with McDonnell.

Alexander McDonnell was born in Belfast, 22 May 1798. He wrote several works on economics, had ambitions of becoming a member of parliament, and was employed in London by the Committee of West Indian Merchants to monitor parliamentary bills that affected them.

These two met from noon to around 7pm almost every day, bar Sundays, from June to October 1834. The matches resulted thus:

1	Bourdonnais	16	McDonnell	5	Drawn	4
2		4		5		0
3		6		5		1
4		8		3		7
5		7		4		1
6		4		5		0

Total	Bourdonnais 45	McDonnell 27	Drawn 13	

The 85 games are known. Some accounts speak of 88 games being played, others conjecture that this figure arises because McDonnell may have had three games start in the unfinished last match. Bourdonnais had to return to Paris and they never met again.

Bourdonnais was heavy but lively, even boisterous and something of a bohemian. After each day's play against McDonnell he would remain at the table, grabbing a quick meal, and playing until well past midnight against anyone and everyone. According to George Walker he did not speak a word of English, but as he had an English wife this may be sheer hyperbole.

McDonnell was the complete opposite — a quiet, orderly and somewhat reserved man. At the end of each session he would return home to his bachelor apartment and exhausted but unable to sleep, paced his room for much of the night. He died in London, on 14 September 1835, of Bright's disease, accelerated, it is said, by the exertions of the great competition.

Bourdonnais returned to London in 1840 but after two days became too ill with dropsy to keep working as the 'pro' at Simpson's Divan, and died penniless on 13 December.

Women's World Championship

Instituted by FIDE in 1927 the winner was to be decided by a tournament run alongside the Olympiad team event. Menchik was dominant. Of her 83 championship tournament games she won 78, drew 4 and lost only 1. She won 1 title match also, but with a less brilliant result of +9=5−2.

With Menchik's death, in an air raid on London in 1944, the procedure changed. After a tournament of leading contenders, 1949−50, to find a new champion, the title came up for challenge by match play on a regular cycle.

London *1927*

	1	2	3	4	5	6	7	8	9	10	11	12	Total
1 Menchik	♛	1	1	1	½	1	1	1	1	1	1	1	10½
2 Beskow	0	♛	0	1	1	1	1	1	1	1	1	1	9
3 Wolf-Kalmar	0	1	♛	1	1	1	0	½	0	1	½	1	7
4 Holloway	0	0	0	♛	½	1	½	1	½	1	1	½	6
5 Michell	½	0	0	½	♛	0	1	0	1	1	1	1	6
6 Price	0	0	0	0	1	♛	1	1	1	0	½	1	5½
7 Harum	0	0	1	½	0	0	♛	0	1	0	1	1	4½
8 Stirling	0	0	½	0	1	0	1	♛	0	1	0	½	4
9 Frigard	0	0	1	½	0	0	0	1	♛	0	1	0	3½
10 Stevenson	0	0	0	0	0	1	1	0	1	♛	½	0	3½
11 Synnewaag	0	0	½	0	0	½	0	1	0	½	♛	1	3½
12 Daunke	0	0	0	½	0	0	0	½	1	1	0	♛	3

Hamburg *1930*

	1	2	3	4	5	Total
1 Menchik	♛	½ 1	0 1	1 1	1 1	6½
2 Wolf-Kalmar	½ 0	♛	1 0	1 1	1 1	5½
3 Henschel	1 0	0 1	♛	1 1	0 ½	4½
4 Beskow	0 0	0 0	0 0	♛	1 1	2
5 Stevenson	0 0	0 0	1 ½	0 0	♛	1½

Prague *1931*

	1	2	3	4	5	Total
1 Menchik	♛	1 1	1 1	1 1	1 1	8
2 Wolf-Kalmar	0 0	♛	0 1	0 1	1 1	4
3 Stevenson	0 0	1 0	♛	1 ½	1 0	3½
4 Beskow	0 0	1 0	0 ½	♛	1 0	2½
5 Henschel	0 0	0 0	0 1	0 1	♛	2

Folkestone *1933*

	1	2	3	4	5	6	7	8	Total
1 Menchik	♛	1 1	1 1	1 1	1 1	1 1	1 1	1 1	14
2 Price	0 0	♛	1 ½	0 ½	1 1	0 1	1 1	1 1	9
3 Gilchrist	0 0	0 ½	♛	1 1	1 ½	½ ½	1 ½	1 1	8½
4 Michell	0 0	1 ½	0 0	♛	½ 1	1 1	0 1	1 1	9
5 Tonini	0 0	0 0	0 ½	½ 0	♛	1 1	0 1	1 1	6
6 Schwartzmann	0 0	1 0	½ ½	0 0	0 0	♛	1 ½	1 1	5
7 D'Autremont	0 0	0 0	0 ½	1 0	1 0	0 ½	♛	1 1	5
8 Harum (absent)	0 0	0 0	0 0	0 0	0 0	0 0	0 0	♛	0

From a book published in 1800.
(Author)

Warsaw *1935*

	1	2	3	4	5	6	7	8	9	10	Total
1 Menchik	♛	1	1	1	1	1	1	1	1	1	9
2 Gerlecka	0	♛	½	½	1	1	1	½	1	1	6½
3 Harum	0	½	♛	½	1	1	1	1	0	1	6
4 Menchik, O	0	½	½	♛	½	½	½	1	1	1	5½
5 Thierry	0	0	0	½	♛	1	1	½	1	1	5
6 Hermanova	0	0	0	½	0	♛	0	1	1	1	3½
7 Holloway	0	0	0	½	0	1	♛	0	1	1	3½
8 Skjönsberg	0	½	0	0	½	0	1	♛	1	0	3
9 Kowalska	0	0	1	0	0	0	0	0	♛	½	1½
10 Shannon	0	0	0	0	0	0	0	1	½	♛	1½

Semmering *June–16 July 1937*

Menchik beat Sonja Graf +9=5−2

Stockholm *1937*

After the first round drawn by lot, the best scorers meet each other in list order, with a different opponent each round. Fourteen rounds were decided upon.

1 Menchik	14	8 Gilchrist	7½	15 Farago	7	22 Larsen	6
2 Benini	10	9 Andersson, I	7½	16 Holloway	7	23 Beskow	5½
3 Lauberte	9	10 Hermanova	7	17 Florow-Bulhak	6½	24 Shannon	5
4 Graf	9	11 Roodzant	7	18 Harum	6½	25 Bloch-Nakkerud	2
5 Bain	8½	12 St. John	7	19 Reischer	6½	26 Mellbye	1
6 Karff	8	13 Andersson, A	7	20 Menchik, O	6½		
7 Fischerova	8	14 Gerlecka	7	21 Thomson	6		

Buenos Aires *1939*

	1	2	3	4	5	6	7	8	9	10	11	12	13	14	15	16	17	18	19	20	Total
1 Menchik	♛	1	1	1	1	½	1	1	½	1	1	1	1	1	1	1	1	1	1	1	18
2 Graf	0	♛	0	1	0	1	1	1	1	1	1	1	1	1	1	1	1	1	1	1	16
3 Carrasco	0	1	♛	0	1	1	1	1	1	1	1	0	1	½	1	1	1	1	1	1	15½
4 Rinder	0	0	1	♛	1	½	1	1	1	1	1	½	1	1	1	1	0	1	1	1	15
5 Karff	0	1	0	0	♛	1	1	½	1	½	1	1	1	1	0	1	1	1	1	1	14
6 Lauberte	½	0	0	½	0	♛	1	½	½	1	½	1	½	1	1	1	½	1	1	½	12½
7 Mora	0	0	0	0	0	0	♛	1	½	0	1	1	1	1	1	½	1	1	1	1	11
8 Roodzant	0	0	0	0	½	½	0	♛	½	1	½	1	1	½	1	½	1	1	1	1	11
9 Schwartzmann	½	0	0	0	0	½	½	½	♛	½	½	1	½	½	½	½	0	1	1	1	9
10 Janecek	0	0	0	0	½	0	1	0	½	♛	½	1	1	1	½	0	1	1	0	1	9
11 Larsen	0	0	0	0	0	½	0	½	½	½	♛	½	1	1	1	0	0	1	1	1	8½
12 Trepat	0	0	1	½	0	0	0	0	0	0	½	♛	½	1	½	0	½	1	1	1	7½
13 Andersson	0	0	0	0	0	½	0	0	½	0	0	½	♛	½	½	1	1	1	1	1	7½
14 Reischer	0	0	½	0	0	0	0	½	½	0	0	0	½	♛	1	1	1	0	1	1	7
15 Berea	0	0	0	0	1	0	0	0	½	½	0	½	½	0	♛	1	½	1	½	1	7
16 Stöffels	0	0	0	0	0	0	½	½	½	1	1	0	0	0	0	♛	1	1	½	½	6½
17 Vigil	0	0	0	1	0	½	0	0	1	0	1	½	0	0	½	0	♛	0	½	1	6
18 Raclauskiene	0	0	0	0	0	0	0	0	0	0	0	0	0	1	0	0	1	♛	½	1	3½
19 Nakkerud	0	0	0	0	0	0	0	0	0	1	0	0	0	0	½	½	½	½	♛	0	3
20 Lougheed	0	0	0	0	0	½	0	0	0	0	0	0	0	0	0	½	0	0	1	♛	2

Moscow *1949–50*

		1	2	3	4	5	6	7	8	9	10	11	12	13	14	15	16	Total
1	Rudenko	♛	1	½	1	½	½	½	1	1	1	1	1	0	1	½	1	11½
2	Rubtsova	0	♛	1	1	½	½	½	0	½	1	1	1	1	1	1	½	10½
3	Belova	½	0	♛	½	1	1	1	0	0	0	1	1	1	1	1	1	10
4	Bykova	0	0	½	♛	1	1	1	1	0	1	½	½	1	1	½	1	10
5	Chaudé de Silans	½	½	0	0	♛	1	0	1	0	½	1	1	1	1	1	1	9½
6	Keller	½	½	0	0	0	♛	1	1	1	½	1	0	1	1	1	1	9½
7	Trammer	½	½	0	0	1	0	♛	1	1	½	½	1	1	1	½	1	9½
8	Heemskerk	0	1	1	0	0	0	0	♛	1	½	½	1	1	½	1	½	8
9	Benini	0	½	1	1	1	0	0	0	♛	0	0	½	0	1	1	1	7
10	Langos	0	0	1	0	½	½	½	½	1	♛	½	0	0	0	1	½	6
11	Mora	0	0	0	½	0	0	½	½	1	½	♛	1	1	1	0	0	6
12	Hruskova-Belska	0	0	0	½	0	1	0	0	½	1	0	♛	0	½	1	½	5
13	Gresser	1	0	0	0	0	0	0	0	1	1	0	1	♛	0	0	1	5
14	Karff	0	0	0	0	0	0	0	½	0	1	0	½	1	♛	1	1	5
15	Larsen	½	0	0	½	0	0	½	0	0	0	1	0	1	0	♛	1	4½
16	Hermanova	0	½	0	0	0	0	0	½	0	½	1	½	0	0	0	♛	3

Gaprindasvili. (Novosti)

15 August–20 September 1953 *Leningrad*

Bykova	0 0 1 1 ½ 1 1 ½ 0 0 1 1 0 1	9
Rudenko	1 1 0 0 ½ 0 0 ½ 1 1 0 0 1 0	6

22 August–23 September 1956 *Moscow*

	Rubtsova	Bykova	Rudenko	
Rubtsova	♛ ♛ ♛	½ ½ ½ 1 ½ 0 1 ½	½ 1 0 1 0 1 1 1	10
Bykova	½ ½ ½ 0 ½ 1 0 ½	♛ ♛ ♛	1 ½ 1 ½ 1 1 0 1	9½
Rudenko	½ 0 1 0 1 0 0 0	0 ½ 0 ½ 0 0 1 0	♛ ♛ ♛	4½

2 February–14 March 1958 *Moscow*

Bykova	0 1 0 ½ 0 ½ 1 1 1 1 1 1 0 ½	8½
Rubtsova	1 0 1 ½ 1 ½ 0 0 0 0 0 0 1 ½	5½

4 December 1959–4 January 1960 *Moscow*

Bykova	0 1 ½ 1 0 ½ 1 ½ ½ 1 1 1 ½	8½
Zvorikina	1 0 ½ 0 1 ½ 0 ½ ½ 0 0 0 ½	4½

18 September–17 October 1962 *Moscow*

Gaprindashvili	½ 1 1 1 ½ 1 1 ½ ½ 1 1	9
Bykova	½ 0 0 0 ½ 0 0 ½ ½ 0 0	2

18 September–23 October 1965 *Riga*

Gaprindashvili	1 0 ½ 1 1 ½ 1 1 ½ 0 1 0 1	8½
Kushnir	0 1 ½ 0 0 ½ 0 0 ½ 1 0 1 0	4½

8 April–18 May 1969 *Tbilisi and Moscow*

Gaprindashvili	0 ½ 1 0 1 1 ½ 1 ½ 1 ½ 1 ½	8½
Kushnir	1 ½ 0 1 0 0 ½ 0 ½ 0 ½ 0 ½	4½

Women's world champion Chiburdanidze at Lloyds Bank 1985. (John Stone/Lloyds Bank)

10 May – 26 June 1972 *Riga*

Gaprindashvili
1 1 0 1 $\frac{1}{2}$ 1 $\frac{1}{2}$ 0 1 $\frac{1}{2}$ 0 $\frac{1}{2}$ $\frac{1}{2}$ 0 $\frac{1}{2}$ $\frac{1}{2}$ 8$\frac{1}{2}$
Kushnir
0 0 1 0 $\frac{1}{2}$ 0 $\frac{1}{2}$ 1 0 $\frac{1}{2}$ 1 $\frac{1}{2}$ $\frac{1}{2}$ 1 $\frac{1}{2}$ $\frac{1}{2}$ 7$\frac{1}{2}$

20 October – 27 November 1975 *Pitsunda/Tbilisi*

Gaprindashvili	1 0 1 1 $\frac{1}{2}$ 1 1 1 0 1 0 1 1	8$\frac{1}{2}$
Alexandriya	0 1 0 0 $\frac{1}{2}$ 0 0 1 0 1 0 0	3$\frac{1}{2}$

August – October 1978 *Pitsunda*

Chiburdanidze
$\frac{1}{2}$ $\frac{1}{2}$ $\frac{1}{2}$ 1 1 $\frac{1}{2}$ 0 $\frac{1}{2}$ 1 $\frac{1}{2}$ 0 $\frac{1}{2}$ 1 $\frac{1}{2}$ $\frac{1}{2}$ 8$\frac{1}{2}$
Gaprindashvili
$\frac{1}{2}$ $\frac{1}{2}$ $\frac{1}{2}$ 0 0 $\frac{1}{2}$ 1 $\frac{1}{2}$ 0 $\frac{1}{2}$ 1 $\frac{1}{2}$ 0 $\frac{1}{2}$ $\frac{1}{2}$ 6$\frac{1}{2}$

8 September – 27 October 1981 *Borzhomi/Tbilisi*

Chiburdanidze
$\frac{1}{2}$ $\frac{1}{2}$ $\frac{1}{2}$ $\frac{1}{2}$ 0 1 1 $\frac{1}{2}$ 1 0 0 $\frac{1}{2}$ $\frac{1}{2}$ $\frac{1}{2}$ 1 0 8
Alexandriya
$\frac{1}{2}$ $\frac{1}{2}$ $\frac{1}{2}$ $\frac{1}{2}$ 1 0 0 $\frac{1}{2}$ 0 1 1 $\frac{1}{2}$ $\frac{1}{2}$ $\frac{1}{2}$ 0 1 8

11 September – 22 October 1984 *Volgograd*

Chiburdanidze	$\frac{1}{2}$ $\frac{1}{2}$ 0 1 $\frac{1}{2}$ $\frac{1}{2}$ $\frac{1}{2}$ 0 1 1 $\frac{1}{2}$ 1 1 $\frac{1}{2}$	8$\frac{1}{2}$
Levitina	$\frac{1}{2}$ $\frac{1}{2}$ 1 0 $\frac{1}{2}$ $\frac{1}{2}$ $\frac{1}{2}$ 1 0 0 $\frac{1}{2}$ 0 0 $\frac{1}{2}$	5$\frac{1}{2}$

World Junior Championship

Launched in England in 1951, this competition was held every two years until 1973 and annually since then. If not already one, the winner becomes an International Master.

1951	Coventry/ Birmingham	Ivkov (Yugoslavia)
1953	Copenhagen	Panno (Argentina)
1955	Antwerp	Spassky (USSR)
1957	Toronto	Lombardy (USA)
1959	Munchenstein	Bielicki (Argentina)
1961	The Hague	Parma (Yugoslavia)
1963	Vrnjacka Banja	Gheorghiu (Romania)
1965	Barcelona	Kurajica (Yugoslavia)
1967	Jerusalem	Kaplan (Puerto Rico)
1969	Stockholm	Karpov (USSR)
1971	Athens	Hug (Switzerland)
1973	Teesside	Belyavsky (USSR)
1974	Manila	Miles (England)
1975	Tjentiste	Chekhov (USSR)
1976–7	Groningen	Diesen (USA)
1977	Innsbruck	Yusupov (USSR)
1978	Graz	Dolmatov (USSR)
1979	Skien	Seirawan (USA)
1980	Dortmund	Kasparov (USSR)
1981	Mexico City	Cvitan (Yugoslavia)
1982	Copenhagen	Sokolov (USSR)
1983	Belfort	Georgiev (Bulgaria)
1984	Kiljava	Hansen (Denmark)
1985	Sharjah	Dlugy (USA)

Dlugy. (Stephane Bureau)

France v GB, 1843

Staunton was a giant in the chess world, a hero to some, a villain to others. Not much is known about his early life and though he denied the rumour that he was the illegitimate son of the Earl of Carlisle cynics thought he did so in order to further it. He said that his name was Howard (the Earl's family name) and that he was born in Westmorland in 1810. Probably his true origin was quite humble, but he succeeded thanks to a good brain and a huge capacity for work.

One of the many inspired by the Bourdonnais-McDonnell games, Staunton was a first-class player by 1840. He launched *Chess Player's Chronicle* and when the editor of *Le Palamède* visited London in April and May 1843 they contested a fighting match which hung in the balance until the end. The six games averaged more than 50 moves each.

The winner was Pierre Charles Fournier de Saint-Amant (born 12 September 1800 at Château Latour, died 29 October 1872 at Birmandreis Hydra, Algeria). After the death of Bourdonnais Saint-Amant had shown himself to be the strongest player in Paris. Staunton challenged him to a formal match, for a stake of £100, the victor being the first to win eleven games, draws excluded. The ensuing match has been classed, many years later, as being equivalent to a world championship.

Play was at the Paris Chess Club from 14 November to 20 December 1843. The epic struggle seized the attention of fans all over the world, especially in Britain where they badgered newspapers to give the games. Spectators crammed into the small playing room and as the match reached its climax and public excitement grew, gendarmes had to be posted at the club doors to refuse further admittance.

Except for the drawn third game Staunton won all up to game nine, when, in a lost position, Saint-Amant found a desperate resource and it was Staunton, making a reply which he himself said 'can be attributed only to overweening confidence', who lost. Staunton came back to win the tenth but then blundered again in the eleventh in an easily won pawn endgame, won game twelve, lost game thirteen. Fourteen was drawn and then Staunton won the fifteenth to be within one game of victory.

All was not over. Saint-Amant won the sixteenth. The seventeenth and eighteenth were bitterly fought draws and the Frenchman won the next two. Amid scenes of great excitement Staunton secured game twenty-one and won 'The Grand Chess Match between France and England'.

A further match was arranged for October 1844. It never took place but seems to have ended the top level careers of both champions. Staunton went to Paris for the match, caught pneumonia, came close to death and was left with a permanent heart weakness. Saint-Amant may have lost his chess enthusiasm, or perhaps his business interests had become too demanding, for he took only a passing interest for the rest of his days.

Staunton continued to write about chess until his death in London on 22 June 1874, but more than that he neglected no opportunity to popularize the game. He travelled throughout the country to visit clubs or embryo associations, and undertook much detailed work in an effort to establish a unified set of laws for the game. It was his vision that led to the world's first international tournament, London 1851, although he was knocked out by the eventual winner, Anderssen. Becoming increasingly involved in other literary work Staunton sold *Chess Player's Chronicle* in 1854 and concentrated on an edition of Shakespeare's works, published in monthly parts.

Then, in 1858, came the events which blighted Staunton's reputation. The young American genius, Morphy (see page 36), came to Europe to challenge the leading players, Staunton among them. Staunton accepted in principle, but was never pinned down to a firm commitment. He entered a tournament at Birmingham where Morphy had promised to play (indeed the date was chosen specifically for him) but Morphy was persuaded not to appear

Staunton.

in case Staunton beat him and then refused to play a match. In fact Staunton played so poorly that he realized that he had no chance against Morphy unless he took time off from his Shakespearian work, and Routledge, the publisher, threatened him with legal action if he were to break his contract.

He may have entertained hopes of playing a match eventually, he may just have become irritated with being nagged about it (he had become rather grouchy in the 1850s), but Staunton did not tell Morphy plainly that there would be no match. It would have been of little consequence that they did not play — Morphy would have won well enough — were it not for the fact that the American's mental health became impaired years later and some of his admirers sought a cause in the frustrated match. Although that theory is discredited the damage has been done to Staunton's reputation.

World Junior Women's Championship (under-21)

Shortly after its foundation FIDE sponsored a championship, but the pre-war entry was almost entirely British.

1926	Menchik	1932	Bullen
1927	Menchik	1933	Bullen
1928	Gregory	1934	Ballard
1929	Gregory	1935	Dew
1930	Gregory	1936	Saunders
1931	Bullen	1937	Saunders

1982	Senta	Brustman (Poland)
1983	Mexico	Khasanova (USSR)
1985	Dobrna	Arakhamia (USSR)

World Under-16 Championship

The brain-child of the French, this was called the Cadet championship at first. After one year as an under-16 event it became under-18 for the next two years. Recognized by FIDE, it became under-17 in 1977 and remained so until 1981 when it finally reverted to under-16. In the same year a girls' event was introduced, although some girls had entered the open championship in earlier years.

1974	Pont St Maxence	Mestel (England)
1975	Creil	Goodman (England)

Rojas. (Roger Blackmore)

1976	Wattignies	Grinberg (Israel)
1977	Cagnes sur Mer	Arnason (Iceland)
1978–9	Sas van Gent	Motwani (Scotland)
1979	Belfort	Tempone (Argentina)
1980	Le Havre	Salov (USSR)
1981	Embulse	Conquest (England)
1982	Guayaquil	Bareyev (USSR)
1983	Bucaramanga	Dreyev (USSR)
1984	Paris	Dreyev (USSR)
1985	Petach Tikua	Rojas (Chile)

Women

1981	Chichester (unofficial)	Polgár (Hungary)
1983	Paris	Madl (Hungary)
1985	Petach Tikua	Marić, M (Yugoslav)
1986		Arakhamia (USSR)

World Amateur Championship

In its year of formation FIDE tried to link chess with the Olympic games and embraced amateurism. The chess world does not readily make the distinction to which the world of athletics pretends, and only two championships were held

1924	Paris	Mattison (Latvia)
1928	The Hague	Euwe (Netherlands)

World Team Championship

A new competition in 1985: the idea is to have ten teams (six players) comprising the continental champions of Europe, Asia, Africa and the Americas, the five leading teams from the previous Olympiad (additional to any already qualified) and a team from the host country. USA declined for financial reasons. The only African country of even modest chess prowess is South Africa, banned from FIDE competition for political reasons, and so a team selected from all African countries played.

Luzern *16–27 November 1985*

		1	2	3	4	5	6	7	8	9	10	**Total**
1	USSR	♛	2½	4	4½	3½	4	5	4½	3½	6	**37½**
2	Hungary	3½	♛	3½	4½	4½	3½	2½	3½	4	5	**34½**
3	England	2	2½	♛	4	2½	2	4	3½	4	6	**30½**
4	France	1½	1½	2	♛	3	4½	3½	4	3½	5	**28½**
5	Romania	2½	1½	3½	3	♛	2½	3½	3	4	5	**28½**
6	Switzerland	2	2½	4	1½	3½	♛	2½	3½	3	5	**27½**
7	China PR	1	3½	2	2½	2½	3½	♛	3½	3	5½	**27**
8	Argentina	1½	2½	2½	2	3	2½	2½	♛	4	5	**25½**
9	W. Germany	2½	2	2	2½	2	3	3	2	♛	4½	**23½**
10	Africa Select	0	1	0	1	1	1	½	1	1½	♛	**7**

Olympiads

Olympiads are international team tournaments open to all members of FIDE. Thus England, Scotland, Wales and the Channel Islands, as separate members, enter teams, but USSR, as one member, is allowed only one team. Four players and up to two reserves compete. Placings are based on points for games rather than matches. The fixture soon became every second year, interrupted by the war.

Originally all teams met but numbers grew larger and a system of preliminaries and finals was introduced in 1939. Entries continued to grow and from 1976 Swiss system pairings have been used. The host country may enter a 'B' team to make the number of teams even.

Before the war the women's world championship was always held at the same time but women have played in the Olympiads and indeed there were smiles one year because a member of the Virgin Islands team was in a late stage of pregnancy. However a women-only Olympiad series was introduced in 1957 for two boards, raised to three in 1974, and a reserve. Below is a list of all Olympiads. The tables show placings.

Year			No. of teams
1927	London	18–29 Jul	16
1928	The Hague	5 Jul–21 Aug	17
1930	Hamburg	13–27 Jul	18
1931	Prague	11–26 Jul	19
1933	Folkestone	12–23 Jun	15
1935	Warsaw	15–31 Aug	20
1937	Stockholm	31 July–14 Aug	19
1939	Buenos Aires	21 Aug–19 Sep	26
1950	Dubrovnik	20 Aug–11 Sep	16
1952	Helsinki	9–31 Aug	25
1954	Amsterdam	4–25 Sep	26
1956	Moscow	31 Aug–15 Sep	34
1958	Munich	30 Sep–23 Oct	36
1960	Leipzig	16 Oct–9 Nov	40
1962	Varna	16 Sep–10 Oct	37
1964	Tel Aviv	2–25 Nov	50
1966	Havana	23 Oct–20 Nov	52
1968	Lugano	17 Oct–7 Nov	53
1970	Siegen	5–27 Sep	60
1972	Skopje	18 Sep–13 Oct	62
1974	Nice	6–30 Jun	73
1976	Haifa	24 Oct–10 Nov	48
1978	Buenos Aires	25 Oct–12 Nov	65
1980	Malta	20 Nov–8 Dec	82
1982	Luzern	30 Oct–16 Nov	92
1984	Thessalonika	19 Nov–4 Dec	88

Reshevsky at the 1964 Olympiad, Tel Aviv.
(Brian Reilly)

Olympiad Placings

Year	27	28	30	31	33	35	37	39	50	52	54	56	58	60	62	64	66	68	70	72	74	76	78	80	82	84	**Total**
Albania													28	26			38							37	41	40	6
Algeria																					70			55	68	60	4
Andorra																		53	56	58	71	42	60	74	72	66	9
Angola																								82	89	80	3
Arab Emirates																							64	61	69	36	4
Argentina	12	8				8	4	5	2	2	2	4	3	7	3	9	5	7	8	14	14	4	17	14	13	14	23
Australia																43	29	15	32	33	19	30	34	25	23		10
Austria	7	4	4	8	6	7			7	17	15	13	12	15	12	20	17	17	22	23	18	18	19	21	14	39	24
Bahamas																					72						1
Bahrain																									87	69	2
Bangladesh																									61		1
Belgium	14	12		13		17		6		19	16	24	33	19	25	26	33	30	30	24	47	40	52	43			20
Bermuda																						41	62	77	90	85	5
Bolivia								25					36			45	45		46	40	52						7

Year	27	28	30	31	33	35	37	39	50	52	54	56	58	60	62	64	66	68	70	72	74	76	78	80	82	84	*Total*
Botswana																									91		1
Brazil									14		19						25	28	36	35		27	26	39	20		10
Bulgaria									20			10	6	10	6	6	8	7	3	7	6	4	13	19	6	11	16
Canada									17		14		15		12	23	13	11	19	24	8	11		9	18	19	14
Chile									12	8		22		22		24	37				38	17	29	33	21	22	12
China																							20	38	40	13	4
Colombia												18	18	16		31	22		23	25	20	10	23	32	20	30	13
Costa Rica														49						32							2
Cuba								11		15			18	16	21	14	20	21	22	25		18	13	9	10		14
Cyprus													37	50	51	51	57	56	68			70	66	58			10
Czechoslovakia	5	7	5	3	2	5	5	6	4	4	7	5	5	10	5	6	9	5	4	9			5		2	17	23
Denmark	2	5	11	17	12	16	15	15	13	14	16	10	18	16	24	17	10	12	19	13	26	25	7	15	8	18	26
Dominican R																	49	47	48	45	50	27	38	45	33	46	10
Dutch Antilles																	66	48									2
Ecuador								21					29		26	39			46			51			63		7
Egypt																							60	47	47		3
England	3		8	9	10	12	13		16	9	8	11	12	14	18	21	16	25	17	10	3	12	6	10	2		23
Estonia				11	8	3																					3
Faroes																			55	54	58	44	46	73	57	64	8
Finland	15		17			13	12		10	9	20	17	21	17	20	32	20	23	20	33	15	16	22	20	23	38	22
France	13	11	12	14	8	10		10	9		21	21	23	31	30	34	26	44		48	28	26	36	17	28	7	23
Germany	6	9	3	5			1																				5
Germany E										13		20	6	9	8	15	9	10	9	10							10
Germany W								3	8	5	5	7	8	7	3		5	6	5	7	5	4	24	16	6		17
Greece									16	20	24	32	30	35	33	35	32	34	31	29	40			28	35	29	16
Guatemala							22														37	48		46			4
Guernsey/Jer																	59	60	62	34			69	71	81		7
Guyana																					43	54					2
Honduras																					29				86	67	3
Hong Kong																	52	48	53	51	57	39	40	68	58	53	10
Hungary	1	1	2	10	5	4	2		6	6	3	13	4	5	4	3	6	2	2	6			1	2	5	4	23
Iceland			15		14		16	16		23	12	14	22	23	23	29	11	22	27	24	22	22	28	23	22	15	21
India													27		24	28	37						36	42	33		7
Indonesia													26		27		24	26	39			26	44	29	31		9
Iran												28	32		29	36			32	35	34	31					8
Iraq																			61	65					55		3
Ireland						20		23		25	33	34	38	36	41	40	38	42	39	37	35		41	32	57		17
Israel										11	7	12	17	14	15	13	19	18	13	18	17	6	5	8	12	12	17
Italy	10	15		16	11	18	14		12	18	17		28	32			29	31	30	27	19	13		22	43	28	20
Jamaica																							55	62	81	76	4
Japan																			47	47	67	38	44	52	62	82	8
Jordan																				61			54	67	82	77	5
Kenya																								71	88	73	3
Latvia		14	10	6	9	9	11	7																			7
Lebanon														36	40		50	50	45	52	52			58	60	65	10
Libya																							58	75	80	74	4
Lithuania			14	13	7	14	7	13																			6
Luxemburg										25	26	34		34	48	42	39	46	53	51	36	45	53	76	68		15
Malaysia																				59	59		57	49	59	50	6
Mali																									86		1
Malta										39							52	50	56					59	64	63	7
Mauretania																							59				1
Mexico																	40	44	46	44	41	41	21	35	38	41	10

Year	27	28	30	31	33	35	37	39	50	52	54	56	58	60	62	64	66	68	70	72	74	76	78	80	82	84	Total
Monaco													37		42	46	42	60		55	43			79	73	84	10
Mongolia												30	27	21	23	30	27	16	28	36			46	37			11
Morocco																47	41	54	57	60		49			37		7
Netherlands	4	10	7	11		6	8	5	10	8	19	14	10	11	11	15	15	18	8	5	2	14	10	15	9		24
New Guinea																					45			80	74	79	4
New Zealand																		49	44	45	21	25	56	49	45		8
Nicaragua																	48										1
Nigeria																							76	77	72		3
Norway		18	18			18	18	15	21	23	24	25	19	25	22	13	30	29	21	21	11	31	27	24	26		22
Pakistan																				48			42	56	54		4
Palestine						15		9																	88		3
Panama																49			54								2
Paraguay							26								27		45				15	32	48	53	56		8
Peru						24	14								19			39	31			42					6
Philippines												25	26	25		25	31	14	26	20	11	20	24	16	19	16	14
Poland		3	1	2	3	3	3	2	12			23	19	21	18	10	16	11	14	12	23		8	7	7	21	22
Portugal													31	30		47	38	35	41	37	31			39	51	32	11
Puerto Rico												29	33		31	38	41	40	36	40	49		56	63	61	52	13
Romania		16	13	15		17							11		11	9	7	8	8	10	7	8	6	11	11	5	17
S Africa													27			44	43	36	43								5
Saar											24	22	26														3
San Marino																									87		1
Scotland				15		19						31	29			28	28	28	34	34	29	33	33	51	34	24	15
Senegal																								83			1
Singapore																	43	40	49	43				44	42		6
Spain	16	17	16	19									9	20	13	14	12	19	12	11	12	9	9	25	27	27	18
Sri Lanka																						39		48	51		3
Surinam																							75	75			2
Sweden	11	13	9	7	4	2	10	4	11	7	11	15	20	13	17	16	24	24	17	15	13	12	16	12	17	25	26
Switzerland	8	6	12		19						22	13	9	8	22	30	18	21	37	16	27	7	10	31	26	49	20
Syria																			55	47			35	30	54		5
Thailand																					30			43	55	62	4
Trinidad/Tob																				69			53	50	67	71	5
Tunisia												35	34	27		34	37	35	42	32			50	57	65	48	12
Turkey													35	39	35	33	51	38	42				47	50	34		10
Uganda																							81	79	59		3
Uruguay							19							32	46	33				53	28	37		45			8
USA		2	6	1	1	1	1		4	5			4	2	4	6	2	4	4	9	3	1	3	4	3	3	22
USSR											1	1	1	1	1	1	1	1	1	1	1	1	2	1	1	1	16
Venezuela															33	36	32				44	23	34	29	36		8
Virgin I (Brit)																					73	47	65	72	84	78	6
Virgin I (US)																					63	46	61	65	85	83	6
Virgin Isles																		52	58	62							3
Wales																				43	16	14	41	18	30	35	7
Yugoslavia	9			4			6	9	1	3	3	2	2	3	2	4	2	3	3	2			15	3	4	8	21
Zaire																					63	78	78				3
Zambia																								92			1
Zimbabwe/Rhod																		50		64				64	70	70	5
Host B Team																							66	31	44		3

Year	27	28	30	31	33	35	37	39	50	52	54	56	58	60	62	64	66	68	70	72	74	76	78	80	82	84	
Total teams	16	17	18	19	15	20	19	26	16	25	26	34	36	40	37	50	52	53	60	62	73	48	65	82	92	88	

Nick Grant, managing director of Duncan Lawrie bank needs sunglasses against the winter sunshine at Heathrow, but the English team returning from Thessaloniki find overcoats more in order. Chandler, Mestel, Short, Nunn and Speelman show the silver medals they had just won at the 1984 Olympiad while non-playing captain David Anderton thanks the bank for its sponsorship. Nunn also won the prize for best score (10/11) on 2nd board and on a rest day won the problem-solving championship! England top board Miles had gone directly to another event. (Duncan Lawrie)

Women's Olympiads

1957	Emmen	2–21 Sep	21	1976	Haifa	24 Oct–10 Nov	23
1963	Split	21 Sep–10 Oct	15	1978	Buenos Aires	25 Oct–12 Nov	32
1966	Oberhausen	3–15 Oct	14	1980	Malta	20 Nov–8 Dec	42
1969	Lublin	7–23 Sep	15	1982	Luzern	30 Oct–16 Nov	45
1972	Skopje	25 Sep–13 Oct	23	1984	Thessalonika	19 Nov–4 Dec	51
1974	Medellin	15 Sep–7 Oct	26				

Women's Olympiad

	1957	1963	1966	1969	1972	1974	1976	1978	1980	1982	1984	Total
Arab Emirates									40		46	2
Argentina							11	12	12	24	34	5
Australia					16		7	16	16	19	35	6
Austria	17	12	14	13	11	16	18		33	29	31	10
Belgium	20	13		14					37	34	37	6
Bolivia								28				1
Brazil					14	13		20	10	16	19	6
Bulgaria	5	5	8	5	4	3		7	9	14	2	10
Canada						10	9	18	20	18	17	6
China									6	6	5	3
Colombia						17	15	19	18	15	23	6
Cuba											11	1
Czechoslovakia	11		6	3	5	6						5
Denmark	13		13	12			8	17	30		24	7
Dominican R									24		26	2
E. Germany	3	3	3	6	7							5
Egypt									35	42	44	3

	1957	1963	1966	1969	1972	1974	1976	1978	1980	1982	1984	Total
England	7		9	10	8	8	2	8	14	11	8	10
Finland	18				21	18	13	21	34	31	30	8
France	16						14	13	15	12	18	6
Greece									23	21	28	3
Guatemala											45	1
Hong Kong											47	1
Hungary	4	6	7	2	3	4		2	2	3	6	10
Iceland								26	22	26	32	4
India								15	25	9	16	4
Indonesia										23	25	2
Iraq						23					43	2
Ireland	14			15	20	20	12		26	40	38	8
Israel					18	12	1		7	30		5
Italy							10		19	20	29	4
Jamaica											49	1
Japan					23	19	20	23	36	35	41	7
Luxemburg	21											1
Malaysia											33	1
Malta									38			1
Mexico						21		24	32	33	39	5
Monaco		14				26		31				3
Mongolia		10			15					22		3
Netherlands	9	7	5	9	12	5	5	11	17	8	13	11
New Zealand							23	30	29	28	40	5
Nigeria									42			1
Norway	19									41	27	3
Panama						25						1
Philippines							16			27		2
Poland	12	8	11	7	9			5	3	4	7	9
Portugal										21		1
Puerto Rico						22		32	39			3
Romania	2	4	2	8	2	2		10	4	2	3	10
Scotland	15	15			22		21	22	28	32	20	8
Singapore					19							1
Spain						11	3	6	11	10	10	6
Sweden					13	15	19	9	21	7	15	7
Switzerland					17		17		31	25	14	5
Trinidad/Tob										43	48	2
Turkey										37	42	2
Uruguay								29				1
US Virgin I									41	45	51	3
USA	10	9	10			14	4	14	13	17	12	9
USSR	1	1	1	1	1	1		1	1	1	1	10
Venezuela								27		38		2
W. Germany	8	11	12	11	6	9	6	3	5	5	4	11
Wales							22	25	27	39	22	5
Yugoslavia	6	2	4	4	10	7		4	8	13	9	10
Zambia										44		1
Zimbabwe											50	1
Host B Team										36	36	2
Number of teams	21	15	14	15	23	25	23	32	42	45	51	

World Youth Team Championship

After the first students' congress, in Liverpool, 1952 (won jointly by Bronstein and Taimanov), a team event for students was launched, originally for under-30s. Later this changed to under-27 and from 1978 it was re-styled as a youth event (many competitors appeared to be studying only chess), and the age limit reduced to 25.

1954	Oslo	Czechoslovakia
1955	Lyons	USSR
1956	Uppsala	USSR
1957	Reykjavik	USSR
1958	Varna	USSR
1959	Budapest	Bulgaria
1960	Leningrad	USA
1961	Helsinki	USSR
1962	Marianske Lazne	USSR
1963	Budva	Czechoslovakia
1964	Cracow	USSR
1965	Sinaia	USSR
1966	Orebro	USSR
1967	Harrachov	USSR
1968	Vienna	USSR
1969	Dresden	USSR
1970	Haifa	USA
1971	Mayaguez	USSR
1972	Graz	USSR
1974	Teesside	USSR
1976	Caracas	USSR
1977	Mexico City	USSR
1978	Mexico City	England
1980	Mexico City	USSR
1981	Graz	USSR
1983	Chicago	USSR
1985	Mendoza	USSR

World Correspondence Championship

Controlled by the International Correspondence Chess Federation (ICCF), formed from the ICCA which itself sprang from the IFSB in 1946, these contests take the form of preliminaries and a final. The ICCF also runs an Olympiad, a world championship confined to women, and an Olympiad for women (the first of these is not yet completed). The dates below are when the final ended.

Champion

1953	1	Purdy, 2 – 3 Malmgren & Napolitano
1959	1	Ragozin, 2 – 3 Endzelins & Schmid
1962	1	O'Kelly, 2 Dubinin, 3 Lundqvist
1965	1	Zagorovsky, 2 Borisenko, 3 Arlauskas
1968	1	Berliner, 2 – 3 Hybl & Husak
1971	1	Rittner, 2 Zagorovsky, 3 Estrin
1975	1	Estrin, 2 Boey, 3 – 4 Zagorovsky & Richardson
1980	1	Sloth, 2 Zagorovsky, 3 Kosenkov
1983	1	Oim, 2 – 3 Baumbach & Mikhailov
1984	1	Palciauskas, 2 Morgado, 3 Richardson & Sanakoyev

Women

1972	1	Rubtsova, 2 Schoisswohl, 3 Yakovleva
1977	1	Yakovleva, 2 Rubtsova, 3 Rotova
1984	1	Kristol, 2 Rotova, 3 Yakovleva

Olympiads

1952	Hungary
1955	Czechoslovakia
1961	USSR
1964	USSR
1968	Czechoslovakia
1972	USSR
1976	USSR
1982	USSR

Telex Olympiad

Conceived by FIDE and ICCF as a knock-out team match to be played by telephone, telex, telegraph, or radio, the event suffers because unfinished games have to be adjudicated. The expectation that the players would come from the correspondence chess fraternity has proved false. In both competitions to date USSR beat E. Germany in the final, but narrowly. In the second final E. Germany led by one win and three draws at the end of play but adjudication gave USSR a win and three draws from the unfinished games, and as the win was on board 2 whereas the E. German one was on board 3, USSR won on tie-break.

1977 – 8	USSR
1981 – 2	USSR

World Championships for Blind Players

The blind English player R.W. Bonham created the International Braille Chess Association in 1951. Affiliated to FIDE in 1964, it runs world championships for individuals, over-the-board and by correspondence, as well as Olympiads. Originally called Braille championships, these have been re-styled as for the visually handicapped.

World Championship

The first below was simply the championship of IBCA while the second was the European championship.

1958	Rheinbreitbach	Bonham
1966	Timmendorfer Strand	Čabarkapa (Yug)
1970	Ermelo	Čabarkapa
1975	Bad Berleburg	Rudensky (USSR)
1978	Bruges	Krylov (USSR)
1982	Hastings	Krylov

Correspondence World Championship

1955 – 7	Bonham
1957 – 9	Bonham
1959 – 61	Bonham
1961 – 3	Bonham
1963 – 4	Bonham & Kristensen (Denmark)
1965 – 6	Bonham
1966 – 8	Kristensen
1969 – 70	Kristensen
1971 – 2	Zeitler (W. Germany)
1973 – 4	Zeitler
1975 – 6	Fiter (Spain)
1977 – 8	Zeitler

Olympiads

		Winner	No. of teams
1961	Meschede	Yugoslavia	7
1964	Kuehkungsborn	Yugoslavia	9
1968	Weymouth	USSR	19
1972	Pula	USSR	22
1976	Kuortana	USSR	21
1980	Noorwijkerhout	USSR	23
1985	Benidorm	USSR	20

World Chess Oscar

Instituted in 1967 by Jordi Puig (Spain), the award is made to the player voted most outstanding of the year by chess journalists. In 1982 an award was instituted confined to women, although they are not excluded from the original Oscar.

	Oscar
1967	Larsen
1968	Spassky
1969	Spassky
1970	Fischer
1971	Fischer
1972	Fischer
1973	Karpov
1974	Karpov
1975	Karpov
1976	Karpov
1977	Karpov
1978	Korchnoi
1979	Karpov

	Oscar	Womens' Oscar
1980	Karpov	
1981	Karpov	
1982	Kasparov	Gaprindashvili
1983	Kasparov	Cramling
1984	Karpov	Chiburdanidze
1985	Kasparov	Chiburdanidze

Problems

World Problem Solving Championship

Originated during the 20th meeting of the FIDE Composition Commission, this is for teams of two.

1977	Finland
1978	Finland
1979	W. Germany
1980	Israel
1981	Finland
1982	Yugoslavia
1983	Finland
1984	Finland
1985	Finland

World Chess Composition Tournament

This has seven sections for ten composition themes, judged neutrally.

1	1975	USSR
2	1977(?)	USSR
3	1986	

World Computer Championship

The first world championship for computers was at Stockholm in 1974, when a Russian program won. Since then the event has taken place every three years, Toronto 1977, Linz 1980 and New York 1983, all three won by American programs. In 1966 computer programs made their first feeble attempt at competition with humans. The current world champion program is at approximately master level, and at speed chess is rated at approximately Elo 2600, which means that only a handful of humans could match it.

The computers used in these contests cost many millions of pounds. Since 1980 there have been regular world championships for the ordinary domestic chess computer. In a rapidly changing area there is little point in giving the names of machines, but the most successful programmers to date have been Dan and Kathy Spracklen and Richard Lang.

Morphy

'The pride and sorrow of chess' was how the Scotsman W.C. Spens styled Paul Charles Morphy, born 22 June 1837, New Orleans. Qualifying as a lawyer when still too young to practise, Morphy took a year off to play chess. He had a phenomenal memory: he knew the laws of Louisiana by heart, and just about every chess game score he had ever played through.

Morphy first became widely known after his clear win in the first American tournament, New York 1857. Visiting England he defeated a leading player, Löwenthal, by 9 – 3, with 2 draws and wanted to play Staunton, no longer active but still the most powerful voice in the chess world. Taking bad advice Morphy dodged playing in a tournament at Birmingham where Staunton had gone specifically to meet him, and in turn Staunton dodged Morphy for ever.

Morphy's popularity knew no bounds. He would play anyone prepared to face him, was gracious in victory and took his rare defeats well. Above all his play showed an unmatched tactical brilliance in an age when defensive play was hardly known. His next port of call, Paris, was a happy one, French being a natural second language for him.

Morphy's first serious opponent in Paris, Daniel Harrwitz (born 29 April 1823, Breslau, died 9 January 1884, Bolzano) was then at the height of his powers. Harrwitz won the first two games of their match and, having a sarcastic nature, mocked his opponent. Morphy, stung, won the next four games and, after a draw, the eighth game. Harrwitz resigned the match with an ill-grace which cost him his popularity and ultimately his job as a chess professional.

Possibly the Harrwitz match contained the best games that Morphy ever played but in the eyes of the public his next and last opponent, Anderssen, a maths teacher, was the one who counted. After his victory in the London 1851 tournament and Staunton's retirement Anderssen was held to be the foremost player. He was so keen to meet Morphy that he travelled to Paris during the school Christmas

Morphy as seen in 1859.

holiday 1858, although Morphy, with no demands on his time, could have made the opposite journey more easily.

Morphy had been ill and the match (for the first to win seven games) opened in his hotel room. Morphy lost the first game, drew the second, won five games in a row, drew another and won the next. Then Anderssen scored his second victory before losing the final game to end the match. For one of the few times in chess history there was unanimity as to the best player in the world.

Morphy promised to play a return match in Breslau, but his brother-in-law was sent to Paris to make him return home. In New York Morphy had a hero's welcome. He wrote a chess column in the *New York Ledger* where the first thing he did was to annotate 35 of the Bourdonnais-McDonnell games (see page 21).

What Morphy was unable to do was to set up a legal practice. The Civil War made it an inauspicious time but the real obstacle was that nobody would treat him as anything other than the world's greatest chess player. He withdrew from chess and eventually from all society when he developed a persecution complex. He died in his home in New Orleans, 10 July 1884.

International Tournaments

We are living in an age of unprecedented quality and quantity of tournaments. In his *Chess Tournaments, a checklist* covering 1849–1980 Jeremy Gaige cites 10,626 tournaments of all kinds, a quarter of them in the 1970s. The first real international tournament was in London in 1851, at the time of the Great Exhibition. It was run on a knock-out basis because it was assumed that once a player was out of the running he could not be expected to exert himself fully. A few days later an all-play-all tournament was held in London and indeed several players returned to their own countries after losing a few games. However by the 1870s there had been a shift to all-play-all, although knock-outs were retained for some types of competition.

Here are the details of a little more than 100 of the strongest international events to date excluding those already given in connection with world championships. Although these are all super-tournaments it is worth noting that the USSR championship is regularly of comparable strength, and so was the Hungarian championship in 1981.

A composed engraving from The Graphic, *17 July 1886, shows the leading players of the day. Standing l. to r., G.H. Mackenzie, Kolisch, Winawer, Bird, Riviére, Rosenthal, Mason, Potter, Schallopp, L. Paulsen, G.A. Macdonnell and Gunsberg. Seated, Blackburne, Steinitz, Zukertort and Englisch.* (Mary Evans)

Vienna *10 May – 26 June 1882*

		1	2	3	4	5	6	7	8	9	10	11	12	13	14	15	16	17	18	Total
1	Steinitz	♛	1½	½½	½1	0½	10	½½	11	01	1½	01	11	10	11	11	01	11*	11*	**24**
2	Winawer	0½	♛	00	½0	1½	10	11	10	01	1½	11	11	11	11	11	11	11*	01*	**24**
3	Mason	½½	11	♛	½1	0½	½½	½½	11	11	10	01	½1	11	1½	0½	11	01*	½1	**23**
4	Mackenzie	½0	½1	½0	♛	½½	10	½1	1½	½0	11	11	01	01	11	10	1½	11*	11*	**22½**
5	Zukertort	1½	0½	1½	½½	♛	0½	0½	11	11	00	11	01	01	11	11	11	11*	01*	**22½**
6	Blackburne	01	01	½½	01	1½	♛	½½	0½	10	01	10	1½	11	11	10	11	01*	11*	**21½**
7	Englisch	½½	00	½½	½0	1½	½½	♛	11	½0	½½	½½	½½	0½	01	11	11	11*	½1	**19½**
8	Paulsen	00	01	00	0½	00	1½	00	♛	½½	½1	½1	½1	11	½1	11	½1*	½1*	11	**18½**
9	Wittek	10	10	00	½1	00	01	½1	½½	♛	½0	01	½½	10	½½	½1	1½	½1*	11*	**18**
10	Weiss	0½	0½	01	·00	11	10	½½	½0	½1	♛	0½	0½	11	0½	01	00	11*	11*	**16½**
11	Hruby	10	00	10	00	00	01	½½	½0	10	1½	♛	½½	10	11	01	10	01*	11*	**16**
12	Schwarz	00	00	½0	10	10	0½	½½	.½0	½½	1½	½½	♛	00	½0	11	½0	01*	11*	**14**
13	Chigorin	01	00	00	10	10	00	00	1½	01	00	01	11	♛	00	11	1½	01*	01	**14**
14	Meitner	00	00	0½	00	00	00	10	½0	½½	1½	00	½1	11	♛	01	01	01*	11	**13**
15	Bird	00	00	1½	01	00	01	00	½0	½0	10	10	00	00	10	♛	11	½1*	01	**12**
16	Ware, Jr.	10	00	00	0½	00	00	00	00	0½	11	01	½1	0½	10	00	♛	01*	11*	**11**
17	Noa	00*	00*	10*	00*	00*	10*	00*	½0*	½0*	00*	10*	10*	10*	10*	½0*	10*	♛	½0*	**9**
18	Fleissig, B	00*	10*	½0*	00*	10*	00*	½0	½0*	00*	00*	00*	00*	10	00*	10	00*	½1*	♛	**7**

*scored by default
Winawer won the first game of the play-off match, Steinitz the second. The prizes were then shared.

London *26 April – 23 June 1883*

		1	2	3	4	5	6	7	8	9
1	Zukertort	♛	01	d11	1d1	dd11	1d0	11	11	d1d1
2	Steinitz	10	♛	10	00	0dd1	11	1d1	d0d0	11
3	Blackburne	d00	01	♛	01	1dd0	d00	1d1	d1d1*	dd½dd1
4	Chigorin	0d0	11	10	♛	0d1	11	d01	0dd1	10
5	Englisch	dd00	1dd0	0dd1	1d0	♛	dd½dd½	dd00	dd½dd1	01
6	Mackenzie	0d1	00	d11	00	dd½dd½	♛	0d1	d0d1	01
7	Mason	00	0d0	0d0	d10	dd11	1d0	♛	d10	d10
8	Rosenthal	00	d1d1	d0d0*	1dd0	dd½dd0	d1d0	d01	♛	dd½dd1
9	Winawer	d0d0	00	dd½dd0	01	10	10	d01	dd½dd0	♛
10	Bird	00	00	1d0	01	d10	1d0	00	d01	d10
11	Noa	00	0d0	0d0	d01	00	0d0	dd½0	10	dd01
12	Sellman	01	00	d00	0d0	d00	dd½d0	0dd0	d10	0d0
13	Mortimer	01	0d0	00	01	00	d00	d00	00	00
14	Skipworth	00	00	00	00	00	00	00	d00	00

*scored by default
d = 1st or 2nd draw, which did not count and had to be replayed. Skipworth retired early in the 2nd round.

Hastings *5 August – 2 September 1895*

		1	2	3	4	5	6	7	8	9	10	11	12	13	14	15	16	17	18	19	20	21	22	Total
1	Pillsbury	♛	0	0	1	1	1	1	1	0	½	½	1	1	1	1	1	1	½	1	1	1	1	**16½**
2	Chigorin	1	♛	1	1	0	0	1	1	1	1	½	1	0	1	½	1	½	1	1	½	1	1	**16**
3	Lasker	1	0	♛	0	1	1	0	1	1	0	1	1	1	½	1	1	½	1	1	½	1	1	**15½**
4	Tarrasch	0	0	1	♛	1	1	½	0	½	1	1	1	1	0	1	½	1	1	0	½	1	1	**14**
5	Steinitz	0	1	0	0	♛	1	1	½	½	1	1	½	0	1	0	1	1	1	0	½	1	1	**13**
6	Schiffers	0	1	0	0	0	♛	½	½	0	1	1	½	1	½	1	1	0	½	1	½	1	1	**12**
7	Bardeleben	0	0	1	½	0	½	♛	½	½	0	0	1	½	1	½	1	½	1	1	1	0	1	**11½**
8	Teichmann	0	0	0	1	½	½	½	♛	½	0	0	1	½	1	1	0	½	1	½	1	1	1	**11½**
9	Schlechter	1	0	0	½	½	1	½	½	♛	½	½	1	0	1	½	½	½	½	½	½	1	0	**11**
10	Blackburne	½	0	1	0	0	0	1	1	½	♛	0	1	1	0	½	0	1	0	1	0	1	1	**10½**
11	Walbrodt	½	½	0	0	0	0	1	1	½	1	♛	0	0	½	½	½	0	½	½	1	1	1	**10**
12	Burn	0	0	0	0	½	½	0	0	0	0	1	♛	1	0	½	0	1	1	1	1	1	1	**9½**
13	Janowski	0	1	0	0	1	0	½	½	1	0	1	0	♛	½	½	0	0	1	½	1	0	1	**9½**
14	Mason	0	0	½	1	0	½	0	0	0	1	½	1	½	♛	1	0	½	0	1	1	0	1	**9½**
15	Bird	0	½	0	0	1	0	½	0	½	½	½	½	½	0	♛	1	1	½	0	½	½	1	**9**
16	Gunsberg	0	0	0	½	0	0	0	1	½	1	½	1	1	1	0	♛	1	½	0	1	0	0	**9**
17	Albin	0	½	½	0	0	1	½	½	½	0	1	0	1	½	0	0	♛	0	0	1	1	½	**8½**
18	Marco	½	0	0	0	0	½	0	0	½	1	½	0	0	1	½	½	1	♛	1	1	0	½	**8½**
19	Pollock	0	0	0	1	1	0	0	½	½	0	½	0	½	0	1	1	1	0	♛	0	0	1	**8**
20	Mieses	0	½	½	½	½	½	0	0	½	1	0	0	0	0	½	0	0	0	1	♛	1	1	**7½**
21	Tinsley	0	0	0	0	0	0	1	0	0	0	0	0	1	1	½	1	0	1	1	0	♛	1	**7½**
22	Vergani	0	0	0	0	0	0	0	0	1	0	0	0	0	0	0	1	½	½	0	0	0	♛	**3**

St Petersburg *13 December 1895 – 27 January 1896*

		1	2	3	4	Total
1	Lasker	♛♛	11½01½	00½1½½	1½11½1	**11½**
2	Steinitz	00½10½	♛♛	1½½111	01100½	**9½**
3	Pillsbury	11½0½½	0½½000	♛♛	11100½	**8**
4	Chigorin	0½00½0	10011½	00011½	♛♛	**7**

10	11	12	13	14	Total
11	11	10	10	11	**22**
11	1*d*1	11	1*d*1	11	**19**
0*d*1	1*d*1	*d*11	11	11	**17½**
10	*d*10	1*d*1	10	11	**16**
*d*01	11	*d*11	11	11	**15½**
0*d*1	1*d*1	*dd*½*d*1	*d*11	11	**15½**
11	*dd*½1	1*dd*1	*d*11	11	**15½**
*d*10	01	*d*01	11	*d*11	**14**
*d*01	*dd*10	1*d*1	11	11	**13**
♛	00	11	*d*11	*d*11	**12**
11	♛	01	11	01	**9½**
00	10	♛	11	01	**6½**
*d*00	00	00	♛	01	**3**
*d*00	10	10	10	♛	**3**

Pillsbury.

Budapest 4 – 28 October 1896

	1	2	3	4	5	6	7	8	9	10	11	12	13	Total
1 Charousek	♛	1	1	0	½	½	1	½	1	1	0	1	1	8½
2 Chigorin	0	♛	½	1	0	1	½	1	1	1	1	½	1	8½
3 Pillsbury	0	½	♛	½	½	1	1	0	0	1	1	1	1	7½
4 Janowsky	1	0	½	♛	0	0	1	0	1	1	½	1	1	7
5 Schlechter	½	1	½	1	♛	½	1	½	0	½	1	½	0	7
6 Walbrodt	½	0	0	1	½	♛	1	0	1	0	½	1	1	6½
7 Winawer	0	½	0	0	0	0	♛	1	1	1	1	1	1	6½
8 Tarrasch	½	0	1	1	½	1	0	♛	½	0	0	½	1	6
9 Albin	0	0	1	0	1	0	0	½	♛	0	1	½	1	5
10 Maróczy	0	0	0	0	½	1	0	1	1	♛	½	0	1	5
11 Marco	1	0	0	½	0	½	0	1	0	½	♛	1	0	4½
12 Noa	0	½	0	0	½	0	0	½	½	1	0	♛	1	4
13 Popiel	0	0	0	0	0	1	0	0	0	0	1	0	♛	2

In play-off, Chigorin beat Charousek, +3, =0, −1.

London 30 May – 10 July 1899

	1	2	3	4	5	6	7	8	9	10	11	12	13	14	15	Total
1 Lasker	♛	1½	½1	½1	½1	01	11	11	1½	1½	½1	11	11	11	*1−	22½
2 Janowsky	0½	♛	01	10	11	1½	11	½1	00	11	10	11	01	1½	*1−	18
3 Maróczy	½0	10	♛	½½	½½	½1	01	1½	10	11	½1	½1	1½	11	*1−	18
4 Pillsbury	½0	01	½½	♛	½1	00	10	½½	11	11	11	1½	11	½−		18
5 Schlechter	½0	00	½½	½0	♛	1½	10	½1	½1	0½	11	11	11	11	*1−	17
6 Blackburne	10	0½	½0	11	0½	♛	½0	01	1½	01	10	1½	11	11	½−	15½
7 Chigorin	00	00	10	01	01	½1	♛	1½	1½	01	½1	10	11	10	1−	15
8 Showalter	00	½0	0½	½½	½0	10	0½	♛	0½	0½	1½	11	11	01	*1−	12½
9 Mason	0½	11	01	00	½0	0½	0½	1½	♛	00	01	00	11	½1	*1−	12
10 Cohn, W	0½	00	00	00	1½	10	10	1½	11	♛	0½	1½	10	00	*1−	11½
11 Steinitz	½0	01	½0	00	00	01	½0	0½	10	1½	♛	½0	½1	11	*1−	11½
12 Lee	00	00	½0	00	00	0½	01	00	11	0½	½1	♛	½1	½½	*1−	9½
13 Bird	00	10	0½	0½	00	00	00	00	00	01	½0	½0	♛	11	*1−	7
14 Tinsley	00	0½	00	00	00	00	01	10	½0	11	00	½½	00	♛	0−	6
15 Teichmann	*0−	*0−	*0−	½−	*0−	½−	0−	*0−	*0−	*0−	*0−	*0−	*0−	1−	♛	2

*scored by default
Teichmann retired ill after playing four games.

Engraving from a German book of 1616. (Author)

St Petersburg *15 February – 12 March 1909*

	1	2	3	4	5	6	7	8	9	10	11	12	13	14	15	16	17	18	19	Total
1 Lasker	♛	0	1	½	½	1	1	1	1	½	1	1	0	1	1	1	1	1	1	**14½**
2 Rubinstein	1	♛	1	1	½	½	½	1	1	1	1	½	0	1	½	1	1	1	1	**14½**
3 Duras	0	0	♛	0	0	1	½	0	1	½	1	0	1	1	1	1	1	1	1	**11**
4 Spielmann	½	0	1	♛	0	1	1	½	½	1	½	½	1	0	½	1	½	½	1	**11**
5 Bernstein	½	½	1	1	♛	0	1	0	1	1	1	1	½	0	0	0	½	½	1	**10½**
6 Teichmann	0	½	0	0	1	♛	0	½	½	½	1	½	1	½	1	½	1	1	½	**10**
7 Perlis	0	½	½	0	0	1	♛	½	1	½	1	½	1	½	1	½	0	0	1	**9½**
8 Cohn, E	0	0	1	½	1	½	½	♛	0	0	½	1	½	0	½	½	½	1	1	**9**
9 Salwe	0	0	0	½	0	½	0	1	♛	0	1	½	1	1	½	0	1	1	1	**9**
10 Schlechter	½	0	½	0	0	½	½	1	1	♛	0	0	1	1	½	0	1	½	1	**9**
11 Mieses	0	0	0	½	0	0	0	½	0	1	♛	1	½	1	1	1	0	1	1	**8½**
12 Tartakower	0	½	1	½	0	½	½	0	½	1	0	♛	0	0	½	1	1	1	½	**8½**
13 Dus-Khotimirski	1	1	0	0	½	0	0	½	0	0	½	1	♛	½	½	½	1	0	1	**8**
14 Forgács	0	0	0	1	1	½	½	1	0	0	0	1	½	♛	½	½	½	0	½	**7½**
15 Burn	0	½	0	½	1	0	0	½	½	½	0	½	½	½	♛	1	½	½	0	**7**
16 Vidmar	0	0	0	0	1	½	½	½	1	1	0	0	½	½	0	♛	½	1	0	**7**
17 Speijer	0	0	0	½	½	0	1	½	0	0	1	0	0	½	½	½	♛	½	½	**6**
18 Freymann	0	0	0	½	½	0	1	0	0	½	0	0	1	1	½	0	½	♛	0	**5½**
19 Znosko-Borowski	0	0	0	0	0	½	0	0	0	0	0	½	0	½	1	1	½	1	♛	**5**

San Sebastian *19 February – 17 March 1911*

	1	2	3	4	5	6	7	8	9	10	11	12	13	14	15	Total
1 Capablanca	♛	0	½	½	1	½	½	1	1	½	1	½	1	½	1	9½
2 Rubinstein	1	♛	½	½	½	½	½	½	½	½	1	½	½	1	1	9
3 Vidmar	½	½	♛	0	½	½	½	1	½	½	1	½	1	1	1	9
4 Marshall	½	½	1	♛	½	½	½	½	½	1	1	½	½	0	1	8½
5 Nimzowitsch	0	½	½	½	♛	½	0	½	1	1	½	½	½	½	1	7½
6 Schlechter	½	½	½	½	½	♛	½	0	½	½	1	½	½	1	½	7½
7 Tarrasch	½	½	½	½	1	½	♛	1	½	0	½	½	1	0	½	7½
8 Bernstein	0	½	0	½	½	1	0	♛	1	1	½	1	0	1	0	7
9 Spielmann	0	½	½	½	0	½	½	0	♛	½	½	1	½	1	1	7
10 Teichmann	½	½	½	0	0	½	1	0	½	♛	0	½	½	1	1	6½
11 Janowski	0	0	0	0	½	0	½	½	½	1	♛	0	1	1	1	6
12 Maroczy	½	½	½	½	½	½	½	0	0	½	1	♛	½	½	0	6
13 Burn	0	½	0	½	½	½	0	1	½	½	0	½	♛	0	½	5
14 Duras	½	0	0	1	½	0	1	0	0	0	0	½	1	♛	½	5
15 Leonhardt	0	0	0	0	0	½	½	1	0	0	0	1	½	½	♛	4

San Sebastian *19 February – 20 March 1912*

		1	2	3	4	5	6	7	8	9	10	11	Total
1	Rubinstein	♛	½1	01	½1	½½	1½	01	11	½½	½1	½	12½
2	Nimzowitsch	½0	♛	01	1½	0½	11	11	½½	½½	11	½	12
3	Spielmann	10	10	♛	10	1½	½1	½½	½1	½½	1½	1	12
4	Tarrasch	½0	0½	01	♛	11	01	½0	½½	11	11	1	11½
5	Perlis	½½	1½	0½	00	♛	1½	½1	½½	½½	1½	½	10
6	Marshall	0½	00	½0	10	0½	♛	½1	1½	½½	11	1	9½
7	Duras	10	00	½½	½1	½0	½0	♛	½½	½1	01	½	8½
8	Schlechter	00	½½	½0	½½	½½	0½	½½	♛	½½	1½	½	8
9	Teichmann	½½	½½	½½	00	½½	½½	½0	½½	♛	½½	½	8
10	Leonhardt	½0	00	0½	00	0½	00	10	0½	½½	♛	1	5
11	Forgács	½	½	0	0	½	0	½	½	½	0	♛	3

St Petersburg *21 April – 22 May 1914*
Preliminary Section

		1	2	3	4	5	6	7	8	9	10	11	Total
1	Capablanca	♛	½	½	1	½	1	½	1	1	1	1	8
2	Lasker	½	♛	½	½	½	0	1	½	1	1	1	6½
3	Tarrasch	½	½	♛	½	½	1	½	1	1	0	1	6½
4	Alekhine	0	½	½	♛	1	½	1	½	½	½	1	6
5	Marshall	½	½	½	0	♛	1	½	½	1	1	½	6
6	Bernstein	0	1	0	½	0	♛	½	½	½	1	1	5
7	Rubinstein	½	0	½	0	½	½	♛	½	½	1	1	5
8	Nimzowitsch	0	½	0	½	½	½	½	♛	0	½	1	4
9	Blackburne	0	0	0	½	0	½	½	1	♛	0	1	3½
10	Janowski	0	0	1	½	0	0	0	½	1	♛	½	3½
11	Gunsberg	0	0	0	0	½	0	0	0	0	½	♛	1

Final Section

		1	2	3	4	5	Total
1	Lasker	♛	½1	11	1½	11	7
2	Capablanca	½0	♛	½1	10	11	5
3	Alekhine	00	½0	♛	11	1½	4
4	Tarrasch	0½	01	00	♛	0½	2
5	Marshall	00	00	0½	1½	♛	2

Final Standing
(Based on cumulative scores from preliminary and final sections)

		W	D	L	Total
1	Lasker	10	7	1	13½
2	Capablanca	10	6	2	13
3	Alekhine	6	8	4	10
4	Tarrasch	5	7	6	8½
5	Marshall	4	8	6	8

Schlechter in 1909.

New York   *16 March – 19 April 1924*

	1	2	3	4	5	6	7	8	9	10	11	*Total*
1 Dr E. Lasker	♛	½0	1½	½1	11	11	11	½1	½1	½1	11	16
2 Capablanca	½1	♛	½½	½½	01	½1	11	11	1½	½1	½1	14½
3 Alekhine	0½	½½	♛	½½	10	1½	½½	½½	11	½½	11	12
4 Marshall	½0	½½	½½	♛	½1	0½	01	½0	½1	1½	11	11
5 Reti	00	10	01	½0	♛	½½	01	11	10	10	11	10½
6 Maróczy	00	½0	0½	1½	½½	♛	01	½½	11	½1	10	10
7 Bogoljubow	00	00	½½	10	10	10	♛	01	11	½1	01	9½
8 Tartakower	½0	00	½½	½1	00	½½	10	♛	10	½0	½1	8
9 Yates	½0	0½	00	½0	01	00	00	01	♛	11	½1	7
10 Ed Lasker	½0	½0	½½	0½	01	½0	½0	½1	00	♛	0½	6½
11 Janowski	00	½0	00	00	00	01	10	½0	½0	1½	♛	5

New York   *19 February – 22 March 1927*

	1	2	3	4	5	6	*Total*
1 Capablanca	♛	1½½½	1½1½	½½1½	½½1½	11½1	14
2 Alekhine	0½½½	♛	½01½	½½½½	1½½1	½1½1	11½
3 Nimzowitsch	0½0½	½10½	♛	100½	11½½	1½½1	10½
4 Vidmar	½½0½	½½½½	011½	♛	½½½½	½01½	10
5 Spielmann	½½0½	0½½0	00½½	½½½½	♛	½½1½	8
6 Marshall	00½0	½0½0	0½½0	½10½	½½0½	♛	6

Berlin   *11–29 October 1928*

	1	2	3	4	5	6	7	*Total*
1 Capablanca	♛	½½	½½	½½	1½	11	11	8½
2 Nimzowitsch	½½	♛	½0	½½	01	11	1½	7
3 Spielmann	½½	½1	♛	½0	11	½0	½½	6½
4 Tartakower	½½	½½	½1	♛	00	½0	1½	5½
5 Rubinstein	0½	10	00	11	♛	01	0½	5
6 Reti	00	00	½1	½1	10	♛	½½	5
7 Marshall	00	0½	½½	0½	1½	½½	♛	4½

Bled   *23 August – 20 September 1931*

	1	2	3	4	5	6	7	8	9	10	11	12	13	14	*Total*
1 Alekhine	♛	1½	11	1½	½½	11	1½	1½	1½	½½	11	11	½½	11	20½
2 Bogoljubow	0½	♛	½0	11	11	1½	0½	10	01	0½	00	11	½1	11	15
3 Nimzowitsch	00	½1	♛	11	00	0½	½½	½½	½½	½1	1½	1½	11	0½	14
4 Flohr	0½	00	00	♛	1½	½½	½1	10	1½	½1	11	½0	½1	½½	13½
5 Kashdan	½½	00	11	0½	♛	1½	½½	00	1½	½½	10	11	½½	½½	13½
6 Stoltz	00	0½	1½	½½	0½	♛	½1	11	½½	½1	½1	00	01	1½	13½
7 Vidmar	0½	1½	½½	½0	½½	½0	♛	½½	11	½0	½½	½1	½1	½½	13½
8 Tartakower	0½	01	½½	01	11	00	½½	♛	½0	½½	½½	11	½½	½½	13
9 Kostić	0½	10	½½	0½	0½	½½	00	½1	♛	½½	½½	01	1½	11	12½
10 Spielmann	½½	1½	½0	½0	½½	½0	½1	½½	½½	♛	0½	00	1½	11	12½
11 Maróczy	00	11	0½	00	01	½0	½½	½½	½½	1½	♛	½1	½½	½½	12
12 Colle	00	00	0½	½1	00	11	½0	00	10	11	½0	♛	0½	11	10½
13 Asztalos	½½	½0	00	½0	½½	10	½0	½½	0½	0½	½½	1½	♛	0½	9½
14 Pirc	00	00	1½	½½	½½	0½	½½	½½	00	00	½½	00	1½	♛	8½

Moscow *14 May – 8 June 1936*

		1	2	3	4	5	6	7	8	9	10	Total
1	Capablanca	♛	1½	½½	1½	1½	½1	½1	½½	11	½1	13
2	Botvinnik	0½	♛	½1	1½	½1	½1	11	½½	½1	½½	12
3	Flohr	½½	½0	♛	½1	0½	½1	0½	½0	½1	11	9½
4	Lilienthal	0½	0½	½0	♛	½½	½1	½1	½1	½½	½½	9
5	Ragozin	0½	½0	1½	½½	♛	1½	0½	1½	½½	½0	8½
6	Lasker	½0	½0	½0	½0	0½	♛	½½	½1	1½	1½	8
7	Kan	½0	00	1½	½0	1½	½½	♛	½½	0½	½½	7½
8	Levenfisch	½½	½½	½1	½0	0½	½0	½½	♛	½0	10	7½
9	Ryumin	00	½0	½0	½½	½½	0½	1½	½1	♛	½½	7½
10	Eliskases	½0	½½	00	½½	½1	0½	½½	01	½½	♛	7½

Nottingham *10–28 August 1936*

		1	2	3	4	5	6	7	8	9	10	11	12	13	14	15	Total
1	Botvinnik	♛	½	½	½	½	½	½	½	1	1	1	1	1	1	½	10
2	Capablanca	½	♛	½	½	1	1	0	½	1	½	½	1	1	1	1	10
3	Euwe	½	½	♛	½	1	0	½	0	1	½	1	1	1	1	1	9½
4	Fine	½	½	½	♛	½	½	½	1	½	1	½	1	1	½	1	9½
5	Reshevsky	½	0	0	½	♛	1	½	1	1	1	½	1	1	1	½	9½
6	Alekhine	½	0	1	½	0	♛	1	½	½	1	1	½	1	½	1	9
7	Flohr	½	1	½	½	½	0	♛	1	1	1	½	0	0	1	1	8½
8	Lasker	½	½	1	0	0	½	0	♛	½	1	½	1	1	1	1	8½
9	Vidmar	0	0	0	½	0	½	0	½	♛	1	½	½	1	½	1	6
10	Bogoljubow	0	½	½	0	0	0	0	0	0	♛	½	1	1	1	1	5½
11	Tartakower	0	½	0	½	½	0	½	½	½	½	♛	0	0	1	1	5½
12	Tylor	0	0	0	0	0	½	1	0	½	0	1	♛	½	½	½	4½
13	Alexander	0	0	0	0	0	0	1	0	0	0	1	½	♛	½	½	3½
14	Thomas	0	0	0	½	0	½	0	0	½	0	0	½	½	♛	½	3
15	Winter	½	0	0	0	½	0	0	0	0	0	0	½	½	½	♛	2½

Semmering–Baden *8–27 September 1937*

		1	2	3	4	5	6	7	8	Total
1	Keres	♛	½½	½½	10	½1	10	½1	11	9
2	Fine	½½	♛	½½	½½	½½	½½	1½	1½	8
3	Capablanca	½½	½½	♛	½½	1½	½0	½1	½½	7½
4	Reshevsky	01	½½	½½	♛	½½	11	½0	10	7½
5	Flohr	½0	½½	0½	½½	♛	1½	½½	1½	7
6	Eliskases	01	½½	½1	00	0½	♛	½1	0½	6
7	Ragozin	½0	0½	½0	½1	½½	½0	♛	1½	6
8	Petrov	00	0½	½½	01	0½	1½	0½	♛	5

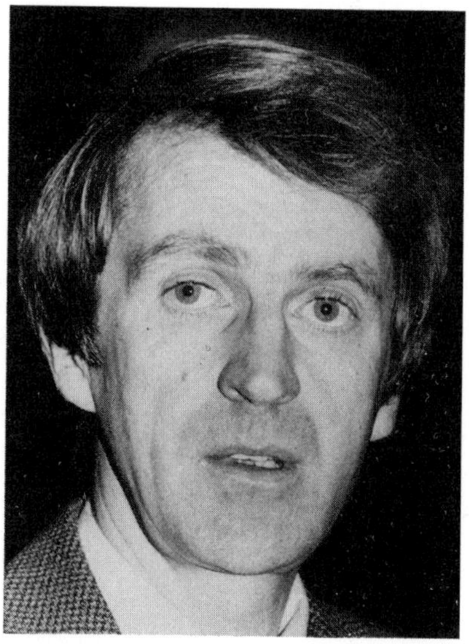

Fridrik Olafsson, former President of FIDE, now secretary to the Icelandic parliament. (Agterdenbos)

AVRO (= Algemeene Vereeniging 'Radio Omroep', a Dutch radio station)
6–27 November 1938 Each round was played in a different city – Amsterdam, The Hague, Rotterdam, Groningen, Zwolle, Haarlem, Amsterdam, Utrecht, Arnhem, Breda, Rotterdam, The Hague, Leiden and Amsterdam.

	1	2	3	4	5	6	7	8	Total
1 Keres	♛	1½	½½	½½	½½	1½	1½	½½	8½
2 Fine	0½	♛	1½	11	10	10	½½	1½	8½
3 Botvinnik	½½	0½	♛	1½	½0	1½	½1	½½	7½
4 Alekhine	½½	00	0½	♛	1½	½½	½1	½1	7
5 Euwe	½½	01	½1	0½	♛	0½	01	1½	7
6 Reshevsky	0½	01	0½	½½	1½	♛	½½	1½	7
7 Capablanca	0½	½½	½0	½0	10	½½	♛	½1	6
8 Flohr	½½	0½	½½	½0	0½	0½	½0	♛	4½

Smyslov. (Acorn Computers)

Moscow (Alekhine Memorial) *7 October – 3 November 1956*

	1	2	3	4	5	6	7	8	9	10	11	12	13	14	15	16	Total
1 Botvinnik	♛	½	½	½	½	1	0	½	½	1	1	1	1	1	1	1	11
2 Smyslov	½	♛	½	½	½	½	½	½	½	1	1	1	1	1	1	1	11
3 Taimanov	½	½	♛	½	1	1	½	½	½	½	½	1	½	1	1	1	10½
4 Gligorić	½	½	½	♛	0	½	½	½	1	½	½	1	1	1	1	1	10
5 Bronstein	½	½	0	1	♛	½	½	½	½	½	1	½	1	½	1	1	9½
6 Najdorf	0	½	0	½	½	♛	½	½	1	½	½	½	1	1	1	1	9
7 Keres	1	½	½	½	½	½	♛	1	0	½	0	½	½	½	1	1	8½
8 Pachman	½	½	½	½	½	½	0	♛	½	½	½	½	½	1	1	1	8½
9 Unzicker	½	½	½	0	½	0	1	½	♛	1	½	½	½	1	0	1	8
10 Ståhlberg	0	0	½	½	½	½	½	½	0	♛	½	½	1	1	1	1	8
11 Szabó	0	0	½	½	0	½	1	½	½	½	♛	½	½	½	0	½	6
12 Padevsky	0	0	0	0	½	½	½	½	½	½	½	♛	0	½	1	½	5½
13 Uhlmann	0	0	½	0	0	0	½	½	½	0	½	1	♛	1	½	½	5½
14 Chiocaltea	0	0	0	0	½	0	½	0	0	0	½	½	0	♛	1	½	3½
15 Sliwa	0	0	0	0	0	0	0	0	1	0	1	0	½	0	♛	½	3
16 Golombek	0	0	0	0	0	0	0	0	0	0	½	½	½	½	½	♛	2½

Dallas *30 November – 16 December 1957*

	1	2	3	4	5	6	7	8	Total
1 Gligorić	♛	½½	0½	½1	1½	½1	½½	½1	8½
2 Reshevsky	½½	♛	½½	½½	½0	01	11	11	8½
3 Szabó	1½	½½	♛	½½	½½	0½	½½	1½	7½
4 Larsen	½0	½½	½½	♛	1½	01	10	1½	7½
5 Yanofsky	0½	½1	½½	0½	♛	10	½½	½1	7
6 Olafsson, F	½0	10	1½	10	01	♛	½½	0½	6½
7 Najdorf	½½	00	½½	01	½½	½½	♛	½0	5½
8 Evans	½0	00	0½	0½	½0	1½	½1	♛	5

Moscow *6–21 April 1959*

	1	2	3	4	5	6	7	8	9	10	11	12	Total
1 Bronstein	♛	½	½	½	½	1	½	½	1	½	1	½	7
2 Smyslov	½	♛	1	½	½	½	½	1	½	½	½	1	7
3 Spassky	½	0	♛	1	½	½	½	½	1	1	½	1	7
4 Vasyukov	½	½	0	♛	½	½	½	½	½	1	1	½	6
5 Portisch	½	½	½	½	♛	0	½	½	½	½	1	1	6
6 Filip	0	½	½	½	1	♛	1	½	½	½	½	½	6
7 Aronin	½	½	½	½	½	0	♛	1	½	½	½	0	5
8 Milev	½	0	½	½	½	½	0	♛	½	1	½	½	5
9 Olafsson	0	½	0	½	½	½	½	½	♛	0	1	1	5
10 Simagin	½	½	0	0	½	½	½	0	1	♛	½	½	4½
11 Larsen	0	½	½	0	0	½	½	½	0	½	♛	1	4
12 Lutikov	½	0	0	½	0	½	1	½	0	½	0	♛	3½

Ivkov. (Bénédictine)

Bled *2 September – 4 October 1961*

	1	2	3	4	5	6	7	8	9	10	11	12	13	14	15	16	17	18	19	20	Total
1 Tal	♛	0	½	½	½	½	½	1	1	1	½	1	1	1	½	1	1	1	1	1	14½
2 Fischer	1	♛	1	½	½	1	1	½	1	½	½	½	½	1	1	½	½	1	½	½	13½
3 Petrosyan	½	0	♛	½	1	½	½	1	½	½	½	½	1	1	0	½	1	1	1	1	12½
4 Keres	½	½	½	♛	½	½	½	½	0	½	½	1	½	1	1	1	1	½	1	1	12½
5 Gligorić	½	½	0	½	♛	½	½	½	1	1	½	½	½	½	½	1	1	1	1	1	12½
6 Geller	½	0	½	½	½	♛	½	1	0	½	½	½	½	0	1	1	½	1	1	½	10½
7 Trifunović	½	0	½	½	½	½	♛	½	½	½	½	½	½	½	½	½	1	½	1	1	10½
8 Parma	0	½	0	½	½	0	½	♛	½	½	½	½	½	1	½	1	½	½	1	1	10
9 Bisguier	0	0	½	1	0	1	½	½	♛	0	½	0	1	0	½	1	½	½	1	1	9½
10 Matanović	0	½	½	½	0	½	½	½	1	♛	½	½	0	1	½	½	0	1	1	½	9½
11 Darga	½	½	½	½	½	½	½	½	½	½	♛	½	½	0	½	0	½	1	0	1	9
12 Donner	0	½	½	0	½	½	½	½	1	½	½	♛	1	0	½	1	½	0	0	1	9
13 Najdorf	0	½	0	½	½	½	½	½	0	1	½	0	♛	1	½	0	½	1	1	½	9
14 Olafsson	0	0	0	0	½	1	½	0	1	0	1	1	0	♛	1	½	½	½	½	½	8½
15 Portisch	½	0	1	0	½	0	½	½	½	½	½	½	½	0	♛	0	½	½	½	1	8
16 Ivkov	0	½	½	0	0	0	½	0	0	½	1	0	1	½	1	♛	1	½	½	½	8
17 Pachman	0	½	0	0	0	½	0	½	½	1	½	½	½	½	½	0	♛	½	½	½	7
18 Bertok	0	0	0	½	0	0	½	½	½	0	0	1	0	½	½	½	½	♛	½	1	6½
19 Germek	0	½	0	0	0	0	0	0	0	0	1	1	0	½	½	½	½	½	♛	½	5½
20 Udovčić	0	½	0	0	0	½	0	0	0	½	0	0	½	½	0	½	½	0	½	♛	4

Los Angeles (Piatigorsky Cup) *2–27 July 1963*

	1	2	3	4	5	6	7	8	Total
1 Keres	♛	½½	½0	11	00	½1	11	½1	8½
2 Petrosyan	½½	♛	½½	½½	½½	01	11	½1	8½
3 Najdorf	½1	½½	♛	½0	1½	½½	0½	1½	7½
4 Olafsson	00	½½	½1	♛	½1	½1	10	½½	7½
5 Reshevsky	11	½½	0½	½0	♛	½½	1½	0½	7
6 Gligorić	½0	10	½½	½0	½½	♛	½0	1½	6
7 Benkö	00	00	1½	01	0½	½1	♛	10	5½
8 Panno	½0	½0	0½	½½	1½	0½	01	♛	5½

Belgrade *22 September – 14 October 1964*

	1	2	3	4	5	6	7	8	9	10	11	12	13	14	15	16	17	18	Total
1 Spassky	♛	½	½	½	1	½	½	1	1	½	1	½	1	½	1	1	1	1	13
2 Korchnoi	½	♛	0	1	1	1	0	1	½	½	½	1	0	1	1	½	1	1	11½
3 Ivkov	½	1	♛	0	½	½	½	½	½	½	½	½	1	1	1	1	1	1	11½
4 Gligorić	½	0	1	♛	1	1	½	1	0	0	½	½	½	1	1	1	1	½	11
5 Larsen	0	0	½	0	♛	1	1	1	1	½	½	½	½	1	0	½	1	1	10
6 Matanović	½	0	½	0	0	♛	½	½	½	1	½	½	1	1	1	½	1	1	10
7 Bronstein	½	1	½	½	0	½	♛	½	1	0	½	½	½	½	1	½	1	½	9½
8 Benko	0	0	½	0	0	½	½	♛	½	1	1	1	1	½	½	1	½	1	9½
9 Cirić	0	½	½	1	0	½	0	½	♛	½	½	½	½	½	½	1	1	1	9
10 Janosević	½	½	½	1	½	0	1	0	½	♛	0	½	0	½	½	1	0	1	8
11 Parma	0	½	½	½	½	½	½	0	½	1	♛	½	½	½	0	0	1	½	7½
12 Trifunović	½	0	½	½	½	½	½	0	½	½	½	♛	½	½	0	½	½	½	7
13 Flesch	0	1	0	½	½	0	½	0	½	1	½	½	♛	½	0	½	½	½	7
14 Minić	½	0	0	0	0	0	½	½	½	½	½	½	½	♛	1	½	1	½	7
15 Szabo	0	0	0	0	1	0	0	½	½	½	1	1	1	0	♛	1	0	0	6½
16 Matulović	0	½	0	0	½	½	½	0	0	0	1	½	½	½	0	♛	½	½	5½
17 Zuidema	0	0	0	0	0	0	0	½	0	1	0	½	½	0	1	½	♛	1	5
18 Milić	0	0	0	½	0	0	½	0	0	0	½	½	½	½	1	½	0	♛	4½

Zagreb *12 April – 9 May 1965*

	1	2	3	4	5	6	7	8	9	10	11	12	13	14	15	16	17	18	19	20	Total
1 Ivkov	♛	½	½	½	0	1	1	½	½	½	1	½	1	1	1	½	1	½	1	1	13½
2 Uhlmann	½	♛	½	½	0	½	1	½	1	1	1	½	½	½	1	1	½	1	1	1	13½
3 Petrosyan	½	½	♛	½	0	½	1	½	½	1	½	½	½	½	½	1	1	1	1	1	12½
4 Parma	½	½	½	♛	½	½	1	½	½	½	½	½	1	½	½	½	½	1	1	1	12
5 Portisch	1	1	1	½	♛	½	1	½	1	1	½	½	½	½	½	½	0	½	½	½	12
6 Bronstein	0	½	½	½	½	♛	½	½	½	1	½	½	½	1	1	½	½	½	1	1	11½
7 Larsen	0	0	0	0	0	½	♛	1	1	½	1	½	½	0	1	1	1	1	½	1	10½
8 Filip	½	½	½	½	½	½	0	♛	1	½	½	½	½	½	½	½	0	1	½	½	9½
9 Matanović	½	0	½	½	0	½	0	0	♛	1	½	½	1	½	1	½	½	½	1	½	9½
10 Padevsky	½	0	0	½	0	0	½	½	0	♛	½	1	½	½	½	1	1	1	1	½	9½
11 Antoshin	0	0	½	½	½	½	0	½	½	½	♛	1	½	1	0	½	½	½	½	1	9
12 Marović	½	½	½	½	½	½	½	½	½	0	0	♛	½	½	½	½	1	½	0	1	9
13 Minić	0	½	½	0	½	½	½	½	0	½	½	½	♛	½	1	½	½	½	½	1	9
14 Bisguier	0	½	½	½	½	0	1	½	½	½	0	½	½	♛	0	0	½	1	1	½	8½
15 Damjanović	0	0	½	½	½	0	0	½	0	½	1	½	0	1	♛	0	½	1	1	1	8½
16 Gipslis	½	0	0	½	½	½	0	½	½	0	½	½	½	1	1	♛	½	0	1	½	8½
17 Gligorić	0	½	0	½	1	½	0	1	½	0	½	0	½	½	½	½	♛	1	½	½	8½
18 Udovčić	½	0	0	0	½	½	0	0	½	0	½	½	½	0	0	1	0	♛	½	1	6
19 Golombek	0	0	0	0	½	0	½	½	0	0	½	1	½	0	0	0	½	½	♛	½	5
20 Bertok	0	0	0	0	½	0	0	½	½	½	0	0	0	½	0	½	½	0	½	♛	4

Yerevan *17 September – 6 October 1965*

	1	2	3	4	5	6	7	8	9	10	11	12	13	14	*Total*
1 Korchnoi	♛	½	½	½	½	½	1	½	1	1	½	1	1	1	9½
2 Petrosyan	½	♛	½	½	½	1	½	½	1	½	½	1	1	½	8½
3 Stein	½	½	♛	1	0	½	½	1	½	1	1	½	½	1	8½
4 Liberzon	½	½	0	♛	1	1	½	½	½	½	½	½	1	1	8
5 Portisch	½	½	1	0	♛	½	½	0	½	1	½	1	0	1	7
6 Nei	½	0	½	0	½	♛	1	½	½	½	½	½	½	1	6½
7 Averbakh	0	½	½	½	½	0	♛	1	½	½	½	½	½	½	6
8 Matanović	½	½	0	½	1	½	0	♛	½	½	½	½	½	½	6
9 Filip	0	0	½	½	½	½	½	½	♛	½	½	½	½	1	6
10 Fuchs	0	½	0	½	0	½	½	½	½	♛	½	½	1	1	6
11 Stålhberg	½	½	0	½	½	½	½	½	½	½	♛	½	1	0	6
12 Schmid	0	0	½	½	0	½	½	½	½	½	½	♛	1	½	5½
13 Mhatsakanyan	0	0	½	0	1	½	½	½	½	0	0	0	♛	1	4½
14 Shashin	0	½	0	0	0	0	½	½	0	0	1	½	0	♛	3

Moscow *14–28 January 1966*

	1	2	3	4	5	6	*Total*
1 Petrosyan	♛	10	11	1½	1½	11	8
2 Boleslavsky	01	♛	1½	½½	11	0½	6
3 Simagin	00	0½	♛	1½	1½	01	4½
4 Averbakh	0½	½½	0½	♛	00	11	4
5 Korchnoi	0½	00	0½	11	♛	½½	4
6 Shamkovich	00	1½	10	00	½½	♛	3½

Santa Monica (Piatigorsky Cup) *17 July – 15 August 1966*

	1	2	3	4	5	6	7	8	9	10	*Total*
1 Spassky	♛	1½	½1	½½	1½	½½	½½	½½	1½	½1	11½
2 Fischer	0½	♛	01	½1	½½	½½	½1	01	11	½1	11
3 Larsen	½0	10	♛	1½	½0	11	½1	1½	01	½0	10
4 Portisch	½½	½0	0½	♛	½½	1½	½½	½½	½1	½1	9½
5 Unzicker	0½	½½	½1	½½	♛	½½	½½	½½	1½	½½	9½
6 Petrosyan	½½	½½	00	0½	½½	♛	½½	11	½½	½1	9
7 Reshevsky	½½	½0	½0	½½	½½	½½	♛	½1	½½	1½	9
8 Najdorf	½½	10	0½	½½	½½	00	½0	♛	1½	½1	8
9 Ivkov	0½	00	10	½0	0½	½½	½½	0½	♛	½1	6½
10 Donner	½0	½0	½1	½0	½½	½0	0½	½0	½0	♛	6

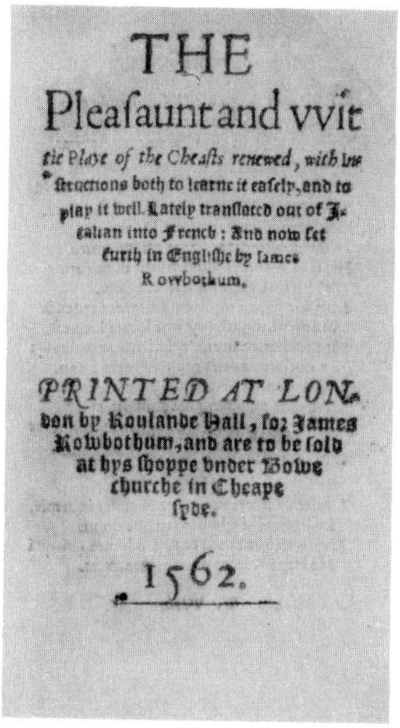
THE
Pleasaunt and wittie Playe of the Cheasts renewed, with instructions both to learne it easely, and to play it well. Lately translated out of Italian into French: And now set furth in Englishe by James Rowbothum.

PRINTED AT LONdon by Roulande Hall, for James Rowbothum, and are to be sold at hys shoppe under Bowe churche in Cheape syde.

1562.

Title page of the first instructional book on chess published in England (a translation of Damiano). (Author)

Moscow *21 May – 18 June 1967*

		1	2	3	4	5	6	7	8	9	10	11	12	13	14	15	16	17	18	Total
1	Stein	♛	½	½	½	½	1	½	½	½	1	½	½	0	1	1	1	½	1	**11**
2	Gipslis	½	♛	½	½	½	½	½	½	½	½	½	½	1	1	½	½	½	1	**10**
3	Bobotsov	½	½	♛	½	½	½	½	½	½	½	½	½	1	1	½	½	½	1	**10**
4	Smyslov	½	½	½	♛	½	1	½	½	½	½	½	½	1	½	1	½	0	1	**10**
5	Tal	½	½	½	½	♛	0	1	½	½	0	1	½	½	½	1	1	½	1	**10**
6	Portisch	0	½	½	0	1	♛	½	1	0	1	1	½	0	½	1	½	1	½	**9½**
7	Bronstein	½	½	½	½	0	½	♛	½	½	½	½	½	½	1	½	1	1	½	**9½**
8	Spassky	½	½	½	½	½	0	½	♛	0	½	½	1	½	½	1	½	1	1	**9½**
9	Geller	½	½	½	½	½	1	½	1	♛	½	½	0	0	½	½	½	½	½	**8½**
10	Keres	0	½	½	½	1	0	½	½	½	♛	½	½	½	½	½	½	1	½	**8½**
11	Petrosyan	½	½	½	½	0	0	½	½	½	½	♛	1	1	0	½	½	1	½	**8½**
12	Najdorf	½	½	½	½	½	½	½	0	1	½	0	♛	½	½	½	½	1	½	**8½**
13	Gheorghiu	1	0	0	0	½	1	½	½	1	½	0	½	♛	½	½	½	½	½	**8**
14	Gligorić	0	0	0	½	½	½	0	½	½	½	1	½	½	♛	½	1	½	½	**7½**
15	Bilek	0	½	½	0	0	0	½	0	½	½	½	½	½	½	♛	½	½	½	**6**
16	Filip	0	½	½	½	0	½	0	½	½	½	½	½	½	0	½	♛	½	0	**6**
17	Pachman	½	½	½	1	½	0	0	0	½	0	0	0	½	½	½	½	♛	½	**6**
18	Uhlmann	0	0	0	0	0	½	½	0	½	½	½	½	½	½	½	1	½	♛	**6**

Budva *22 June – 5 July 1967*

		1	2	3	4	5	6	7	8	9	10	11	12	Total
1	Korchnoi	♛	½	½	½	1	½	½	1	1	1	½	1	**8**
2	Tal	½	♛	½	½	0	1	½	½	½	1	1	½	**6½**
3	Gligorić	½	½	♛	½	0	½	½	½	1	½	1	1	**6½**
4	Gipslis	½	½	½	♛	½	½	1	½	½	½	½	½	**6**
5	Bukić	0	1	1	½	♛	0	½	0	1	½	½	1	**6**
6	Geller	½	0	½	½	1	♛	½	1	0	½	½	1	**6**
7	Cirić	½	½	½	0	½	½	♛	½	½	½	½	½	**5**
8	Ivkov	0	½	½	½	1	0	½	♛	0	½	½	1	**5**
9	Taimanov	0	½	0	½	0	1	½	1	♛	½	½	½	**5**
10	Bogdanović	0	0	½	½	½	½	½	½	½	♛	½	1	**5**
11	Minić	½	0	0	½	½	½	½	½	½	½	♛	½	**4½**
12	Suetin	0	½	0	½	0	0	½	0	½	0	½	♛	**2½**

Winnipeg *3–14 October 1967*

		1	2	3	4	5	6	7	8	9	10	Total
1	Darga	♛	1	½	½	½	½	½	½	1	1	**6**
2	Larsen	0	♛	½	½	1	½	1	1	½	1	**6**
3	Keres	½	½	♛	½	½	½	½	½	1	1	**5½**
4	Spassky	½	½	½	♛	½	½	½	½	1	1	**5½**
5	Benko	½	0	½	½	♛	½	½	1	½	1	**5**
6	Szabo	½	½	½	½	½	♛	½	½	0	1	**4½**
7	Gheorghiu	½	0	½	½	½	½	♛	½	½	1	**4½**
8	Matanović	½	0	½	½	0	½	½	♛	½	1	**4**
9	Yanofsky	0	½	0	0	½	½	½	½	♛	½	**3½**
10	Kagan	0	0	0	0	0	0	0	0	½	♛	**½**

Bobtosov. (Reproduced by courtesy of B.T. Batsford)

Lugano *1–20 March 1970*

		1	2	3	4	5	6	7	8	Total
1	Larsen	♛	1½	10	10	½1	1½	11	½½	9½
2	Olafsson	0½	♛	10	½½	1½	½1	1½	½1	8½
3	Unzicker	01	01	♛	½½	½½	½½	½½	1½	7½
4	Gligorić	01	½½	½½	♛	½½	½½	½½	½1	7½
5	Byrne, R	½0	0½	½½	½½	♛	½½	½½	11	7
6	Szabo	0½	½0	½½	½½	½½	♛	½½	½½	6
7	Kavalek	00	0½	½½	½½	½½	½½	♛	½½	5½
8	Donner	½½	½0	0½	½0	00	½½	½½	♛	4½

Rovinj–Zagreb *11 April – 6 May 1970*

		1	2	3	4	5	6	7	8	9	10	11	12	13	14	15	16	17	18	Total
1	Fischer	♛	1	½	½	½	½	1	½	1	1	0	½	1	1	1	1	1	1	13
2	Gligorić	0	♛	1	½	½	1	½	½	½	½	½	½	½	½	1	1	1	1	11
3	Smyslov	½	0	♛	½	½	½	½	1	1	½	½	1	½	1	½	1	½	1	11
4	Hort	½	½	½	♛	½	½	½	1	½	½	1	1	½	½	½	½	1	1	11
5	Korchnoi	½	½	½	½	♛	½	0	1	½	0	1	1	1	1	½	½	1	1	11
6	Petrosyan	½	0	½	½	½	♛	½	½	½	½	1	1	1	½	½	½	1	1	10½
7	Minić	0	½	½	½	1	½	♛	½	1	½	½	½	½	½	½	0	½	1	9
8	Ivkov	½	½	0	0	0	½	½	♛	½	½	½	1	1	½	½	½	1	1	9
9	Uhlmann	0	½	0	½	½	½	0	½	♛	½	0	1	½	1	1	1	1	0	8½
10	Bertok	0	½	½	½	1	½	½	½	½	♛	0	½	½	½	½	½	½	1	8½
11	Kovačević	1	½	½	0	0	0	½	½	1	1	♛	0	½	½	½	½	1	½	8½
12	Browne	½	½	0	0	0	0	½	0	0	½	1	♛	½	½	½	1	1	1	7½
13	Parma	0	½	½	½	0	0	½	0	½	½	½	½	♛	½	½	½	½	½	6½
14	Kurajica	0	½	0	½	0	½	½	½	0	½	½	½	½	♛	½	½	½	½	6½
15	Ghitescu	0	0	½	½	½	½	½	½	0	½	½	½	½	½	♛	½	0	½	6½
16	Marović	0	0	0	½	½	½	1	½	0	½	½	0	½	½	½	♛	0	½	6
17	Udovčić	0	0	½	0	0	0	½	0	0	½	0	0	½	½	1	1	♛	1	5½
18	Ničevski	0	0	0	0	0	0	0	0	1	0	½	0	½	½	½	½	0	♛	3½

Leiden *16 April – 7 May 1970*

		1	2	3	4	Total
1	Spassky	♛	1½½½	½½½½	½½1½	7
2	Donner	0½½½	♛	½½½½	1½½½	6
3	Botvinnik	½½½½	½½½½	♛	01½0	5½
4	Larsen	½½0½	0½½½	10½1	♛	5½

Hort likes the menu. (Stephane Bureau)

Palma de Mallorca *8 November – 13 December 1970*

		1	2	3	4	5	6	7	8	9	10	11	12	13	14	15	16	17	18	19	20	21	22	23	24	Total
1	Fischer	♛	0	1	½	1	1	½	1	½	1	1	1	1	1	1	1	1	½	1	1	½	½	1	½	**18½**
2	Larsen	1	♛	½	½	0	1	½	½	½	½	1	1	0	½	½	1	½	1	½	1	1	½	1	½	**15**
3	Geller	0	½	♛	1	½	1	½	1	½	½	½	1	½	½	1	½	1	½	½	½	1	1	½	½	**15**
4	Hübner	½	½	0	♛	½	1	½	0	½	½	0	½	½	1	½	1	1	1	1	½	1	1	1	1	**15**
5	Taimanov	0	1	½	½	♛	½	½	½	½	½	½	0	½	0	1	1	½	1	½	1	½	1	1	1	**14**
6	Uhlmann	0	0	0	0	½	♛	1	½	½	1	½	½	1	½	0	1	½	1	1	½	1	1	1	1	**14**
7	Portisch	½	½	½	½	½	0	♛	½	0	1	½	1	1	½	½	½	1	½	½	1	½	1	1	0	**13½**
8	Smyslov	0	½	0	1	½	½	½	♛	1	½	½	0	½	½	½	½	½	½	1	1	½	1	1	1	**13½**
9	Polugayevsky	½	½	½	½	½	½	1	0	♛	½	1	½	½	½	½	1	0	½	1	1	½	½	½	½	**13**
10	Gligorić	0	½	½	½	½	0	0	½	½	♛	1	½	1	½	1	½	½	1	0	½	1	½	1	1	**13**
11	Panno	0	0	½	1	½	½	½	½	0	0	♛	½	½	½	1	1	½	½	½	½	1	1	½	1	**12½**
12	Mecking	0	0	0	½	1	½	0	1	½	½	½	♛	1	½	½	½	½	0	½	½	1	1	1	1	**12½**
13	Hort	0	1	½	½	½	0	0	½	½	0	½	0	♛	1	½	1	½	½	½	½	1	½	1	½	**11½**
14	Ivkov	0	½	½	0	1	½	½	½	½	½	½	½	0	♛	½	½	0	½	½	½	½	1	½	½	**10½**
15	Suttles	0	½	0	½	0	1	½	½	½	0	0	½	½	½	♛	0	½	½	1	½	0	1	½	1	**10**
16	Minić	0	0	½	0	0	0	½	½	0	½	0	½	0	½	1	♛	1	½	½	½	1	½	1	1	**10**
17	Reshevsky	0	½	0	0	½	½	0	½	1	½	½	½	½	1	½	0	♛	½	½	½	0	0	½	1	**9½**
18	Matulović	½	0	½	0	0	0	½	½	½	0	½	1	½	½	½	½	½	♛	½	½	0	0	½	1	**9**
19	Addison	0	½	½	0	½	0	½	0	0	1	½	½	½	½	0	½	½	½	♛	½	0	0	1	1	**9**
20	Filip	0	0	½	½	0	½	0	0	0	½	½	½	½	½	½	½	½	½	½	♛	½	1	½	0	**8½**
21	Naranja	½	0	0	0	½	0	½	½	½	0	0	0	0	½	1	0	1	1	1	½	♛	0	0	1	**8½**
22	Ujtumen	½	½	0	0	0	0	0	0	½	½	0	0	½	0	0	½	1	1	1	0	1	♛	1	½	**8½**
23	Rubinetti	0	0	½	0	0	0	0	0	½	0	½	0	0	½	½	0	½	½	0	½	1	0	♛	1	**6**
24	Jimenez	½	½	½	0	0	0	1	0	½	0	0	0	½	½	0	0	0	0	0	1	0	½	0	♛	**5½**

Wijk aan Zee *11–30 January 1971*

		1	2	3	4	5	6	7	8	9	10	11	12	13	14	15	16	Total
1	Korchnoi	♛	½	½	½	1	½	1	0	½	1	1	½	0	1	1	1	**10**
2	Ivkov	½	♛	½	½	½	½	0	1	½	½	1	½	½	1	1	1	**9½**
3	Gligorić	½	½	♛	½	1	1	½	½	½	½	½	½	1	½	½	1	**9½**
4	Petrosyan	½	½	½	♛	½	1	½	½	1	½	½	½	1	½	½	1	**9½**
5	Olafsson	0	½	0	½	♛	½	1	1	½	1	½	½	1	½	1	1	**9½**
6	Hort	½	½	0	0	½	♛	½	1	0	1	½	½	1	½	1	1	**8½**
7	Hübner	0	1	½	½	0	½	♛	½	0	1	½	½	½	1	1	1	**8½**
8	Andersson	1	0	½	½	0	0	½	♛	½	½	1	½	½	½	1	1	**8½**
9	Mecking	½	½	½	0	½	1	1	0	♛	½	1	½	1	½	0	1	**8½**
10	Langeweg	0	½	½	½	0	0	0	½	½	♛	1	½	½	1	½	1	**7**
11	Donner	0	0	½	½	½	½	½	0	0	0	♛	1	1	½	1	½	**6½**
12	Lengyel	½	½	½	½	½	½	½	½	½	½	0	♛	½	½	0	½	**6½**
13	Ree	1	½	0	0	0	0	½	½	0	½	0	½	♛	1	1	1	**6½**
14	Najdorf	0	0	½	½	½	½	0	½	½	0	½	½	0	♛	½	½	**5**
15	Kuijpers	0	0	½	½	0	0	0	0	1	½	0	1	0	½	♛	½	**4½**
16	Van Den Berg	0	0	0	0	0	0	0	0	0	0	½	½	0	½	½	♛	**2**

Moscow *24 November – 19 December 1971*

		1	2	3	4	5	6	7	8	9	10	11	12	13	14	15	16	17	18	Total
1	Karpov	♛	½	½	½	½	½	½	½	1	1	1	1	½	½	½	½	½	1	**11**
2	Stein	½	♛	½	½	½	½	½	½	½	1	½	½	1	½	1	½	1	1	**11**
3	Smyslov	½	½	♛	½	1	½	½	½	½	½	½	½	½	1	1	½	1	½	**10½**
4	Tukmakov	½	½	½	♛	½	½	½	½	½	½	1	½	½	½	½	1	1	½	**10**
5	Petrosyan	½	½	0	½	♛	½	1	½	½	½	1	½	½	½	½	1	1	½	**10**
6	Tal	½	½	½	½	½	♛	½	1	½	½	0	½	½	0	1	½	1	1	**9½**
7	Spassky	½	½	½	½	0	½	♛	½	½	½	0	1	1	1	½	½	½	1	**9½**
8	Byrne, R	½	½	½	½	½	0	½	♛	1	½	0	1	½	½	½	1	½	½	**9**
9	Hort	0	½	½	½	½	½	½	0	♛	½	1	½	½	1	½	½	½	1	**9**
10	Bronstein	0	0	½	½	½	½	½	½	½	♛	0	½	½	½	1	1	1	1	**9**
11	Korchnoi	0	½	½	0	0	1	1	1	0	1	♛	0	1	½	0	1	½	½	**8½**
12	Savon	0	½	½	½	½	½	0	0	½	½	1	♛	½	0	½	½	½	1	**7½**
13	Gheorghiu	½	0	½	½	½	½	0	½	½	½	0	½	♛	1	½	½	½	½	**7½**
14	Olafsson	½	½	0	½	½	1	0	½	0	½	½	1	0	♛	½	0	½	1	**7½**
15	Uhlmann	½	0	0	½	½	0	½	½	½	0	1	½	½	½	♛	0	½	½	**6½**
16	Balashov	½	½	½	0	0	½	½	0	½	0	0	½	½	1	1	♛	0	½	**6½**
17	Parma	½	0	0	0	0	0	½	½	½	0	½	½	½	½	½	1	♛	½	**6**
18	Lengyel	0	0	½	½	½	0	0	½	0	0	½	0	½	0	½	½	½	♛	**4½**

Hilversum *12–19 June 1973*

		1	2	3	4	5	6	7	8	Total
1	Szabó	♛	10	1½	½½	½1	1½	½1	1½	**9½**
2	Geller	01	♛	½½	½½	1½	1½	1½	11	**9½**
3	Ljubojević	0½	½½	♛	½1	½1	½½	½½	11	**8½**
4	Andersson	½½	½½	½0	♛	½1	½½	½0	½½	**6½**
5	Sax	½0	0½	½0	½½	♛	½½	10	1½	**6**
6	Ivkov	0½	0½	½½	½½	½½	♛	0½	½1	**6**
7	Polugayevsky	½0	0½	½½	½½	01	1½	♛	0½	**6**
8	Timman	0½	00	00	½½	½0	½0	1½	♛	**4**

Sochi *11–30 September 1973*

		1	2	3	4	5	6	7	8	9	10	11	12	13	14	15	16	Total
1	Tal	♛	½	½	½	½	½	1	½	½	1	1	1	½	1	1	1	**11**
2	Spassky	½	♛	½	½	½	1	½	1	½	½	½	½	1	1	½	1	**10**
3	Krogius	½	½	♛	½	½	½	½	½	½	½	½	½	1	1	1	½	**9**
4	Smejkal	½	½	½	♛	½	½	½	½	1	½	1	½	0	½	1	1	**9**
5	Andersson	½	½	½	½	♛	½	½	½	½	½	½	½	½	½	1	1	**8½**
6	Timman	½	0	½	½	½	♛	½	½	1	½	1	½	0	½	1	1	**8½**
7	Suetin	0	½	½	½	½	½	♛	½	½	½	1	½	½	1	½	½	**8**
8	Kholmov	½	0	½	½	½	½	½	♛	0	1	1	1	1	1	0	0	**8**
9	Balashov	½	½	½	0	½	0	½	1	♛	½	½	½	1	½	1	0	**7½**
10	Filip	0	½	½	½	½	½	½	0	½	♛	0	½	½	1	1	½	**7**
11	Rashkovsky	0	½	½	0	½	0	0	0	½	1	♛	1	½	½	½	1	**6½**
12	Szabo	0	½	½	½	½	½	½	0	½	½	0	♛	½	½	½	1	**6½**
13	Hennings	½	0	0	1	½	0	½	0	0	½	½	½	♛	½	0	1	**6½**
14	Rukavina	0	0	0	½	½	½	0	0	½	0	½	½	½	♛	½	1	**5**
15	Spiridinov	0	½	0	0	0	0	½	1	0	0	½	½	1	½	♛	½	**5**
16	Korenski	0	0	½	0	0	0	½	1	1	½	0	0	0	0	½	♛	**4**

Steinitz & Zukertort

Steinitz was the most profound researcher chess has ever known. His early fame was in Vienna, whence he had moved from his native Prague and for a while he was known as the 'Viennese Morphy', after the style of his play. In 1862 he settled in London and revolutionized chess, but it was a quiet revolution and some remained unaware of it. In retrospect we can see that he created modern chess, and also chess analysis.

In 1866 Steinitz won a fine match against Anderssen by 8 – 6. It has been called, much later, a world championship, for after Morphy's disappearance Anderssen would probably have held the title had it existed at the time. But Steinitz still played in the old style and continued to do so until the early 1870s.

Steinitz developed his theory of chess slowly. (The world 'theory' has another meaning in chess, its opposite, practice. 'Opening theory' means what has happened in competitive games.) Steinitz evolved a real theory, too elaborate to detail here. Grossly to oversimplify, games are not won, they are lost.

Instead of an all-out attack from the opening, the correct technique, according to Steinitz, was to develop the pieces harmoniously, strengthen one's position, and seize upon the opponent's mistakes. Only when an advantage had been secured should an attack be launched. The effect of these ideas was a great rise in the quality of chess. For less skilled onlookers the game lost its romance. They thought that Morphy had conjured wins from level positions and any suggestion that he needed opponent's blunders was an insult to their idol.

Until Steinitz's time, and to some extent since, annotators, relying on hindsight, praised the winner's moves and condemned the loser's. He took an objective view and in the pages of *The Field* and the London *Figaro* set a new standard of analysis that has seldom been surpassed.

While he was doing this Steinitz acquired a mastery of English that enabled him to defend himself briskly against those who found him lacking in the kind of servility they expected

from a professional. A group of his enemies brought Zukertort to London to bring the 'Bohemian Caesar' down a peg. That did not happen, but Zukertort remained in London, and he, too, became fluent in English.

Other than the fact that these were the best pair of players in the world they had little in common. Steinitz was a great seeker for the truth. Anderssen said of Zukertort that if he made an off-hand unpremeditated remark he might tell the truth, but if he made a deliberate statement you could bet your bottom thaler it was a lie. The Munchhausen of chess, it is possible that Zukertort may have believed his own stories, such as being a doctor of medicine, a theologian, big-game hunter, music critic, etc.

Zukertort's attempt to squash Steinitz in 1872 failed. He won only one game to his opponent's seven (four draws), but he continued to improve and had his finest hour when he won the London 1883 tournament by a handsome margin. Meanwhile he had become joint editor of *Chess Monthly* with Leopold Hoffer of Budapest who had arrived a penniless refugee in 1879 and also mastered English.

Steinitz, after living in England '20 years as a foreigner', had emigrated to the USA (where he changed his forename from Wilhelm to William and was to become naturalized on 6 October 1888). He had an outlet for his pen, his own *International Chess Magazine*. Zukertort said that Steinitz prided himself on the scurrility of his speech and was told in reply that he was vulgar, untruthful and malicious. Despite the verbal battle, the matadors did agree to meet.

In 1886 the great match began in the USA, the first for the championship of the world, the victor needing to win ten games (see page 12 for details). It left Zukertort a broken man. Two years later he collapsed while playing at Simpson's Divan and died the following day. After ten weeks together the two great players had reconciled their differences, but Steinitz's hatred of Hoffer continued to grow leading to many vehement slanging matches.

Montilla *20–31 August 1974*

	1	*2*	*3*	*4*	*5*	*6*	*7*	*8*	*9*	*10*	***Total***
1 Radulov	♛	½	½	½	½	½	½	½	1	1	5½
2 Kavalek	½	♛	½	½	½	1	½	½	½	½	5
3 Pfleger	½	½	♛	½	½	½	1	½	½	½	5
4 Quinteros	½	½	½	♛	½	½	0	1	½	½	4½
5 Gheorghiu	½	½	½	½	♛	½	½	½	½	½	4½
6 Andersson	½	0	½	½	½	♛	½	½	½	1	4½
7 Ribli	½	½	0	1	½	½	♛	½	½	0	4
8 Keene	½	½	½	0	½	½	½	♛	½	½	4
9 Parma	0	½	½	½	½	½	½	½	♛	½	4
10 Diez Del Corral	0	½	½	½	½	0	1	½	½	♛	4

Kavalek. (Reproduced by courtesy of B.T. Batsford)

Manila *2–24 October 1974*

	1	*2*	*3*	*4*	*5*	*6*	*7*	*8*	*9*	*10*	*11*	*12*	*13*	*14*	*15*	***Total***
1 Vasyukov	♛	½	1	1	½	½	1	0	½	½	1	1	1	1	1	10½
2 Petrosyan	½	♛	½	½	1	½	1	½	½	1	½	½	1	1	½	9½
3 Larsen	0	½	♛	½	1	0	½	0	½	1	1	1	1	1	1	9
4 Gheorghiu	0	½	½	♛	½	½	1	½	1	½	0	½	1	1	1	8½
5 Gligorić	½	0	0	½	♛	½	½	½	1	0	1	1	1	1	1	8½
6 Kavalek	½	½	1	½	½	♛	½	½	½	½	½	½	½	½	1	8
7 Ljubojević	0	0	½	0	½	½	♛	½	½	1	1	1	½	1	1	8
8 Pfleger	1	½	1	½	½	½	½	♛	½	0	0	0	1	½	1	7½
9 Andersson	½	½	½	0	0	½	½	½	♛	½	1	½	½	1	1	7½
10 Quinteros	½	0	0	½	1	½	0	1	½	♛	0	0	1	1	1	7
11 Portisch	0	½	0	1	0	½	0	1	0	1	♛	1	½	0	1	6½
12 Torre	0	½	0	½	0	½	0	1	½	1	0	♛	½	1	1	6½
13 Kraidman	0	0	0	0	0	½	½	0	½	0	½	½	♛	1	½	4
14 Cardoso	0	0	0	0	0	½	0	½	0	0	1	0	0	♛	1	3
15 Naranja	0	½	0	0	0	0	0	0	0	0	0	0	½	0	♛	1

Wijk aan Zee *13 January – 1 February 1975*

	1	*2*	*3*	*4*	*5*	*6*	*7*	*8*	*9*	*10*	*11*	*12*	*13*	*14*	*15*	*16*	***Total***
1 Portisch	♛	1	½	½	1	½	½	½	½	½	½	½	1	1	1	1	10½
2 Hort	0	♛	1	½	½	½	½	1	½	½	½	1	½	1	1	1	10
3 Smejkal	½	0	♛	½	½	1	½	1	½	½	½	1	½	1	1	½	9½
4 Kavalek	½	½	½	♛	½	½	½	½	½	½	½	1	1	½	½	1	9
5 Gligorić	0	½	½	½	♛	½	½	0	½	½	½	½	1	1	1	1	8½
6 Hübner	½	½	0	½	½	♛	½	½	1	0	½	1	½	1	1	½	8½
7 Sosonko	½	½	½	½	½	½	♛	½	0	1	½	0	1	½	1	1	8½
8 Browne	½	0	0	½	1	½	½	♛	½	0	1	½	½	½	1	1	8
9 Geller	½	½	½	½	½	0	1	½	♛	½	½	½	½	½	½	1	8
10 Timman	½	½	½	½	½	1	0	1	½	♛	½	1	½	½	½	0	8
11 Furman	½	½	½	½	½	½	½	0	½	½	♛	½	½	½	0	1	7
12 Langeweg	½	0	0	0	½	0	1	½	½	0	½	♛	1	1	½	½	6½
13 Ree	0	½	½	0	0	½	0	½	½	½	½	0	♛	½	½	1	5½
14 Donner	0	0	0	½	0	0	½	½	½	½	½	0	½	♛	1	½	5
15 Kuijpers	0	0	0	½	0	0	0	0	½	½	1	½	½	0	♛	½	4
16 Popov, L	0	0	½	0	0	½	0	0	0	1	0	½	0	½	½	♛	3½

Montilla *19–29 August 1975*

		1	2	3	4	5	6	7	8	9	10	*Total*
1	Polugayevsky	♕	½	0	½	1	1	1	½	1	½	6
2	Radulov	½	♕	½	½	½	½	1	½	1	1	6
3	Pfleger	1	½	♕	½	½	½	½	½	½	1	5½
4	Kavalek	½	½	½	♕	½	½	½	1	½	1	5½
5	Csom	0	½	½	½	♕	1	½	½	½	1	5
6	Bellon	0	½	½	½	0	♕	1	½	1	1	5
7	Szabó	0	0	½	½	½	0	♕	½	1	1	4
8	Toran	½	½	½	0	½	½	½	♕	½	½	4
9	Byrne, R	0	0	½	½	½	0	0	½	♕	1	3
10	Medina	½	0	0	0	0	0	0	½	0	♕	1

Milan *20 August – 14 September 1975*

		1	2	3	4	5	6	7	8	9	10	11	12	*Total*
1	Portisch	♕	½	½	½	½	½	1	½	0	1	1	1	7
2	Karpov	½	♕	½	1	½	½	½	1	0	1	½	½	6½
3	Petrosyan	½	½	♕	½	½	½	½	½	½	1	1	½	6½
4	Ljubojević	½	0	½	♕	½	1	½	0	1	½	1	1	6½
5	Smejkal	½	½	½	½	♕	½	1	½	½	0	1	½	6
6	Tal	½	½	½	0	½	♕	0	0	1	½	1	1	5½
7	Browne	0	½	½	½	0	1	♕	½	½	½	½	1	5½
8	Unzicker	½	0	½	1	½	1	½	♕	½	0	0	½	5
9	Andersson	1	1	½	0	½	0	½	½	♕	0	0	1	5
10	Gligorić	0	0	0	½	1	½	½	1	1	♕	0	½	5
11	Larsen	0	½	0	0	0	0	½	1	1	1	♕	1	5
12	Mariotti	0	½	½	0	½	0	0	½	0	½	0	♕	2½

Sax. (Agterdenbos)

Semi-final Matches

Karpov	½	½	½	½	2
Petrosyan	½	½	½	½	2

Portisch	½	½	1	½	2½
Ljubojević	½	½	0	½	1½

Final Matches

1	Karpov	½	1	½	½	½	½	3½
2	Portisch	½	0	½	½	½	½	2½

3	Petrosyan	1	½	½	½	0	½	3
4	Ljubojević	0	½	½	½	1	½	3

Ljubojevíc. (Stephane Bureau)

Teesside *1–16 September 1975*

	1	*2*	*3*	*4*	*5*	*6*	*7*	*8*	*9*	*10*	*11*	*12*	*13*	*14*	*15*	***Total***
1 Geller	♛	½	½	½	½	1	1	½	1	½	½	½	1	½	1	9½
2 Smyslov	½	♛	0	½	½	½	½	½	½	1	½	1	½	1	1	8½
3 Bronstein	½	1	♛	½	½	1	0	½	½	0	½	1	½	1	½	8
4 Hort	½	½	½	♛	½	½	½	½	½	½	½	½	½	1	1	8
5 Hübner	½	½	½	½	♛	½	1	½	½	0	½	½	1	½	1	8
6 Sax	0	½	0	½	½	♛	½	½	½	1	1	1	0	½	1	7½
7 Timman	0	½	1	½	0	½	♛	½	½	1	½	0	1	1	½	7½
8 Kavalek	½	½	½	½	½	½	½	♛	½	½	½	½	½	½	½	7
9 Olafsson	0	½	½	½	½	½	½	½	♛	1	½	½	½	½	½	7
10 Miles	½	0	1	½	1	0	0	½	0	♛	1	½	½	½	½	6½
11 Gheorghiu	½	½	½	½	½	0	½	½	½	0	♛	½	½	½	½	6
12 Lombardy	½	0	0	½	½	0	1	½	½	½	½	♛	½	0	1	6
13 Stean	0	½	½	½	0	1	0	½	½	½	½	½	♛	½	½	6
14 Keene	½	0	0	0	½	½	0	½	½	½	½	1	½	♛	½	5½
15 Hartston	0	0	½	0	0	0	½	½	½	½	½	0	½	½	♛	4

Manila *2–31 October 1975*

	1	*2*	*3*	*4*	*5*	*6*	*7*	*8*	*9*	*10*	*11*	***Total***
1 Ljubojević	♛	½	½	½	1	1	½	½	½	1	1	7
2 Polugayevsky	½	♛	1	½	½	0	1	1	½	0	1	6
3 Mecking	½	0	♛	½	1	1	½	½	1	½	½	6
4 Larsen	½	½	½	♛	½	0	1	½	1	1	½	6
5 Pfleger	0	½	0	½	♛	1	½	1	½	1	1	6
6 Balinas	0	1	0	1	0	♛	½	0	1	½	1	5
7 Gligorić	½	0	½	0	½	½	♛	½	½	1	1	5
8 Karaklajić	½	0	½	½	0	1	½	♛	½	0	0	3½
9 Kavalek	½	½	0	0	½	0	½	½	♛	½	½	3½
10 Torre	0	1	½	0	0	½	0	1	½	♛	0	3½
11 Øgaard	0	0	½	½	0	0	0	1	½	1	♛	3½

Wijk aan Zee *15–29 January 1976*

	1	*2*	*3*	*4*	*5*	*6*	*7*	*8*	*9*	*10*	*11*	*12*	***Total***
1 Ljubojević	♛	½	0	½	1	½	1	1	½	½	1	1	7½
2 Olafsson	½	♛	½	½	1	½	½	½	1	1	1	½	7½
3 Kurajica	1	½	♛	1	½	0	0	1	½	½	½	1	6½
4 Tal	½	½	0	♛	½	½	½	½	½	1	1	1	6½
5 Browne	0	0	½	½	♛	1	½	½	0	1	½	1	5½
6 Smejkal	½	½	1	½	0	♛	½	1	1	0	½	0	5½
7 Andersson	0	½	1	½	½	½	♛	½	½	0	½	½	5
8 Dvoretsky	0	½	0	½	½	0	½	♛	½	1	½	1	5
9 Ree	½	0	½	½	1	0	½	½	♛	½	½	½	5
10 Langeweg	½	0	½	0	0	1	1	0	½	♛	½	½	4½
11 Sosonko	0	0	½	0	½	½	½	½	½	½	♛	1	4½
12 Böhm	0	½	0	0	0	1	½	0	½	½	0	♛	3

In a Browne study.

Amsterdam *13–23 May 1976*

	1	*2*	*3*	*4*	*Total*
1 Karpov	♛	1½	½1	½½	4
2 Browne	0½	♛	½1	01	3
3 Olafsson	½0	½0	♛	1½	2½
4 Timman	½½	10	0½	♛	2½

Soviet emigré Sosonko jokes with Karpov and Tal. (Stephane Bureau)

Manila *13–21 July 1976*

	1	*2*	*3*	*4*	*Total*
1 Torre	♛	1½	½1	1½	4½
2 Karpov	0½	♛	½1	½½	3
3 Ljubojević	½0	½0	♛	1½	2½
4 Browne	0½	½½	0½	♛	2

Bad Lauterberg *5–23 March 1977*

	1	*2*	*3*	*4*	*5*	*6*	*7*	*8*	*9*	*10*	*11*	*12*	*13*	*14*	*15*	*16*	*Total*
1 Karpov	♛	1	½	1	½	1	½	1	½	1	½	½	1	1	1	1	12
2 Timman	0	♛	½	½	½	½	1	1	½	1	½	1	1	1	0	1	10
3 Furman	½	½	♛	½	½	½	½	½	1	1	½	0	0	1	1	1	9
4 Sosonko	0	½	½	♛	½	½	½	½	½	½	½	½	½	1	1	1	8½
5 Olafsson	½	½	½	½	♛	½	½	½	½	½	1	½	½	1	0	½	8
6 Csom	0	½	½	½	½	♛	½	1	½	1	½	½	½	½	½	½	8
7 Hübner	½	0	½	½	½	½	♛	½	½	0	½	½	½	1	1	1	8
8 Liberzon	0	0	½	½	½	0	½	♛	½	1	½	½	1	½	1	1	8
9 Gligorić	½	½	0	½	½	½	½	½	♛	0	½	½	1	½	½	1	7½
10 Miles	0	0	0	½	½	0	1	0	1	♛	½	½	1	½	1	1	7½
11 Andersson	½	½	½	½	0	½	½	½	½	½	♛	½	½	½	½	½	7
12 Keene	½	0	1	½	½	½	½	½	½	½	½	♛	0	½	0	1	7
13 Torre	0	0	1	½	½	½	½	0	0	0	½	1	♛	½	1	½	6½
14 Hermann	0	0	0	0	0	½	0	½	½	½	½	½	½	♛	1	½	5
15 Gerusel	0	1	0	0	1	½	0	0	½	0	½	1	0	0	♛	0	4½
16 Wockenfuss	0	0	0	0	½	½	0	0	0	0	½	0	½	½	1	♛	3½

Geneva *26 March – 11 April 1977*

	1	*2*	*3*	*4*	*5*	*6*	*7*	*8*	*9*	*10*	*11*	*12*	*13*	*14*	*Total*
1 Larsen	♛	½	½	1	0	0	½	½	1	½	½	1	1	1	8½
2 Andersson	½	♛	½	½	0	1	½	½	½	½	1	1	½	1	8
3 Dzindzikhashvili	½	½	♛	½	½	1	½	½	½	1	½	½	½	½	7½
4 Sosonko	0	½	½	♛	½	½	1	½	½	½	½	½	1	1	7½
5 Pachman	1	1	½	½	♛	½	½	½	0	½	½	½	½	½	7
6 Torre	1	0	0	½	½	♛	0	½	1	½	½	1	½	1	7
7 Liberzon	½	½	½	0	½	1	♛	½	1	½	½	½	0	½	6½
8 Ivkov	½	½	½	½	½	½	½	♛	½	0	½	½	½	1	6½
9 Sigurjónsson	0	½	½	½	1	0	0	½	♛	1	½	½	½	1	6½
10 Timman	½	½	0	½	½	½	½	1	0	♛	½	½	1	0	6
11 Byrne	0	0	½	½	½	½	½	½	½	½	♛	1	½	½	6
12 Olafsson	0	0	½	½	½	0	½	½	½	½	0	♛	1	1	5½
13 Hug	0	½	½	0	½	½	1	½	½	0	½	0	♛	½	5
14 Westerinen	0	0	½	0	½	0	½	0	0	1	½	0	½	♛	3½

Ljubljana–Portorož *2–20 June 1977*

		1	2	3	4	5	6	7	8	9	10	11	12	13	14	**Total**
1	Larsen	♛	½	½	1	0	½	½	½	1	1	1	1	1	1	9½
2	Hort	½	♛	½	½	½	½	1	½	½	½	1	1	1	1	9
3	Savon	½	½	♛	0	½	1	1	1	1	½	1	½	1	½	9
4	Tseshkovsky	0	½	1	♛	½	½	½	½	1	½	1	0	½	1	7½
5	Kurajica	1	½	½	½	♛	½	½	½	0	½	½	1	½	½	7
6	Parma	½	½	0	½	½	♛	½	1	½	1	½	½	½	½	7
7	Sosonko	½	0	0	½	½	½	♛	½	½	1	½	1	1	½	7
8	Bukić	½	½	0	½	½	0	½	♛	½	½	0	½	½	1	5½
9	Gligorić	0	½	0	0	1	½	½	½	♛	1	0	½	½	½	5½
10	Planinc	0	½	½	½	½	0	0	½	0	♛	1	1	0	1	5½
11	Barle	0	0	0	0	½	½	½	1	1	0	♛	0	1	½	5
12	Jelen	0	0	½	1	0	½	0	½	½	0	1	♛	0	1	5
13	Sax	0	0	0	½	½	½	0	½	½	1	0	1	♛	½	5
14	Sigurjónsson	0	0	½	0	½	½	½	0	½	0	½	0	½	♛	3½

Uhlmann. (Reproduced by courtesy of B.T. Batsford)

Leningrad *24 June – 20 July 1977*

		1	2	3	4	5	6	7	8	9	10	11	12	13	14	15	16	17	18	**Total**
1	Romanishin	♛	½	½	1	½	1	1	½	0	1	½	0	½	1	1	½	1	1	11½
2	Tal	½	♛	½	0	½	½	1	½	½	½	1	1	1	½	1	1	½	1	11½
3	Smyslov	½	½	♛	½	½	½	½	½	½	½	½	1	½	½	½	1	1	1	10½
4	Vaganyan	0	1	½	♛	½	1	½	0	1	½	½	½	1	½	1	½	½	½	10
5	Karpov	½	½	½	½	♛	½	½	½	0	1	0	1	1	1	½	½	½	1	10
6	Balashov	0	½	½	0	½	♛	½	½	½	½	½	½	½	1	1	½	½	1	9
7	Kochiyev	0	0	½	½	½	½	♛	1	1	1	½	0	½	½	1	½	½	½	9
8	Ribli	½	½	½	1	½	½	0	♛	½	½	0	1	½	½	0	1	½	1	9
9	Taimanov	1	½	½	0	1	½	0	½	♛	0	½	½	1	0	½	½	1	1	9
10	Smejkal	0	½	½	½	0	½	0	½	1	♛	½	½	½	½	½	1	0	1	8
11	Belyavsky	½	0	½	½	1	½	½	1	½	½	♛	0	0	1	½	0	½	0	7½
12	Garcia, G	1	0	0	½	0	½	1	0	½	½	1	♛	0	½	½	½	0	1	7½
13	Kuzmin	½	0	½	0	0	½	½	½	0	½	1	1	♛	1	½	½	½	0	7½
14	Gheorghiu	0	½	½	½	0	0	½	½	1	½	0	½	0	♛	½	½	½	1	7
15	Knežević	0	0	½	0	½	0	0	1	½	½	½	½	½	½	♛	½	1	½	7
16	Radulov	½	0	0	½	½	½	½	0	½	0	1	½	½	½	½	♛	½	½	7
17	Vogt	0	½	0	½	½	½	½	½	0	1	½	1	½	½	0	½	♛	0	7
18	Mariotti	0	0	0	½	0	0	½	0	0	0	1	0	1	0	½	½	1	♛	5

Tilburg *22 September – 6 October 1977*

		1	2	3	4	5	6	7	8	9	10	11	12	**Total**
1	Karpov	♛	1	½	½	½	1	½	1	1	½	½	1	8
2	Miles	0	♛	½	½	½	½	1	0	1	1	1	1	7
3	Hort	½	½	♛	½	½	½	½	½	½	½	1	½	6
4	Kavalek	½	½	½	♛	½	½	½	½	½	½	½	1	6
5	Timman	½	½	½	½	♛	1	½	½	0	½	½	1	6
6	Hübner	0	½	½	½	0	♛	1	1	½	½	½	1	6
7	Gligorić	½	0	½	½	½	0	♛	½	1	½	1	½	5½
8	Andersson	0	1	½	½	½	0	½	♛	½	½	½	½	5
9	Balashov	0	0	½	½	1	½	0	½	♛	1	½	½	5
10	Smyslov	½	0	½	½	½	½	½	½	0	♛	½	½	4½
11	Sosonko	½	0	0	½	½	½	0	½	½	½	♛	½	4
12	Olafsson	0	0	½	0	0	0	½	½	½	½	½	♛	3

Wijk aan Zee *19 January – 2 February 1978*

		1	*2*	*3*	*4*	*5*	*6*	*7*	*8*	*9*	*10*	*11*	*12*	***Total***
1	Portisch	♛	½	½	½	1	1	½	½	1	1	½	1	**8**
2	Korchnoi	½	♛	½	½	½	1	1	1	1	½	1	0	**7½**
3	Andersson	½	½	♛	½	½	½	1	½	0	½	1	1	**6½**
4	Ree	½	½	½	♛	½	½	½	½	½	½	½	1	**6**
5	Timman	0	½	½	½	♛	½	1	1	½	½	½	½	**6**
6	Panno	0	0	½	½	½	♛	½	½	½	1	½	1	**5½**
7	Mecking	½	0	0	½	0	½	♛	1	½	½	½	1	**5**
8	Miles	½	0	½	½	0	½	0	♛	1	½	1	½	**5**
9	Najdorf	0	0	1	½	½	½	½	0	♛	½	½	1	**5**
10	Sosonko	0	½	½	½	½	0	½	½	½	♛	½	½	**4½**
11	Kavalek	½	0	0	½	½	½	½	0	½	½	♛	½	**4**
12	Van Der Sterren	0	1	0	0	½	0	0	½	0	½	½	♛	**3**

Bugojno *26 February – 15 March 1978*

		1	*2*	*3*	*4*	*5*	*6*	*7*	*8*	*9*	*10*	*11*	*12*	*13*	*14*	*15*	*16*	***Total***
1	Karpov	♛	½	0	1	½	1	1	½	½	1	½	1	½	½	½	1	**10**
2	Spassky	½	♛	½	0	½	1	1	½	½	1	½	½	½	1	1	1	**10**
3	Timman	1	½	♛	½	½	0	½	1	1	½	0	1	½	½	½	1	**9**
4	Ljubojević	0	1	½	♛	½	1	½	0	½	0	½	½	½	1	1	1	**8½**
5	Tal	½	½	½	½	♛	½	½	½	½	½	½	½	½	1	1	½	**8½**
6	Larsen	0	0	1	0	½	♛	1	½	1	½	1	1	½	½	0	½	**8**
7	Hort	0	0	½	½	½	0	♛	1	½	1	½	½	1	1	½	½	**8**
8	Hübner	½	½	0	1	½	½	0	♛	½	½	½	1	0	½	1	½	**7½**
9	Balashov	½	½	0	½	½	0	½	½	♛	1	½	½	1	½	½	½	**7½**
10	Miles	0	0	½	1	½	½	0	½	0	♛	½	½	1	½	1	½	**7**
11	Ivkov	½	½	1	½	½	0	½	½	½	½	♛	½	½	½	0	0	**6½**
12	Portisch	0	½	0	½	½	0	½	0	½	½	½	♛	1	½	1	½	**6½**
13	Vukić	½	½	½	½	½	½	0	1	0	0	½	0	♛	½	½	½	**6**
14	Byrne	½	0	½	0	0	½	0	½	½	½	½	½	½	♛	½	1	**6**
15	Gligorić	½	0	½	0	0	1	½	0	½	0	1	0	½	½	♛	½	**5½**
16	Bukić	0	0	0	0	½	½	½	½	½	½	1	½	½	0	½	♛	**5½**

Nikšić *6–22 June 1978*

		1	*2*	*3*	*4*	*5*	*6*	*7*	*8*	*9*	*10*	*11*	*12*	***Total***
1	Gulko	♛	½	½	1	1	1	½	1	½	1	½	½	**8**
2	Timman	½	♛	1	1	½	½	1	½	½	½	1	1	**8**
3	Vaganyan	½	0	♛	½	½	½	½	1	½	½	1	1	**6½**
4	Portisch	0	0	½	♛	1	½	½	½	½	½	1	1	**6**
5	Hort	0	½	½	0	♛	½	½	1	½	½	1	1	**6**
6	Uhlmann	0	½	½	½	½	♛	1	½	0	1	0	1	**5½**
7	Ribli	½	0	½	½	½	0	♛	½	½	1	1	½	**5½**
8	Gligorić	0	½	0	½	0	½	½	♛	1	1	½	1	**5½**
9	Andersson	½	½	½	½	½	1	½	0	♛	½	½	0	**5**
10	Ljubojević	0	½	½	½	½	0	0	0	½	♛	1	1	**4½**
11	Velimirović	½	0	0	0	0	1	0	½	½	0	♛	1	**3½**
12	Ivanović	½	0	0	0	0	0	½	0	1	0	0	♛	**2**

Ribli. (David Fowler)

Amsterdam *12–29 July 1978*

		1	2	3	4	5	6	7	8	9	10	11	12	13	14	*Total*
1	Timman	♕	1	½	½	1	1	½	0	1	1	½	½	1	1	9½
2	Ribli	0	♕	1	1	½	1	½	1	1	½	0	½	1	½	8½
3	Dzindzikhashvili	½	0	♕	½	½	1	½	1	½	½	½	½	1	½	7½
4	Hort	½	0	½	♕	½	0	½	½	½	½	1	1	1	1	7½
5	Pfleger	0	½	½	½	♕	1	½	½	1	½	½	½	1	½	7½
6	Romanishin	0	0	0	1	0	♕	½	1	½	1	½	½	1	1	7
7	Andersson	½	½	½	½	½	½	♕	½	½	1	½	½	0	1	7
8	Ljubojević	1	0	0	½	½	0	½	♕	1	1	½	1	0	½	6½
9	Langeweg	0	0	½	½	0	½	½	0	♕	1	½	½	1	1	6
10	Adorjan	0	½	½	½	½	0	0	0	0	♕	1	½	1	1	5½
11	Miles	½	1	½	0	½	½	½	½	½	0	♕	½	0	½	5½
12	Ree	½	½	½	0	½	½	½	0	½	½	½	♕	½	0	5
13	Nikolac	0	0	0	0	0	0	1	1	0	0	1	½	♕	1	4½
14	Browne	0	½	½	0	½	0	0	½	0	0	½	1	0	♕	3½

Tilburg *31 August – 15 September 1978*

		1	2	3	4	5	6	7	8	9	10	11	12	*Total*
1	Portisch	♕	½	½	1	1	1	½	½	½	0	1	½	7
2	Timman	½	♕	½	½	½	½	½	½	1	1	½	½	6½
3	Dzindzikhashvili	½	½	♕	1	0	½	½	½	½	½	½	1	6
4	Hübner	0	½	0	♕	½	½	½	1	1	1	½	½	6
5	Miles	0	½	1	½	♕	0	0	½	1	½	1	1	6
6	Browne	0	½	½	½	1	♕	1	½	½	1	0	0	5½
7	Hort	½	½	½	½	1	0	♕	½	0	½	½	1	5½
8	Spassky	½	½	½	0	½	½	½	♕	0	1	1	½	5½
9	Larsen	½	0	½	0	0	½	1	1	♕	½	½	½	5
10	Ljubojević	1	0	½	0	½	0	½	0	½	♕	½	1	4½
11	Sosonko	0	½	½	½	0	1	½	0	½	½	♕	½	4½
12	Ribli	½	½	0	½	0	1	0	½	½	0	½	♕	4

Wijk aan Zee *18 January – 1 February 1979*

		1	2	3	4	5	6	7	8	9	10	11	12	*Total*
1	Polugayevsky	♕	½	½	½	1	½	½	½	½	1	1	1	7½
2	Miles	½	♕	½	½	1	½	½	½	½	½	1	½	6½
3	Andersson	½	½	♕	½	½	½	½	½	½	½	1	1	6½
4	Sosonko	½	½	½	♕	½	½	½	1	½	½	½	1	6½
5	Timman	0	0	½	½	♕	½	½	½	1	½	1	1	6
6	Hübner	½	½	½	½	½	♕	1	½	0	½	½	1	6
7	Hort	½	½	½	½	½	0	♕	½	½	½	1	1	6
8	Ree	½	½	½	0	½	½	½	♕	1	½	0	½	5
9	Dzindzikhashvili	½	½	½	½	0	1	½	0	♕	1	½	0	5
10	Garcia, G	0	½	½	½	½	½	½	½	0	♕	0	½	4
11	Nikolac	0	0	0	½	0	½	0	1	½	1	♕	0	3½
12	Gaprindashvili	0	½	0	0	0	0	0	½	1	½	1	♕	3½

Miles reflects on his position.
(Stephane Bureau)

Montreal *10 April – 7 May 1979*

	1	2	3	4	5	6	7	8	9	10	**Total**
1 Tal	♛	½½	½1	½½	½½	11	½1	1½	½½	1½	**12**
2 Karpov	½½	♛	½½	11	11	11	½½	1½	½½	½0	**12**
3 Portisch	½0	½½	♛	½½	½½	½½	1½	½½	1½	11	**10½**
4 Ljubojević	½½	00	½½	♛	½½	½0	½½	10	11	1½	**9**
5 Timman	½½	00	½½	½½	♛	½½	½½	½0	½1	1½	**8½**
6 Spassky	00	00	½½	½1	½½	♛	½1	1½	½½	01	**8½**
7 Hübner	½0	½½	0½	½½	½½	½0	♛	10	½½	1½	**8**
8 Kavalek	0½	0½	½½	01	½1	0½	01	♛	½½	01	**8**
9 Hort	½½	½½	0½	00	½0	½½	½½	½½	♛	11	**8**
10 Larsen	0½	½1	00	0½	0½	10	0½	10	00	♛	**5½**

Pretoria, Durban, Cape Town, Johannesburg *5–26 May 1979*

	1	2	3	4	**Total**
1 Korchnoi	♛	½½01	111½	11½½	**8½**
2 Unzicker	½½10	♛	1½½½	½10½	**6½**
3 Miles	000½	0½½½	♛	1110	**5**
4 Lein	00½½	½01½	0001	♛	**4**

Bled, Portorož *31 May – 22 June 1979*

	1	2	3	4	5	6	7	8	9	10	11	12	13	14	15	16	**Total**
1 Timman	♛	½	½	1	1	½	1	1	½	½	1	½	1	½	½	1	**11**
2 Larsen	½	♛	½	0	1	1	1	1	0	½	1	½	1	1	1	0	**10**
3 Ribli	½	½	♛	½	0	½	1	½	1	½	½	1	1	½	1	1	**10**
4 Tseshkovsky	0	1	½	♛	½	½	½	1	½	0	½	½	1	1	1	1	**9½**
5 Marjanović	0	0	1	½	♛	½	1	½	0	½	½	1	1	1	½	1	**9**
6 Miles	½	0	½	½	½	♛	0	0	1	½	0	1	1	1	1	1	**8½**
7 Quinteros	0	0	0	½	0	1	♛	½	1	1	0	½	1	1	1	1	**8½**
8 Ivkov	0	0	½	0	½	1	½	♛	1	½	½	1	0	½	1	1	**8**
9 Kuzmin	½	1	0	½	1	0	0	0	♛	1	0	½	1	1	1	½	**8**
10 Parma	½	½	½	1	½	½	0	½	0	♛	½	½	½	½	½	1	**7½**
11 Gligorić	0	0	½	½	½	1	1	½	1	½	♛	½	0	½	½	0	**7**
12 Jelen	½	½	0	½	0	0	½	0	½	½	½	♛	1	½	½	1	**6½**
13 Barle	0	0	0	0	0	0	0	1	0	½	1	0	♛	1	0	1	**4½**
14 Marangunić	½	0	½	0	0	0	0	½	0	½	½	½	0	♛	½	1	**4½**
15 Šahović	½	0	0	0	½	0	0	0	0	½	½	½	1	½	♛	0	**4**
16 Chi Chinghsuan	0	1	0	0	0	0	0	0	½	0	1	0	0	0	1	♛	**3½**

Waddinxveen *11–26 June 1979*

	1	2	3	4	**Total**
1 Karpov	♛	1½	½1	11	5
2 Kavalek	0½	♛	½½	½1	3
3 Hort	½0	½½	♛	½½	2½
4 Sosonko	00	½0	½½	♛	1½

Amsterdam *11–28 July 1979*

		1	2	3	4	5	6	7	8	9	10	11	12	13	14	Total
1	Hort	♛	½	1	½	½	½	1	1	1	½	½	½	½	1	9
2	Sax	½	♛	½	1	½	½	0	1	1	1	½	½	1	1	9
3	Andcrsson	0	½	♛	½	½	1	½	1	1	1	½	1	½	½	8½
4	Smejkal	½	0	½	♛	½	½	1	½	1	1	1	0	1	1	8½
5	Sosonko	½	½	½	½	♛	½	½	0	½	½	½	1	½	1	7
6	Byrne	½	½	0	½	½	♛	½	½	½	½	½	1	½	1*	7
7	Torre	0	1	½	0	½	½	♛	½	½	½	1	1	½	½	7
8	Ree	0	0	0	½	1	½	½	♛	½	1	½	½	1	0	6
9	Lein	0	0	0	0	½	½	½	½	♛	1	½	½	1	1	6
10	Donner	½	0	0	0	½	½	½	0	0	♛	1	1	½	½	5
11	Ligterink	½	½	½	0	½	½	0	½	½	0	♛	½	½	0	4½
12	Farago	½	½	0	1	0	0	0	½	½	0	½	♛	½	½	4½
13	Stean	½	0	½	0	½	½	½	0	0	½	½	½	♛	½	4½
14	Šahović	0	0	½	0	0	0*	½	1	0	½	1	½	½	♛	4½

*Scored by default

Tilburg *31 August – 15 September 1979*

		1	2	3	4	5	6	7	8	9	10	11	12	Total
1	Karpov	♛	½	½	½	1	1	½	½	½	1	½	1	7½
2	Romanishin	½	♛	½	½	0	½	1	1	½	1	½	1	7
3	Portisch	½	½	♛	½	½	1	½	0	½	½	1	1	6½
4	Sax	½	½	½	♛	½	0	½	1	½	½	½	1	6
5	Sosonko	0	1	½	½	♛	1	½	0	1	0	½	½	5½
6	Larsen	0	½	0	1	0	♛	½	1	½	1	1	0	5½
7	Spassky	½	0	½	½	½	½	♛	½	1	½	½	½	5½
8	Timman	½	0	1	0	1	0	½	♛	½	½	½	1	5½
9	Hübner	½	½	½	½	0	½	0	½	♛	½	½	1	5
10	Hort	0	0	½	½	1	0	½	½	½	♛	½	1	5
11	Kavalek	½	½	0	½	½	0	½	½	½	½	♛	½	4½
12	Smyslov	0	0	0	0	½	1	½	0	0	0	½	♛	2½

Bad Kissingen *28 January – 8 February 1980*

		1	2	3	4	Total
1	Karpov	♛	½ ½	1½	11	4½
2	Spassky	½ ½	♛	½ ½	½ ½	3
3	Hübner	0½	½ ½	♛	1½	3
4	Unzicker	00	½ ½	0½	♛	1½

Romanishin (seated) and Ljubojević. (Brian Reilly)

London *10–25 April 1980*

	1	2	3	4	5	6	7	8	9	10	11	12	13	14	Total
1 Miles	♛	1	½	0	1	1	½	½	0	½	1	1	1	½	8½
2 Andersson	0	♛	½	½	1	0	½	½	½	1	1	1	1	1	8½
3 Korchnoi	½	½	♛	½	½	½	1	½	1	1	0	½	1	1	8½
4 Sosonko	1	½	½	♛	0	½	½	½	½	½	1	0	1	1	7½
5 Speelman	0	0	½	1	♛	1	½	½	½	0	1	1	½	1	7½
6 Gheorghiu	0	1	½	½	0	♛	½	½	½	1	1	½	0	1	7
7 Ljubojević	½	½	0	½	½	½	♛	½	1	½	0	1	½	1	7
8 Timman	½	½	½	½	½	½	½	♛	0	1	1	0	1	½	7
9 Sax	1	½	0	½	½	½	0	1	♛	0	½	½	½	1	6½
10 Browne	½	0	0	½	1	0	½	0	1	♛	0	½	½	1	5½
11 Larsen	0	0	1	0	0	0	1	0	½	1	♛	½	½	1	5½
12 Stean	0	0	½	1	0	½	0	1	½	½	½	♛	½	½	5½
13 Nunn	0	0	0	0	½	1	½	0	½	½	½	½	♛	½	4½
14 Short	½	0	0	0	0	0	0	½	0	0	0	½	½	♛	2

Bugojno *3–24 May 1980*

	1	2	3	4	5	6	7	8	9	10	11	12	Total
1 Karpov	♛	½	1	½	½	½	½	1	½	1	1	1	8
2 Larsen	½	♛	½	½	½	½	1	½	½	1	1	1	7½
3 Timman	0	½	♛	½	½	1	½	½	1	½	½	1	6½
4 Andersson	½	½	½	♛	½	½	½	½	0	½	1	½	5½
5 Ljubojević	½	½	½	½	♛	0	½	½	1	½	½	½	5½
6 Polugayevsky	½	½	0	½	1	♛	½	½	½	½	½	½	5½
7 Hort	½	0	½	½	½	½	♛	½	½	½	½	½	5
8 Ivkov	0	½	½	½	½	½	½	♛	½	½	½	½	5
9 Kurajica	½	½	0	1	0	½	½	½	♛	0	½	1	5
10 Tal	0	0	½	½	½	½	½	½	1	♛	½	½	5
11 Kavalek	0	0	½	0	½	½	½	½	½	½	♛	½	4
12 Gligorić	0	0	0	½	½	½	½	½	0	½	½	♛	3½

Amsterdam *6 June – 14 July 1980*

	1	2	3	4	5	6	7	8	Total
1 Karpov	♛	½½	½½	½1	1½	01	11	11	10
2 Timman	½½	♛	½½	1½	1½	½½	½1	½1	9
3 Sosonko	½½	½½	♛	½½	½½	½½	½1	½1	8
4 Hort	½0	0½	½½	♛	½½	1½	11	½1	7½
5 Dolmatov	0½	0½	½½	½½	♛	0½	1½	11	7
6 Ribli	10	½½	½½	0½	1½	♛	01	10	7
7 Van der Wiel	00	½0	½0	½0	0½	10	♛	01	4
8 Larsen	00	½0	½0	½0	00	01	10	♛	3½

Puerto Madryn *19–27 July 1980*

	1	2	3	4	Total
1 Miles	♛	10	½1	1½	4
2 Ljubojević	01	♛	½½	11	4
3 Panno	½0	½½	♛	1½	3
4 Quinteros	0½	00	0½	♛	1

Smyslov in 1935 with his father, a strong player. (Reproduced by courtesy of B.T. Batsford)

Tilburg *18 September – 3 October 1980*

		1	2	3	4	5	6	7	8	9	10	11	12	Total
1	Karpov	♛	½	1	½	1	½	½	0	1	1	1	½	7½
2	Portisch	½	♛	½	½	½	1	½	1	½	½	½	1	7
3	Timman	0	½	♛	½	½	½	½	1	½	½	1	1	6½
4	Sosonko	½	½	½	♛	½	½	½	½	½	1	½	½	6
5	Spassky	0	½	½	½	♛	0	½	1	1	1	½	½	6
6	Tal	½	0	½	½	1	♛	½	½	½	½	½	½	5½
7	Hort	½	½	½	½	½	½	♛	0	½	½	½	½	5
8	Larsen	1	0	0	½	0	½	1	♛	½	0	1	½	5
9	Andersson	0	½	½	½	0	½	½	½	♛	½	½	½	4½
10	Ribli	0	½	½	0	0	½	½	1	½	♛	½	½	4½
11	Hübner	0	½	0	½	½	½	½	0	½	½	♛	1	4½
12	Kavalek	½	0	0	½	½	½	½	½	½	½	0	♛	4

Adorján. (Stephane Bureau)

Vrbas *5–17 October 1980*

		1	2	3	4	5	6	7	8	9	10	11	12	Total
1	Miles	♛	½	½	1	1	½	½	1	1	½	½	0	7
2	Petrosyan	½	♛	½	½	½	½	½	½	½	1	½	1	6½
3	Adorján	½	½	♛	½	½	½	½	½	½	1	½	1	6½
4	Yusupov	0	½	½	♛	½	1	1	½	1	1	½	0	6½
5	Ivanović	0	½	½	½	♛	1	½	½	½	0	1	1	6
6	Sax	½	½	½	0	0	♛	1	½	½	1	½	1	6
7	Gligorić	½	½	½	0	½	0	♛	½	½	½	1	1	5½
8	Kurajica	0	½	½	½	½	½	½	♛	½	½	½	1	5½
9	Ivkov	0	½	½	0	½	½	½	½	♛	½	½	½	4½
10	Velimirović	½	0	0	0	1	0	½	½	½	♛	1	½	4½
11	Bukić	½	½	½	½	0	½	0	½	½	0	♛	1	4½
12	Popović	1	0	0	1	0	0	0	0	½	½	0	♛	3

Buenos Aires *15 October – 4 November 1980*

		1	2	3	4	5	6	7	8	9	10	11	12	13	14	Total
1	Larsen	♛	½	0	½	0	1	1	1	1	1	½	1	1	1	9½
2	Timman	½	♛	1	1	½	½	0	1	1	1	½	½	1	½	9
3	Ljubojević	1	0	♛	½	½	½	½	1	½	½	½	1	1	½	8
4	Karpov	½	0	½	♛	1	½	½	½	½	0	1	1	½	1	7½
5	Andersson	1	½	½	0	♛	½	½	½	1	½	½	½	½	1	7½
6	Hort	0	½	½	½	½	♛	½	½	1	½	½	½	½	1	7
7	Najdorf	0	1	½	½	½	½	♛	0	1	½	½	½	1	½	7
8	Balashov	0	0	0	½	½	½	1	♛	0	1	½	½	1	½	6
9	Kavalek	0	0	½	½	0	0	0	1	♛	1	1	0	1	1	6
10	Olafsson	0	0	½	1	½	½	½	0	0	♛	½	1	½	1	6
11	Quinteros	½	½	½	0	½	½	½	½	0	½	♛	½	0	1	5½
12	Panno	0	½	0	0	½	½	½	½	1	0	½	♛	½	½	5
13	Browne	0	0	0	½	½	½	0	0	0	½	1	½	♛	½	4
14	Giardelli	0	½	½	0	0	0	½	½	0	0	0	½	½	♛	3

Baden bei Wien *27 October – 15 November 1980*

		1	2	3	4	5	6	7	8	9	10	11	12	13	14	15	16	Total
1	Spassky	♕	1	½	½	½	½	½	½	½	½	½	1	1	1	1	1	10½
2	Belyavsky	0	♕	½	1	½	½	1	1	1	½	1	½	½	½	1	1	10½
3	Nunn	½	½	♕	½	1	½	½	½	½	½	½	1	1	½	1	1	10
4	Byrne	½	0	½	♕	½	½	½	1	½	½	½	1	½	1	½	1	9
5	Vaganyan	½	½	0	½	♕	1	½	1	½	½	½	½	½	½	1	1	9
6	Smejkal	½	½	½	½	0	♕	½	½	½	½	½	1	½	½	1	1	8½
7	Liberzon	½	0	½	½	½	½	♕	½	½	0	1	1	0	1	½	1	8
8	Seirawan	½	0	½	0	0	½	½	♕	½	½	½	½	1	1	1	1	8
9	Gheorghiu	½	0	½	½	½	½	½	½	♕	½	½	½	½	1	0	1	7½
10	Stean	½	½	½	0	½	½	1	½	½	♕	½	0	½	0	½	1	7
11	Adorján	½	0	½	½	½	½	0	½	½	½	♕	½	½	½	1	½	7
12	Miles	0	½	0	½	½	0	0	½	½	1	½	♕	½	½	1	1	7
13	Gligorić	0	0	½	½	½	½	1	0	½	½	½	½	♕	0	1	½	6½
14	Van der Wiel	0	½	½	0	½	½	0	0	0	1	½	½	1	♕	0	1	6
15	Hölzl	0	0	0	½	0	0	½	0	1	½	0	0	0	1	♕	0	3½
16	Janetschek	0	0	0	0	0	0	0	0	0	0	½	0	½	0	1	♕	2

Wijk aan Zee *16 January – 1 February 1981*

		1	2	3	4	5	6	7	8	9	10	11	12	13	Total
1	Sosonko	♕	1	½	½	½	½	1	½	½	1	½	½	1	8
2	Timman	0	♕	0	1	½	½	½	1	½	1	1	1	1	8
3	Sveshnikov	½	1	♕	½	1	½	½	½	1	½	½	½	0	7
4	Taimanov	½	0	½	♕	1	½	½	½	1	½	½	1	½	7
5	Browne	½	½	0	0	♕	½	1	½	1	½	½	½	1	6½
6	Sax	½	½	½	½	½	♕	0	½	½	½	½	½	1	6
7	Gheorghiu	0	½	½	½	0	1	♕	½	½	½	1	½	½	6
8	Andersson	½	0	½	½	½	½	½	♕	½	0	½	1	1	6
9	Ree	½	½	0	0	0	½	½	½	♕	1	1	½	½	5½
10	Miles	0	0	½	½	½	½	½	1	0	♕	½	½	½	5
11	Torre	½	0	½	½	½	½	0	½	0	½	♕	0	1	4½
12	Unzicker	½	0	½	0	½	½	½	0	½	½	1	♕	0	4½
13	Langeweg	0	0	1	½	0	0	½	0	½	½	0	1	♕	4

Linares *16 January – 1 February 1981*

		1	2	3	4	5	6	7	8	9	10	11	12	Total
1	Karpov	♕	1	½	½	½	½	1	1	½	1	½	1	8
2	Christiansen	0	♕	½	½	1	½	1	½	1	1	1	1	8
3	Larsen	½	½	♕	0	0	1	1	½	1	½	1	1	7
4	Ribli	½	½	1	♕	½	½	½	½	1	1	0	½	6½
5	Spassky	½	0	1	½	♕	½	½	½	½	½	1	½	6
6	Kavalek	½	½	0	½	½	♕	½	½	½	½	1	1	6
7	Portisch	0	0	0	½	½	½	♕	½	½	1	1	1	5½
8	Ljubojević	0	½	½	½	½	½	½	♕	0	½	1	½	5
9	Gligorić	½	0	0	0	½	½	½	1	♕	1	0	1	5
10	Quinteros	0	0	½	0	½	½	0	½	0	♕	1	1	4
11	Bellon	½	0	0	1	0	0	0	0	1	0	♕	1	3½
12	Garcia, G	0	0	0	½	½	0	0	½	0	0	0	♕	1½

Belyavsky, interviewed, considers his reply. (Jaeg)

Moscow *3–25 April 1981*

	1	2	3	4	5	6	7	8	9	10	11	12	13	14	Total
1 Karpov	♛	½	1	½	½	½	1	1	½	½	½	½	1	1	9
2 Polugayevsky	½	♛	½	½	½	½	½	½	1	½	½	1	½	½	7½
3 Smyslov	0	½	♛	½	½	½	½	1	½	½	½	1	1	½	7½
4 Kasparov	½	½	½	♛	½	½	½	1	0	½	½	1	½	1	7½
5 Gheorghiu	½	½	½	½	♛	½	½	½	½	½	½	½	1	½	7
6 Portisch	½	½	½	½	½	♛	½	0	½	1	1	1	0	½	7
7 Balashov	0	½	½	½	½	½	♛	½	½	½	1	½	0	1	6½
8 Belyavsky	0	½	0	0	½	1	½	♛	1	1	½	½	½	½	6½
9 Petrosyan	½	0	½	1	½	½	½	0	♛	½	½	½	½	½	6
10 Andersson	½	½	½	½	½	0	½	0	½	♛	½	½	½	1	6
11 Smejkal	½	½	½	½	½	0	0	½	½	½	♛	0	1	½	5½
12 Torre	½	0	0	0	½	0	½	½	½	½	1	♛	1	½	5½
13 Timman	0	½	0	½	0	1	1	½	½	½	0	0	♛	1	5½
14 Geller	0	½	½	0	½	½	0	½	½	0	½	½	0	♛	4

Bad Kissingen *25 April – 5 May 1981*

	1	2	3	4	5	6	Total
1 Korchnoi	♛	1½	1½	11	11	11	9
2 Hort	0½	♛	0½	½½	11	11	6
3 Seirawan	0½	1½	♛	10	11	01	6
4 Sosonko	00	½½	01	♛	½0	½½	3½
5 Wirthensohn	00	00	00	½1	♛	1½	3
6 Lobron	00	00	10	½½	0½	♛	2½

Amsterdam *15–29 May 1981*

	1	2	3	4	5	6	7	8	9	10	11	12	Total
1 Timman	♛	½	½	½	½	½	1	½	½	1	1	1	7½
2 Karpov	½	♛	½	0	½	½	½	1	1	½	1	1	7
3 Portisch	½	½	♛	½	1	0	½	½	1	½	1	1	7
4 Hort	½	1	½	♛	½	½	½	½	½	½	1	½	6½
5 Kavalek	½	½	0	½	♛	½	½	1	½	½	1	1	6½
6 Smyslov	½	½	1	½	½	♛	½	½	½	½	½	1	6½
7 Ree	0	½	½	½	½	½	♛	½	1	1	½	½	6
8 Ljubojević	½	0	½	½	0	½	½	♛	½	½	1	½	5
9 Miles	½	0	0	½	½	½	0	½	♛	½	1	1	5
10 Polugayevsky	0	½	½	½	½	½	0	½	½	♛	½	½	4½
11 Donner	0	0	0	0	0	½	½	0	0	½	♛	1	2½
12 Langeweg	0	0	0	½	0	0	½	½	0	½	0	♛	2

Las Palmas *June 1981*

	1	2	3	4	5	6	Total
1 Timman	♛	½1	1½	½1	11	11	8½
2 Larsen	½0	♛	½½	1½	½1	11	6½
3 Seirawan	0½	½½	♛	10	11	½1	6
4 Korchnoi	½0	0½	01	♛	11	11	6
5 Bellon	00	½0	00	00	♛	10	1½
6 Garcia Padron	00	00	½0	00	01	♛	1½

Korchnoi finds the position drawish. (Bénédictine)

Lasker & Tarrasch

In 1892 the German Jew, Tarrasch, won his fourth consecutive tournament. In the last three he lost only one game out of 53. He was the logical challenger for the world title, now that Zukertort was dead, but had to turn down an invitation to play Steinitz in Havana because of his work as a doctor of medicine in Nuremberg.

Meanwhile another German Jew, Lasker, won a few matches and minor tournaments and challenged Tarrasch, six years his senior, to a match. The older man was offended and told Lasker to go away and prove himself by winning a strong tournament. Instead he went to America and challenged Steinitz. Lasker's victory (see page 12) only embittered Tarrasch further and a hostility developed between the two.

Tension often exists between a world champion and his challenger, but in this case it was made worse because some thought that Lasker had simply caught Steinitz in his decline, and Tarrasch, who meanwhile had won another tournament, was rightly the champion. In 1903 a match was agreed, but Tarrasch had to withdraw after a minor accident.

In 1905 Tarrasch scored 8 − 1 with 8 draws against Marshall, the winner of a strong tournament at Cambridge Springs in 1904. The doctor suggested that it was easier to beat the declining Steinitz than to achieve such a staggering win against Marshall at the height of his powers. Early in 1907 Lasker, who also became a doctor in 1900 (but in mathematics), beat Marshall 8 − 0 with 7 draws.

Tarrasch came back by winning a powerful tournament, Ostend 1907, described as being for the world tournament championship (although such a title has yet to be recognized). By the time the two doctors came face to face in 1908 the interest and excitement had reached a level never before known in chess history.

At the beginning of the match Tarrasch told Lasker that the only words he would say were 'check' and 'mate'. He managed only the first of these. Lasker won 8 − 3 with 5 draws (see page

Lasker at the outset of his career. Later he rejected optical aids.

12). His opponent never again won an important event.

Over their careers they met 30 times. Lasker won 18 and lost 4 games. Tarrasch was always able to advance reasons showing that he was really a better player, but Lasker said that results were the only truth.

Tarrasch, a fine writer, although little translated, was called the chess teacher of the German nation and generations have modelled their play on his clear logical principles. Lasker is said to have left no school, and in a sense it is true, because much of his pre-eminence was due to his remarkable tactical ability, rather than any new theory. However, players like Kasparov and Korchnoi owe much to him. Tarrasch was excellent at analysing positions, but Lasker saw that a game is a struggle, not a series of positions. The way to disconcert the opponent and create opportunities was, frequently, to disturb the balance. This technique gave birth to the legend that Lasker deliberately played bad moves.

Johannesburg *1–21 August 1981*

		1	2	3	4	Total
1	Andersson	♛	½0½½	½½½1	1½1½	7
2	Korchnoi	½1½½	♛	101½	001½	6½
3	Hübner	½½½0	010½	♛	11½1	6½
4	Nunn	0½0½	110½	00½0	♛	4

Van der Wiel. (Agterdenbos)

Tilburg *1–16 October 1981*

		1	2	3	4	5	6	7	8	9	10	11	12	Total
1	Belyavsky	♛	½	0	1	½	½	½	½	1	1	1	1	7½
2	Petrosyan	½	♛	½	½	½	½	1	½	½	½	1	1	7
3	Portisch	1	½	♛	½	1	0	½	½	1	0	1	½	6½
4	Timman	0	½	½	♛	½	½	1	1	1	0	½	1	6½
5	Ljubojević	½	½	0	½	♛	½	½	½	1	½	1	½	6
6	Andersson	½	½	1	½	½	♛	0	½	0	½	½	1	5½
7	Kasparov	½	0	½	0	½	1	♛	0	½	1	1	½	5½
8	Spassky	½	½	½	0	½	½	1	♛	½	½	½	½	5½
9	Larsen	0	½	0	0	0	1	½	½	♛	1	0	1	4½
10	Sosonko	0	0	1	1	½	½	0	½	0	♛	½	½	4½
11	Hübner	0	½	0	½	0	½	0	½	1	½	♛	½	4
12	Miles	0	0	½	0	½	0	½	½	0	½	½	♛	3

Wijk aan Zee *14–31 January 1982*

		1	2	3	4	5	6	7	8	9	10	11	12	13	14	Total
1	Balashov	♛	½	½	½	½	½	½	½	½	1	½	1	1	1	8½
2	Nunn	½	♛	1	1	½	½	0	½	1	½	1	½	1	½	8½
3	Hort	½	0	♛	½	½	½	½	½	½	½	½	1	1	1	7½
4	Van der Wiel	½	0	½	♛	½	½	½	1	0	1	1	1	0	1	7½
5	Hübner	½	½	½	½	♛	½	½	½	0	½	0	1	1	1	7
6	Kavalek	½	½	½	½	½	♛	½	½	½	1	½	½	½	½	7
7	Nikolić, P	½	1	½	½	½	½	♛	½	½	½	1	½	0	½	7
8	Sosonko	½	½	½	0	½	½	½	♛	0	½	1	1	½	1	7
9	Tal	½	0	½	1	1	½	½	1	♛	0	0	1	1	0	7
10	Ree	0	½	½	0	½	0	½	½	1	♛	½	½	1	1	6½
11	Timman	½	0	½	0	1	½	0	0	1	½	♛	½	0	1	5½
12	Christiansen	0	½	0	0	0	½	½	0	0	½	½	♛	1	1	4½
13	Sunye	0	0	0	1	0	½	1	½	0	0	1	0	♛	0	4
14	Chandler	0	½	0	0	0	½	½	0	1	0	0	0	1	♛	3½

Mar del Plata *8–27 February 1982*

		1	*2*	*3*	*4*	*5*	*6*	*7*	*8*	*9*	*10*	*11*	*12*	*13*	*14*	*Total*
1	Timman	♛	1	1	½	0	½	0	1	1	½	1	1	1	1	9½
2	Portisch	0	♛	½	1	1	½	0	½	½	1	½	1	1	½	8
3	Karpov	0	½	♛	½	½	½	1	0	1	1	½	1	½	½	7½
4	Polugayevsky	½	0	½	♛	0	½	½	½	½	1	1	1	½	1	7½
5	Seirawan	1	0	½	1	♛	½	0	½	½	0	½	1	1	1	7½
6	Andersson	½	½	½	½	½	♛	½	1	½	½	½	½	½	½	7
7	Larsen	1	1	0	½	1	½	♛	½	1	0	½	½	0	0	6½
8	Garcia Palermo	0	½	1	½	½	0	½	♛	½	½	0	1	½	½	6
9	Najdorf	0	½	0	½	½	½	0	½	♛	1	½	1	½	½	6
10	Braga	½	0	0	0	1	½	1	½	0	♛	½	0	1	½	5½
11	Panno	0	½	½	0	½	½	½	1	½	½	♛	0	½	½	5½
12	Franco	0	0	0	0	0	½	½	0	0	1	1	♛	1	1	5
13	Quinteros	0	0	½	½	0	½	1	½	½	0	½	0	♛	1	5
14	Giardelli	0	½	½	0	0	½	1	½	½	½	½	0	0	♛	4½

Chicago *9–21 April 1982*

		1	*2*	*3*	*4*	*5*	*6*	*Total*
1	Hübner	♛	1½	½1	1½	11	½1	8
2	Browne	0½	♛	1½	½1	½0	½1	5½
3	Korchnoi	½0	0½	♛	½½	½1	1½	5
4	Dzindzikhashvili	0½	½0	½½	♛	½½	½1	4½
5	Lein	00	½1	½0	½½	♛	½½	4
6	Martz	½0	½0	0½	½0	½½	♛	3

London (Phillips & Drew) *15–30 April 1982*

		1	*2*	*3*	*4*	*5*	*6*	*7*	*8*	*9*	*10*	*11*	*12*	*13*	*14*	*Total*
1	Andersson	♛	½	1	½	1	0	½	½	½	1	½	1	1	½	8½
2	Karpov	½	♛	0	½	½	1	½	1	1	½	1	½	1	½	8½
3	Seirawan	0	1	♛	0	½	½	1	0	1	½	1	1	½	1	8
4	Speelman	½	½	1	♛	1	0	½	½	½	½	½	½	½	½	7
5	Timman	0	½	½	0	♛	1	0	½	1	½	½	½	1	1	7
6	Portisch	1	0	½	1	0	♛	½	1	½	½	0	1	0	1	7
7	Ljubojević	½	½	0	½	1	½	♛	1	0	0	1	½	½	1	7
8	Spassky	½	0	1	½	½	0	0	♛	½	½	½	½	1	1	6½
9	Miles	½	0	0	½	0	½	1	½	♛	1	1	1	½	0	6½
10	Geller	0	½	½	½	½	½	1	½	0	♛	½	½	½	½	6
11	Nunn	½	0	0	½	½	1	0	½	0	½	♛	1	½	½	5½
12	Christiansen	0	½	0	½	½	0	½	½	0	½	0	♛	1	1	5
13	Mestel	0	0	½	½	0	1	½	0	½	½	½	0	♛	1	5
14	Short	½	½	0	½	0	0	0	0	1	½	½	0	0	♛	3½

Bugojno *6–25 May 1982*

		1	*2*	*3*	*4*	*5*	*6*	*7*	*8*	*9*	*10*	*11*	*12*	*13*	*14*	***Total***
1	Kasparov	♛	½	½	½	½	½	1	1	½	½	1	1	1	1	9½
2	Polugayevsky	½	♛	½	½	1	½	0	½	½	1	½	1	1	½	8
3	Ljubojević	½	½	♛	½	½	½	½	½	1	1	½	½	½	1	8
4	Spassky	½	½	½	♛	½	½	1	½	½	½	½	½	1	½	7½
5	Hübner	½	0	½	½	♛	½	½	½	1	½	½	½	1	1	7½
6	Andersson	½	½	½	½	½	♛	0	½	½	1	½	½	1	½	7
7	Larsen	0	1	½	0	½	1	♛	½	0	0	1	1	1	½	7
8	Petrosyan	0	½	½	½	½	½	½	♛	½	1	½	½	½	1	7
9	Ivanović	½	½	0	½	0	½	1	½	♛	1	½	0	0	1	6
10	Timman	½	0	0	½	½	0	1	0	0	♛	1	1	½	½	5½
11	Kavalek	0	½	½	½	½	½	0	½	½	0	♛	½	½	½	5
12	Najdorf	0	0	½	½	½	½	0	½	1	0	½	♛	½	½	5
13	Gligorić	0	0	½	0	0	0	0	½	1	½	½	½	♛	1	4½
12	Ivkov	0	½	0	½	0	½	½	0	0	½	½	½	0	♛	3½

Turin *4–22 June 1982*

		1	*2*	*3*	*4*	*5*	*6*	***Total***
1	Andersson	♛	½½	½½	½½	½½	1½	5½
2	Karpov	½½	♛	01	1½	½½	½½	5½
3	Ljubojević	½½	10	♛	0½	½1	½½	5
4	Portisch	½½	0½	1½	♛	0½	½1	5
5	Spassky	½½	½½	½0	1½	♛	½½	5
6	Kavalek	0½	½½	½½	½0	½½	♛	4

Tilburg *30 September – 16 October 1982*

		1	*2*	*3*	*4*	*5*	*6*	*7*	*8*	*9*	*10*	*11*	*12*	***Total***
1	Karpov	♛	½	½	½	½	1	½	1	0	1	1	1	7½
2	Timman	½	♛	½	½	½	½	½	½	½	1	1	1	7
3	Sosonko	½	½	♛	½	1	0	½	0	1	1	½	1	6½
4	Andersson	½	½	½	♛	½	½	1	½	½	½	½	1	6½
5	Smyslov	½	½	0	½	♛	½	½	1	½	½	1	½	6
6	Petrosyan	0	½	1	½	½	♛	1	0	1	½	½	½	6
7	Browne	½	½	½	0	½	0	♛	½	1	½	0	1	5
8	Nunn	0	½	1	½	0	1	½	♛	½	½	½	0	5
9	Portisch	1	½	0	½	½	0	0	½	♛	½	½	1	5
10	Torre	0	0	0	½	½	½	½	½	½	♛	½	1	4½
11	Hübner	0	0	½	½	0	½	1	½	½	½	♛	½	4½
12	Larsen, B	0	0	0	0	½	½	0	1	0	0	½	♛	2½

Yusupov. (Agterdenbos)

Sochi *1–21 December 1982*

		1	2	3	4	5	6	7	8	9	10	11	12	13	14	15	16	*Total*
1	Tal	♛	½	1	½	½	½	½	½	½	½	1	1	½	½	1	1	10
2	Nikolić, P	½	♛	½	1	½	1	½	0	½	½	½	½	½	1	1	1	9½
3	Romanishin	0	½	♛	½	1	½	½	1	½	½	1	½	½	1	1	0	9
4	Dvoiris	½	0	½	♛	0	½	½	1	0	½	1	1	1	½	1	1	9
5	Vaiser	½	½	0	1	♛	½	½	½	½	½	1	1	½	½	½	1	9
6	Speelman	½	0	½	½	½	♛	1	½	½	½	½	½	½	1	½	½	8
7	Panchenko	½	½	½	½	½	0	♛	½	½	½	½	½	½	½	1	1	8
8	Averkin	½	1	0	0	½	½	½	♛	1	1	0	0	½	½	1	½	7½
9	Geller, E	½	½	½	1	½	½	½	0	♛	½	1	½	½	½	0	½	7½
10	Razuvayev	½	½	½	½	½	½	½	0	½	♛	½	0	½	½	½	1	7
11	Psakhis	0	½	0	0	0	½	½	1	0	½	♛	1	1	½	½	1	7
12	Ftáčnik	0	½	½	0	0	½	½	1	½	1	0	♛	1	½	0	½	6½
13	Hazai	½	½	½	0	½	½	½	½	½	½	0	0	♛	½	½	1	6½
14	Pigusov	½	0	0	½	½	0	½	½	½	½	½	½	½	♛	½	1	6½
15	Chandler, M	0	0	0	0	½	½	0	0	1	½	½	1	½	½	♛	½	5½
16	Semkov	0	0	1	0	0	½	0	½	½	0	0	½	0	0	½	♛	3½

Wijk aan Zee *13–30 January 1983*

		1	2	3	4	5	6	7	8	9	10	11	12	13	14	*Total*
1	Andersson	♛	½	1	½	½	½	1	1	½	½	½	1	1	½	9
2	Ribli	½	♛	½	1	½	½	½	1	1	½	½	1	½	½	8½
3	Browne	0	½	♛	½	½	½	1	½	½	1	½	1	1	½	8
4	Hort	½	0	½	♛	½	½	0	1	1	1	½	½	1	1	8
5	Nunn	½	½	½	½	♛	½	½	0	1	½	½	1	1	½	7½
6	Seirawan	½	½	½	½	½	♛	½	1	0	½	1	0	1	½	7
7	Hulak	0	½	0	1	½	½	♛	1	½	0	1	½	½	½	6½
8	Korchnoi	0	0	½	0	1	0	0	♛	1	1	½	1	0	1	6
9	Olafsson, F	½	0	½	0	0	1	½	0	♛	½	1	0	½	1	5½
10	Ree	½	½	0	0	½	½	1	0	½	♛	½	1	½	0	5½
11	Scheeren	½	½	½	½	½	0	0	½	0	½	♛	½	½	1	5½
12	Van der Wiel	0	0	0	½	0	1	½	0	1	0	½	♛	1	½	5
13	Kuligowski	0	½	0	0	0	0	½	1	½	½	½	0	♛	1	4½
14	Speelman	½	½	½	0	½	½	½	0	0	1	0	½	0	♛	4½

Linares *11–25 February 1983*

		1	2	3	4	5	6	7	8	9	10	11	*Total*
1	Spassky	♛	½	½	½	½	½	1	½	½	1	1	6½
2	Karpov	½	♛	½	½	½	1	½	½	½	½	1	6
3	Andersson	½	½	♛	½	½	½	½	½	½	1	1	6
4	Yusupov	½	½	½	♛	½	½	1	½	½	1	0	5½
5	Miles	½	½	½	½	♛	½	½	½	0	1	1	5½
6	Sax	½	0	½	½	½	♛	0	½	1	1	1	5½
7	Timman	0	½	½	0	½	1	♛	1	1	½	0	5
8	Hort	½	½	½	½	½	½	0	♛	½	½	1	5
9	Geller, E	½	½	½	0	1	0	½	½	♛	½	1	5
10	Seirawan	0	½	0	½	0	0	0	½	½	♛	1	3
11	Larsen, B	0	0	0	1	0	0	1	0	0	0	♛	2

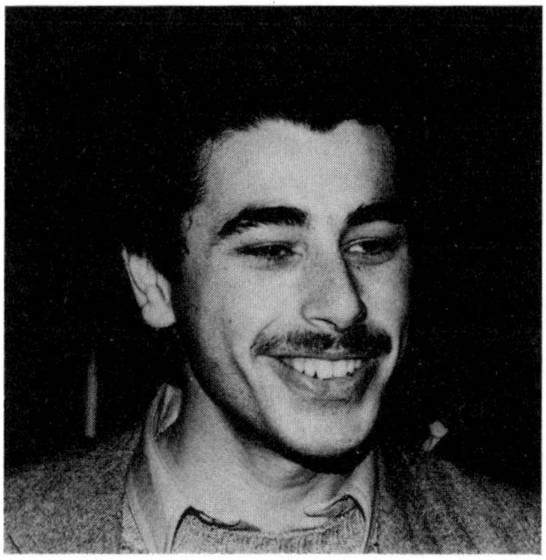

Seirawan. (Agterdenbos)

Gjøvik *12–21 August 1983*

		1	2	3	4	5	6	7	8	9	10	Total
1	Nunn	♛	1	½	½	½	½	1	½	1	½	6
2	Adorján	0	♛	1	1	1	½	½	½	½	1	6
3	Browne	½	0	♛	½	1	½	1	1	½	1	6
4	Miles	½	0	½	♛	1	½	½	½	1	1	5½
5	Agdestein	½	0	0	0	♛	1	½	1	1	1	5
6	Spassky	½	½	½	½	0	♛	½	½	1	½	4½
7	Ftáčnik	0	½	0	½	½	½	♛	1	½	1	4½
8	Karlsson	½	½	0	½	0	½	0	♛	½	1	3½
9	Helmers	0	½	½	0	0	0	½	½	♛	½	2½
10	Øgaard	½	0	0	0	0	½	0	0	½	♛	1½

Nikšić *23 August – 13 September 1983*

		1	2	3	4	5	6	7	8	9	10	11	12	13	14	15	Total
1	Kasparov	♛	1	1	0	½	½	½	1	1	1	1	1	1	½	1	11
2	Larsen, B	0	♛	½	½	1	0	½	1	½	1	1	½	½	1	1	9
3	Portisch	0	½	♛	½	½	½	½	½	½	0	½	1	1	1	1	8
4	Spassky	1	½	½	♛	½	½	½	½	½	0	½	½	1	½	1	8
5	Andersson	½	0	½	½	♛	1	½	½	½	½	0	1	1	½	½	7½
6	Miles	½	1	½	½	0	♛	0	½	1	½	½	½	½	1	½	7½
7	Tal	½	½	½	½	½	1	♛	½	½	0	½	½	½	½	½	7
8	Timman	0	0	½	½	½	½	½	♛	1	½	½	1	½	½	½	7
9	Ljubojević	0	½	½	½	½	0	½	0	♛	1	½	0	½	1	1	6½
10	Seirawan	0	0	1	1	½	½	1	½	0	♛	½	½	0	0	1	6½
11	Gligorić	0	0	½	½	1	½	½	0	½	½	♛	½	½	½	½	6
12	Petrosyan	0	½	0	½	0	½	½	½	1	½	½	♛	½	½	½	6
13	Nikolić, P	0	½	0	0	0	½	½	½	½	½	1	½	♛	½	½	5½
14	Sax	½	0	0	½	½	0	½	½	0	1	½	½	½	♛	0	5
15	Ivanović	0	0	0	0	½	½	½	½	0	0	½	½	½	1	♛	4½

Tilburg *12–25 October 1983*

		1	2	3	4	5	6	7	8	9	10	11	12	Total
1	Karpov	♛	½	½	½	½	½	1	½	½	½	1	1	7
2	Ljubojević	½	♛	½	½	½	½	1	½	½	1	1	0	6½
3	Portisch	½	½	♛	½	½	1	½	½	½	½	½	1	6½
4	Sosonko	½	½	½	♛	½	½	0	½	½	1	1	½	6
5	Vaganyan	½	½	½	½	♛	1	½	1	½	0	0	1	6
6	Hübner	½	½	0	½	0	♛	½	½	½	½	1	1	5½
7	Polugayevsky	0	0	½	1	½	½	♛	½	½	1	½	½	5½
8	Spassky	½	½	½	½	0	½	½	♛	½	½	½	1	5½
9	Andersson	½	½	½	½	½	½	½	½	♛	½	½	0	5
10	Timman	½	0	½	0	1	½	0	½	½	♛	½	1	5
11	Seirawan	0	0	½	0	1	0	½	½	½	½	♛	½	4
12	Van der Wiel	0	1	0	½	0	0	½	0	1	0	½	♛	3½

Wijk aan Zee *13–29 January 1984*

		1	*2*	*3*	*4*	*5*	*6*	*7*	*8*	*9*	*10*	*11*	*12*	*13*	*14*	***Total***
1	Belyavsky	♛	½	1	½	½	½	1	½	1	1	1	½	1	1	10
2	Korchnoi	½	♛	1	½	½	½	1	½	1	1	½	1	1	1	10
3	Nikolić, P	0	0	♛	1	½	½	0	1	½	½	1	1	½	1	7½
4	Andersson	½	½	0	♛	½	½	½	½	½	½	½	1	1	½	7
5	Adorján	½	½	½	½	♛	½	1	½	½	0	½	½	½	½	6½
6	Hübner	½	½	½	½	½	♛	0	1	0	½	0	½	1	1	6½
7	Miles	0	0	1	½	0	1	♛	½	1	½	0	½	1	½	6½
8	Tukmakov	½	½	0	½	½	0	½	♛	½	½	½	½	1	1	6½
9	Van der Wiel	0	0	½	½	½	1	0	½	♛	½	1	½	½	1	6½
10	Sosonko	0	0	½	½	1	½	½	½	½	♛	½	½	½	½	6
11	Ree	0	½	0	½	½	1	1	½	0	½	♛	0	½	½	5½
12	Torre	½	0	0	0	½	½	½	½	½	½	1	♛	0	½	5
13	Ligterink	0	0	½	0	½	0	0	0	½	½	½	1	♛	½	4
14	Van der Sterren	0	0	0	½	½	0	½	0	0	½	½	½	½	♛	3½

Sarajevo *18 March – 4 April 1984*

		1	*2*	*3*	*4*	*5*	*6*	*7*	*8*	*9*	*10*	*11*	*12*	*13*	*14*	***Total***
1	Korchnoi	♛	½	½	½	½	1	½	½	1	1	1	½	1	½	9
2	Timman	½	♛	½	½	1	½	0	1	1	1	1	1	0	1	9
3	Yusupov	½	½	♛	½	1	½	½	0	½	0	1	½	1	1	7½
4	Van der Wiel	½	½	½	♛	½	1	½	0	½	½	½	½	1	1	7½
5	Draško	½	0	0	½	♛	½	½	½	1	½	½	½	1	1	7
6	Kurajica	0	½	½	0	½	♛	0	½	1	½	1	½	1	1	7
7	Popović	½	1	½	½	½	1	♛	1	0	½	½	½	½	0	7
8	Romanishin	½	0	1	1	½	½	0	♛	½	½	0	½	½	1	6½
9	Dizdar	0	0	½	½	0	0	1	½	♛	½	0	½	1	1	5½
10	Hulak	0	0	1	½	½	½	½	½	½	♛	½	½	0	½	5½
11	Djurić	0	0	0	½	½	0	½	1	1	½	♛	1	0	0	5
12	Marjanović	½	0	½	½	½	½	½	½	½	½	0	♛	½	0	5
13	Velimirović	0	1	0	0	0	0	½	½	0	1	1	½	♛	½	5
14	Lobron	½	0	0	0	0	0	1	0	0	½	1	1	½	♛	4½

Predrag Nikolić presses his clock at Wijk aan Zee 1984, where he was third. Behind him is Belyavsky, joint winner, and the bearded Van der Wiel. (Stephane Bureau)

Oslo *12–22 April 1984*

		1	2	3	4	5	6	7	8	9	10	Total
1	Karpov	♛	1	½	½	½	½	½	½	1	1	6
2	Miles	0	♛	1	½	1	½	1	0	½	1	5½
3	Makarichev	½	0	♛	½	1	1	½	1	½	½	5½
4	Adorján	½	½	½	♛	½	½	½	½	½	½	4½
5	Arnason, J	½	0	0	½	♛	1	½	½	½	1	4½
6	De Firmian	½	½	0	½	0	♛	½	1	½	1	4½
7	Hübner	½	0	½	½	½	½	♛	½	½	½	4
8	Wedberg	½	1	0	½	½	0	½	♛	½	0	3½
9	Hort	0	½	½	½	½	½	½	½	♛	0	3½
10	Agdestein	0	0	½	½	0	0	½	1	1	♛	3½

Speelman. (BCF)

London *26 April – 11 May 1984*

		1	2	3	4	5	6	7	8	9	10	11	12	13	14	Total
1	Karpov	♛	1	½	1	½	½	1	½	½	1	1	1	½	0	9
2	Chandler	0	♛	½	½	1	½	0	1	1	0	1	½	1	1	8
3	Polugayevsky	½	½	♛	½	½	1	½	½	1	½	0	½	1	1	8
4	Timman	0	½	½	♛	½	½	½	1	1	½	½	1	½	½	7½
5	Ribli	½	0	½	½	♛	½	½	1	½	1	½	½	½	½	7
6	Seirawan	½	½	0	½	½	♛	1	1	0	½	1	1	0	½	7
7	Korchnoi	0	1	½	1	½	0	♛	½	½	½	½	½	½	½	6½
8	Vaganyan	½	0	½	0	0	0	½	♛	½	1	½	1	1	1	6½
9	Andersson	½	0	0	0	½	1	½	½	♛	½	½	½	½	½	5½
10	Miles	0	1	½	½	0	½	½	0	½	♛	½	0	1	½	5½
11	Speelman	0	0	1	½	½	0	½	½	½	½	♛	½	½	½	5½
12	Mestel	0	½	½	0	½	0	½	0	½	1	½	♛	½	½	5
13	Nunn	½	0	0	½	½	1	0	0	½	0	½	½	♛	1	5
14	Torre	1	0	0	½	½	½	½	0	½	½	½	½	0	♛	5

Bugojno *24 May – 11 June 1984*

		1	2	3	4	5	6	7	8	9	10	11	12	13	14	Total
1	Timman	♛	½	1	½	½	½	½	½	½	½	1	1	1	½	8½
2	Ribli	½	♛	½	½	½	½	½	½	1	½	½	1	1	½	8
3	Torre	0	½	♛	0	½	1	½	½	½	1	1	½	1	½	7½
4	Spassky	½	½	1	♛	½	½	½	½	½	0	½	½	½	1	7
5	Andersson	½	½	½	½	♛	½	½	½	½	1	½	½	0	½	6½
6	Belyavsky	½	½	0	½	½	♛	½	½	½	1	½	½	½	½	6½
7	Gligorić	½	½	½	½	½	½	♛	½	½	½	½	1	½	0	6½
8	Ljubojević	½	½	½	½	½	½	½	♛	½	1	½	½	½	0	6½
9	Tal	½	0	½	½	½	½	½	½	♛	0	½	½	1	1	6½
10	Miles	½	½	0	1	0	0	½	0	1	♛	½	½	1	½	6
11	Smyslov	0	½	0	½	½	½	½	½	½	½	♛	½	½	1	6
12	Kovacević	0	0	½	½	½	½	0	½	½	½	½	♛	½	1	5½
13	Ivanović	0	0	0	½	1	½	½	½	0	0	½	½	♛	1	5
14	Larsen, B	½	½	½	0	½	½	1	1	0	½	0	0	0	♛	5

Tilburg *2–18 October 1984*

		1	2	3	4	5	6	7	8	9	10	11	12	*Total*
1	Miles	♛	½	½	½	½	½	1	1	½	1	1	1	8
2	Belyavsky	½	♛	½	½	½	1	0	½	½	½	1	1	6½
3	Hübner	½	½	♛	½	½	½	½	½	1	1	½	½	6½
4	Ribli	½	½	½	♛	0	½	½	1	½	1	1	½	6½
5	Tukmakov	½	½	½	1	♛	½	½	½	½	½	½	1	6½
6	Ljubojević	½	0	½	½	½	♛	1	½	½	½	1	½	6
7	Portisch	0	1	½	½	½	0	♛	½	½	0	1	1	5½
8	Timman	0	½	½	0	½	½	½	♛	1	½	½	1	5½
9	Andersson	½	½	0	½	½	½	½	0	♛	½	½	1	5
10	Smyslov	0	½	0	0	½	½	1	½	½	♛	1	0	4½
11	Sosonko	0	0	½	0	½	0	0	½	½	0	♛	1	3
12	Van der Wiel	0	0	½	½	0	½	0	0	0	1	0	♛	2½

Novi Sad *10–23 October 1984*

		1	2	3	4	5	6	7	8	9	10	11	12	*Total*
1	Nikolić, P	♛	½	½	½	½	1	½	1	1	½	½	1	7½
2	Popović	½	♛	½	½	½	1	½	½	0	1	1	1	7
3	Sokolov, A	½	½	♛	½	½	½	½	½	1	½	1	1	7
4	Smejkal	½	½	½	♛	½	½	0	1	0	1	½	1	6
5	Torre	½	½	½	½	♛	½	½	½	1	0	1	½	6
6	Ftáčnik	0	0	½	½	½	♛	1	1	½	½	1	½	6
7	Cebalo	½	½	½	1	½	0	♛	0	1	½	½	1	6
8	Velimirović	0	½	½	0	½	0	1	♛	½	1	½	1	5½
9	Ivanović	0	1	0	1	0	½	0	½	♛	0	1	1	5
10	Marjanović	½	0	½	0	1	½	½	0	1	♛	½	½	5
11	Kurajica	½	0	0	½	0	0	½	½	0	½	♛	½	3
12	Kovacević	0	0	0	0	½	½	0	0	0	½	½	♛	2

'Cross my heart' says Adorján, but what did Portisch ask? (Agterdenbos)

Titograd *17–21 December 1984*

		1	2	3	4	5	6	7	8	9	10	11	12	Total
1	Velimirović	♛	½	½	½	½	½	1	1	1	½	½	1	7½
2	Korchnoi	½	♛	1	½	0	½	½	1	½	1	1	1	7½
3	Tal	½	0	♛	1	½	½	½	½	1	½	1	½	6½
4	Popović	½	½	0	♛	1	½	1	½	½	½	½	½	6
5	Ivanović	½	1	½	0	♛	½	½	1	0	1	0	1	6
6	Taimanov	½	½	½	½	½	♛	½	½	½	½	½	½	5½
7	Marjanović	0	½	½	0	½	½	♛	0	½	1	1	1	5½
8	Cebalo	0	0	½	½	0	½	1	♛	1	1	0	½	5
9	Zapata	0	½	0	½	1	½	½	0	♛	½	½	1	5
10	Kudrin	½	0	½	½	0	½	0	0	½	♛	1	1	4½
11	Djurić	½	0	0	½	1	½	0	1	½	0	♛	0	4
12	Csom	0	0	½	½	0	½	0	½	0	0	1	♛	3

Vaganyan. (Jaeg)

Reggio Emilia *27 December 1984 – 7 January 1985*

		1	2	3	4	5	6	7	8	9	10	11	12	Total
1	Portisch	♛	1	1	½	1	1	0	1	½	½	½	½	7½
2	Hort	0	♛	½	1	½	½	½	½	½	½	1	1	6½
3	Timman	0	½	♛	½	0	1	½	1	½	½	1	1	6½
4	Adorjan	½	0	½	♛	½	1	1	0	1	½	½	½	6
5	Toth	0	½	1	½	♛	½	1	0	½	½	1	½	6
6	Kurajica	0	½	0	0	½	♛	1	1	½	1	½	1	6
7	Rogers	1	½	½	0	0	0	♛	½	½	½	1	1	5½
8	Miles	0	½	0	1	1	0	½	♛	1	½	0	1	5½
9	Lobron	½	½	½	0	½	½	½	0	♛	½	1	½	5
10	Mokry	½	½	½	½	½	0	½	½	½	♛	0	½	4½
11	Ivanović	½	0	0	½	0	½	0	1	0	1	♛	1	4½
12	Garcia, S	½	0	0	½	½	0	0	0	½	½	0	♛	2½

Wijk aan Zee *18 January – 13 February 1985*

		1	2	3	4	5	6	7	8	9	10	11	12	13	14	Total
1	Timman	♛	½	1	½	½	1	1	½	½	½	½	1	½	1	9
2	Nunn	½	♛	1	½	½	0	1	½	1	½	½	½	½	1	8
3	Belyavsky	0	0	♛	½	½	1	½	1	½	1	½	½	1	1	8
4	Georgiev	½	½	½	♛	½	½	1	½	1	0	½	½	1	½	7½
5	Portisch	½	½	½	½	♛	½	0	½	1	0	1	½	1	½	7
6	Romanishin	0	1	0	½	½	♛	½	½	½	½	1	½	½	½	6½
7	Lobron	0	0	½	0	1	½	♛	1	1	1	½	0	½	½	6½
8	Ree	½	½	0	½	½	½	0	♛	0	1	½	1	½	1	6½
9	Korchnoi	½	0	½	0	0	½	0	1	♛	½	1	1	1	½	6½
10	Spraggett	½	½	0	1	1	½	0	0	½	♛	½	½	½	0	5½
11	Ftàčnik	½	½	½	½	0	0	½	½	0	½	♛	½	½	1	5½
12	Van der Wiel	0	½	½	½	½	½	1	0	0	½	½	♛	½	0	5
13	Ligterink	½	½	0	0	0	½	½	½	0	½	½	½	♛	1	5
14	Kudrin	0	0	0	½	½	½	½	0	½	1	0	1	0	♛	4½

Linares *8–22 March 1985*

	1	2	3	4	5	6	7	8	9	10	11	12	*Total*
1 Hübner	♛	½	1	½	½	½	0	½	1	1	1	½	7
2 Ljubojević	½	♛	1	½	½	1	1	0	½	1	½	½	7
3 Korchnoi	0	0	♛	0	½	1	1	1	1	½	½	1	6½
4 Portisch	½	½	1	♛	½	½	½	½	½	½	½	1	6½
5 Spassky	½	½	½	½	♛	½	½	½	½	½	1	½	6
6 Miles	½	0	0	½	½	♛	½	0	1	½	1	1	5½
7 Polugayevsky	1	0	0	½	½	½	♛	½	½	1	½	½	5½
8 Timman	½	1	0	½	½	1	½	♛	0	0	1	½	5½
9 Rivas	0	½	0	½	½	0	½	1	♛	½	½	1	5
10 Christiansen	0	0	½	½	½	½	0	1	½	♛	0	½	4
11 Vaganyan	0	½	½	½	0	0	½	0	½	1	♛	½	4
12 Adorjan	½	½	0	0	½	0	½	½	0	½	½	♛	3½

Moscow *12–28 April 1985*

	1	2	3	4	5	6	7	8	9	10	11	12	*Total*
1 Romanishin	♛	½	½	½	½	1	½	1	1	½	1	1	8
2 Vaganyan	½	♛	½	0	1	½	½	1	½	1	1	1	7½
3 Tukmakov	½	½	♛	1	½	½	½	½	½	½	1	1	7
4 Sveshnikov	½	1	0	♛	½	½	1	½	½	½	½	½	6
5 Geller, E	½	0	½	½	♛	½	½	½	1	½	½	½	5½
6 Razuvayev	0	½	½	½	½	♛	1	½	½	½	½	½	5½
7 Polugayevsky	½	½	½	0	½	0	♛	½	½	1	½	½	5
8 Ivkov	0	0	½	½	½	½	½	♛	1	½	½	½	5
9 Dolmatov	0	½	½	½	0	½	½	0	♛	1	½	1	5
10 Ftáčnik	½	0	½	½	½	½	0	½	0	♛	½	½	4
11 Speelman	0	0	0	½	½	½	½	½	½	½	♛	½	4
12 Am. Rodriguez	0	0	0	½	½	½	½	½	0	½	½	♛	3½

Portorož/Ljubljana *5–21 June 1985*

	1	2	3	4	5	6	7	8	9	10	11	12	*Total*
1 Portisch	♛	½	1	½	1	0	½	1	½	½	½	1	7
2 Ribli	½	♛	½	½	1	½	½	½	½	½	1	1	7
3 Miles	0	½	♛	½	½	1	1	½	1	½	1	½	7
4 Christiansen	½	½	½	♛	0	1	½	½	½	½	1	1	6½
5 Nikolić, P	0	0	½	1	♛	½	½	½	½	½	1	1	6
6 Popović	1	½	0	0	½	♛	½	½	½	1	½	½	5½
7 Gligorić	½	½	0	½	½	½	♛	½	½	½	½	½	5
8 Parma	0	½	½	½	½	½	½	♛	½	½	½	½	5
9 Karlsson	½	½	0	½	½	½	½	½	♛	½	½	½	5
10 Smyslov	½	½	½	½	½	0	½	½	½	♛	0	½	4½
11 Barle	½	0	0	0	0	½	½	½	½	1	♛	½	4
12 Cigan	0	0	½	0	0	½	½	½	½	½	½	♛	3½

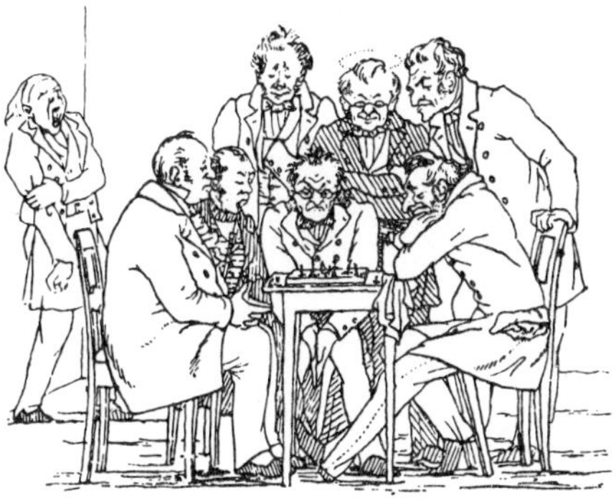

Amsterdam (OHRA) *15–26 July 1985*

		1	2	3	4	5	6	Total
1	Karpov	♕	½½	11	1½	½½	1½	7
2	Timman	½½	♕	½½	01	11	½1	6½
3	Nunn	00	½½	♕	½½	½1	11	5½
4	Miles	0½	10	½½	♕	10	½½	4½
5	Martinović	½½	00	½0	01	♕	½½	3½
6	Sunye Neto	0½	½0	00	½½	½½	♕	3

Tilburg *28 August – 17 September 1985*

		1	2	3	4	5	6	7	8	Total
1	Miles	♕	0½	11	11	10	0½	½1	½½	8½
2	Hübner	1½	♕	½½	01	½½	½1	½½	½1	8½
3	Korchnoi	00	½½	♕	½½	½1	½1	11	1½	8½
4	Ljubojević	00	10	½½	♕	1½	1½	01	01	7
5	Polugayevsky	01	½½	½0	0½	♕	½1	0½	½½	6
6	Romanishin	1½	½0	½0	0½	½0	♕	½½	1½	6
7	Timman	½0	½½	00	10	1½	½½	♕	01	6
8	Dzindzikhashvili	½½	½0	0½	10	½½	0½	10	♕	5½

Naestved *13–28 September 1985*

		1	2	3	4	5	6	7	8	9	10	11	12	Total
1	Vaganyan	♕	½	1	0	½	1	0	½	1	1	1	0	6½
2	Browne	½	♕	½	1	½	1	½	½	0	½	1	½	6½
3	Larsen	0	½	♕	1	½	1	½	½	½	0	1	1	6½
4	Short	1	0	0	♕	½	½	½	½	1	1	½	½	6
5	Tal	½	½	½	½	♕	½	½	0	1	½	½	1	6
6	Nikolić, P	0	0	0	½	½	♕	1	½	½	1	1	1	6
7	Andersson	1	½	½	½	½	0	♕	½	½	½	½	½	5½
8	Nunn	½	½	½	½	1	½	½	♕	0	½	0	1	5½
9	Ftáčnik	0	1	½	0	0	½	½	1	♕	½	1	½	5½
10	Agdestein	0	½	1	0	½	0	½	½	½	♕	½	½	4½
11	Chandler, M	0	0	0	½	½	0	½	1	0	½	♕	1	4
12	Hansen, C	1	½	0	½	0	0	½	0	½	½	0	♕	3½

Chandler (left) and Tal.
(Courtesy of B.T. Batsford)

Reggio Emilia *27 December 1985 – 8 January 1986*

	1	2	3	4	5	6	7	8	9	10	11	12	Total
1 Andersson	♛	½	½	1	½	½	½	½	1	½	½	1	7
2 Ljubojević	½	♛	½	½	0	½	1	1	1	½	1	½	7
3 Romanishin	½	½	♛	1	½	0	½	½	½	1	1	1	7
4 Portisch	0	½	0	♛	1	½	1	½	1	½	½	1	6½
5 Sosonko	½	1	½	0	♛	½	½	½	½	½	½	½	5½
6 Nogueiras	½	½	1	½	½	♛	1	½	0	½	0	½	5½
7 Lobron	½	0	½	0	½	0	♛	1	½	1	1	0	5
8 Kavalek	½	0	½	½	½	½	0	♛	½	½	½	1	5
9 Smejkal	0	0	½	0	½	1	½	½	♛	½	½	1	5
10 Ribli	½	½	0	½	½	½	0	½	½	♛	½	½	4½
11 Marjanović	½	0	0	½	½	1	0	½	½	½	♛	½	4½
12 Cebalo	0	½	0	0	½	½	1	0	0	½	½	♛	3½

Glenn Flear creating one of the greatest sporting upsets. Brought in as a last minute reserve he won the strong London 1986 tournament (see below). During the course of his game against Speelman he married Christine Leroy, French women's champion. (Jaeg)

Wijk aan Zee *17 January – 2 February 1986*

	1	2	3	4	5	6	7	8	9	10	11	12	13	14	Total
1 Short	♛	½	½	½	1	½	1	½	½	½	1	1	1	1	9½
2 Ljubojević	½	♛	½	1	½	½	½	½	½	0	1	½	1	1	8
3 Nikolić	½	½	♛	0	½	1	0	½	½	1	½	1	1	1	8
4 Van der Wiel	½	0	1	♛	½	½	1	½	½	½	½	1	1	½	8
5 Hübner	0	½	½	½	♛	½	½	½	½	½	1	½	1	1	7½
6 Hodgson	½	½	0	½	½	♛	0	½	1	1	½	1	0	1	7
7 Sosonko	0	½	1	0	½	1	♛	½	½	½	½	½	½	1	7
8 Chernin	½	½	½	½	½	½	½	♛	½	½	½	½	1	0	6½
9 Hort	½	½	½	½	½	0	½	½	♛	½	1	½	½	½	6½
10 Seirawan	½	1	0	½	½	0	½	½	½	♛	½	1	½	½	6½
11 Hellers	0	0	½	½	0	½	½	½	0	½	♛	½	0	1	4½
12 Ree	0	½	0	0	½	0	½	½	½	0	½	♛	½	1	4½
13 Van der Sterren	0	0	0	0	0	1	½	0	½	½	1	½	♛	½	4½
14 De Firmian	0	0	0	½	0	0	0	1	½	½	0	0	½	♛	3

London *11–27 March 1986*

	1	2	3	4	5	6	7	8	9	10	11	12	13	14	Total
1 Flear	♛	½	½	½	½	0	½	½	1	1	½	1	1	1	8½
2 Chandler	½	♛	1	½	½	½	0	½	1	½	1	0	1	1	8
3 Short	½	0	♛	½	½	1	½	½	½	½	1	1	1	½	8
4 Nunn	½	½	½	♛	½	½	0	½	1	½	0	1	1	1	7½
5 Ribli	½	½	½	½	♛	½	½	½	½	½	½	1	1	½	7½
6 Polugayevsky	1	½	0	½	½	♛	½	½	½	½	1	0	½	1	7
7 Portisch	½	1	½	1	½	½	♛	½	½	½	0	1	0	½	7
8 Spassky	½	½	½	½	½	½	½	♛	½	½	½	1	½	½	7
9 Vaganyan	0	0	½	0	½	½	½	½	♛	1	½	0	1	1	6
10 Speelman	0	½	½	½	½	½	½	½	0	♛	½	1	½	½	6
11 Larsen	½	0	0	1	½	0	1	½	½	½	♛	0	0	1	5½
12 Plaskett	0	1	0	0	0	1	0	0	1	0	1	♛	1	0	5
13 Mestel	0	0	0	0	0	½	1	½	0	½	1	0	♛	½	4
14 Dlugy	0	0	½	0	½	0	½	½	0	½	0	1	½	♛	4

USSR v Rest of the World

There have been two so far, both excellent competitive struggles. Four rounds were played.

1970 Belgrade

Board	*USSR*		*Rest of World*	
1	Spassky	½ 1 0	Larsen	½ 0 1 1
	Stein	0		
2	Petrosyan	0 0 ½ ½	Fischer	1 1 ½ ½
3	Korchnoi	½ ½ 0 ½	Portisch	½ ½ 1 ½
4	Polugayevsky	0 ½ ½ ½	Hort	1 ½ ½ ½
5	Geller	1 ½ ½ ½	Gligorić	0 ½ ½ ½
6	Smyslov	½ 1 0 1	Reshevsky	½ 0 1
			Olafsson	0
7	Taimanov	1 1 ½ 0	Uhlmann	0 0 ½ 1
8	Botvinnik	1 ½ ½ ½	Matulović	0 ½ ½ ½
9	Tal	½ 0 1 ½	Najdorf	½ 1 0 ½
10	Keres	½ 1 ½ 1	Ivkov	½ 0 ½ 0
	20½	(5½ 6 4 5)	19½	(4½ 4 6 5)

1984 London

Board	*USSR*		*Rest of World*	
1	Karpov	1 ½ ½ ½	Andersson	0 ½ ½ ½
2	Kasparov	½ ½ ½ 1	Timman	½ ½ ½ 0
3	Polugayevsky	½ 0 ½	Korchnoi	½ 1 ½ ½
	Tukmakov	½		
4	Smyslov	0 ½	Ljubojević	1 0 ½ ½
	Tukmakov	1 ½		
5	Vaganyan	½ ½ ½ 0	Ribli	½ ½ ½ 1
6	Belyavsky	1 1 ½ 1	Seirawan	0 0
			Larsen	½ 0
7	Tal	½ 1 ½	Nunn	½ ½ 0
	Romanishin	½	Chandler	½
8	Razuvayev	½ ½ ½ ½	Hübner	½ ½ ½ ½
9	Yusupov	½ ½ ½	Miles	½ ½ ½ 1
	Romanishin	0		
10	Sokolov	0 1 0	Torre	1 0 1
	Romanishin	½	Chandler	½
	21	(5 6 5½ 4½)	19	(5 4 4½ 5½)

USSR team (v. Rest of World) 1984. Seated l. to r. Yusupov, Polugayevsky, official, Smyslov, Tal. Standing Razuvayev, Romanishin, Vaganyan, Karpov, Kasparov, Belyavsky, Tukmakov and Sokolov. (Reproduced by courtesy of B.T. Batsford)

Rest of the World (v. USSR) 1984. Seated l. to r. Korchnoi, Larsen, official, Timman, Torre. Standing Hübner, Miles, Seirawan, Chandler, Ljubojevic, Ribli, Andersson, Nunn. (Reproduced by courtesy of B.T. Batsford)

EEC (Common Market) Team Championship

An informal competition for teams of four players.

1975	Ostend	Netherlands
1978	Middlesbrough	West Germany
1980	Berlin	Great Britain

European Cup

A knock-out competition for club teams of six players. The national club champion or an accepted nominee is eligible. Some clubs include foreign professionals in their teams and so the prestige of the title has been questioned. Finals to date:–

1976 Burevestnik (USSR) beat
Solingen (W. Germany)
1979 Burevestnik beat Volmac (Netherlands)
1982 Spartacus (Hungary) beat Burevestnik
1984 Trud (USSR) beat Burevestnik

European Team Championship

For national teams of eight players and a reserve. A series of knock-outs reduces the number of teams to eight for an all-play-all final. In 1957 there were four, and 1961 and 1965 six, teams in the final.

1957 Vienna 1 USSR 2 Yugoslavia
3 Czechoslovakia
1961 Oberhausen 1 USSR 2 Yugoslavia
3 Hungary
1965 Hamburg 1 USSR 2 Yugoslavia
3 Hungary
1970 Kapfenberg 1 USSR 2 Hungary
3 East Germany
1973 Bath 1 USSR 2 Yugoslavia
3 Hungary
1977 Moscow 1 USSR 2 Hungary
3 Yugoslavia
1980 Skara 1 USSR 2 Hungary
3 England
1983 Plovdiv 1 USSR 2 Yugoslavia
3 Hungary

European Junior Championship

Known at first as the Niemiejer International Junior Championship, this event, held over the New Year holiday, became recognized by FIDE in 1971–2. It has always taken place in Groningen, Netherlands, for competitors up to the age of 21. In 1976–7 it was combined with the World Junior Championship and won by an American. The European title went to the player who finished second.

1962–3	Zuidema (Netherlands)
1963–4	Sloth (Denmark) & Hartoch (N-lands)
1964–5	Hübner (W. Germany) & Ree (N-lands)
1965–6	Ree (N-lands) & Whiteley (England)
1966–7	Steinberg (USSR)
1967–8	Karpov (USSR)
1968–9	Maeder (W. Germany), Ribli (Hungary) & Vaganyan (USSR)
1969–70	Adorjan (Hungary)
1970–1	Ribli (Hungary)
1971–2	Sax (Hungary)
1972–3	Romanishin (USSR)
1973–4	Makarychev (USSR)
1974–5	Nunn (England)
1975–6	Kochyev (USSR)
1976–7	Ftačnik (Czechoslovakia)
1977–8	Taulbut (England)
1978–9	Van der Wiel (Netherlands)
1979–80	Chernin (USSR)

Ioseliani. (Agterdenbos)

1980–1	Akesson (Sweden)
1981–2	Curt Hansen (Denmark)
1982–3	Ehlvest (USSR)
1983–4	Salov (USSR)
1984–5	Hellers (Sweden)
1985–6	Khalifman (USSR)

European Junior Women's Championship

The first was not representative because many countries were not invited.

1977	Novi Sad	Sikora (Poland) & Kas (Hungary)
1978	Kikinda	Ioseliani (USSR)
1979	Kula	Ioseliani (USSR)
1980	Backa Topola	Brustman (Poland)
1981	Panonija	Stupina (USSR)
1984	Katowice	Madl (Hungary)

Chernin. (Agterdenbos)

Commonwealth Championship

The idea of a Commonwealth Championship is old. One was planned for New Zealand, 1949 but abandoned because the BCF could not compete. In 1950 the strongest players of Canada, New Zealand and South Africa (Yanofsky, Wade and Heidenfeld) happened to be in England and the opportunity was taken to hold an informal a-p-a championship, adding a promising Australian and a player from each of England and Scotland. The Commonwealth Chess Association, formed in 1981, planned a championship to be held in Nigeria in 1982, but it was to be 1983 before their first competition took place, held on the Swiss system.

1950	Oxford	Fairhurst (Scotland)
1983	Melbourne	Rogers, Hjorth (both Australia)
1984	Hong Kong	Spraggett (Canada) & Chandler (England)
1985	London	Thipsay (India) & Spraggett

Nordic Championship

1897	Stockholm	Svensson, S
1899	Copenhagen	Møller, J
1901	Göteborg	Møller
1903	Christiana	Giersing
1905	Stockholm	Pettersson, A.H.
1907	Copenhagen	Leonhardt
1909	Göteborg	Vidmar
1912	Stockholm	Alekhine
1916	Copenhagen	Johner, P
1917	Christiana	Nyholm, G
1919	Göteborg	Spielmann & Olson
1924	Copenhagen	Nimzowitsch
1928	Oslo	Berndtsson
1929	Göteborg	Ståhlberg
1930	Stockholm	Andersen, E
1934	Copenhagen	Nimzowitsch
1936	Helsinki	Lundin
1938	Orebro	Ståhlberg
1939	Oslo	Ståhlberg & Lundin
1946	Copenhagen	Kaila
1947	Helsinki	Böök & Stoltz
1948	Orebro	Möller, B
1950	Reykjavik	Möller, B
1953	Esbjerg	Olafsson
1955	Oslo	Larsen
1957	Helsinki	Sterner
1959	Orebro	Johanessen, S
1961	Reykjavik	Jóhannsson, I
1963	Odense	Brinck-Claussen
1965	Oslo	Thorbergsson*
1967	Hangö	Hoen*
1969	Lidköping	Jakobsen, O
1971	Reykjavik	Olafsson

Grandmasters at the 1983 Lloyds Bank tournament. The bank chairman, Sir Jeremy Morse, is the top figure. The others, l. to r. are Tarjan, Nunn, Quinteros, Keene, Matanović, Razuvayev and Bilek. (John Stone/Lloyds Bank)

1973	Grenà	Larsen
1975	Sandefjord	Holm*
1977	Rajamäki	Pettersson, L-E*
1979	Sundsvall	Niklasson
1981	Reykjavik	Helmers
1983	Esbjerg	Hansen
1985	Gjøvik	Agdestein*

Mitropa Cup

The cup, presented by Austria, was played as a knock-out in the first year, and a-p-a subsequently, by teams of four (plus reserve) from central Europe.

1976	Innsbruck	West Germany
1977	Bad Kohlgrub	Austria
1978	Il Ciocco	Yugoslavia
1979	Bern	Yugoslavia
1980	Rovinj	West Germany
1981	Luxemburg	Yugoslavia
1982	Bourgoin–Jallieu	France
1983	Lienz	Yugoslavia
1984	Bad Lauterberg	West Germany
1985	Arandjelovac	Yugoslavia

Balkaniad

A team tournament for the Balkan countries Bulgaria, Greece, Romania, Turkey, Yugoslavia, and, since 1979, Albania. The series really began at the third attempt, in 1971, and is played over six boards. In recent years there have been parallel events for women and juniors.

1971	Athens	Romania
1972	Sofia	Yugoslavia
1973	Poiana Brasov	Bulgaria
1974	Porec	Bulgaria
1975	Istanbul	Yugoslavia
1976	Athens	Yugoslavia
1977	Albena	Romania
1978	Baile Herculane	Yugoslavia
1979	Bihac	Yugoslavia
1980	Istanbul	Yugoslavia
1981	Athens	Yugoslavia
1982	Plovdiv	Bulgaria
1983	Baile Herculane	Yugoslavia
1985	Heraklion	Yugoslavia

Clare Benedict Tournament

A tournament for teams of four, sponsored by Clare Benedict (1871–1961), an American who lived the latter part of her life in Luzern. Exceptionally, in 1954 the competition was for individuals.

1953	Mont Pélerin	Netherlands
1955	Mont Pélerin	Netherlands
1956	Lenzerheide	West Germany
1957	Gurten-Kulm	West Germany
1958	Chaumont	Switzerland
1959	Lugano	West Germany
1960	Biel	West Germany
1961	Neuhausen	Austria
1962	Gurten-Kulm	West Germany
1963	Luzern	West Germany
1964	Lenzerheide	West Germany
1965	Berlin	West Germany
1966	Brunnen	Netherlands
1967	Leysin	West Germany
1968	Bad Aibling	West Germany
1969	Adelboden	Netherlands
1970	Paignton	Spain, England & West Germany
1971	Madrid	Netherlands
1972	Vienna	West Germany
1973	Gstaad	West Germany
1974	Menorca	England
1975	Copenhagen	Denmark
1979	Middlesbrough	England

Asian Championships

Asian Team Championship
1974	Philippines
1977	Philippines
1979	Philippines
1981	Philippines
1983	China
1984	China

Asian Cities Championship
1981	Shanghai
1983	Beijing (=Peking)
1984	Shanghai
1985	Shanghai

Cable Matches

At one time these seized public interest and three different series of transatlantic matches were contested. In addition there was a unique match between the House of Commons and the House of Representatives, on 31 May and 1 June 1897. Each side won two games and the other one was drawn.

The most important series was between Great Britain and the United States for the Newnes Trophy. After thirteen contests it was won outright by Britain thanks to three consecutive wins, but in total each side had won six matches while one was drawn. In terms of games it was 64:64. In addition to the annual score an analysis of results taken from the *British Chess Magazine* of 1911 shows exactly who did what in every match.

1896	GB 3.5	USA 4.5		
1897	5.5	4.5		
1898	5.5	4.5		
1899	4	6		
1900	4	6		
1901	5	5		
1902	4.5	5.5		
1903	4.5	5.5		
1907	5.5	4.5		
1908	3.5	6.5		
1909	6	4		
1910	6.5	3.5		
1911	6	4		

English Team

		Times Played	Score	Average	Average Position
Atkins, H E	a7D, b3w, c4D, d2L, e3L, f5L, g3w, h4L, i2w, j2D, l2w, m2D	12	6	.5	3.25
Bellingham, G E H	b6D, c5L, d9D, e4L, f6D, g6D, h5w	7	3	.43	5.86
Bird, H E	a3L	1	0	.0	3.
Blackburne, J H	a1w, b1D, c1D, d1w, e1D, f1L, h2L, i4D, j1D, k1L, l1L	11	4½	.41	1.33
Blake, J H	b7L, g8D, k5w, l8L	4	1½	.375	7.
Burn, A	a2L, c2L, i1D, m1w	4	1½	.375	1.5
Caro, H	c3L	1	0	0.	3.
Cole, H G	m10L	1	0	0.	10.
Cole, H H	b9w	1	1	1.	9.
England, P R	j7L	1	0	0.	7.
Girdlestone, T B	g10L	1	0	0.	10.
Gunston, W H	h9w	1	1	1.	9.
Holmes, Dr	i8D, k8D	2	1	.5	8.
Hooke, G A	h10L	1	0	0.	10.
Jacobs, H	b10w, c9w, d6D, e8w, f9L, h8D, k10w	7	5	.714	8.57
Jackson, E M	a8w, b8w, c8w, d4L, e7w, f8D	6	4½	.75	7.16
Lawrence, T F	b4L, d3L, e6L, g1D, h1D, i3D, j3D, k2D, l3D, m3L	10	3	.3	2.9
Lee, F J	e2D, f3D, g4L, i6D	4	1½	.375	3.75
Locock, C D	a5D, b2L, c7D, d7D	4	1½	.375	5.25
Mason, J	f2w, g2D	2	1½	.75	2.
Michell, R P	f10w, g9L, h7w, i9L, j8L, k6w, l10D, m9D	8	4	.5	8.5
Mills, D Y	a6D, b5D, c6w, d5D, e5D, f4D, g5D, h3D	8	4½	.506	4.87
Palmer, Rev. W C	j9L	1	0	0.	9.
Richmond, G W	i5w, j4D, m6L	3	1½	.5	5.
Sergeant, E G	j10D, k9w	2	1½	.75	9.5
Thomas, G A	l9w, m8w	2	2	1.	8.5
Tinsley, S	a4D	1	0	0.	4.
Trenchard, H W	c10w, d10D, e10L, g7w, k6L	5	2½	.5	8.6
Wahltuch, V L	k7w, l4w, m4w	3	3	1.	5.
Wainwright, G E	d8D, i10w, j5D, k4L, l6w	5	3	.6	6.6
Ward, W	e9D, f7w, i7L, j6D, k3L, l7D, m7w	7	3½	.5	6.57
Yates, F D	l5w, m5w	2	2	1.	5.

American Team

		Times Played	Score	Average	Average Position
Baird, D G	a8L, c7D, d10D	3	1	.33	8.3
Bampton, S W	e8L, f8D, i7w	3	1½	.5	7.66
Barry, J F	a4w, b4w, c3w, d3w, e3w, f3D, g2D, h2w, i2L, k2D, l2L, m4L	12	7½	.625	2.8
Black, R T	l8w, m6w	2	2	1.	7.
Burille, C F	a3w, b3L	2	1	.5	3.
Delmar, E	a7D, b7w, c6L, e10w, g7L, h8D, j4D	7	3½	.5	7.

85

		Times Played	Score	Average	Average Position
Fox, A W	i6D, m3w	2	1½	.75	4.5
Galbraith, J A	c10L	1	0	0.	10.
Helms, H	b8L, g10w, h10w, j3D, k6L	5	2½	.5	7.4
Hodges, A B	a6D, b6D, c5w, d4w, e4w, f4D, g4w, h3D, i3D, j1D, k3w, l3D, m2D	13	9	.69	3.7
Howell, C S	f10L, g9w, h9L, i9w, j6D, k5L	6	2½	.416	8.
Hymes, E	a5D, b5D, c4D, d5D, e5D, f5w, g5D, h5L	8	4	.5	4.87
Johnston, S P	d7D	1	½	.5	7.
Libaire, E W	j9w	1	1	1.	9.
Marshall, F J	d8D, e7L, f7L, g3L, h4w, i1D, k1w, l1w, m1L	9	4	.44	3.66
McCutcheon, J L	b10L	1	0	0.	10.
Meyer, J B	l10D, m10w	2	1½	.75	10.
Milnes, B C	m8L	1	0	0.	8.
Mlotkowski, S	k9L	1	0	0.	9.
Morgan, M	i5L	1	0	0.	5.
Newman, C J	d9D, e9D, f9w, g8D, h7L	5	2½	.5	8.4
Pillsbury, H N	a1L, b1D, c1D, d1L, e1D, f1w, g1D, h1D	8	3½	.437	1.
Robinson, A K	c9L, i10L, j10D	3	½	.166	9.66
Rosenfeld, H	l9L	1	0	0.	9.
Ruth, W A	k10L	1	0	0.	10.
Schweitzer, G L	j7w, k7L, l7D, m9D	4	2	.5	7.5
Showalter, J W	a2w, b2w, c2w, d2w, e2D, f2L	6	4½	.75	2.
Stadelman, S L	j5D, k8D, l6L	3	1	.33	6.33
Teed, F M	b9L	1	0	0.	9.
Voight, H G	d6D, e6w, f6D, g6D, h6w, i4D, j2D, k4w, l4L, m5L	10	5½	.55	4.9
Walcott, J H	m7L	1	0	0.	7.
Wolbrecht, G H	i8D, j8w, l5L	3	1½	.5	7.
Young, F K	c8L	1	0	0.	8.

a = 1896	d = 1899	g = 1902	j = 1908	m = 1911
b = 1897	e = 1900	h = 1903	k = 1909	w = won game
c = 1898	f = 1901	i = 1907	l = 1910	L = lost game

D = drawn game
The figure = position in team.

The second series was fought by combined teams from Oxford and Cambridge Universities (and London in the final match) against combined teams from American universities. As in the senior matches the series was broken after 1903 because the Russo-Japanese war made cabling facilities unavailable.

	Oxford & Cambridge	America
1899	3.5	2.5
1900	4.5	1.5
1901	3	3
1902	4.5	1.5
1903	3.5	2.5
1906	3	3
1907	3	3
1908	2.5	3.5
1909	1.5	4.5
1910	1.5	4.5
1924	2.5	3.5

The final series, for the Insull Trophy, was between London and an American city.

1926	London 4	Chicago 2
1927	4	New York 2
1928	3.5	Washington 2.5*
1930	3	Washington 3
1931	3.5	Philadelphia 2.5

*There was a dispute due to a transmission error and the match was annulled. A game shown as drawn in these totals was involved. Washington claimed a win.

National & City Championships

These lists of the major national and city championships may disagree with those printed elsewhere. New controlling bodies sometimes discount earlier titles although they were accepted as such in their time. Commonly the establishment of championships evolved slowly and some events came to be regarded as such retrospectively. Countries may allow foreign entries in their championships but in some of these cases the title is restricted to nationals.

A few women's championships are here, but increasingly the stronger women players are refusing to play in segregated events and the titles noted may not indicate the strongest active female player. The brilliant young Hungarian, Zsuzsa Polgar, rated as the world's strongest woman at the age of 15, refuses even to enter the Women's World Championship competition, having her eyes on the full title.

The locations indicate where a tournament was played. Matches are marked differently. The years are of the competition or, in the case of correspondence events, the end of play.

* = after play-off with other player(s) with the same score.
** = a tie-break method applied.

Argentine Championship

1921	match	Reca
1922	match	Villegas
1923	match	Reca
1924	match	Reca
1925	match	Reca
1926	match	Grau
1927	match	Reca
1928	match	Reca
1929	match	Reca
1930	match	Pleci
1931	match	Pleci
1932	match	Bolbochan, Jácobo
1933	match	Bolbochan, Jácobo
1934	match	Piazzini
1935	match	Grau
1936	match	Grau
1937	match	Guimard
1938	match	Guimard
1939	match	Grau
1940	match	Maderna
1941	match	Guimard
1942	match	Rossetto
1943	Buenos Aires	Iliesco
1944	Buenos Aires	Rossetto
1945	Buenos Aires	Pilnik
1946	Buenos Aires	Bolbochan, Julio
1947	Buenos Aires	Rossetto

Polgar. (Agterdenbos)

1948	Buenos Aires	Bolbochan, Julio
1949	match	Najdorf
1950 – 1	Buenos Aires	Maderna*
1951	Buenos Aires	Najdorf
1952	Buenos Aires	Shocron
1953	Buenos Aires	Panno
1954	Buenos Aires	unfinished

1955	Buenos Aires	Najdorf
1956	Buenos Aires	Sanguineti
1957	Buenos Aires	Sanguineti
1958	Buenos Aires	Pilnik
1959	Buenos Aires	Wexler
1960	Buenos Aires	Rossetto
1962	Buenos Aires	Sanguineti
1963	Buenos Aires	Garcia, R
1964	Buenos Aires	Najdorf
1965	Buenos Aires	Sanguineti
1966	Buenos Aires	Quinteros
1967	Mar del Plata	Najdorf
1969	Buenos Aires	Juarez
1969	Buenos Aires	Sanguineti
1971–2	Buenos Aires	Rubinetti
1972	Buenos Aires	Rossetto
1973	Santa Fe	Sanguineti
1974	Caseros	Sanguineti
1975	Buenos Aires	Najdorf
1976	Buenos Aires	Szmetan
1978	Buenos Aires	Emma
1980	Quilmes	Quinteros
1982	Buenos Aires	Rubinetti*
1983	Buenos Aires	Gomez-Baillo*
1984	Buenos Aires	Barbero
1985	Buenos Aires	Panno

Rogers. (Agterdenbos)

Australian Championship

1885	Melbourne	Esling
1887	Adelaide	Charlick
1888	Melbourne	Crane*
1893	Sydney	Wallace
1895	Melbourne	Wallace
1896	Sydney	Wallace
1897(1)	Warrnambool	Crane
1897(2)	Sydney	Jacobsen
1906	Perth	Viner
1912–13	Sydney	Viner
1913	Bellingen	Viner
1922	Melbourne	Watson
1924	Brisbane	Viner*
1926	Sydney	Crackanthorp
1927	Perth	Crackanthorp
1930–1	Melbourne	Watson
1932–3	Sydney	Koshnitsky
1934–5	Melbourne	Purdy, C
1936–7	Perth	Purdy, C*
1938–9	Sydney	Koshnitsky
1945	Sydney	Steiner
1946–7	Adelaide	Steiner
1948–9	Melbourne	Purdy, C
1951	Brisbane	Purdy, C
1952–3	Hobart	Steiner
1954–5	Perth	Purdy, J
1956–7	Melbourne	Ozols & Lazare
1958–9	Sydney	Steiner
1960	Adelaide	Endzelins
1962–3	Perth	Purdy, J
1964–5	Hobart	Hamilton*
1967	Brisbane	Hamilton
1968–9	Melbourne	Browne
1969–70	Sydney	Flatow
1971–2	Melbourne	Fuller & Hay
1973–4	Cooma	Jamieson
1975–6	Sydney	Rubanraut
1977–8	Perth	Shaw
1979–80	Adelaide	Rogers
1981–2	Melbourne	Hamilton
1983–4	Sydney	Johansen & Solomon
1985–6	Toowoomba	Rogers

Austrian Championship

1921	Vienna	Sämisch
1922	Vienna	Rubinstein
1924	Vienna	Dünmann
1925	Vienna	Becker & Wolf
1929	Innsbruck	Eliskases & Glass
1930	Graz	Künert
1931	Bregenz	Berghofer & Palda
1933	Vienna	Fuss
1934	Vienna	Podhorzer
1947	Ischl	Lenner
1948	Horn	Galia
1949	Efferding	Platt
1950	Melk	Palme

1951	Vienna	Lokvenc*
1952	Steyr	Poschauko
1953	Wolfsberg	Lokvenc
1954	Baden/Wien	Dückstein
1955	Prein	Auer
1956	Prein	Dückstein
1957	St Johann	Auer
1958	Ripp/Hallein	Prameshuber*
1960	Prein	Robatsch
1963	Ottenstein	Schwarzbach
1965	Ottenstein	Struner
1967	Graz	Janetschek
1969	Haag	Röhrl*
1971	Hartberg	Röhrl
1973	Leoben	Janetschek
1975	Mösern ob Telfs	Hölzl
1977	Mösern ob Telfs	Dückstein
1979	Lienz	Herzog*
1981	Lienz	Hölzl*
1983	Seckau	Herzog
1985	Wolfsberg	Klinger

Brazilian Championship

1925		Souza Mendes
1928		Souza Mendes
1929		Souza Mendes
1930		Souza Mendes
1932		Rocas
1933		Rocas

Klinger. (Roger Blackmore)

1935		Borges
1938		Cruz
1939		Trompowsky
1940		Cruz
1941		da Silva Rocha
1942		Cruz
1943	Rio de Janeiro	Souza Mendes
1944		Rocas
1947	Porto Alegre	De Freitas
1948	Rio de Janeiro	Cruz
1949	Rio de Janeiro	Cruz
1950		Mangini
1951	Fortaleza	German
1952		Carvahlo
1953	Rio de Janeiro	Cruz
1954	São Paulo	Souza Mendes
1956		Mangini
1957		da Silva
1958		Souza Mendes
1959		Gadia
1960	São Paulo	Camara
1961	Fortaleza	Camara
1962	Vitoria	Gadia
1963	Recife	Camara
1964	Brasilia	Rocha
1965	Rio de Janeiro	Mecking
1966	Belo Horizonte	Paiva
1967	São Paulo	Mecking
1968	San Bernardo	Camara
1969	São Paulo	Rocha
1970	Recife	van Riemsdijk
1971	Fortalexa	Paiva
1972		German
1973	Salvador	van Riemsdijk
1974	Tijuca	Miranda & Segal
1975	Caxias do Sul	Gouveia
1976	João Pessoa	Sunye Neto
1977	Curitiba	Sunye Neto
1978	Natal	Segal
1979		Sunye Neto
1980	Novo Friburgo	Sunye Neto
1981	São Luis	Sunye Neto
1982	Brasilia	Sunye Neto
1983		
1984	Cabo Prio	Milos
1985	Brasilia	Milos

British Championship

The first series was for a championship cup, provided by the British Chess Association, to become the property of anyone winning it twice in succession. This is exactly what happened on the fourth contest in 1872.

The next series, begun in 1886, was confined to amateurs and was, particularly in the early years, unrepresentative. George Newnes (later Sir George) donated a cup for annual competition. The first winner refused the second year 'to compete in an open tournament for a position which I already hold' and thought it 'monstrous' that he should be asked to enter 'into competition with every amateur, of whatever strength, who might think fit to present himself'.

The present series is linked to the British Chess Federation. It was not held in war years, nor in 1919, 1922, 1927 and 1930, when it would have clashed with major international events in England. Nor was it held in 1939 when the British team were in Buenos Aires for the Olympiad. A women's event took place in most of those years. Until 1958 the championship clashed regularly with Olympiads. Increasingly in recent years the strongest women have played in the championship and the women's titleholder is not necessarily the best. In 1922 and again in 1985 the women's tournament was open to all nationalities, and in the latter the British champion was the one who finished third.

Symbols: * after play-off. ** after tie-break (sum of opponents' scores). *** Blackburne could not play-off.

British Championship

Champion	Women's Champion
London *20 Jun – 1866*	
de Vere	
London *23 Nov – 1868*	
Blackburne*	
London *10 Oct – 1870*	
Wisker*	
London *2 – 14 Jul 1872*	
Wisker*	
London *Jul – Oct 1886*	
Gattie	
London *29 Nov – 12 Dec 1887*	
Locock*	
Bradford *6 – 18 Aug 1888*	
Guest	
London *25 Nov – 1889*	
Wainwright	
Manchester *25 Aug – 30 Sep 1890*	
Mills	
London *7 – 18 Mar 1892*	
Jones-Bateman	
Hastings *19 – 24 Aug 1895*	
Atkins	
Southampton *30 Aug – 8 Sep 1897*	
Atkins	
Bath *2 – 13 Sep 1900*	
Atkins	
Norwich *1 – 10 Sep 1902*	
Michell	
Hastings *22 Aug – 3 Sep 1904*	
Napier*	Finn

Champion	Women's Champion
Southport *14 – 26 Aug 1905*	
Atkins	Finn
Shrewsbury *6 – 18 Aug 1906*	
Atkins	Herring
London *12 – 26 Aug 1907*	
Atkins	Herring*
Tunbridge Wells *10 – 22 Aug 1908*	
Atkins	Curling*
Scarborough *9 – 21 Aug 1909*	
Atkins*	Anderson
Oxford *15 – 27 Aug 1910*	
Atkins	Houlding
Glasgow *14 – 25 Aug 1911*	
Atkins*	Houlding
Richmond (Sy) *12 – 24 Aug 1912*	
Griffith	Anderson
Cheltenham *6 – 21 Jul 1913*	
Yates	Moseley*
Chester *10 – 22 Aug 1914*	
Yates***	Houlding
Hastings *11 – 23 Aug 1919*	
	Holloway
Edinburgh *9 – 21 Aug 1920*	
Scott	Stevenson*
Malvern *8 – 20 Aug 1921*	
Yates	Anderson*
London *31 Jul – 18 Aug 1922*	
	Price
Southsea *13 – 24 Aug 1923*	
Thomas	Price
Southport *11 – 23 Aug 1924*	
Atkins	Price
Stratford on Avon *17 – 29 Aug 1925*	
Atkins	Stevenson
Edinburgh *2 – 13 Aug 1926*	
Yates	Stevenson
Tenby *2 – 13 Jul 1928*	
Yates	Price
Ramsgate *29 Jul – 10 Aug 1929*	
Sultan Khan	Gilchrist
Scarborough *23 Jun – 5 Jul 1930*	
	Stevenson*
Worcester *10 – 22 Aug 1931*	
Yates	Michell & Wheelwright
London *15 – 27 Aug 1932*	
Sultan Khan	Michell*
Hastings *31 Jul – 12 Aug 1933*	
Sultan Khan	Fatima
Chester *30 Jul – 11 Aug 1934*	
Thomas	Gilchrist

Champion	Women's Champion	Champion	Women's Champion
Yarmouth *8 – 20 Jul 1935*		**Chester** *18 – 29 Aug 1952*	
Winter	Michell	Wade	
Nottingham *10 – 28 Aug 1936*		**Hastings** *10 – 22 Aug 1953*	
	Holloway	Yanofsky	Tranmer
Bournemouth *8 – 20 Jun 1936*		**Nottingham** *16 – 29 Aug 1954*	
Winter		Barden & Phillips	Bruce
Blackpool *5 – 17 Jul 1937*		**Aberystwyth** *22 Aug – 3 Sep 1955*	
Fairhurst	Dew	Golombek	Doulton & Bruce
Brighton *8 – 19 Aug 1938*		**Blackpool** *20 – 31 Aug 1956*	
Alexander	Musgrave	Alexander	Pritchard
Bournemouth *14 – 25 Aug 1939*		**Plymouth** *19 – 30 Aug 1957*	
	Saunders	Fazekas	Sunnucks
Nottingham *12 – 24 Aug 1946*		**Leamington** *18 – 29 Aug 1958*	
Combe	Saunders*	Penrose*	Sunnucks*
Harrogate *11 – 22 Aug 1947*		**York** *10 – 22 Aug 1959*	
Golombek*	Tranmer	Penrose*	Bruce
London *31 Aug – 11 Sep 1948*		**Leicester** *15 – 27 Aug 1960*	
Broadbent	Price	Penrose	Bruce
Felixstowe *8 – 20 Aug 1949*		**Aberystwyth** *14 – 25 Aug 1961*	
Golombek	Tranmer	Penrose	Tranmer
Buxton *21 Aug – 2 Sep 1950*		**Whitby** *13 – 24 Aug 1962*	
Broadbent	Bruce*	Penrose	Bruce
Swansea *20 Aug – 1 Sep 1951*		**Bath** *12 – 23 Aug 1963*	
Klein	Bruce	Penrose	Bruce

Penrose at the time he was the foremost British player.
(Brian Reilly)

Golombek, the patriarch of British chess.
(Roger Blackmore)

Champion	Women's Champion	Champion	Women's Champion
Whitby 17 – 29 Aug 1964		**Morecambe** 4 – 15 Aug 1975	
Haygarth	Sunnucks	Hartston	Jackson*
Hastings 9 – 20 Aug 1965		**Portsmouth** 9 – 20 Aug 1976	
Lee	Pritchard	Mestel	Hartston
Sunderland 8 – 20 Aug 1966		**Brighton** 8 – 19 Aug 1977	
Penrose	Clarke M.E.E. & Moore	Botterill	Hartston*
Oxford 7 – 19 Aug 1967		**Ayr** 7 – 19 Aug 1978	
Penrose	Bruce & Dobson	Speelman	Jackson*
Bristol 5 – 17 Aug 1968		**Chester** 6 – 18 Aug 1979	
Penrose	Dobson	Bellin**	Miles*
Rhyl 11 – 23 Aug 1969		**Brighton** 4 – 16 Aug 1980	
Penrose	Bruce & Dobson	Nunn*	Jackson
Coventry 10 – 21 Aug 1970		**Morecambe** 3 – 15 Aug 1981	
Wade	Hartston	Littlewood	Jackson
Blackpool 9 – 21 Aug 1971		**Torquay** 2 – 14 Aug 1982	
Keene	Hartston	Miles	Garwell
Brighton 14 – 26 Aug 1972		**Southport** 8 – 20 Aug 1983	
Eley	Hartston	Mestel	Hamid & Milligan
Eastbourne 6 – 18 Aug 1973		**Brighton** 30 Jul – 11 Aug 1984	
Hartston*	Hartston	Short	Unni*
Clacton 5 – 16 Aug 1974		**Edinburgh** 29 Jul – 10 Aug 1985	
Botterill*	Hartston	Speelman	Hamid

Hartston. (BCF)

Nunn holding the British Championship trophy after defeating Hartston in the play-off (1980–1). (Grieveson Grant)

Mestel. (Lars Grahn)

Stewart Reuben (see p 124) presents the trophy to British women's champion Rani Hamid. (BCF)

British Correspondence Championship

The British Chess Federation ran a national championship from 1921, but later asked the British Correspondence Chess Association (founded in 1906) to take over the task with effect from 1940. The names of the winners for 1938 and 1939 are not known, but some lists wrongly give here the winners of the BCCA's own competition.

1921 Hamond
1922 Blake
1923 Hooper
1924 Gunston
1925 Gossett
1926 Macdonald
1927 Macdonald
1928 Gunston
1929 West
1930 Macdonald
1931 Whicher
1932 Tylor
1933 Tylor
1934 Tylor
1935 Wheatcroft
1936 Roche
1937 Roche
1938 ?
1939 ?
1940 Roche
1941 Wolstenholme
1942 Morry
1943 Bonham
1944 Hooper
1945 Wood, B H
1946 Wood, G
1947 Bonham & Cairncross
1948 Wood, G & Parr
1949 Israel & Parr
1950 Parr

1951 Bonham & Brown
1952 Hallmark
1953 Rhodes
1954 Fuller
1955 Fuller
1956 Parr
1957 Davey
1958 Oakley
1959 Milan
1960 Cafferty
1961 Davey & Hunter
1962 Milan
1963 Milan

The British Postal Chess Foundation, formed in 1962, was made responsible for running the national championship from 1964 on.

1964 Dodson
1965 Milan
1966 Milan & Hollis
1967 Hollis
1968 Timperley
1969 Milan
1970 Hopewell
1971 Hollis
1972 Boyd
1973 Walker
1974 Stewart
1975 Davies & Ebbett
1976 Footner
1977 Clarke
1978 Shephard
1979 Shephard, Cunliffe & Stewart
1980 Stewart
1981 Woodford
1982 Chandler
1983 Bryson
1984 Bryson
1985 Bryson

Grand Prix (UK)

Since the early 1960s there has been a boom in weekend tournaments in Britain. One factor has been the award of prizes on the grand prix principle, as for example in motor racing and skiing. Performances in specific events, many of them weekenders, are aggregated. From 1974 to 1980 the grand prix was sponsored by Cutty Sark who gave cash and samples of their product, whisky. From 1981 the sponsor was Leigh, specialists in waste management, whose ever-increasing support naturally lacked a product sample. After the first year a petit prix was instituted followed in 1976 by the infelicitously named grande prixette. In 1982 a new category, amateur prix, began.

	G Prix	P Prix	Prixette
1974	Bennett & Miles		
1975	Miles	Bennett	
1976	Rumens	McKay	Wright
1977	Botterill	Horner	Jackson
1978	Rumens	Short	Jackson
1979	Nunn	Hebden	Jackson
1980	Nunn	Miles	Jackson
1981	Hebden	Arkell	Jackson
1982	Miles	Horner	Miles
1983	Plaskett	Short	Jackson & Miles
1984	Miles	Arkell	Jackson
1985	Large	Hebden	Jackson

Plaskett. (Bénédictine)

Bulgarian Championship

In 1940 Tsvetkov did not play-off. He was equal first with Neikirch who was not then a Bulgarian citizen and could not take the title. Neikirch was also first in 1937 and 1938, the title going to the player finishing second. In 1983 Ermenkov was excluded after three rounds because he ignored a ban on smoking.

Bulgarian Championship

1933	Varna	Geshev*
1934	Sofia	Geshev
1935	Ruse	Geshev
1936	Sofia	Geshev
1937	Sofia	Kantardzhiev
1938	Varna	Tsvetkov
1940	Sofia	Tsvetkov*
1942	Sofia	Toshev
1943	Sofia	Neikirch
1945	Sofia	Tsvetkov*
1946	Sofia	Petrov P S
1947	Sofia	Piskov & Toshev
1948	Sofia	Neikirch & Tsvetkov
1949	Sofia	Dimitrov
1950	Sofia	Tsvetkov
1951	Sofia	Tsvetkov*
1952	Sofia	Milev
1953	Sofia	Minev*
1954	Sofia	Padevsky
1955	Sofia	Padevsky
1957	Sofia	Neikirch
1958	Sofia	Bobotsov
1959	Sofia	Popov
1960	Sofia	Milev
1961	Sofia	Milev
1962	Sofia	Padevsky
1963	Sofia	Tringov
1964	Sofia	Padevsky*
1965	Varna	Minev
1966	Sofia	Minev*
1967	Sofia	Peev*
1969	Plovdiv	Spiridinov*
1970	Sofia	Popov
1971	Sofia	Radulov
1972	Sofia	Bokhosyan
1973	Sofia	Ermenkov
1974	Asenovgrad	Radulov*
1975	Pernik	Ermenkov*
1976	Sofia	Ermenkov
1977	Sofia	Radulov*
1978	Vratza	Kirov*
1979	Sofia	Ermenkov*
1980 – 1	Sofia	Radulov*
1981	Sofia	Tringov
1982	Sofia	Inkiov*
1983	Pernik	Donchev*
1984	Sofia	Georgiev & Ermenkov
1985	Sofia	Tringov

Kasparov. (Jaeg)

Kasparov. (Jaeg)

Korchnoi.

Yusupov.

Adams. (BCF)

Plaskett. (BCF)

Jackson. (BCF)

Typical of many ordinary players, the Rev K.S. Proctor, a tournament stalwart. (BCF)

Chilean Championship

1920	Valparaiso	Peralta
1924	Valparaiso	Castillo
1926	Valparaiso	Castillo
1927	Valparaiso	Castillo
1929	Vina del Mar	Castillo
1931	Vina del Mar	Flores
1932	Valparaiso	Reed
1934	Santiago	Castillo
1935	Santiago	Flores
1937	Santiago	Salas
1940	Santiago	Castillo
1941	Santiago	Flores
1944	Santiago	Flores
1946	Santiago	Pizzi
1948	Santiago	Castillo
1949	Santiago	Castillo
1950	Santiago	Flores
1952	Santiago	Flores
1953	Santiago	Castillo
1954	Santiago	Salas
1955	Santiago	Salas
1956	Santiago	Flores
1957	Santiago	Letelier
1958	Santiago	Stekel
1959	Santiago	Letelier
1960	Santiago	Letelier
1961	Santiago	Flores
1962	Santiago	Salas
1964	Santiago	Letelier
1965	Santiago	Flores
1966	Santiago	Ader
1968	Santiago	Godoy
1969	Santiago	Silva*
1970	Santiago	Donoso
1971	Santiago	Silva
1972	Santiago	Letelier
1974	Santiago	Silva
1975	Santiago	Silva
1976	Santiago	Silva
1977	Santiago	Donoso
1978	Santiago	Donoso
1979	Santiago	Campos*
1980	Santiago	Campos*
1981	Santiago	Morovic
1982	Santiago	Cifuentes
1983	Santiago	Cifuentes
1984	Santiago	Cifuentes
1985	Santiago	Cifuentes

Cuban Championship

1902	Havana	Corzo, Juan
1939		Aleman
1942		Gonzalez
1943		Gonzalez
1944		Fernandez
1950		Romero & Cobo
1951		Gonzalez
1952	Havana	Gonzalez
1955	Havana	Calero
1956		Cabrera
1957		Jiménez
1958		Ortega
1960	Havana	Jiménez
1963	Havana	Jiménez
1965	Havana	Jiménez
1966	Havana	Ortega
1967	Havana	Jiménez*
1968	various	Garcia, S*
1969	Matazanas	Rodriguez
1970	Havana	Garcia, S
1971	Havana	Rodriguez
1972	Playa Larga	Rodriguez
1973	Cienfuegos	Garcia, S
1974	Varadero	Garcia, G
1975	Las Villas	Estevez
1976	Holguin	Fernandez
1976	Pinar del Rio	Garcia, G
1977	Sancti Spiritus	Lebredo & Vilela
1978	Camaguey	Nogueiras
1979–80		Garcia, S
1981–2	Sagua la Grande	Hernandez
1983	Sagua de T.	Garcia, G*
1984	Holguin	Nogueiras & Rodriguez

Czech Championship

1905	Prague	Duras
1907	Brno	Treybal
1909	Prague	Duras
1911	Plzen	Duras (as Raz)
1913	Mlada Boleslav	Hromadka
1919	Prague	Schubert
1921	Brno	Hromadka, Prokes, Treybal
1923	Pardubice	Walter
1925	Bratislava	Reti
1927	C.Budejovice	Opocensky*
1929	Brno	Opocensky
1931	Prague	Zobel
1933	Mnichovo H.	Flohr*
1936	Podebrady	Flohr
1938	Prague	Opocensky
1940	Rakovnik	Foltys
1943	Prague	Foltys, Opocensky, Zita
1944	Brno	Opocensky
1946	Ostrava	Pachman
1948	Bratislava	Richter*
1950	Gottwaldow	Fichtl & Filip
1952	Tat.Lom./Prague	Filip
1953	Prague	Pachman*

Kiril Georgiev. (Stephane Bureau)

Canadian Championship

1873	Toronto	Ensor
1874	Montreal	Hicks
1875	Ottawa	Jackson
1876	Hamilton	Sanderson
1877	Quebec	Howe
1878 – 9	Montreal	Ascher
1879	Ottawa	Pope
1881	Ottawa	Shaw
1881 – 2	Quebec	Sanderson
1882 – 3	Montreal	Ascher & Howe
1884	Ottawa	Lambert
1886	Quebec	MacLeod
1887	Montreal	Barry*
1888	Quebec	MacLeod*
1889	Montreal	Flemming*
1890	Quebec	Short
1891	Montreal	Davison
1892	Toronto	Boultbee
1893	Quebec	Narraway
1894	Montreal	Davison
1897	Orillia	Narraway
1898	Toronto	Narraway
1899	Montreal	Smith
1904	Winnipeg	Smith
1906	Montreal	Smith
1908 – 9	Toronto	Sawyer
1910	Montreal	Morrison
1913	Winnipeg	Morrison*
1920	Toronto	Gale
1922	Montreal	Morrison
1924	Hamilton	Morrison
1926	Montreal	Morrison
1927	Toronto	Fox
1929	Montreal	Fox
1931	Hamilton	Fox*
1932	Haileybury	Fox
1933	Winnipeg	Martin
1934	Toronto	Belson
1935	Montreal	Fox
1936	Toronto	Blumin
1937	Quebec	Blumin
1938	Toronto	Fox
1940	Montreal	Fox
1941	Winnipeg	Yanofsky
1943	Dalhousie	Yanofsky
1945	Saskatoon	Yanofsky & Yerhoff
1946	Toronto	Belson
1947	Quebec	Yanofsky
1948	Arvida	Fox
1951	Vancouver	Vaitonis
1953	Winnipeg	Anderson & Yanofsky
1955	Ottawa	Anderson
1957	Vancouver	Vaitonis
1959	Montreal	Yanofsky
1961	Brockville	Joyner
1963	Winnipeg	Yanofsky
1965	Vancouver	Yanofsky
1969	Pointe Claire	Suttles*
1972	Toronto	Biyiasas
1975	Calgary	Biyiasas
1978	Toronto	Biyiasas
1981	Montreal	Ivanov
1984	Ottawa	Spraggett
1985	Edmonton	Stone & Ivanov

Ivanov supports Gulko's campaign for an exist visa from the USSR. (Stephane Bureau)

Taulbot. (BCF)

Speelman, unusually without glasses.
(BCF)

McNab. (BCF)

Hebden. (BCF)

Bellin. (BCF)

The Duncan Lawrie Olympiad awards, designed by Wedgwood and presented for the best games played in the Olympiad and Women's Olympiad. (Josiah Wedgwood & Sons Limited, Barlaston)

Hort. (Stephane Bureau)

1954	Prague	Filip
1955	Prague	Sefc
1956	Podebrady	Alster
1957	Prague	Pachman
1958	Prague	Pachman
1960	Ostrava	Fichtl*
1961	Kosice	Pachman
1962	Prague	Kavalek
1963	Prague	Pachman
1964	Brno	Jansa*
1965	Pardubice	Augustin
1966	Harrachov	Pachman
1967	Bratislava	Kozma
1968	Luhacovice	Kavalek
1970	Havirov	Hort
1971	Havirov	Hort
1972	Trinec	Hort
1973	Luhacovice	Smejkal
1974	Rimavska S.	Jansa
1975	Brno	Hort
1976	Ostrava	Prandstetter
1977	Decin	Hort
1978	Marianske Lazne	Prandstetter
1979	Trenc.Teplice	Smejkal
1980	Trnava	Ambroz
1981		Ftačnik
1982	Fremstat	Ftačnik
1983	Bratislava	Ftačnik
1984	Sumperk	Hort & Jansa
1985		Ftačnik

Danish Championship

The Danish chess union (DSU) held its first championship in 1910, but the players from Copenhagen did not join in until 1922 and some regard that as the first true championship.
Symbols: * play-off. ** tie-break by lottery. *** no play-off because Nielsen died.

1910	Randers	Kruse
1911	Odense	Jørgensen
1912	Lemvig	Weye
1913	Slagelse	Kier
1914	Aarhus	Salskov
1915	Horsens	Giersing
1916	Copenhagen	Juhl
1917	Grenaa	Jacobsen, E
1918	Nykøbing	Karlsson
1919	Middlefart	Weilbach
1920	Aalborg	Pedersen, J
1921	Roskilde	Thomsen, F
1922	Copenhagen	Jacobsen, E
1923	Copenhagen	Andersen, Erik
1924	Randers	Kier
1925	Aarhus	Andersen
1926	Sønderborg	Andersen*
1927	Vordingborg	Andersen
1928	Horsens	Gemzøe
1929	Copenhagen	Andersen
1930	Svendborg	Andersen
1931	Frederikshavn	Andersen
1932	Esbjerg	Andersen*
1933	Naskov	Andersen
1934	Vejle	Andersen
1935	Copenhagen	Andersen
1936	Herning	Andersen*
1937	Odense	Hage
1938	Aalborg	Hage
1939	Naestved	Norman-Hansen*
1940	Randers	Enevoldsen, J*
1941	Copenhagen	Nielsen, B
1942	Nørresundby	Nielsen
1943	Helsingør	Enevoldsen, J
1944	Odense	Nielsen
1945	Odense	Poulsen
1946	Nykøbing	Nielsen
1947	Esbjerg	Enevoldsen*
1948	Aarhus	Enevoldsen
1949	Copenhagen	Hage***
1950	Aalborg	Hage**
1951	Odense	Pedersen, E*
1952	Herning	Poulsen
1953	Horsens	Pedersen
1954	Aarhus	Larsen
1955	Aalborg	Larsen
1956	Copenhagen	Larsen
1957	Odense	Ravn
1958	Herning	Andersen, B
1959	Aarhus	Larsen
1960	Aalborg	Enevoldsen
1961	Nykøbing	Pedersen
1962	Copenhagen	Kølvig
1963	Odense	Larsen
1964	Holsterbro	Larsen
1965	Aalborg	Holm
1966	Aarhus	Brinck-Claussen
1967	Vejle	Andersen, B
1968	Copenhagen	Andersen, B
1969	Odense	Jakobsen*

1970	Flensborg	Brinck-Claussen*
1971	Hjørring	Jakobsen
1972	Esbjerg	Hamann
1973	Copenhagen	Andersen, B
1974	Vejle	Rath
1975	Odense	Iskov
1976	Aarhus	Jacobsen
1977	Copenhagen	Brinck-Claussen
1978	Horsens	Høi
1979	Aalborg	Kristiansen
1980	Odense	Jakobsen
1981	Aarhus	Mortensen*
1982	Vejle	Kristiansen*
1983	Copenhagen	Hansen
1984	Aalborg	Hansen*
1985	Naestved	Hansen*

Estonian Championship

1922–3	Tallinn	Rinne
1932	Tallinn	Laurentius & Rinne
1932–3	Tallinn	Friedemann
1934	Tallinn	Raud
1934–5	Tallinn	Keres*
1936	Tallinn	Schmidt, P
1937	Tallinn	Schmidt, P
1938–9	Tallinn	Raud
1941	Tallinn	Kibbermann & Türn
1942	Tallinn	Keres
1943	Tallinn	Keres
1944	Viljandi	Türn & Eller
1945	Tallinn	Keres
1946	Tallinn	Renter
1947–8	Tallinn	Randviir
1948	Tallinn	Arulaid
1949	Pärnu	Randviir & Renter
1950	Tallinn	Randviir
1951	Tallinn	Nei
1952	Tallinn	Nei
1953	Tartu	Keres
1954	Tallinn	Randviir
1955	Tallinn	Arulaid
1956	Tartu	Nei
1957	Tartu	Randviir*
1958	Tallinn	Uusi
1959	Tartu	Uusi
1960	Viljandi	Nei
1961	Tallinn	Nei
1962	Tartu	Nei
1963	Tallinn	Uusi
1964	Tallinn	Arulaid
1965	Tartu	Etruk*
1966	Viljandi	Uusi
1967	Tallinn	Luik
1968	Tartu	Hermlin
1969	Tallinn	Etruk
1970	Viljandi	
1971	Tallinn	Nei

1972	Tartu	
1973		
1974		Nei
1975	Pärnu	Kärner, Rotov & Veingold
1976	Haapsalu	Heuer
1977	Tallinn	Kärner
1978		
1979	Tartu	Uusi
1980		
1981		
1982		Oll

Finnish Championship

1922	Helsinki	Chepurnov
1928	Helsinki	Chepurnov
1931	Helsinki	Böök
1932	Helsinki	Krogius
1933	Helsinki	Rasmusson
1934	Helsinki	Böök
1934–5	Helsinki	Böök
1936	Helsinki	Böök
1937	Helsinki	Gauffin
1938	Helsinki	Salo
1938–9	Helsinki	Kaila*
1945	Helsinki	Solin
1945–6	Helsinki	Böök
1946–7	Helsinki	Fred
1947–8	Turku	Niemalä
1949	Helsinki	Salo
1950	Helsinki	Ojanen
1951	Helsinki	Ojanen
1951–2	Helsinki	Ojanen
1952–3	Helsinki	Ojanan
1953–4	Helsinki	Kaila
1955	Helsinki	Fred*
1956	Helsinki	Salo*
1957	Helsinki	Ojanen
1958	Helsinki	Ojanen
1959	Turku	Ojanen
1960	Helsinki	Ojanen
1961	Helsinki	Ojanen
1962	Helsinki	Ojanen
1963	Helsinki	Böök
1964	Helsinki	Kanko
1965	Helsinki	Westerinen
1966	Naantali	Westerinen
1967	Helsinki	Ojanen
1968	Helsinki	Westerinen
1969	Helsinki	Sirkiä
1970	Helsinki	Westerinen
1971	Helsinki	Sarén
1972	Helsinki	Ojanen
1974	Helsinki	Poutiainen
1976	Helsinki	Poutiainen & Rantanen
1978	Helsinki	Rantanen
1980	Järvenpää	Aijälä

1982	Helsinki	Mäki
1983	Helsinki	Ojanen*
1984	Helsinki	Binham
1985	Espoo	Yrjölä

French Championship

1914	Lyons	Goetz
1923	Paris	Renaud
1924	Strasbourg	Crépeaux
1925	Nice	Crépeaux
1926	Biarritz	Chéron
1927	Chamonix	Chéron
1928	Marseille	Gibaud
1929	St Claude	Chéron
1930	Rouen	Gibaud
1931	Lille	Muffang
1932	La Baule	Raizman
1933	Sarreguemines	Gromer
1934	Paris	Kahn
1935	St Alban-les-Eaux	Gibaud
1936	Paris	Raizman
1937	Toulouse	Gromer
1938	Nice	Gromer
1940		Gibaud
1941		Crépeaux
1942	Paris	Daniel
1943	Pau	Bigot
1945	Roubaix	Boutteville
1946	Bourdeaux	Raizman
1947	Rouen	Raizman
1948	Paris	Rossolimo
1949	Besançon	Hugot
1950	Aix	Boutteville
1951	Vichy	Raizman
1952	Charleville	Raizman
1953	Paris	Tartakower*
1954	Marseille	Boutteville
1955	Toulouse	Boutteville
1956	Vittel	Rolland
1957	Bordeaux	Bergraser
1958	Le Touquet	Lemoine
1959	Reims	Boutteville
1961	Paris	Mazzoni
1962	Paris	Thiellement
1963	Paris	Thiellement
1964	Montpellier	Roos
1965	Dunkerque	Mazzoni
1966	Grenoble	Bergraser
1967	Dieppe	Boutteville
1968	Lyon-Charbonniers	Letzelter
1969	Pau	Planté
1970	Mulhouse	Maclès
1971	Merignac	Letzelter
1972	Rosny-sur-Bois	Haik
1973	Vittel	Benoit
1974	Chambery	Letzelter
1975	Dijon	Todorcevic
1976	St Jean de Monts	Chevaldonnet
1977	Le Touquet	Roos
1978	Castelnaudry	Giffard
1979	Courcheval	Sellos & Kouatly
1980	Puteaux	Roos
1981	Virolles	Seret & Goldenberg
1982	Strasbourg	Giffard
1983	Belfort	Herb & Haik
1984	Alès	Seret
1985	Clermont-Ferrand	Seret*

German Championship

1879	Leipzig	Englisch
1881	Berlin	Blackburne
1883	Nuremberg	Winawer
1885	Hamburg	Gunsberg
1887	Frankfurt	Mackenzie
1889	Breslau	Tarrasch
1892	Dresden	Tarrasch
1893	Kiel	Walbrodt & Bardeleben
1894	Leipzig	Tarrasch
1898	Cologne	Burn
1900	Munich	Pillsbury & Schlechter
1902	Hanover	Janowski
1904	Coburg	Bardeleben, Schlechter & Swiderski
1906	Nuremberg	Marshall
1908	Düsseldorf	Marshall
1910	Hamburg	Schlechter
1912	Breslau	Duras & Rubinstein
1914	Mannheim	Alekhine (unfinished)
1921	Hamburg	Post
1922	Bad Oeynhausen	Post
1923	Frankfurt	Grünfeld
1925	Breslau	Bogoljubow
1927	Magdeburg	Spielmann
1929	Duisburg	Ahues
1931	Swinemünde	Bogoljubow
1933	Bad Pyrmont	Bogoljubow
1934	Aachen	Carls
1935	Aachen	Richter
1937	Bad Oeynhausen	Kieninger
1938	Bad Oeynhausen	Eliskases
1939	Bad Oeynhausen	Eliskases
1940	Bad Oeynhausen	Kieninger
1941	Bad Oeynhausen	Schmidt, P & Junge
1942	Bad Oeynhausen	Rellstab
1943	Vienna	Lokvenc

Capablanca

Capablanca, nicknamed the Chess Machine, was perhaps the greatest natural chess genius. He was not taught to play and read little on the subject, but came to be so invincible that his rare losses made headlines, and at least two books have been written about his few defeats. He was imperturbable and charming (especially to the opposite sex).

As soon as he played in Europe, in 1911, it was clear that he was a potential challenger, but war intervened and it was 1921 before he could play and beat a lacklustre Lasker. Despite the ease of his victory, with no game going against him, he lost 5 kilos in weight.

The Cuban government then gave him a diplomatic appointment which appears to have

Capablanca c.1929. (David Hooper)

involved little work, but facilitated his travels. Like most top chess players he was multi-lingual but he differed from many by having the social graces expected in diplomatic circles.

Learning from bitter experience the leading players agreed a set of requirements in 1922, known as the London Rules, which any challenger for the world title had to meet. Among them was the obligation to raise a purse of $10,000. The winner was to be the first to win six games. Potential challengers were Rubinstein and Nimzowitsch but, in 1927, it was Alekhine who had first shot, and to general amazement he won.

The new champion formed a marked contrast to Capablanca. A Russian, resident in Paris from the early 1920s, Alekhine lived for chess. He read everything and forgot nothing. He took an interest in games played by all levels of players, ever on the alert for ideas. His games were imaginative, and if, like everyone else, he lacked Capablanca's quick sight of the board, he had greater creativity.

He was also more devious. Suddenly Capablanca was no longer a suitable person to be allowed another tilt at the title, and one of Alekhine's weapons was the London Rules. After the Depression $10,000 became a much bigger obstacle. It has been said that Alekhine was willing to accept a challenge only if he felt he had an easy victim, but in truth only one player fell outside that category.

Capablanca's play was a model of perfection; it seemed so effortless, but for some the very ease of it was boring. Alekhine's games were full of surprises and excitement. To this day there is no consensus as to who was the better player. On the other hand Alekhine was much the better writer, perhaps because he was much more enthusiastic, but he had a tendency to 'improve' his games, perhaps because he wrote whole books from memory, without playing through games on a board or checking sources. And, as we shall see, there were unlikable traits in his character.

West German Championship

1947	Weidenau	Kieninger
1948	Essen	Unzicker
1949	Bad Pyrmont	Bogoljubow
1950	Bad Pyrmont	Unzicker
1951	Düsseldorf	Teschner
1952	Berlin	Unzicker
1953	Leipzig	Unzicker (with E Germany)
1955	Frankfurt	Darga
1957	Bad Neuenahr	Tröger
1959	Nuremberg	Unzicker
1961	Bad Pyrmont	Darga
1963	Bad Pyrmont	Unzicker*
1965	Bad Aibling	Unzicker & Pfleger
1967	Kiel	Hübner & Besser
1969	Königsfeld	Christoph
1970	Völklingen	Hecht
1971	Berlin	Gligoric
1972	Oberursel	Kestler
1973	Dortmund	Hecht, Andersson & Spassky
1974	Menden	Ostermeyer
1975	Mannheim	Browne
1976	Bad Pyrmont	Wockenfuss
1977	Bad Lauterburg	Karpov
1978	Bad Neuenahr	Pachman
1979	Munich	Spassky
1980	Bad Neuenahr	Lobron
1981	Bochum	Kavalek
1982	Bad Neuenahr	Glienke
1983	Hanover	Karpov
1984	Bad Neuenahr	Lobron

German Women's Championship

1947	Seesen	Keller-Herrmann
1948		Keller-Herrmann
1949	Munich	Rinder
1951	Klosterlausnitz	Keller-Herrmann
1952	Schwerin	Keller-Herrmann
1953	Waldkirch	Keller-Herrmann
1955	Krefeld	Rinder
1956	Wolfratshausen	Rinder
1957	Lindau	Axt
1958	Giessen	Axt
1959	Dahn/Pfalz	Rinder
1960	Büdingen	Scheffold
1961	Wennigsen	Axt
1962	Eckernförde	Brandler
1963	Krefeld	Lucht
1964	Bremen	Karner
1965	Wangen	Stibaner
1968	Fürstenfeldbruck	Wasnetsky
1970	Lauterbach	Laakmann
1972	Burg/Fehmarn	Laakmann
1974	Kassel	Laakmann
1976	Brilon	Laakmann*

1978		Hund, B
1980		Hund, I
1982		Kübel
1984	Bad Aibling	

German Correspondence Championship

1952	Schmid
1954	Heemsoth
1956	Rittner
1958	Hübener
1959	Koch
1960	Schönherr
1962	Mainz
1964	Flum
1967	Flatau
1969	Heemsoth
1971	Tiemeyer
1973	Schmaus
1975	Dünhaupt
1976	Merz
1980 (1)	Maeder
1980 (2)	Ahlers
1982	Kern

East German Championship

1948	Bad Doberan	Teschner
1949	Klosterausnitz	Pietzsch
1950	Sömmerda	Elstner
1951	Schwerin	Stein
1952	Binz	Koch*
1953	Leipzig	Unzicker (with W Ger)
1954	Jena	Fuchs*
1955	Zwickau	Uhlmann
1956	Leipzig	Fuchs
1957	Sömmerda	Malich
1958	Schkopau	Uhlmann
1960	Leipzig	Pietzsch*
1961	Premnitz	Zinn
1962	Gera	Pietzsch
1963	Aschersleben	Möhring
1964	Magdeburg	Uhlmann
1965	Annaberg-Buchholz	Zinn
1967	Colditz	Pietzsch
1968	Weimar	Uhlmann
1969	Schwerin	Espig
1970	Freiberg	Baumbach
1971	Strausberg	Espig
1972	Görlitz	Schöneberg
1973	Erfurt	Malich
1974	Potsdam	Knaak
1975	Stralsund	Uhlmann*
1976	Gröditz	Uhlmann*
1977	Frankfurt/Oder	Vogt
1978	Eggesin	Knaak
1979	Suhl	Vogt

1980	Plauen	Grünberg*
1981	Fürstenwalde	Uhlmann
1982	Salzwedel	Knaak
1983	Cottbus	Knaak*
1984	Eilenberg	Knaak
1985	Juterbog	Uhlmann

Hungarian Championship

1906	Györ	Balla
1907	Székesfehérvár	Forgács
1911	Budapest	Balla & Barasz
1912	Temesvar	Breyer
1913	Debrecen	Asztalos
1922	Budapest	Havasi
1924	Györ	Nagy
1928	Budapest	Vajda
1931	Budapest	Steiner, L
1932	Budapest	Maroczy
1933	Budapest	Canal
1934	Budapest	Eliskases
1935	Tatatovaros	Szabó
1936	Budapest	Steiner, L
1937	Budapest	Szabó
1941	Budapest	Füstér
1942	Budapest	Barcza
1943	Diosgyor	Barcza
1945	Budapest	Florian
1946	Budapest	Szabó
1947	Budapest	Barcza
1948	Budapest	Benko
1950(1)	Budapest	Barcza
1950(2)	Budapest	Szabó
1951	Budapest	Barcza
1952	Budapest	Szabó
1953	Budapest	Sándor
1954	Budapest	Szabó
1955	Budapest	Barcza
1957	Budapest	Barcza
1958(1)	Budapest	Portisch
1958(2)	Budapest	Portisch*
1959	Budapest	Szabó*
1961	Budapest	Portisch*
1962	Budapest	Portisch*
1963	Budapest	Bilek
1964	Budapest	Portisch
1965(1)	Budapest	Bilek
1965(2)	Budapest	Portisch
1966	Budapest	Barcza
1967–8	Budapest	Szabó
1968–9	Budapest	Forintos
1969	Budapest	Dely
1970	Budapest	Bilek
1971	Budapest	Portisch
1972	Budapest	Csom
1973	Budapest	Adorjan, Ribli, Csom
1974	Budapest	Ribli
1975	Budapest	Portisch

Bilek. (Bénédictine)

1976	Budapest	Sax
1977	Budapest	Sax & Ribli
1978	Budapest	Pintér
1979	Budapest	Pintér
1980	Budapest	Lukacs
1981	Budapest	Portisch**
1982	Budapest	Schneider & Horvath
1984	Budapest	Adorjan
1985	Kecskemet	Perenyi

Icelandic Championship

1913		Zophróniasson
1914		Zophróniasson
1915		Zophróniasson
1916		Zophróniasson
1917		Zophróniasson
1918		Gilfer
1919		Olafsson, S
1920		Gilfer
1921		Olafsson, S
1922		Olafsson, S
1923		Olafsson, Fm
1924		Jónsson
1925		Gilfer
1926		Jónsson
1927		Gilfer
1928		Thorvaldsen
1929		Gilfer

1930		Hafstein
1931		Asgeirsson
1932		Gudmundsson, J
1933	Reykjavik	Asgeirsson
1934		Asgeirsson
1935	Reykjavik	Gilfer
1936	Reykjavik	Gudmundsson, J
1937		Gudmundsson, J
1938		Möller
1940		Thorvaldsen
1941		Möller
1942		Gilfer
1943		Möller
1944		Asgeirsson
1945	Reykjavik	Asgeirsson
1946	Reykjavik	Asgeirsson*
1947	Reykjavik	Möller
1948	Reykjavik	Möller
1949	Reykjavik	Arnlaugsson
1950	Reykjavik	Möller
1951	Reykjavik	Johnsen
1952	Reykjavik	Olafsson, Fd
1953	Reykjavik	Olafsson, Fd
1954	Reykjavik	Gudmundsson, G
1956	Reykjavik	Jóhannsson
1957	Reykjavik	Olafsson, Fd
1958	Reykjavik	Jóhannsson
1959	Reykjavik	Jóhannsson
1960	Reykjavik	Thorbergsson
1961	Reykjavik	Olafsson, Fd
1962	Reykjavik	Olafsson, Fd
1963	Reykjavik	Jóhannsson
1964	Reykjavik	Olafsson, H
1965	Reykjavik	Sigurjónsson
1966	Reykjavik	Gunnarsson
1967	Reykjavik	Thorsteinsson
1968	Reykjavik	Sigurjónsson
1969	Reykjavik	Olafsson, Fd
1970	Reykjavik	Magnusson
1971	Reykjavik	Kristinsson
1972	Reykjavik	Sigurjónsson
1973	Reykjavik	Magnusson
1974	Reykjavik	Kristinsson
1975	Reykjavik	Thorsteinsson
1976	Reykjavik	Angantysson
1977	Reykjavik	Arnason
1978		Olafsson, H
1979		Asmundsson
1980	Reykjavik	Hjartarson
1981	Reykjavik	Olafsson, H
1983	Reykjavik	Karlsson
1984	Reykjavik	Hjartarson

Irish Championship

These records are patchy. A championship in 1865 was run alongside a master tournament and the winner's name has been given as J.A. Porterfield Rynd, but he was supposedly born in 1855! The Hibernian Chess Association ran championships in 1885 and 1886. The results are not known for the 1889 competition, apparently run on handicap lines. From 1912 and 1938 the annual competition was usually between the champions of the four provinces (Ulster, Munster, Leinster and Connacht) but since then a larger tournament has been the custom. There have also been Oireachtas Championships, of no special chess significance, confined to Irish speakers.

Women's championships are rarely reported, and are ignored by some of the stronger players.

1865	Dublin	Rynd
1885	Dublin	Pollock
1886	Belfast	Pollock
1889	Dublin	
1912		O'Hanlon
1915	Dublin	O'Hanlon
1922	Portadown	Cranston
1924	Dublin	Baker
1925	Dublin	O'Hanlon
1926	Belfast	O'Hanlon*
1927		Baker
1928		Baker
1929	Dublin	Baker
1930		O'Hanlon
1931		Cranston
1932		O'Hanlon
1933	Dublin/Cork	Creevey
1934		Creevey
1935		O'Hanlon
1936		O'Hanlon
1937		Cox
1938		Cox
1939		O'Sullivan, B
1940		O'Hanlon
1946		O'Sullivan, B
1947		Duignan
1948		O'Sullivan, D
1949	Galway	Kennedy
1950	Belfast	Maher
1951	Cork	Bourke
1952	Dublin	Schuster
1953	Galway	Mulcahy
1954	Belfast	Kelly
1955	Cork	Maher
1956	Dublin	O'Sullivan, D
1957	Galway	O'Sullivan, D
1958	Belfast	Heidenfeld
1959	Killarney	Reilly
1960	Dublin	Reilly
1961	Galway	Reid
1962	Derry	Reid & Littleton
1963	Cork	Heidenfeld
1964	Dublin	Heidenfeld
1965	Galway	Littleton
1966	Belfast	Moles
1967	Cork	Heidenfeld
1968	Dublin	Heidenfeld

1969	Dublin	Patterson
1970	Belfast	Henry
1971	Cork	Moles
1972	Dublin	Heidenfeld
1973	Cork	McGrillen
1974	Dublin	Doyle
1975	Dublin	Keogh & Ludgate
1976	Coleraine	Kernan
1977	Cork	Ludgate & Devanney
1978	Galway	Ludgate
1979	Dublin	Dunne & Keogh
1980	Cork	Delaney, P
1981	Dublin	Dunne & Short
1982	Cork	Delaney, J
1983	Castlebar	Dunne
1984	Newcastle	Curtin
1985	Dublin	Orr & Curtin

Israeli Championship

1936	Tel Aviv	Czerniak
1937	Jerusalem	Porat
1938	Tel Aviv	Czerniak
1940	Tel Aviv	Porat*
1945	Tel Aviv	Aloni
1951	Tel Aviv etc	Oren
1953	Tel Aviv etc	Porat
1955	Tel Aviv etc	Czerniak
1957	Tel Aviv	Porat
1959	Tel Aviv	Porat
1961–2	Tel Aviv	Aloni*
1963	Tel Aviv	Porat
1965	Tel Aviv	Aloni
1967	Tel Aviv	Kagan
1969–70	Tel Aviv	Kagan
1971–2	Tel Aviv, Haifa	Geller, U
1974	Tel Aviv	Liberzon
1976	Haifa	Birnboim
1977	Tel Aviv	Dzindzikhashvili
1980	Tel Aviv	Birnboim
1982	Tel Aviv	Gruenfeld

Italian Championship

1875	Rome	Seni
1878	Livorno	Sprega
1881	Milan	Salvioli
1883	Venice	Zannoni
1886	Rome	Zannoni
1892	Turin	Torre, V
1900	Rome	Reggio
1901	Venice	Reggio
1905	Florence	Reggio
1906	Milan	Martinolich
1911	Rome	Gladig
1913	Bologna	Reggio

1916	Milan	Reggio
1920	Viareggio	Rosselli
1921	Viareggio	Marotti
1923	Naples	Rosselli
1929	Florence	Monticelli
1931	Milan	Rosselli
1934	Milan	Monticelli
1935	Florence	Sacconi
1936	Florence	Castaldi
1937	Naples	Castaldi
1939	Rome	Monticelli
1943	Florence	Nestler
1947	Rome	Castaldi*
1948	Florence	Castaldi*
1950	Sorrento	Porreca*
1951	Venice	Paoli
1952	Ferrara	Norcia
1953	Florence	Castaldi
1954	Trieste	Nestler*
1956	Rovigo	Porreca
1957	Reggio Emilia	Paoli
1959	Rimini	Castaldi*
1960	Perugia	Cappello
1961	S Benedetto	Giustolisi
1962	Forte dei Marmi	Tatai
1963	Imperia	Contedini
1964	Naples	Giustolisi
1965	Florence	Tatai
1966	Rovigo	Giustolisi
1967	Savona	Tatai
1968	Milan	Paoli
1969	S Benedetto	Mariotti
1970	Chioggia	Tatai
1971	S Benedetto	Tatai
1972	Recoaro-Terme	Micheli
1973	Chioggia	Micheli
1974	Castelvecchio	Tatai
1975	Pesaro	Toth
1976	Il Ciocco	Toth
1977	Il Ciocco	Tatai
1979	Venice	Tatai
1981(1)	Naples	Toth
1982(2)	Barcellona	Messa
1982	Arco	Toth
1983	Arco	Tatai
1984	Arcidosso	Torh
1985	Arcidosso	Zichichi

Latvian Championship

1924	Riga	Matison
1926–7	Riga	Apseniek
1930–1	Riga	Petrov
1932	Jelgava	Feigin*
1934	Riga	Apseniek*
1935	Riga	Petrov
1937	Riga	Petrov
1938–9	Riga	Petrov

1941	Riga	Koblenc
1943	Riga	Zdanov
1945	Riga	Alatortsev
1946	Riga	Koblenc
1947	Riga	Solmanis
1948	Riga	Strautmanis*
1949	Riga	Taimanov
1950	Riga	Mezgailis
1951	Riga	Pasman
1952	Riga	Klavin
1953	Riga	Tal
1954	Riga	Klovan
1955	Riga	Gipslis
1956	Riga	Gipslis
1957	Riga	Gipslis
1958	Riga	Zilber*
1959	Riga	Klasup*
1960	Riga	Gipslis
1961	Riga	Gipslis
1962	Riga	Klovan
1963	Riga	Gipslis
1964	Riga	Gipslis
1965	Riga	Tal
1966	Riga	Gipslis
1967	Riga	Klovan
1968	Riga	Klovan
1969	Riga	Petkevic & Smit
1970	Riga	Klovan
1971	Riga	Klovan
1972	Riga	Gutman
1973	Daugavpils	Vitolin*
1974	Riga	Kirpichnikov & Petkevic
1975	Riga	Klovan & Smit
1976	Riga	Vitolin
1977	Riga	Vitolin
1978	Riga	Vitolin
1979	Riga	Klovan
1980	Riga	Zhuravlev
1981	Riga	Voitkevic
1982	Riga	Vitolin
1983	Riga	Vitolin
1984	Riga	Kengis
1985	Riga	Vitolin & Petkevic

Leningrad City Championship

1920	Rabinovich, I
1922	Levenfish
1924	Levenfish
1925	Rabinovich, I, Romanovsky, Ilyin-Genevsky, & Levenfish
1926	Ilyin-Genevsky
1928	Rabinovich, I
1929	Ilyin-Genevsky
1931	Botvinnik

1932	Botvinnik
1933 – 4	Alatortsev & Lisitsin
1936	Ragozin
1937	Rovner, Tolush, Chekhover
1938	Tolush
1939	Lisitsin
1940 – 1	Rabinovich, I
1941	unfinished
1943	Sklyarov
1944	Model
1945	Ragozin
1946	Tolush
1947	Lisitsin & Tolush
1948	Taimanov
1949	Chekhover
1950	Taimanov
1951	Taimanov
1953	Furman
1954	Kopilov*
1955	Korchnoi
1956	Kondratiev
1957	Korchnoi & Furman
1958	Rubel
1959	Spassky
1960	Shishkin
1961	Spassky & Taimanov
1962 – 3	Klaman
1963	Vladimirov
1964	Korchnoi
1965	Faibisovich*
1966	Ruban
1967	Cherepkov
1968	Cherepkov*
1969	Faibisovich
1970	Karasev
1971	Osnos
1972	Lukin
1973	Taimanov
1974	Karasev
1975	Tseitlin, Mark
1976	Tseitlin, Mark
1977	Faibisovich
1978	Tseitlin, Mark
1979	Polovodin*
1980	Osnos
1981	Lukin
1982	Cherepkov*
1983	Lukin
1984	Yudasin
1985	Aseyev

London Championship

There is now no London championship, partly because there is no body which could be made to take the responsibility for its organization. At one time the championship of the powerful City of London Club was regarded as being equivalent to a London championship. Over the New Year 1923–4 the London Chess League held its annual meeting and planned to hold a tournament which it hoped would be regarded as an unofficial championship. The entry was too weak (it clashed with the Hastings congress), but the following year the series began its run up to the outbreak of war in 1939.

After the war ended an official London Championship was inaugurated, open to all residents. A series of knock-outs reduced the vast number of entries to a size that could be handled by an all-play-all tournament held towards the end of the year. It was efficiently run by the Lud Eagle Club whose members no doubt believed that the burden would have been taken up by the ill-fated National Chess centre when it opened in 1952.

1924–5	Birnberg
1926	Winter
1927	Drewitt
1928	Drewitt
1928–9	Winter
1929–30	Drewitt
1930–1	Morrison*
1932	Winter
1933	Strachstein
1934	Stronach*
1934–5	Benger
1935–6	Wahltuch, V*
1936–7	Perkins*
1937–8	Benger
1939	Winter
1945	Wood, G
1946	Thomas
1947	Winter
1948	Hooper
1949	Penrose
1950	Aitken
1951	Sergeant, E

Moscow City Championship

1900		Nenarokov
1901		Goncharov & Falk
1902		Boyarkov
1908		Nenarokov
1909		Goncharov
1911		Bernstein
1913		Yordansky
1919–20		Alekhine
1920–1		Zukerman
1921–2		Grigoriev
1922–3		Grigoriev
1923	match(1)	Grigoriev
1923	match(2)	Grigoriev drew
1924	match	Nenarokov
1924		Grigoriev

1924–5		Sergeyev
1926		Rabinovich, A
1927		Zubarev
1928		Verlinsky
1929		Panov
1929	match	Grigoriev
1930		Zubarev
1931		Ryumin
1932		Belavenets, Orlov & Lebedev
1933–4		Ryumin
1935		Ryumin
1936		Alatortsev & Kan
1937		Alatortsev & Belavenets
1938		Belavenets & Smyslov
1939–40		Lilienthal
1941		Kotov
1942		Smyslov
1943–4		Botvinnik
1944–5		Smyslov
1946		Bronstein
1947		Simagin*
1949		Averbakh
1950		Averbakh & Chistyakov
1951		Petrosyan
1952		Zagorovsky
1953		Bronstein
1954		Soloviev
1955		Vasyukov
1956		Petrosyan & Simagin
1957		Bronstein
1958		Vasyukov
1959		Simagin
1960		Vasyukov
1961		Bronstein
1962		Averbakh & Vasyukov
1963		Bikhovsky
1964		Bakulin
1965		Aronin
1966		Bakulin
1967		Volovich
1968		Bronstein & Petrosyan
1969		Zaitsev, I
1970		Balashov
1971		Lein*
1972		Vasyukov
1973		Dvoretsky
1974		Gulko
1975		Grigoryan
1976		Makarichev & Tseitlin, Mik
1977		Tseitlin, Mik
1978		Vasyukov
1979		Grigoryan

1980	Kremenetsky
1981	Arbakov & Sokolov
1982	Bronstein & Rashkovsky
1983	Makarichev & Sveshnikov
1984	Vyzhmanavin
1985	Gorelov

Netherlands Championship

1873	Hague	Gifford*
1874	Amsterdam	De Lelie
1875	Rotterdam	Gifford
1876	Gouda	Vogel
1877	Hague	Daniels
1878	Amsterdam	Van't Kruijs
1879	Rotterdam	Dupré
1880	Gouda	Bird
1881	Hague	Benima
1882	Hague	Messemaker
1883	Rotterdam	Benima
1884	Gouda	Messemaker
1885	Hague	Van Foreest
1886	Utrecht	Van Foreest
1887	Amsterdam	Van Foreest
1888	Rotterdam	Loman
1889	Gouda	Van Foreest
1890	Hague	Loman
1891	Utrecht	Loman
1892	Amsterdam	Van den Berg
1893	Groningen	Van Foreest & Loman
1894	Rotterdam	Loman
1895	Arnhem	Olland
1896	Leiden	Bleijkmans
1897	Utrecht	Loman
1898	Hague	Tresling
1899	Amsterdam	Atkins
1900	Groningen	Oskam*
1901	Haarlem	Olland
1902	Rotterdam	Van Foreest
1903	Hilversum	Leonhardt
1904	Leeuwarden	Bleijkmans
1905	Scheveningen	Marshall
1906	Arnhem	Beffie
1907	Utrecht	Te Kolsté
1908	Haarlem	Esser & Pope
1909	Leiden	Olland
1912	Delft	Loman
1919	Hague	Marchand
1921	Nijmegen	Euwe
1924	Amsterdam	Euwe
1926	Utrecht	Euwe
1929	Amsterdam	Euwe
1933	Hague	Euwe
1936	Rotterdam	Landau
1938	Amsterdam	Euwe

The Dutch giant Donner, now permanently paralysed.
(Reproduced by courtesy of B.T. Batsford)

1939	Amsterdam	Euwe
1942	match	Euwe
1947	match	Euwe
1948	match	Euwe
1950	Amsterdam	Euwe
1952	Enschede	Euwe
1954	Amsterdam	Donner
1955	match	Euwe
1957	Amsterdam	Donner
1958	Amsterdam	Donner
1961	Hague	Tan
1963	Hague	Kuijpers
1965	Hague	Prins*
1967	Zierikzee	Ree*
1969	Leeuwarden	Ree*
1970	Leeuwarden	Scholl*
1971	Leeuwarden	Ree*
1972	Leeuwarden	Zuidema
1973	Leeuwarden	Sosonko*
1974	Leeuwarden	Timman
1975	Leeuwarden	Timman
1976	Leeuwarden	Timman
1977	Leeuwarden	Korchnoi
1978	Leeuwarden	Timman & Sosonko
1979	Leeuwarden	Ligterink

1980	Leeuwarden	Timman
1981	Leeuwarden	Timman
1982	Amsterdam	Ree
1983	Hilversum	Timman
1984	Hilversum	Van der Wiel
1985	Hilversum	Van der Sterren

New Zealand Championship

1879	Christchurch	Hookham*
1888–9	Christchurch	Ollivier
1890	Dunedin	Hookham*
1890–1	Wellington	Barnes
1891–2	Auckland	Siedeberg
1892–3	Christchurch	Siedeberg
1893–4	Dunedin	Edwards
1894–5	Wellington	Mackay
1895–6	Wanganui	Meldrum
1896–7	Christchurch	Barnes
1897–8	Auckland	Barnes
1898–9	Dunedin	Cleland
1900	Wellington	Mason*
1901	Christchurch	Forsyth
1901–2	Auckland	Barnes
1902–3	Dunedin	Grierson
1903–4	Wellington	Mason*
1904–5	Oamaru	Davies
1905–6	Auckland	Barnes*
1906–7	Christchurch	Viner
1908	Wellington	Davies
1908–9	Dunedin	Kelling
1909–10	Auckland	Mason, J*
1910–11	Timaru	Mason
1911–12	Napier	Mason*
1912–13	Nelson	Grierson*
1913–14	Auckland	Mason
1914–15	Christchurch	Kelling
1919–20	Wellington	Mason
1920–1	Dunedin	Dunlop*
1921–2	Auckland	Dunlop
1922–3	Christchurch	Dunlop*
1923–4	Wellington	Crackanthorp
1924–5	Nelson	Purdy, C
1925–6	Dunedin	Crackanthorp
1926–7	Auckland	Davies
1927–8	Christchurch	Davies*
1928–9	Wellington	Erskine
1929–30	Wanganui	Gundersen
1930–1	Rotorua	Gyles*
1931–2	Napier	Gundersen*
1932–3	Auckland	Goldstein
1933–4	Dunedin	Dunlop*
1934–5	Christchurch	Erskine
1935–6	Wellington	Purdy, C
1936–7	Auckland	Abbott
1937–8	Dunedin	Hindin
1938–9	Wanganui	Dunlop

1939–40	Wellington	Dunlop
1940–1	Timaru	Allerhand*
1943–4	Wellington	Wade*
1944–5	Auckland	Wade
1945–6	Christchurch	Lepviikman
1946–7	Palmerston N	Lepviikman
1947–8	Dunedin	Wade
1948–9	Wanganui	Nield
1949–50	Auckland	Allerhand
1950–1	Christchurch	Lynch
1951–2	Napier	Sarapu
1952–3	Timaru	Sarapu
1953–4	Wellington	Sarapu
1954–5	Auckland	Sarapu
1955–6	Dunedin	Foulds
1956–7	Wellington	Feneridis & Phillips
1957–8	Christchurch	Phillips
1958–9	Hamilton	Foulds & Menzies
1959–60	Dunedin	Sarapu
1960–1	Auckland	Sarapu
1961–2	Wellington	Haase
1962–3	Christchurch	Sutton*
1963–4	Auckland	Court
1964–5	Wellington	Phillips
1965–6	Hamilton	Sarapu
1966–7	Christchurch	Sarapu
1967–8	Dunedin	Anderson
1968–9	Wellington	Sarapu & Anderson
1969–70	Auckland	Sarapu
1970–1	Nelson	Sutton
1971–2	Hamilton	Sutton
1972–3	Wellington	Sarapu
1973–4	Christchurch	Sarapu*
1974–5	Dunedin	Garbett
1975–6	Upper Hutt	Chandler*
1976–7	Auckland	Sarapu
1977–8	Wellington	Laird
1978–9	Auckland	Sarapu
1979–80	Upper Hutt	Green, Small, Sarapu
1980–1	Canterbury	Nokes, Small, Sarapu
1981–2	Auckland	Small
1982–3	Dunedin	Gollogly, Garbett
1983–4	Auckland	Garbett
1984–5	Upper Hutt	Small

Norwegian Championship

1918	Christiana	Lilja
1919	Christiana	Brekke
1920	Christiana	Brekke
1921	Bergen	Hansen
1922	Christiana	Erichsen
1923	Christiana	Brekke
1924	Christiana	Lund

Alekhine & Euwe

Alekhine was the first world champion to seize every opportunity to play. He had a succession of fine wins (see the table for Bled 1931 on page 43 for example), but as he gave way to a weakness for food and drink, his edge was blunted. Even so it was something of a surprise in 1935 when he lost his title to Euwe.

In 1928 Euwe was the amateur world champion, and throughout his long career he played substantially as an amateur. He was a teacher of mathematics, and had a doctorate from a university, unlike Alekhine who had one thrust on him by the chess public. Euwe was an upright man and the only criticism ever made of him was towards the end of his life when, as a tireless President of FIDE, he sometimes went along with questionable decisions in order to sustain the organization.

Alekhine pulled himself together before the return match, and in 1937 became the first man to regain the title. Preparations were under way to find a new challenger when war began. During the hostilities Euwe refused to play in German tournaments. Alekhine, on the other hand, took part in many Nazi-sponsored events and was also suspected of writing anti-Semitic propaganda.

It may be that Alekhine knew no higher god than chess, but by the end of the war he had no friends. When he died in 1946 arrangements were under way for him to play the USSR's Mikhail Botvinnik.

A more strident person than Euwe might have insisted that the vacant title of world champion should automatically revert to him, but he readily fell in with the FIDE plan to run a tournament of all eligible challengers. Thus began the Soviet hegemony.

Euwe when he became world champion.

Alekhine around 1930. Note that he signed himself Aljechin, the German form of his Russian name, and also 'Dr', although he never completed his doctorate at the Sorbonne. (David Hooper)

109

1925	Oslo	Brekke	1927	Łodz	Rubinstein
1926	Bergen	Christoffersen	1935	Warsaw	Tartakower
1927	Trondheim	Hansen	1937	Jurata	Tartakower
1929	Drammen	Christoffersen	1946	Sopot	Sliwa
1930	Oslo	Barda (as Olsen)	1948	Kraków	Makarczyk
1931	Stavanger	Gulbrandsen	1949	Poznań	Plater
1932	Bergen	Johnsen	1950	Bielsko	Balcarek
1933	Fredrikstad	Halvorsen	1951	Łodz	Sliwa
1934	Hamar	Halvorsen	1952	Katowice	Sliwa*
1935	Sandefjord	Saurén	1953	Kraków	Sliwa
1936	Oslo	Christoffersen	1954	Łodz	Sliwa*
1937	Trondheim	Krogdahl	1955	Wroclaw	Gromek
1938	Grimstad	Kavlie-Jørgensen	1956	Czestochowa	Plater
1945		Rojahn	1957	Warsaw	Plater
1946	Bergen	Myhre	1959	Łodz	Witkowski*
1947	Kristiansand	Barda	1960	Wroclaw	Sliwa
1948	Fredrikstad	Barda	1961	Katowice	Tarnowski
1949	Oslo	Vestøl	1962	Poznań	Balcerowski*
1950	Trondheim	Myhre	1963	Glucholazy	Bednarski
1951	Stavanger	Kongshavn	1964	Warsaw	Doda
1952	Skien	Barda	1965	Lublin	Balcerowski
1953	Fredrikstad	Barda	1966	Rzeszów	Kostro
1954	Drammen	Haave	1967	Szczecin	Doda*
1955	Stabekk	Myhre	1968	Łodz	Doda
1956	Steinkjer	Morcken	1969	Lublin	Lewi
1957	Lillehammer	Barda	1970	Piotrków	Kostro
1958	Ålesund	Rojahn	1971	Poznań	Schmidt, W
1959	Oslo	Johannessen	1972	Wroclaw	Pytel
1960	Fredrikstad	De Lange	1973	Gdynia	Pytel
1961	Sandefjord	Ofstad	1974	Zielona Góra	Schmidt, W
1962	Hamar	Johannessen	1975	Poznań	Schmidt, W
1963	Moss	Hoen	1976	Bydgoszcz	Sznapik
1964	Oslo	Zwaig	1977	Piotrków Tryb.	Skrobek
1965	Mosjøen	Gulbrandsen	1978	Kraków	Kuligowski**
1966	Bodø	Svedenborg	1979	Tarnów	Przewoznik
1967	Bergen	Svedenborg	1980	Łodz	Sznapik
1968	Oslo	Gulbrandsen	1981	Warsaw	Schmidt & Sznapik
1969	Hamar	Zwaig	1982	Zelena Gora	Adamski*
1970	Kristiansund	Johannessen	1983	Piotrków Tryb.	Sznapik
1971	Skien	Wibe	1984	Poznań	Sznapik
1972	Røros	Kristiansen	1985	Gdynia	Nowak*
1973	Sandnes	Johannessen			
1974	Sandefjord	Øgaard			
1975	Oslo	Øgaard			
1976	Harstad	Helmers			
1977	Bergen	Helmers			
1978	Risör	Hoen			
1979	Molde	Øgaard			
1980	Oslo	Heim			
1981	Kirkenes	Hoen*			
1982	Lillehammer	Agdestein*			
1983	Trondheim	Tiller			
1984	Oslo	Østenstad			
1985	Gausdal	Øgaard			

Polish Championship

1926	Warsaw	Przepiórka

Romanian Championship

1926–7	Sibiu	Tyroler
1927	Bucharest	Tyroler
1929	Iasi	Tyroler
1930	Cernauti	Balogh
1931	Bucharest	Erdelyi
1933–4	Bucharest	Erdelyi
1935	Bucharest	Silberman
1936	Bucharest	Halic
1943	Bucharest	Seimeanu
1946	Bucharest	Troianescu
1947	Brasov	Ichim
1948	Bucharest	Popa
1949	Bucharest	Erdelyi*
1950	Bucharest	Balanel

1951	Bucharest	Flondor & Alexandrescu
1952	Bucharest	Ciocaltea*
1953	Bucharest	Balanel*
1954	Bucharest	Troianescu
1955	Bucharest	Balanel*
1956	Bucharest	Troianescu
1957–8	Bucharest	Troianescu*
1958	Bucharest	Balanel
1959	Bucharest	Ciocaltea*
1960	Bucharest	Gheorghiu
1961	Bucharest	Ciocaltea
1962	Bucharest	Gheorghiu
1963	Bucharest	Ghitescu
1964	Bucharest	Gheorghiu
1965	Bucharest	Gheorghiu
1966	Bucharest	Gheorghiu
1967	Bucharest	Gheorghiu
1968	Bucharest	Troianescu
1969	Bucharest	Ciocaltea*
1970	Bucharest	Ciocaltea*
1971	Bucharest	Ciocaltea
1972	Bucharest	Partos
1973	Bucharest	Gheorghiu*
1974	Bucharest	Urzica
1975	Sinaia	Ciocaltea
1976	Timisoara	Ghinda
1977	Sibiu	Gheorghiu
1978	Herculane	Ghinda*
1979	Bucharest	Ciocaltea*
1980	Bucharest	Suba*
1981	Bucharest	Suba
1982	Bucharest	Foisor
1983	Bucharest	Ghinda
1984	Bucharest	Gheorghiu
1985(1)	Bucharest	Grünberg
1985(2)	Timisoara	Suba

Women

1936	Bucharest	Lutia
1949	Bucharest	Habermann
1950	Brasov	Szathmary
1951	Brasov	Albulet
1952	Sibiu	Grabovietchi
1953	Satu Mare	Giuroiu
1954	Bucharest	Giuroiu
1955	Oradea	Albulet
1956	Cluj	Pogorevici
1957	Ploiesti	Manolescu
1958	Bucharest	Giuroiu
1959	Bucharest	Teodorescu
1960	Timisoara	Nicolau
1961	Bucharest	Nicolau
1962	Brasov	Perevoznic
1963	Ploiesti	Nicolau
1964	Oradea	Nicolau
1965	Herculane	Nicolau
1966	Constanta	Polihroniade
1967	Arad	Baumstark

1968	Oradea	Teodorescu
1969	P. Neamt	Teodorescu
1970	Ploiesti	Polihroniade
1971	Brasov	Polihroniade
1972	Cluj	Polihroniade
1973	Brasov	Nicolau
1974	Timisoara	Teodorescu
1975	Alexandria	Polihroniade
1976	P. Neamt	Polihroniade
1977	Sinaia	Polihroniade
1978	Medias	Nutu
1979	Satu Mare	Nutu
1980	Eforie	Nutu
1981	Herculane	Baumstark
1982	Medias	Ghinda
1983	Herculane	Muresan
1985	Herculane	Muresan

Scottish Championship

Champion

Glasgow *21 – 25 Jul 1884*
Crum

Edinburgh *3 – 8 Aug 1885*
Mills

Glasgow *5 – 9 Apr 1886*
Barbier

Edinburgh *11 – 15 Jul 1887*
Mills

Glasgow *16 – 21 Jul 1888*
Mackenzie G.H.

Edinburgh *29 Jul – 2 Aug 1889*
Marshall

Dundee *14 – 18 Apr 1890*
Walker

Glasgow *20 – 25 Jul 1891*
Chambers

Edinburgh *14 – 19 Apr 1892*
Mills

Dundee *10 – 14 Apr 1893*
Walker

Glasgow *23 – 27 Mar 1894*
Spens

Edinburgh *12 – 16 Apr 1895*
Mills

Dundee *3 – 9 Apr 1896*
Mills

Glasgow *16 – 19 Apr 1897*
Mills

Edinburgh *9 – 16 Apr 1898*
Fraser

Stirling *31 Mar – 4 Apr 1899*
Mills

Champion	Women's Champion
Dundee 13 – 17 Apr 1900	
Mills*	
Glasgow 24 – 29 May 1901	
Macdonald R.C.*	
Perth 27 – 31 Mar 1902	
Macdonald E.	
Edinburgh 20 – 25 Jul 1903	
Borthwick	
Dundee 2 – 6 Apr 1904	
Macdonald R.C.	
Stirling 21 – 26 Apr 1905	
Macdonald R.C.	Hutchison Stirling
Glasgow 13 – 17 Apr 1906	
Macdonald R.C.	Hutchison Stirling
Edinburgh 29 Mar – 1 April 1907	
Gibson	Hutchison Stirling
Dundee 17 – 20 Apr 1908	
Mackenzie A.J.	Cunninghame
Glasgow 9 – 15 Apr 1909	
Mackenzie A.J.	Taylor
Edinburgh 1 – 5 Apr 1910	
Richmond*	Mercer
Glasgow 14 – 18 Apr 1911	
McKee	Taylor
Edinburgh 5 – 10 Apr 1912	
Gibson	Hutchison Stirling
Glasgow 21 – 24 Mar 1913	
Mackenzie A.J.	Hutchison Sterling
Dundee 29 Dec – Jan 1913 – 4	
Gibson	Taylor
Glasgow 31 Dec – 4 Jan 1914 – 5	
Wardhaugh	Cunninghame
Edinburgh 2 – Apr 1920	
Wenman*	Forbes
Glasgow 1921	
Gibson	Gilchrist
Perth 14 – Apr 1922	
Gibson	Gilchrist
Glasgow 28 Dec – 6 Jan 1922 – 3	
Gibson*	Gilchrist
Dundee 28 Dec – 5 Jan 1923 – 4	
Heath	Heard
Edinburgh 10 – 14 Apr 1925	
Page	Ritchie
Glasgow 31 Dec – 7 Jan 1925 – 6	
McKee*	Brockett
Dundee 31 Dec – Jan 1926 – 7	
Macdonald R.C.	Brockett
Edinburgh 30 Dec – Jan 1927 – 8	
Macdonald R.C.	Malcolm
Glasgow 28 Dec – Jan 1928 – 9	
Gibson	Thomson F.F.

Champion	Women's Champion
Dundee 18 – 21 Apr 1930	
Gibson	Thomson F.F.
Edinburgh 31 Dec – Jan 1930 – 1	
Gibson	Thomson J.C.
Glasgow 25 – Mar 1932	
Fairhurst	Thomson F.F.
Edinburgh Dec – Jan 1932 – 3	
Fairhurst	Thomson F.F.
Glasgow 29 Dec – Jan 1933 – 4	
Fairhurst	Thomson F.F.
Aberdeen 22 Apr – 1935	
Aitken	Crum
Edinburgh 30 Dec – Jan 1935 – 6	
Fairhurst	Forbes
Glasgow 31 Dec – Jan 1936 – 7	
Fairhurst	Thomson F.F.
Edinburgh 15 – Apr 1938	
Fairhurst	Gilchrist
Aberdeen 7 – Apr 1939	
Pavey	Brockett
Glasgow 19 – 23 Apr 1946	
Fairhurst	Crum
Dundee 4 – 8 Apr 1947	
Fairhurst	Battrum
Edinburgh 26 – 31 Mar 1948	
Fairhurst	Crum
Aberdeen 15 – 18 Apr 1949	
Fairhurst	Crum
Glasgow 7 – Apr 1950	
Anderson	Gordon
Dundee 23 – 30 Mar 1951	
Thomson	Steedman
Glasgow 11 – 16 Apr 1952	
Aitken	Hogarth
Edinburgh 3 – 11 Apr 1953	
Aitken	Foggie
Stirling 16 – 22 Jul 1954	
Anderson	Hogarth
Aberdeen 15 – 22 Jul 1955	
Aitken	Foggie
Dundee 21 – 28 Jul 1956	
Aitken	Elder & Steedman
Glasgow 12 – 20 Jul 1957	
Aitken	Elder
Edinburgh 5 – 12 Jul 1958	
Aitken	Elder
Glasgow 17 – 24 Jul 1959	
Coast	Steedman
Aberdeen 16 – 22 Jul 1960	
Aitken	Hogarth
Edinburgh 8 – 15 Jul 1961	
Aitken	Elder

Champion	Women's Champion		Champion	Women's Champion
Dundee *21 – 28 Jul 1962*			**Ayr** *6 – 12 Jul 1974*	
Fairhurst	Elder		McKay	Leask
Glasgow *3 – 9 Aug 1963*			**Aberdeen** *12 – 19 Jul 1975*	
Fallone	Elder		Levy & Swanson	Hindle & Leask
Edinburgh *11 – 17 Jul 1964*			**Dundee** *17 – 24 Jul 1976*	
Davie	Elder		McKay*	Forwell
Aberdeen *10 – 16 Jul 1965*			**Glasgow** *16 – 23 Jul 1977*	
Aitken & Jamieson	Thomson S.		Pritchett	Houston
Falkirk *9 – 16 Jul 1966*			**Edinburgh** *15 – 22 Jul 1978*	
Davie	Elder		Motwani	McDougall
Dundee *22 – 28 Jul 1967*			**St Andrews** *28 Jul – 4 Aug 1979*	
Bonner	Elder		McKay	Jackson
Ayr *6 – 13 Jul 1968*			**Troon** *12 – 19 Jul 1980*	
Levy	Elder		Kopec*	Elder
Glasgow *28 Jul – 2 Aug 1969*			**St Andrews** *25 Jul – 1 Aug 1981*	
Davie	Hogarth & Steedman		Morrison*	Jackson
Aberdeen *11 – 18 Jul 1970*			**Troon** *24 – 31 Jul 1982*	
Bonner	Elder		McKay	Milligan
Paisley *5 – 10 Jul 1971*			**St Andrews** *16 – 23 Jul 1983*	
Holt & McKay	Elder		McNab	Coull
Edinburgh *10 – 15 Jul 1972*			**Troon** *12 – 20 Jul 1984*	
Bonner	Elder		Thomson C.	Jackson
Bearsden *14 – 21 Jul 1973*			**St Andrews** *6 – 13 Jul 1985*	
Jamieson	Elder		*	Jackson

McNab. (Bénédictine)

Motwani. (Bénédictine)

South African Championship

1892	Cape Town	Roberts*
1897	Cape Town	Roberts
1899	Durban	Michael
1903	Johannesburg	Lee
1906	Cape Town	Siegheim*
1910	Cape Town	Duhan
1912	Johannesburg	Siegheim
1920	Cape Town	Cameron & Chavkin
1924	Durban	Chavkin
1926	Johannesburg	Blieden
1928	Cape Town	Blieden
1935	Johannesburg	Archer
1937	Cape Town	Dreyer*
1939	Durban	Heidenfeld
1945–6	Johannesburg	Heidenfeld & Holford
1947	Cape Town	Heidenfeld & Dreyer
1949	Durban	Heidenfeld
1951	East London	Heidenfeld
1952–3	Johannesburg	Eriksen
1955	Cape Town	Heidenfeld
1957	Durban	Heidenfeld
1959	Johannesburg	Heidenfeld & Kirby
1961	Cape Town	Gerber
1963	Pretoria	Kirby & van den Meyden
1965	Salisbury	Kroon
1967	Johannesburg	Friedgood
1969	Pretoria	Kroon
1971	Johannesburg	Friedgood
1973	Cape Town	Friedgood
1975	East London	Kroon & De Villiers
1977	Pretoria	Walker & De Villiers
1979	Johannesburg	Korostenski
1981	Cape Town	De Villiers
1983	Pretoria	Macfarlane
1985	Johannesburg	De Villiers & Wolpe

Spanish Championship

1902	Madrid	Golmayo
1912	match	Golmayo
1921	Madrid	Golmayo
1930	match	Rey Ardid
1933	match	Rey Ardid
1935	match	Rey Ardid
1942	match	Rey Ardid
1943	match	Sanz, J
1944	Madrid	Medina
1945	Bilbao	Medina
1946	Santander	Pomar
1947	Valencia	Medina
1948	Murcia	Pérez
1949	Albacete	Medina
1950	San Sebastián	Pomar
1951	Barcelona	Toran
1952	Gijón	Medina
1953	Vigo	Toran
1954	Tarragona	Pérez
1955	Alcoy	Diez del Corral
1956	Barcelona	Lladó
1957	Saragossa	Pomar
1958	Valencia	Pomar
1959	Tenerife	Pomar
1960	Lugo	Pérez
1961	Granada	Llado
1962	Malaga	Pomar
1963	Cadiz	Medina
1964	Las Palmas	Medina
1965	Sevilla	Diez del Corral
1966	Almeria	Pomar
1967	Palma	Fernandez
1968	Reus	Visier
1969	Navalmoral	Bellón
1970	Llarnes	Palacios
1971	Gijon	Bellón
1972	Salamanca	Visier
1973	Tenerife	Sanz, F.J.
1974	Valencia	Bellón
1975	Benidorm	Fraguela
1976	Ceuta	Martin
1977	C'an Picafort	Bellón
1978	Pontevedra	Rivas
1979	Torrevieja	Rivas
1980	Alcoy	Gomez
1981	Sevilla	Rivas
1982	Cartagena	Bellon
1983	Las Palmas	García Padron
1984	Barcelona	Martin
1985	Huesca	De la Villa

Spanish Women's Championship

1950	Madrid	Velat
1951	Valencia	Ruiz
1953	Barcelona	Cifuentes
1955	Valencia	Cifuentes
1957	Madrid	Gutierrez
1959	Barcelona	Gutierrez
1961	Barcelona	Ferrer
1963	Madrid	Ferrer
1965	Arenys de Mar	Gutierrez
1967	Arenys de Mar	Gutierrez
1969	Santander	Ferrer
1971	Candás	Ferrer
1972	Vigo	Ferrer
1973	Gijón	Ferrer
1974	Zaragoza	Ferrer
1975	Sevilla	García
1976	Alicante	Ferrer
1977	Zamora	García
1978	La Toja	García
1979	Vich	Gallego
1980	Reus	García Padrón
1981	Nerja	García
1982	Córdoba	García
1983	Lerida	García Padrón

| 1984 | La Roda | García |
| 1985 | Logroño | Cuevas |

Swedish Championship

Until 1939 there were in effect two championships, one by match play and the other by annual tournament. Now only the tournament survives.

Match

1917	Stockholm	Löwenborg 3; Olson 2
1917	Göteborg	Nyholm 3.5; Berndtsson 1.5
1917	Stockholm	Nyholm 4; Löwenborg 1
1919	Stockholm	Nyholm 2.5; Håkansson 2.5
1919	Stockholm	Nyholm 3.5; Olson 1.5
1919	Göteborg	Nyholm 2.5; Nilsson, A 2.5
1921	Stockholm	Olson, A 3; Nyholm 2
1921	Stockholm	Nyholm 3.5; Olson 1.5
1924	Göteborg	Nilsson, A 3; Nyholm 1
1927	Göteborg	Nilsson, A 2.5; Stoltz 2.5
1929	Göteborg	Ståhlberg 3; Nilsson 0
1931	Göteborg	Ståhlberg 3; Stoltz 3

Tournament

1917	Stockholm	Löwenborg & Olson
1918	Göteborg	Berndtsson
1919	Malmö	Olson, A
1920	Eskilstuna	Berndtsson
1921	Jönköping	Berndtsson & Nyholm
1922	Gävle	Håkanson
1923	Uppsala	Nillson, A & Olson, A
1924	Norrköping	Olson, K
1925	Trollhättan	Kinnmark
1926	Karlstad	Berndtsson
1927	Örebro	Stoltz & Ståhlberg
1928	Hälsingborg	Stoltz
1929	Västerås	Pettersson, E
1931	Uddevalla	Lundin
1932	Karslkrona	Lundin & Ståhlberg
1933	Lund	Bergkvist, Danielsson, Forhaug & Skarp
1934	Falun	Lundin*
1935	Härnösand	Lindberg & Stoltz
1936	Borås	Larsson
1937	Stockholm	Pettersson, W
1938	Kalmar	Lundin
1939	Stockholm	Ståhlberg
1941	Göteborg	Lundin
1942	Ostersund	Lundin
1943	Malmö	Ekenberg
1944	Lidköping	Lundholm
1945	Visby	Lundin
1946	Motala	Lundin
1947	Stockholm	Ekström
1948	Sundsvall	Ekström
1949	Eskilstuna	Sköld
1950	Kristianstad	Sköld
1951	Halmstad	Stoltz*
1952	Hålland	Stoltz*
1953	Örebro	Stoltz*
1954	Hälsingborg	Hörberg
1955	Södertälje	Danielsson
1956	Borås	Stenborg*
1957	Stockholm	Nilsson, Z
1958	Växjö	Johansson
1959	Västerås	Sköld
1960	Kiruna	Lundin*
1961	Avesta	Lundin*
1962	Ornsköldsvik	Ekenberg
1963	Karlskrona	Sköld
1964	Göteborg	Lundin
1965	Falköping	Nilsson, Z*
1966	Malmö	Johansson
1967	Stockholm	Martens
1968	Norrköping	Jansson
1969	Sundsvall	Andersson*
1970	Nässjö	Jansson
1971	Eskilstuna	Malmgren
1972	Skellefteå	Ornstein
1973	Bollnås	Ornstein
1974	Lund	Wahlbohm*
1975	Göteborg	Ornstein
1976	Motala	Schüssler
1977	Stockholm	Ornstein
1978	Degerfors	Renman & Schüssler
1979	Borås	Schneider
1980	Luleå	Renman
1981	Ystad	Cramling, D
1982	Gävle	Schneider
1983	Karlskrona	Schneider
1984	Linköping	Ornstein
1985	Uppsala	Akesson

Swedish Correspondence Championship

1938	Sunberg
1940	Brynhammar
1941	Ekström
1942	Malmgren
1943	Sundberg
1944	Brynhammar
1945	Lundqvist
1947	Sundberg
1948	Lundholm
1950	Johansson
1951	Smith
1952	Eidenfeldt
1953	Arvidsson
1954	Joffe
1955	Pettersson
1956	Smith
1957	Wikström, Bg
1958	Andersson
1959	Åhman
1960	Nättorp
1961	Åhman
1962	Johansson

1963	Ljungdahl
1964	Ekström
1965	Mellgren
1966	Nordström
1967	Ek
1968	Wikström, Bt
1969	Runström
1970	Wikström, Bt
1971	Ekström
1972	Bryntse
1973	Averby
1974	Hernod
1975	Nordström
1976	Hammar
1977	Svenson
1978	Schütz
1979	Varjomaa
1980	Mineur
1981	Wikström, Bt
1982	Welin
1983	Lacko
1984	Rothén
1985	Eszik

Swiss Championship

1889	Zurich	Pestalozzi, Poplawski
1890	Winterthur	Pestalozzi, Poplawski
1892	Basel	Corrodi, Fahrni
1893	Bern	Popoff
1895	Zurich	Bachmann
1896	Luzern	Bachmann, Duhm H
1897	Aarau	Sack
1898	Basel	Bachman
1899	Lausanne	Henneberger M
1900	Bern	Duhm A
1901	St Gallen	Meyer, Pestalozzi, Duhm A, Duhm H
1902	Biel	Meyer, Martin
1903	Zurich	Müller
1904	Luzern	Henneberger W
1905	Neuchatel	Hänni
1906	Basel	Henneberger W, Henneberger M
1907	Schaffhausen	Duhm D, Johner P, Kunz
1908	Bern	Johner P, Johner H
1909	Zurich	Henneberger M
1910	Geneva	Naegeli
1911	Davos	Henneberger M & W, Voellmy, Krantz
1912	Lausanne	Henneberger W
1913	Basel	Duhm A
1914	Montreux	Duhm D, Henneberger W
1920	St Gallen	Voellmy
1922	Neuchatel	Voellmy
1923	Bern	Johner H
1924	Interlaken	Zimmermann
1925	Zurich	Johner P

1926	Geneva	Michel
1927	Biel	Staehelin
1928	Basel	Johner H & P
1929	Schaffhausen	Johner H
1930	Lausanne	Johner P
1931	Winterthur	Johner H
1932	Bern	Johner H & P
1934	Zurich	Johner H
1935	Aarau	Johner H
1936	Luzern	Naegeli
1937	Interlaken	Johner H
1938	Basel	Johner H
1939	Montreux	Grob
1941–2	Aarau etc	Gygli
1942	Lausanne	Ehrat & Christoffel
1943	St Gallen	Christoffel
1944	Vevey	Lob
1945	Lugano	Christoffel
1946	Winterthur	Strehle
1947	Neuchatel	Johner H
1948	Bern	Christoffel*
1949	Schaffhausen	Tordion
1950	Luzern	Johner H
1951	Geneva	Grob
1952	Zurich	Christoffel
1953	Solothurn	Blau
1954	Basel	Kupper
1955	Rapperswill	Blau
1956	Thun	Blau
1957	Lausanne	Kupper*
1958	Lugano	Keller
1959	Biel	Lob*
1960	Balgach	Keller
1961	Interlaken	Keller
1962	St Gallen	Kupper
1963	Basel	Keller
1964	Montreux	Markus
1965	Bern	Markus*
1966	Lugano	Bhend
1967	Biel	Blau
1969	Luzern	Lombard
1970	Riehen	Lombard
1971	Winterthur	Schaufelberger
1972	Locarno	Schaufelberger
1973	Weggis	Lombard
1974	Wettingen	Lombard
1975	Zurich	Hug*
1976	Ascona	Känel
1977	Muttenz	Lombard
1978	St Moritz	Känel
1979	Biel	Wirthensohn
1980	Ascona	Kaenel
1981		Wirthensohn
1982	Silvaplana	Korchnoi
1983	Baden	Huss
1984	Arosa	Korchnoi
1985	Silvaplana	Korchnoi

USA Championship

As in many countries the championship title gradually evolved. Mackenzie played in 13 tournaments and 7 matches in USA, winning all of the tournaments and 6 matches (the other was drawn). He was regarded as the unofficial champion of USA from *c*.1865 to *c*.1885. By a series of victories in United States Chess Association tournaments Showalter claimed the title which then, for nearly half a century, became subject to match play competition.

1888	Cincinnati	Showalter
1890	St Louis	Showalter
1891	Lexington	Showalter
1892	match	Lipschuetz
1895	match	Showalter
1897	match	Pillsbury

Herman Steiner (seated) and Fine. (Brian Reilly)

1898	match	Pillsbury
1906	Pillsbury death	Showalter
1909	match	Marshall
1923	match	Marshall
1936	New York	Reshevsky
1938	New York	Reshevsky
1940	New York	Reshevsky
1942	New York	Reshevsky
1944	New York	Denker
1946	New York	Reshevsky
1948	S. Fallsburg	Steiner
1951	New York	Evans
1954	New York	Bisguier
1957–8	New York	Fischer
1958–9	New York	Fischer
1959–60	New York	Fischer
1960–1	New York	Fischer
1961–2	New York	Evans
1962–3	New York	Fischer
1963–4	New York	Fischer
1965	New York	Fischer
1966	New York	Fischer
1968	New York	Evans
1969	New York	Reshevsky
1972	New York	Byrne, R
1973	El Paso	Kavalek & Grefe
1974	Chicago	Browne
1975	Oberlin	Browne
1977	Mentor	Browne
1978	Pasadena	Kavalek
1980	Greenville	Browne, Evans, Christiansen
1981	South Bend	Browne & Seiraman
1983	Greenville	Dzindzikhashvili, Christiansen, Browne
1984	Berkeley	Alburt
1985	Estes Park	Alburt

USSR Championship

The tournaments before 1920 were obviously not USSR championships. The first five were All-Russian championships, the next two All-Russian amateur championships. The final All-Russian pair were in effect championships but did not bear the name.

USSR Championship

1899	Moscow	Chigorin
1901	Moscow	Chigorin
1903	Kiev	Chigorin
1906	St Petersburg	Salwe
1907–8	Lodz	Rubinstein
1909	St Petersburg	Alekhine
1911	St Petersburg	Levitsky
1912	Vilna	Rubinstein
1914	St Petersburg	Alekhine & Nimzowitsch
1920	Moscow	Alekhine

Keres (left) and Boleslavsky in the Moscow 1957 tournament. Seated behind them is Petrosyan with Taimanov looking on.

1923	Petrograd	Romanovsky		1956	Leningrad	Taimanov*
1924	Moscow	Bogoljubow		1957	Moscow	Tal
1925	Leningrad	Bogoljubow		1958	Riga	Tal
1927	Moscow	Romanovsky,		1959	Tbilisi	Petrosyan
		Bohatirchuk		1960	Leningrad	Korchnoi
1929	Odessa	Verlinsky		1961 Jan	Moscow	Petrosyan
1931	Moscow	Botvinnik		1961 Nov	Baku	Spassky
1933	Leningrad	Botvinnik		1962	Yerevan	Korchnoi
1934	Leningrad	Levenfish,		1963	Leningrad	Stein*
		Rabinovich, I		1964 – 5	Kiev	Korchnoi
1937	Tbilisi	Levenfish		1965	Tallin	Stein*
1939	Leningrad	Botvinnik		1966 – 7	Tbilisi	Stein
1940	Moscow	Bondarevsky,		1967	Kharkov	Polugayevsky, Tal
		Lilienthal		1968 – 9	Alma-Ata	Polugayevsky*
1941	Moscow/	Botvinnik		1969	Moscow	Petrosyan*
	Leningrad			1970	Riga	Korchnoi
1944	Moscow	Botvinnik		1971	Leningrad	Savon
1945	Moscow	Botvinnik		1972	Baku	Tal
1947	Leningrad	Keres		1973	Moscow	Spassky
1948	Moscow	Bronstein & Kotov		1974	Leningrad	Belyavsky & Tal
1949	Moscow	Bronstein & Smyslov		1975	Yerevan	Petrosyan
1950	Moscow	Keres		1976	Moscow	Karpov
1951	Moscow	Keres		1977	Leningrad	Gulko, Dorfman
1952	Moscow	Botvinnik*		1978	Tbilisi	Tal, Tseshkovsky
1954	Kiev	Averbakh		1979	Minsk	Geller
1955	Moscow	Geller*		1980 – 1	Vilnius	Belyavsky, Psakhis

Soviet strength in depth. Behind Korchnoi are Belyavsky and Karpov. Kasparov looks for his nose.
(Agterdenbos)

Taimanov, concert pianist and grandmaster, played a record 23 times in the USSR championship.
(Reproduced by courtesy of B.T. Batsford)

1981	Frunze	Kasparov, Psakhis
1983	Moscow	Karpov
1984	Lvov	Sokolov
1985	Riga	Gurevich*

USSR Women's Championship

1927	Moscow	Rubtsova
1931	Moscow	Rubtsova
1934	Leningrad	Semyenova
1936	Leningrad	Semyenova
1937	Rostov-on-Don	Rubtsova
1945	Moscow	Borisenko
1947	Moscow	Bykova
1948	Moscow	Bykova
1950	Riga	Bykova
1951	Kiev	Zvorykina
1952	Tbilisi	Rudenko
1953	Rostov-on-Don	Zvorykina
1954	Krasnodar	Volpert
1955	Sukhumu	Borisenko
1956	Dnepopetrovsk	Zvorykina
1957	Vilnius	Borisenko & Zvorykina
1958	Kharkov	Volpert & Zvorykina
1959	Lipetsk	Volpert

Botvinnik & Smyslov

Smyslov smiles. (Stephane Bureau)

Botvinnik. (Novosti)

When the unique tournament for the world championship was held in 1948 to find a successor to Alekhine, the popular view was that the winner would be Botvinnik, Keres or Reshevsky. The first of these won relatively easily, four games before the end of play, but the surprise was Smyslov, in second place.

The key to the personalities of each of this pair lies in the title of his autobiography (both available in English). Botvinnik called his *Achieving the Aim*, and few have shown such dedication to the pursuit of their own goals, chess and otherwise. Smyslov's is *In Search of Harmony*, a reflection not merely of his peaceful nature and love of balance but also a nod to his passion for music — he is a baritone of professional standard.

After winning the title Botvinnik neglected chess in order to complete a qualification as doctor of technology. His chess became rusty and he barely scraped home in 1951 against Bronstein. Then came a series of three championship matches against Smyslov, the first drawn, the second won by Smyslov, the final one by Botvinnik. In their four world championship encounters they had won 18 games each, 38 were drawn, and Botvinnik said that he felt that they had been playing each other for a lifetime.

An unsatisfactory aspect of this period was that to beat the champion the challenger not only had to give, in effect, half a point start (because with a drawn match the champion retained the title), but also had to beat the holder twice. The champion's right to a return match was seen by some as an attempt to keep an 'approved' player in office. It was removed at the end of Botvinnik's reign and reinstated during Karpov's. In what other sport is a champion so feather-bedded, so favoured by the authorities that control the sport?

Botvinnik and Smyslov did not strike up a friendship until they had ended their series of matches, but they were not unusually hostile. In 1952 Smyslov made a mildly disparaging remark about Botvinnik who then asked him if he had really said it. 'I didn't know it would all come out', was the reply. Botvinnik wrote, 'Such a frank answer could come only from Smyslov!'

1960	Riga	Borisenko & Zatulovskaya
1962 Jan	Yerevan	Borisenko
1962 Nov	Riga	Zatulovskaya
1963	Baku	Zatulovskaya & Ranniku
1964	Tbilisi	Gaprindashvili
1965	Beltsy	Kozlovskaya
1966	Kiev	Alexandriya
1967	Sochi	Ranniku
1968	Ashkhabad	Alexandriya & Chaikovskaya
1969	Gori	Alexandriya
1970	Beltsy	Kushnir & Ranniku
1971	Sochi	Levitina
1972	Togliatti	Shul
1973–4	Tbilisi	Gaprindashvili
1974	Tbilisi	Fatalibekova
1975	Frunze	Belavenets
1976	Tbilisi	Akhsharumova
1977	Lvov	Chiburdanidze
1978	Nikolayev	Levitina & Semyenova
1979	Tbilisi	Levitina
1980–1	Alma-Ata	Levitina
1981	Ivano-Frankovsk	Gaprindashvili & Ioseliani
1982	Tallin	Ioseliani
1983	Tallin	Gaprindashvili
1984	Kiev	Akhsharumova & Matveyeva
1985	Yerevan	Gaprindashvili

USSR Correspondence Championship

1951	Konstantinopolsky
1955	Atyashev
1957	Borisenko & Dubinin
1960	Sadomsky
1962	Borisenko & Estrin
1964	Simagin
1966	Yudovich, M
1968	Sokolov
1970	Omelchenko
1972	Omelchenko
1975	Voitsekh
1977	Semyenyuk
1978	Umansky
1980	Postovsky

Welsh Championship

The first Welsh championship in modern times was in 1955. The winner was entitled to a place in the British Championship.

In 1970 The Welsh Chess Union seceded from the BCF in order to enter FIDE events as an independent body. Welsh championships were held for a time at the traditional Easter break but in 1979 moved to the New Year holiday although the women's event remained at Easter.

	Champion	*Women*
1955	Griffiths	Kenyon (only woman)
1956	Bourne	Kenyon
1957	Wise & Barnard	Budzinski
1958	Douthwaite	Budzinski & MacLean
1959	Curtis	no competition
1960	Bennett	no competition
1961	Bennett & Mills	MacLean
1962	Jones & Newcombe	no competition
1963	Moore	Mann
1964	Chesters	Southall
1965	Reynolds	Mills (née Mann) & Williams
1966	Sully	Southall
1967	Gilbert	Southall
1968	Williams & Gavrilovic	Southall
1969	Gavrilovic	Southall & Brunker
1970	Gavrilovic & Chesters	Brunker
1971	Williams	Southall
1972	Williams	Brunker
1973	Trevelyan, Hutchings, Botterill & McCarthy	Brunker
1974	Williams	Davies
1975	Williams	Briscombe
1976	Cooper & Rayner	Garwell
1977	Williams	Evans
1978	Cooper & Williams	Garwell
1979	Trevelyan & Sully	Evans
1979–80	Williams	Garwell
1980–1	Williams	Garwell & James
1981–2	Williams	Anson & Brunker
1982–3	James, Jones, Lamford & Williams	Garwell
1983–4	Cooper	Powell
1984–5	Cooper	Brunker
1986	Williams	

Yugoslav Championship

1935	Belgrade	Pirc & Kostić
1936	Novi Sad	Pirc
1937	Rogaska Slatina	Pirc

1938	Ljubljana	Kostić
1939	Zagreb	Vidmar
1945	Novi Sad	Trifunović
1946	Zagreb	Trifunović
1947	Ljubljana	Trifunović & Gligorić
1948 – 9	Belgrade	Gligorić & Pirc
1949	Zagreb	Gligorić
1950 – 1	Ljubljana	Gligorić
1951	Sarajevo	Rabar
1952	Belgrade	Trifunović
1953	Zagreb	Pirc, Rabar & Fuderer
1955	Novi Sad	Karaklajić
1956	Skopje	Gligorić
1957	Sombor	Gligorić
1958	Sarajevo	Ivkov & Gligorić
1959	Kragujevac	Gligorić
1960	Ljubljana	Gligorić
1961	Zagreb	Trifunović
1962	Vrnjačka Banja	Gligorić
1962	Skopje	Matanović & Minić
1963	Zenica	Udovčić & Ivkov
1965	Titograd	Gligorić
1965	Novi Sad	Matulović
1967	Kraljevo	Matulović
1968	Topliče	Stupica & Ostojić
1969	Novo Travnik	Matanović
1970	Vrnjačka Banja	Velimirović & Vukić
1971	Portorož	Vukić & Ostojić
1972	Umag	Ivkov
1973	Sutomore	Ivanović
1974	Porec	Vukic
1975	Novi Sad	Velimirović
1976	Bor	Hulak
1977	Zagreb	Ljubojević & Marangunić
1978	Belgrade	Matanović
1979	Bjelovar	Nemet
1980	Vakuf	Nikolić
1981	Borovo	Ivanović
1982	Vrbaš	Ljubojević
1983	Hercegnovi	Rajković & Ivanović
1984	Subotica	Nikolić
1985	Novi Sad	Marjanović

Yugoslav Women's Championship

1947 – 8	Belgrade	Timofejeva
1948	Novi Sad	Timofejeva
1949	Ljubljana	Cvenkel & Timofejevna
1950	Skopje	Jovanovic V
1951	Zagreb	Jovanovic V
1952	Subotica	Jovanovic V & Lazarevic
1953	Opatija	Nedeljkovic
1954	Osijek	Lazarevic
1955	Celje	Nadj-Radenkovic
1956	Sombor	Lazarevic
1957	Vrnjacka Banja	Lazarevic
1958	Izola	Nedeljkovic
1959	Zagreb	Jocic
1960	Sarajevo	Lazarevic
1961	Tivat	Jovanovic K
1962	Jesenice	Lazarevic
1963	Slavonska Pozega	Lazarevic
1964	Vrnjacka Banja	Stadler
1965	Vrnjacka Banja	Nedeljkovic
1966	Backa Palanka	Ljiljak
1968	Vrnjacka Banja	Konarkowska-Sokolov
1969	Leskovac	Jovanovic R
1971(1)	Radenci	Konarkowska-Sokolov
1971(2)	Belgrade	Jovanovic K
1973	Porec	Kalchbrenner & Stadler
1974(1)	Porec	Pihajlic & Markovic
1974(2)	Belgrade	Jovanovic K
1975	Medulin	Lazarevic
1976	Krk	Lazarevic
1977	Krk	Markovic & Pihajlic
1978	Jajce	Prokopovic**
1979	Bled	Lazarevic
1980	Donji Milanovac	Macek
1981	Arandjelovac	Markovic
1982	Bosanska Krupa	Lazarevic
1983	Arandjelovac	Petrovic
1984	Ostrozac	Petrovic
1985	Kula	
1986	Pucarevo	Marić

The Records

World Champions

Youngest Kasparov, on 9 Nov 1985, age 22 years and 210 days.

Oldest Steinitz, until 26 May 1894, age 58 years and 10 days.

Briefest Tal, 1 year and 5 days

Longest Lasker, 26 years and 337 days.

Most Botvinnik, 3 times. Alekhine is the only other to be champion more than once.

National Champions

Youngest Niaz Murshed, on 18 Mar 1979, champion of Bangladesh age 12 years and 309 days.

Oldest Price, British Women's champion 1948, age 76.

Most Larsen, 17 times Danish Women's champion. Followed by Sarapu, 16 times New Zealand champion.

Others

Olympiads Youngest player. Kiem Tjing-Tjin-Joe, age 12, board 3 for Surinam in 1982.

Most at once In the 1982–3 season Michael Adams was Cornish champion, and also Cornish under-18, under-15, under-13, under-11 and lightning champion. Born 17 Nov 1971, his performance in the Lloyds Bank tournament 1984 was reckoned by Leonard Barden, in *The Guardian*, as probably the best ever by a 12-year-old. In 1986 he won the West of England senior title, becoming the youngest-ever Union champion.

Adams at 14. (Roger Blackmore)

Murshed. (Roger Blackmore)

Interval 1 John Keeble (27 Aug 1855 – 19 Feb 1939), won the Norfolk & Norwich club championship in 1884. He did not enter again until 1933, and then he won it for three consecutive years.

2 John Watkinson (5 Feb 1833 – 19 Dec 1923), founder of the *British Chess Magazine*, was President of the Huddersfield chess club in its formation year, 1853, and again in 1923.

Longevity Strong player Jane Lady Carew lived in three centuries. Born in 1797 she died in November 1901.

Games

Shortest 1 In the last round of Luton 1975 tournament Miles and Reuben, with the blessing of the controller, agreed to draw without making any moves, assuring themselves of 1st and 2nd places respectively.

2 Other than losses by default, the next shortest was at Palma Interzonal 1970 when Fischer, already certain to win, played 1 c4 against Panno who resigned as a protest about hours of play.

3 Unintended shortest. In a tournament at Bela Crkva 1984, between Djordjević and Kovacević (1 d4 Nf6 2 Bg5 c6 3 e3 Qa5+).

4 In a world championship. 21st game between Botvinnik and Petrosyan 1963, agreed drawn after White's 10th move.

Longest 1 The longest game theoretically possible, applying the 50-move draw rule, is 5,949 moves.

2 The longest game known is, like the shortest, a pre-arranged draw, but in this case the players had a bit of fun. Thomas Ristoja (b.19 Sep 1949 Stockholm) and Michael Nykopp (b. 14 Mar 1946 Finland), at Tampere 1971, submitted a draw in 300 moves.

3 Longest real game. In the 1981 Israeli championship Yedael Stepak (b. 21 Aug 1940 Haifa) beat Yaacov Mashian (b. 17 Dec 1938 Teheran) on White's 193rd move.

4 Longest game in a world championship. 124 moves. 5th of the 1978 Karpov-Korchnoi match, also the only one to end in stalemate.

5 Longest game without a capture. Filipowicz-Smederevac, Polanica Zdroj 1966. 70 moves. Drawn under the 50-move rule.

Slowest move Since clocks have been used the record is 2 hrs 20 mins by Francisco Trois (b. 3 Sep 1946 Canoas) for his 7th move against Luis M.C.P. Santos (b. 30 Jun 1955 Lisbon), Vigo 1980. As there were only two moves worth considering Santos said he could not see how it could take so long. Trois replied, 'Yo tampoco' (me neither).

Legends abound from earlier times but one may suspect that they refer to how long it seemed to the opponent. There is no record of any former player taking as long as Trois.

Longest chess game

Stepak – Mashian *Israel 1980*

1 d4 Nf6 2 c4 e6 3 Nf3 b6 4 g3 Bb7 5 Bg2 Be7 6 Nc3 Ne4 7 Qc2 Nxc3 8 Qxc3 0-0 9 0-0 c5 10 Rd1 d6 11 Qc2 Nd7 12 e4 Qc7 13 b3 Rfe8 14 Bb2 Rad8 15 Rd2 e5 16 d5 Bf8 17 Re2 g6 18 Bc1 Bg7 19 Bg5 f6 20 Bd2 Bc8 21 Nh4 Nf8 22 h3 Bd7 23 a4 Qc8 24 Kh2 a5 25 Rf1 Qc7 26 Qd3 g5 27 Nf5 Bxf5 28 exf5 Qf7 29 Re4 Nd7 30 Qe2 Kh8 31 Bf3 Rg8 32 Bh5 Qe7 33 Kg2 Bh6 34 Rh1 Rg7 35 h4 Rdg8 36 Kf1 Nf8 37 Rg4 Qd7 38 Qe4 Qc8 39 Ke2 Qd7 40 Rh2 Qc8 41 Kd3 Qd7 42 Kc2 Qe7 43 Kb2 Qd7 44 hxg5 Bxg5 45 f4 exf4 46 gxf4 Bh6 47 Rxg7 Bxg7 48 Bc3 h6 49 Re2 Nh7 50 Qe6 Nf8 51 Qxd7 Nxd7 52 Re6 Bf8 53 Be8 Rg2+ 54 Kc1 Rg1+ 55 Kd2 Rg2+ 56 Re2 Rxe2+ 57 Kxe2 Kg7 58 Bxd7 Be7 59 Be8 Bd8 60 Bh5 Kf8 61 Kd3 Ke7 62 Ke4 Kf8 63 Bg6 Kg7 64 Bd2 Be7 65 Be3 Bd8 66 b4 axb4 67 Kd3 Kf8 68 Bc1 Ke7 69 Bb2 Kf8 70 Kc2 Ke7 71 Kb3 Kd7 72 Bh5 Ke7 73 Bc1 Kd7 74 Bd2 Ke7 75 Be1 Kd7 76 Bd1 Kc7 77 Kc2 Kd7 78 Kd3 Ke7 79 Bh4 Kd7 80 Kc2 Kc7 81 Kb3 Kb7 82 Bh5 Be7 83 Be8 Kc7 84 Kc2 Kd8 85 a5 bxa5 86 Ba4 Kc7 87 Kd3 Kc8 88 Ke3 Kd8 89 Kf3 h5 90 Kg2 Kc7 91 Kh3 Kd8 92 Bg3 Bf8 93 Kh4 Ke7 94 Kxh5 Kf7 95 Kg4 Bg7 96 Kf3 Ke7 97 Bh4 Kf7 98 Ke4 Bf8 99 Kd3 Bg7 100 Kc2 Ke7 101 Kb3 Kd8 102 Bb5 Kc7 103 Ka4 Kb6 104 Be8 Ka6 105 Bb5+ Kb6 106 Kb3 Kc7 107 Kc2 Kd8 108 Kd2 Ke7 109 Ke3 Kf7 110 Ba4 Bh6 111 Kf3 Bf8 112 Kg4 Be7 113 Kh5 Kg7 114 Bf2 Bf8 115 Bh4 Be7 116 Bg5 Bd8 117 Bd1 Be7 118 Bh6+ Kf7 119 Kh4 Kg8 120 Ba4 Kf7 121 Kg4 Bd8 122 Bg5 Be7 123 Kh5 Kg7 124 Bh4 Bf8 125 Be8 Be7 126 Kg4 Kf8 127 Bd7 Kf7 128 Kf3 Bf8 129 Ke4 Bg7 130 Bc6 Bh6 131 Kd3 Bxf4 132 Kc2 Ke7 133 Kb3 Be5 134 Be1 Kd8 135 Ka4 Kc7 136 Kxa5 Bf4 137 Ba4 Be5 138 Ka6 Bf4 139 Bh4 Be5 140 Bd1 Bd4 141 Bg3 Be3 142 Kb5 Bh6 143 Ka4 Kd7 144 Kb3 Ke7 145 Kc2 Bg5 146 Kd3 Bc1 147 Ke4 Bd2 148 Kf3 Bc1 149 Kg4 Bd2 150 Kh5 Be3 151 Kg6 Bg5 152 Bc2 Bd2 153 Kh5 Bc1 154 Kg4 Bd2 155 Kf3 Bc1 156 Ke2 Bg5 157 Be1 Kf7 158 Bb1 Bf4 159 Bd2 Be5 160 Bc2 Ke7 161 Kf3 Kf7 162 Kg4 Kg7 163 Bf4 Bxf4 164 Kxf4 Kh6 165 Ke3 Kg5 166 Kd2 Kf4 167 Kc1 Ke3 168 Kb2 Kd2 169 Kb3 Kc1 170 Be4 Kd2 171 Ka4 Kc3 172 Kb5 b3 173 Kc6 Kxc4 174 Kxd6 Kd4 175 Bb1 c4 176 Ke6 c3 177 d6 c2 178 Bxc2 bxc2 179 d7 c1=Q 180 d8=Q+ Ke4 181 Qd5+ Kf4 182 Qd4+ Kg3 183 Kf7 Qc2 184 Qxf6 Kf4 185 Qd6+ Kg4 186 f6 Qh7+ 187 Kf8 Qh8+ 188 Ke7 Kf5 189 Qe6+ Kf4 190 f7 Qh7 191 Qe2 Kg3 192 Qe5+ Kf2 193 Ke6 Black resigned.

124

Sequences *1* Wins a) Longest period. Steinitz won every first-class game he played (25 in all) from 4 Aug 1873 to 11 May 1882.

b) In one event. Gustav Richard Ludwig Neumann (b. 15 Dec 1838 Gleiwitz, d. 16 Feb 1881 Allenberg) won all 34 games in Berlin 1865 tournament.

2 Losses. Moreau lost all 26 games at Monte Carlo 1903. Just as the tournament was about to begin a disagreement broke out between the Russian grandmaster Chigorin and his compatriot Prince Dadian who was the main backer. As a result Chigorin was banned. Local player and retired army officer Colonel Moreau had to fill the gap. He fought hard but was quite outclassed.

3 Losses on time. At Linköping 1969 Fritz Sämisch lost all 13 of his games on time.

4 Moves by one piece. Mackenzie-Mason, 2nd match game London 1882. From move 72 to move 144 (just over half of the game) Mason moved only his queen.

5 Checks (see also composition). Westerinen-Keres, Tallinn 1969, 38 queen checks by Keres (moves 38 to 75).

6 Effortless chess. At Slupsk 1979 Bilek drew all of his 10 games in a total of 125 moves taking 109 minutes.

Possibilities *1* If a new version were set up every minute it would take 40,000 years, day and night, to exhaust the 208,089,907,200 ways of placing a standard set on a standard board before play begins!

2 After three moves each more than 9,000,000 positions are possible.

3 The number of different games of 40 moves has been estimated at 25×10^{115} which is much greater than the number of electrons in the universe (estimated at 10^{79}).

Bad luck At Vienna 1890 Albin was the only player not to get a prize.

Coincidences

World Champions In Plymouth 1938 tournament R.M. Bruce lost to World Champion Menchik one morning and World Champion Alekhine in the afternoon. He is the only one to have played two world champions in master chess on the same day.

Games D.A. Fennelly played exactly the same 18-move game against two opponents in the same event, a 1980s correspondence tournament.

Resignation In a game during the 1979 Wyoming State championship both players resigned at exactly the same moment, one because he had a hopeless position, the other because of his conscience. While his opponent was out of the room the player had moved, seen it was a mistake and taken it back substituting another.

Publication The memoirs of Augustus Mongredien (b. 17 Mar 1807 London, d. 30 Mar 1888 London) were received by *British Chess Magazine* shortly after his death. Part was published in May and June 1888 and the manuscript returned to his family. In 1981 the manuscript was rediscovered and sent to the *British Chess Magazine*. Again a part was published, in February 1981, but unknown to the editor it was exactly the part not chosen 93 years earlier.

Marathon A record must be at least 75% against opponents with an average Elo of 1800. Between 9.19 on Friday 13 September 1985 and 5.17 on Monday 16, Erik G. J. Knoppert (b. 20 Sep 1959 Netherlands) scored 82.6% against an average Elo 2000 and completed 500 games.

Blindfold There are no adequate controls to ensure proper records. In 1925 Réti played 29 games blindfold, a world record then, only to hear shortly afterwards that a little-known Spanish player had managed 32. Réti hurried to Spain to verify it. He found that 32 players were invited but 29 did not come and lost by default. Of the 3 games played the blindfold expert drew 1 and lost 2. In 1934 George Koltanowski (b. 17 Sep 1903 Antwerp) played 34 opponents, +24 =10, the last undisputed record. Higher claims since then have been put into doubt by rumours that the master had the games written down, or that large numbers of opponents agreed to resign after a few nominal moves, for example.

Composition

Length *1* Longest. Otto Titusz Blathy (b. 11 Aug 1860 Tata, d. 26 Sep 1939 Budapest) composed a problem with mate in 290 moves, published in his book *Vielzügige Schachaufgaben*, 1889.

2 Longest, all checks. Johan Christoffel van Gool (b. 15 June 1923) and Chéron, mate in 69, every white move check, *Journal de Genève*, 1977.

Mobility *1* Minimum. 32 men in legal position, 2 moves, Thomas Rayner Dawson (b. 28 Nov 1889 Leeds, d. 16 Dec 1951 London), *Chess Amateur* 1923. (A legal position is one that could have arisen in a game.)

30 men in legal position, no moves, Gustavus Charles Reichhelm (b. 6 Nov 1839 Pittsburgh, d. 30 Nov 1905 Philadelphia), *Brentano's Chess Magazine*, 1882.

2 Maximum. 32 men in legal position, no promoted pieces. 164 moves, Oskar E. Vinje (b. Baltimore), *Fairy Chess Review*, 1939.

Legal, with pieces created by pawn promotion, 324 moves, Nenad Petrović (b. 7 Sep 1907 Zagreb), *Fairy Chess Review*, 1946.

3 Maximum mates in 1 move. 47. Pollmächer, Schürig et al. *Illustrirte Zeitung*, 1859.

Retrograde Analysis Alexei Alexeyevich Troitsky (b. 14 Mar 1866 St Petersburg, d. Aug 1942 Leningrad) gave a position and asked 'Who is to move?' The solver had to work backwards 53 moves to the beginning of the 'game' to prove that White was to move. *Deutsche Schachzeitung*, 1914.

Breyer composed a position asking 'Who wins?' By working backwards the solver could show that it was White to move, and as no capture or pawn move could have occurred in the last 50 moves it was a draw. *Chess Amateur*, 1922.

Life and death and all that

Life While in the court of a Muslim ruler, Huon, Duke of Bordeaux, boasted of his chess skill. The king took him up, said he had a daughter who would play Huon. If the Duke lost he would be beheaded, if he won he could have the daughter for the night plus 100 marks. Huon won, but took only the money. The princess said, 'A false fainted heart, Mahomet confound thee; for if I had known thou would thus refuse my company I would have mated thee.'

Death 1 Canute took back a move when playing one of his earls, Ulf, who then knocked over the board and refused to play. Canute had him murdered.

2 Prince John, son of Henry II, smashed a board over the head of his opponent, Fulk, who then almost killed the future king. Later Fulk was among the barons who forced John to seal the Magna Carta in 1215.

3 A case before the London court on 16 August 1254 concerned William de Wendene who stabbed his opponent to death during a chess quarrel.

4 In New York's Greenwich Village in 1960 a spectator criticized the play of a sailor who responded by killing him with a beer glass. The assailant was acquitted of murder.

All that On the eve of the Battle of Trenton, 26 December 1776, the British general, Rall, was sent a note warning him of Washington's planned attack. Playing chess, he put the note in his pocket. It was found unread on his body the next day, after a battle that led to American Independence.

Top Ranking

This is the cream of FIDE's list for January 1986. It is in descending Elo rating order, those with the same rating being in alphabetical order. A world champion is likely to be around 2700, a candidate 2600, and an 'ordinary' grandmaster 2500. The top 103 men appear in the first part, women down to 2200 in the second, and then British players not in the international section, men to 2350, women to 2000. In these latter cases the ranking numbers refer to the British Isles only, and full names are given for those not in the Players section, beginning p. 128.

1	Kasparov	USSR	2720
2	Karpov	USSR	2700
3	Timman	Netherlands	2645
4	Vaganyan	USSR	2645
5	Yusupov	USSR	2645
6	Korchnoi	Switzerland	2635
7	Belyavsky	USSR	2625
8	Hübner	West Germany	2625
9	Miles	England	2610
10	Portisch	Hungary	2610
11	Spassky	France	2610
12	Ljubojević	Yugoslavia	2605
13	Seirawan	USA	2605
14	Tal	USSR	2600
15	Sokolov	USSR	2595
16	Andersson	Sweden	2585
17	Nunn	England	2585
18	Ribli	Hungary	2585
19	Short	England	2585
20	Larsen	Denmark	2575
21	Polugayevsky	USSR	2575
22	Smyslov	USSR	2575
23	Velimirovic	Yugoslavia	2575
24	Chernin	USSR	2570
25	Noguieras	Cuba	2570
26	Tukmakov	USSR	2570
27	Nikolić	Yugoslavia	2565
28	Einhorn	USSR	2560
29	Kavalek	USA	2560
30	Romanishin	USSR	2560
31	Speelman	England	2560
32	Sveshnikov	USSR	2560
33	Van der Wiel	Netherlands	2560
34	Adorjan	Hungary	2555
35	Benjamin	USA	2555
36	Christiansen	USA	2555
37	Pinter	Hungary	2555
38	Psakhis	USSR	2555
39	Garcia-Palermo	Argentina	2550
40	Gavrikov	USSR	2550
41	Sax	Hungary	2550
42	Smejkal	Czechoslovakia	2550
43	Agzamov	USSR	2545
44	Arkhipov	USSR	2545
45	Dlugy	USA	2545
46	Georgiev	Bulgaria	2545
47	Hort	West Germany	2545
48	Lputyan	USSR	2545
49	Olafsson, H	Iceland	2545
50	Popović	Yugoslavia	2545
51	Suba	Romania	2545
52	Dzindzikhashvili	USA	2540
53	Agdestein	Norway	2535
54	Chandler	England	2535
55	Gruenfeld	Israel	2535
56	Lein	USA	2535
57	Spraggett	Canada	2535
58	Campora	Argentina	2530
59	Lerner	USSR	2530
60	Schmid	West Germany	2530
61	Geller	USSR	2525

62	Gheorghiu	Romania	2525
63	Ivkov	Yugoslavia	2525
64	Mestel	England	2525
65	Razuvayev	USSR	2525
66	Salov	USSR	2525
67	Sosonko	Netherlands	2525
68	Tarjan	USA	2525
69	Torre	Philippines	2525
70	Barbero	Argentina	2520
71	De Firmian	USA	2520
72	Dorfman	USSR	2520
73	Farago	Hungary	2520
74	Karlsson	Sweden	2520
75	Petursson	Iceland	2520
76	Ricardi	Argentina	2520
77	Alburt	USA	2515
78	Balashov	USSR	2515
79	Cebalo	Yugoslavia	2515
80	Dolmatov	USSR	2515
81	Ftáčnik	Czechoslovakia	2515
82	Gligorić	Yugoslavia	2515
83	Panno	Argentina	2515
84	Rogers	Australia	2515
85	Ubilava	USSR	2515
86	Zapata	Colombia	2515
87	Browne	USA	2510
88	Gurevich	USSR	2510
89	Hansen	Denmark	2510
90	Knaak	East Germany	2510
91	Mikhalchishin	USSR	2510
92	Quinteros	Argentina	2510
93	Vaiser	USSR	2510
94	Byrne	USA	2505
95	Csom	Hungary	2505
96	Georgadze	USSR	2505
97	Greenfeld	Israel	2505
98	Gulko	USSR	2505
99	Henley	USA	2505
100	Hjartarson	Iceland	2505
101	Hulak	Yugoslavia	2505
102	Rodriguez	Cuba	2505
103	Uhlmann	East Germany	2505

1	Chiburdanidze	USSR	2455
2	Cramling	Sweden	2400
3	Polgar	Hungary	2400
4	Gaprindashvili	USSR	2350
5	Levitina	USSR	2340
6	Alexandriya	USSR	2310
7	Ioseliani	USSR	2310
8	Akhmilovskaya	USSR	2305
9	Litinskaya	USSR	2275
10	Semyenova	USSR	2260
11	Veroci-Petronic	Hungary	2260
12	Zaitseva	USSR	2260
13	Gurieli	USSR	2250
14	Hund, B	West Germany	2245
15	Matveyeva	USSR	2245
16	Terescenco-Nutu	Romania	2245
17	Miletić	Yugoslavia	2240

18	Miles	England	2235
19	Voiska	Bulgaria	2235
20	Rubtsova, T	USSR	2230
21	Lemachko	Switzerland	2225
22	Brustman	Poland	2220
23	Klimova-Richtrova	Czechoslovakia	2220
24	Walker	England	2220
25	Alyekhina	USSR	2215
26	Marković-Jovanović	Yugoslavia	2210
27	Burchardt-Hofmann	East Germany	2205

7	Stean		2500
8	Flear		2485
9	Hodgson		2480
10	Norwood		2460
11	Keene		2455
12	Hebden		2445
13	Littlewood, P.E.		2445
14	Taulbut		2440
15	Hartston		2435
16	King		2435
17	Plaskett		2435
18	Watson		2430
19	Condie		2425
20	Cummings		2415
21	McNab		2415
22	Davies		2410
23	Goodman		2410
24	LeBlancq, Simon		2410
25	Kosten		2405
26	Conquest		2400
27	Hawksworth		2400
28	McKay		2400
29	Pritchett		2400
30	Wells, Peter K.		2400
31	Basman		2395
32	Botterill		2395
33	Cooper		2395
34	Howell		2395
35	Levitt		2395
36	Martin		2390
37	Bellin		2380
38	Arkell		2375
39	Littlewood, John E.		2375
40	Povah		2375
41	Lawton		2365
42	Williams		2360
43	Hindle, Owen M.		2355
44	Horner		2355
45	Large		2355
46	Motwani		2355
47	Potts, Alan		2355
48	Whiteley		2355
49	Penn, Malcolm I.		2350
50	Pigott, John C.		2350

3	Jackson		2200
4	Garwell		2125
5	Needham, Teresa		2120
6	Christopher, Sarah		2075
7	Hepworth, Mandy		2025

The Players

Most of the champions listed here are still active. The symbols b = born, d = died. FIDE titles are abbreviated – IM, International Master; GM, International Grandmaster; WIM, International Woman Master; WGM, International Woman Grandmaster; IMC, International Master Correspondence; GMC, International Grandmaster Correspondence; IMComp, International Master for Chess Composition; GMComp, International Grandmaster for Chess Composition. There can be discrepancies in the published year of title for a player. A qualifying performance in one year may be ratified by FIDE the following year, or FIDE may award the title one year subject to the player

achieving a specified grading in the Elo lists the following year.

'Challenger' means one who played for the world championship. 'Candidate' is a player who reached the candidate stage of the world championship elimination procedure.

A high result in one of the events featured in this book is shown. The date is the end of an event – particularly important for postal competition where a world championship with its preliminaries can take ten years. London 1982 3, means that the player was third in the London 1982 tournament.

Abbott, Hedley Roy *b. 1904 Davenport, England d. 15 Aug 1979 Christchurch, New Zealand* New Zealand champion 1936 – 7.

Adams, Michael *b. 17 Nov 1971.*

Adamski, Jan *b. 11 Nov 1943 Warsaw* IM 1976. Polish champion 1982 (after play-off).

Ader Hausman, Walter *b. 7 Nov 1913 Hodonin* Chilean champion 1966.

Adorján, András *b. 31 Mar 1950 Budapest* IM 1970. GM 1973. Candidate 1980. Vrbas 1980=2. Gjovik 1983=1. European junior champion 1969 – 70. Hungarian champion 1973 (joint), 1984.

Agdestein, Simen *b. 15 May 1967* IM 1983. GM 1985. Nordic champion 1985 (after play-off). Norwegian champion 1982 (after play-off).

Agzamov, Georgy Tadzhikanovich *b. 6 Sep 1954 Almalik* IM 1982. GM 1984.

Ahlers, Klaus Friedrich *b. 1 Jun 1940 Ahrensburg* German correspondence champion 1980 (2).

Åhman, Harry *b. 23 May 1912 Malmberget* IMC 1979. Swedish correspondence champion 1959, 1961.

Ahues, Carl Oscar *b. 26 Dec 1883 Bremen d. 31 Dec 1968 Hamburg* IM 1950. German champion 1929.

Aijälä, Jorma Paavo *b. 21 Mar 1947 Kuusankoski d. 5 Nov 1981 Lahti* Finnish champion 1980.

Aitken, James Macrae *b. 27 Oct 1908 Calderbank,* *Lanarkshire d. 3 Dec 1983 Cheltenham* Scottish champion 1935, 1952, 1953, 1955, 1956, 1957, 1958, 1960, 1961 and jointly 1965. London champion 1950.

Åkesson, Ralf *b. 8 Feb 1961 Oxelösund* IM 1981. Swedish champion 1985. European junior champion 1980 – 1.

Akhmilovskaya, Yelena Bronislavovna *b. 11 Mar 1957 Leningrad* WIM 1977. WGM 1977. Challenger 1986.

Akhsharumova, Anna Markovna (Mrs Gulko) *b. 9 Jan 1957 Moscow* WIM 1977. USSR women's champion 1976, 1984 (joint).

Alatortsev, Vladimir Alexeyevich *b. 14 May 1909 St Petersburg* IM 1950. Emeritus GM 1983. Leningrad champion 1933 – 4 (joint). Moscow champion 1936, 1937 (both joint). Latvian champion (*hors concours*) 1945.

Albulet, Maria *b. 16 Jun 1932 Brăila* WIM 1957. WGM Emeritus 1985. Romanian women's champion 1951, 1955, and, as Pogorevici, 1956.

Alburt, Lev Osipovich *b. 21 Aug 1945 Orenburg* IM 1976. GM 1977. United States champion 1984, 1985.

Alekhine, Alexander Alexandrovich *b. 31 Oct 1892 Moscow d. 24 Mar 1946 Estoril* World champion 1927 – 35, 1937 – 46. St Petersburg 1914 3. New York 1924 3. New York 1927 2. Bled 1931 1.

Nordic champion 1912. German champion 1914 (leading in unfinished event). Russian champion 1909, 1914 (joint), 1920. Moscow champion 1919 – 20.

Aleman, Miguel Cuban champion 1939.

Alexander, Conel Hugh O'Donel *b. 19 Apr 1909 Cork d. 15 Feb 1974 Cheltenham* IM 1950. IMC 1970. British champion 1938, 1956.

Alexandrescu, Gheorghe-Gică *b. 10 Dec 1906 Bucharest* Romanian champion 1951 (joint).

Alexandriya, Nana Georgievna *b. 13 Oct 1949 Poti* WIM 1966. WGM 1976. Women's world championship challenger 1975, 1981. USSR women's champion 1966, 1968 (joint), 1969.

Allen, W J Irish champion =1st 1926, lost play-off.

Allerhand, P *b. 1899 Vienna* New Zealand champion 1940 – 1 (after play-off), 1949 – 50.

Aloni, Itzchak (né Schächter) *b. 5 Apr 1905 d. 1985* Israeli champion 1945, 1961 – 2 (after play-off), 1965.

Alster, Ladislav *b. 2 Apr 1927* Czech champion 1956.

Akhmilovskaya, the 1986 challenger for the women's world championship. (Stephane Bureau)

Alyekhina, Natalia Vladimirovna *b. 3 Nov 1954* USSR WIM 1984.

Ambroz, Jan *b. 18 Jun 1954 Lanskroun* IM 1980. Czech champion 1980.

Andersen, Børge *b. 19 Mar 1934* IM 1964. Danish champion 1958, 1967, 1968, 1973.

Andersen, Erik *b. 10 Apr 1904 Gentofte d. 27 Feb 1938 Copenhagen* Danish champion 1923, 1925, 1926 (play-off), 1927, 1929, 1930, 1931, 1932 (play-off), 1933, 1934, 1935, 1936 (play-off). Nordic champion 1930.

Anderson, Bruce R *b. 4 Sep 1948* New Zealand champion 1967 – 8.

Anderson, Frank Ross *b. 3 Jan 1928 Edmonton d. 18 Sep 1980 San Diego* IM 1954. Canadian champion 1953 (joint), 1955, 1967 – 8, 1968 – 9 (joint).

Anderson, Gertrude Alison *b. c.1876 Hither Green, Kent d. 6 Sep 1924* British women's champion 1909, 1912, and (after play-off) 1921. =1st 1908 but lost play-off.

Anderson, Peter B *b. c.1911 d. 16 Nov 1973 Glasgow* Scottish champion 1950, 1954.

Anderssen, Karl Ernst Adolf *b. 6 Jul 1818 Breslau d. 13 Mar 1879 Breslau.*

Andersson, Anna (Sweden). Women's world championship challenger 1937.

Andersson, Bertil *b. 25 Feb 1915* Swedish correspondence champion 1958.

Andersson, Ingeborg (Sweden). Women's world championship challenger 1937, 1939.

Andersson, Ulf *b. 27 Jun 1951 Västerås* IM 1970. GM 1972. Swedish champion 1969. Geneva 1977 2. Wijk aan Zee 1978 3. Amsterdam 1979 =3. Wijk aan Zee 1979 =2. London 1980 =1. Johannesburg 1981 1. London 1982 =1. Tilburg 1982 =3. Turin 1982 =1. Linares 1983 =2. Wijk aan Zee 1983 1. Reggio Emilia 1985 – 6 =1.

Angantýsson, Haukur *b. 2 Dec 1948 Flateyri* IM 1981. Icelandic champion 1976.

Anger, Frederick British champion (amateur) =1st 1887 but lost play-off.

Anson, Jane *b. 12 Apr 1959 Plymouth* Welsh women's champion 1982 (joint).

Apšeniek, Fricis *b. 7 Apr 1894 Tetele d. 25 Apr 1941 Riga* Latvian champion 1926 – 7, 1934 (after play-off).

Arakhamia, Ketevan Revazovna *b. c.1968 Ochamchira* WIM 1986. World women's under-16 champion 1986.

Arbakov, Valentin Mikhailovich *b. 28 Jan 1952* Moscow champion 1981 (joint).

Archer, John C *b. 4 Jul 1909 d. Oct 1975 Durban* South African champion 1935.

Arkell, Keith Charles *b. 8 Jan 1961 Birmingham*
IM 1985. Petit Prix (UK) champion 1981, 1984.

Arkhipov, Sergey *b. 23 Jun 1954 Moscow* IM
1985.

Arlauskas, Romanas *b. 11 June 1917 Kaunas*
World correspondence championship 1965 3.

Arnason, Jón Loftur *b. 13 Nov 1960* IM 1979.
World under-16 champion 1977. Icelandic
champion 1977.

Arnlaugsson, Gudmundur Icelandic champion
1949.

Aronin, Lev Solomonovich *b. 20 Jul 1920
Kuibyshev d. 1982* IM 1950. Moscow champion
1965.

Arulaid, Alexander *b. 24 May 1924* Estonian
champion 1948, 1955, 1964.

Arvidson, Egon *b. 15 Apr 1915* Swedish
correspondence champion 1953.

Ascher, Jacob Gottschalk *b. 18 Feb 1841 Plymouth
d. 12 Oct 1912 New York* Canadian champion
1878 – 9, 1882 – 3 (joint).

Aseyev, Konstatin N *b. 1960* Leningrad champion
1985.

Asgeirsson, Asmundur Icelandic champion 1931,
1933, 1934, 1944, 1945, 1946 (after play-off).

Asmundsson, Ingvar *b. 10 Jul 1934* Icelandic
champion 1979.

Asztalos, Lajos *b. 29 Jul 1889 Pécs d. 1 Nov 1956
Budapest* IM 1950. Hungarian champion 1913.

Atkins, Henry Ernest *b. 20 Aug 1872 Leicester
d. 31 Jan 1955 Huddersfield* British champion
(amateur) 1895, 1897, 1900. Champion 1905,
1906, 1907, 1908, 1909 (after play-off), 1910, 1911
(after play-off), 1924, 1925. =1st 1904, lost play-
off.

Atyashev, Peter Ivanovich *b. 15 Feb 1918* USSR
correspondence champion 1955.

Auer, Franz *b. Nov 1918* Austrian champion
1955, 1957.

Augustín, Josef *b. 18 May 1942 Kyjov* IM 1976.
Czech champion 1965.

Averbakh, Yuri Lvovich *b. Feb 1922 Kaluga* IM
1950. GM 1952. Candidate 1953. USSR champion
1954. Moscow champion 1949, 1950 (joint), 1962
(joint).

Averby, Rune *b. 25 Oct 1922* Swedish
correspondence champion 1973.

Axt, Helga Ursula *b. 27 Aug 1937 Bad Ems*
German women's champion 1957, 1958, 1961.

Bachmann, Ulrich *b. 1856 Altikon d. 1 Apr 1904
Zurich* Swiss champion 1895, 1896 (joint), 1898.

Bain, Mary *b. 8 Aug 1904 Hungary d. 26 Oct 1972
New York* WIM 1952. Women's world
championship challenger 1937.

Baker, Philip *d. c.May 1932* Irish champion 1924,
1927, 1928, 1929.

Bakulin, Nikolai Ivanovich *b. 9 May 1926
Vologda* Moscow champion 1964, 1966.

Balanel, Ion *b. 7 Jun 1926 Bucharest* IM 1954.
Romanian champion 1950, 1953, 1955, 1958.

Balashov, Yuri Sergeyevich *b. 12 Mar 1949
Shadrinsk* IM 1970. GM 1973. Moscow champion
1970. Wijk aan Zee 1982 =1.

Balcarek, Wiktor *b. 29 Dec 1915 Swietochlowice*
Polish champion 1950.

Balcerowski, Witold *b. 10 Aug 1935 Pińsk* Polish
champion 1962 (after play-off), 1965.

Balla, Zoltán *b. 31 Aug 1883 Budapest d. 1 Apr
1945 Budapest* Hungarian champion 1906, 1911
(joint).

Ballard, Muriel World junior women's champion
1934.

Balogh, János *b. 10 Sept 1892 Tirgu Secuiesc
d. 12 Sep 1980 Budapest* IMC 1953. Romanian
champion 1930.

Barász, Zsigmond *b. c.1877 d. 28 May 1935
Budapest* Hungarian champion 1911 (joint).

Barbero, Gerardo F *b. 21 Aug 1961* IM 1985.
Argentine champion 1984.

Barbier, Georges Émile *b. 24 Feb 1844 Besançon,
France d. 16 Dec 1895 Ecrosville (?), France*
Scottish champion 1886.

Barcza, Gedeon *b. 21 Aug 1911 Kisujszállás
d. 27 Feb 1986 Budapest* IM 1950. GM 1954. IMC
1966. Hungarian champion 1942, 1943, 1947,
1950, 1951, 1955, 1957, 1966.

Barda, Olaf *b. 17 Aug 1909 d. 2 May 1971 Oslo*
IM 1952. GMC 1953. Norwegian champion 1930,
1947, 1948, 1952, 1953, 1957.

Bardeleben, Curt von *b. 4 March 1861 Berlin
d. 31 Jan 1924 Berlin* German champion 1893,
1904 (both joint).

Barden, Leonard William *b. 20 Aug 1929
Croydon, London* British champion (joint) 1954,
equal 1st 1958 but lost play-off.

Bareyev, Yevgeny World under-16 champion
1982.

Barnard, Grahame F Welsh champion 1957 (joint).

Barnes, Richard James *b. 1860 Lal Lal d. 7 Jan
1929 Wellington* New Zealand champion 1890 – 1,
1896 – 7, 1897 – 8, 1901 – 2, 1905 – 6 (after play-
off).

Barry, George Canadian champion 1887 (after
play-off).

Basman, Michael John *b. 16 Mar 1946 St Pancras,
London* IM 1980. British champion =1st 1973 but
lost play-off.

Battrum, M L Scottish women's champion 1947.

Baumbach, Friedrich *b. 8 Sept 1935 Weimar* IMC 1967. GMC 1973. East German champion 1970. World correspondence championship 1983 =2.

Baumstark, Gertrude Rosemaria *b. 21 May 1941 Timişoara* WIM 1970. Romanian women's champion 1967, 1981.

Becker, Georg Albert *b. 5 Sep 1896 Vienna d. 7 May 1984 Vicente Lopez* IM 1953. Austrian champion 1925 (joint).

Bednarski, Boguslaw Jacek *b. 12 Mar 1939 Myślenice* IM 1964. Polish champion 1963.

Belavenets, Lyudmila Sergeyevna *b. 7 Jun 1940 Moscow* IMC 1979. WIM 1977. WIMC 1979. USSR women's champion 1975. Daughter of next.

Belavenets, Sergei Vsevolodovich *b. 1910 d. 7 March 1942 Novgorod* Moscow champion 1932, 1937, 1938 (all joint).

Bellin, Robert *b. 30 Jun 1952 Great Yarmouth* IM 1977. British champion 1979 (on tie-break), equal 1st 1974 but lost play-off.

Bellón López, Juan Manuel *b. 8 May 1950 Valencia* IM 1974. GM 1979. Spanish champion 1969, 1971, 1974, 1977, 1982.

Belova see Borisenko V.

Belson, John Harold *b. 23 Feb 1906 Helsinki d. 13 Mar 1947 Toronto* Canadian champion 1934, 1946.

Belyavsky, Alexander Henrikhovich *b. 17 Dec 1953 Lvov* IM 1973. GM 1975. Candidate 1983, 1985. World junior champion 1973. USSR champion 1974, 1980 – 1 (both joint). Baden 1980 =1. Tilburg 1981 1. Tilburg 1984 =2. Wijk aan Zee 1984 =1. Wijk aan Zee 1985 =2.

Benger, Michael *b. 9 Dec 1910 d. 30 Sep 1980 Wandsworth* London champion 1934 – 5, 1937 – 8.

Benini, Clarice *b. 8 Jan 1905 Florence d. 8 Sep 1976* WIM 1950. Women's world championship challenger 1937, 1949 – 50.

Benjamin, Joel Lawrence *b. 11 March 1964 New York* IM 1980.

Benko, Pal Charles *b. 15 Jul 1928 Amiens* IM 1950. GM 1958. Candidate 1959, 1962. He also qualified as a candidate in 1970 but ceded his place to Fischer. Hungarian champion 1948.

Bennett, Gerald H Grand Prix (UK) champion 1974 (joint), Petit Prix champion 1975.

Bennett, Pat J *b. c.1942* Welsh champion 1960, 1961 (joint).

Benoit, Michel *b. 18 Jan 1949* French champion 1973.

Berea, Maria A *b. 13 Apr 1914 Brazil d. 5 Jul 1983* WIM 1952. Women's world championship challenger 1939.

Berghofer, Herbert Austrian champion 1931 (joint).

Bergkvist, Nils *b. 13 Aug 1900 Södertälje* Swedish champion 1933 (joint).

Bergraser, Volf *b. 4 Jan 1904 Nona Sulita* IMC 1959. GMC 1983. French champion 1957, 1966.

Berliner, Hans Jack *b. 27 Jan 1929 Berlin* GMC 1968. World correspondence champion 1968.

Berndtsson, Karl Mathias *b. 16 Mar 1892 Göteborg d. 29 Sep 1943 Göteborg* Swedish champion (tournament) 1918, 1920, 1921 (joint), 1926. Nordic champion 1928.

Bernstein, Ossip Samuel *b. 2 Oct 1882 Zhitomir d. 30 Nov 1962 France* GM 1950. Moscow champion 1911.

Beskow, Katarina (Sweden). Women's world championship challenger 1927, 1930, 1931, 1937.

Besser, Hans *b. 4 Feb 1935 Meissen* West German champion 1967 (joint).

Bhend, Edwin *b. 9 Sep 1931* IM 1960. Swiss champion 1966.

Bielicki, Carlos *b. 15 May 1940* IM 1959. World junior champion 1959.

Bigot, Louis French champion 1943.

Bikhovsky, Anatoly Avraamovich *b. 30 Apr 1934 Izhevsk* IM 1982. Moscow champion 1963.

Bilek, István *b. 11 Aug 1932 Budapest* IM 1958. GM 1962. Hungarian champion 1963, 1965, 1970.

Binham, Timothy Frank *b. 28 Dec 1956 Helsinki* IM 1983. Finnish champion 1984.

Birnberg, Jonas *b. c.1893 d. 29 May 1970 London* London champion 1924 – 5.

Birnboim, Nathan *b. 27 Nov 1950 Tel Aviv* IM 1978. Israeli champion 1976, 1980.

Bisguier, Arthur Bernard *b. 8 Oct 1929 New York* IM 1950. GM 1957. USA champion 1954.

Biyiasas, Peter *b. 19 Nov 1950 Athens* IM 1972. GM 1978. Canadian champion 1972, 1975, 1978.

Blackburne, Joseph Henry *b. 10 Dec 1841 Chorlton, Manchester d. 1 Sep 1924 Lewisham, London* British champion 1868 (after play-off), =1st 1914 but could not play-off. German champion 1881. London 1883 3.

Blake, Charles W *b. 12 Jun 1880 London d. after 1926 Toronto* Canadian champion =1st 1913 but lost play-off.

Blake, Joseph Henry *b. 3 Feb 1859 Farnborough, Hants d. 11 Dec 1951 Kingston-upon-Thames* British champion =1st 1909 but lost play-off. British correspondence champion 1922.

Blau, Max *b. 19 Dec 1918 Munich d. 1984* IM 1953. Swiss champion 1953, 1955, 1956, 1967.

Blieden, Max *b. 31 Oct 1870 Philadelphia*

d. *26 Aug 1964 Johannesburg* South African champion 1926, 1928.

Blumin, Boris *b. 29 Dec 1907 St Petersburg* Canadian champion 1936, 1937.

Bobotsov, Milko Georgiev *b. 30 Sep 1931 Plovdiv* IM 1960. GM 1961. Bulgarian champion 1958. Moscow 1967 =2.

Boey, Jozef Martin *b. 16 May 1934 Antwerp* IM 1973. IMC 1974. GMC 1975. World correspondence championship 1975 2.

Bogoljubow, Efim Dimitriewitsch *b. 14 Apr 1889 Kiev d. 18 Jun 1952 Triberg* World championship challenger 1929, 1934. German champion 1925, 1931, 1933, 1949. USSR champion 1924, 1925. Bled 1931 2.

Bohatirchuk, Fedor Parfenovich *b. 26 Nov 1892 Kiev d. 4 Sep 1984 Ottawa* IM 1954. IMC 1967. USSR champion 1927 (joint).

Bokhosyán, Sarkis Stepan *b. 27 Mar 1941 Plovdiv* IM 1978. Bulgarian champion 1972.

Bolbochán, Jácobo *b. 26 Dec 1906 Buenos Aires d. 1984* IM 1965. Argentine champion 1932, 1933.

Bolbochán, Julio *b. 20 Mar 1920 Buenos Aires* IM 1955. GM 1977. Argentine champion 1946, 1948.

Boleslavsky, Isaak Efremovich *b. 9 Jun 1919 Zolotonosha d. 15 Feb 1977 Minsk* GM 1950. Candidate 1950, 1953. Moscow 1966 2.

Bondarevsky, Igor Zakharovich *b. 12 May 1913 Rostov on Don d. 14 Jun 1979 Piatigorsk* GM 1950. GMC 1961. USSR champion 1940 (joint).

Bonham, Reginald Walter *b. 31 Jan 1906 St Neots d. 16 Mar 1984 Worcester* Blind world champion 1958. Correspondence blind world champion 1957, 1959, 1961, 1963, 1964 (joint), 1966. British correspondence champion 1943, 1947 (joint), 1951 (joint).

Bonner, Gerald *b. 1 May 1941 Glasgow* Scottish champion 1967, 1970, 1972.

Böök, Eero Einar *b. 9 Feb 1910 Helsinki* IM 1950. Emeritus GM 1984. Nordic champion 1947 (joint). Finnish champion 1931, 1934, 1934–5, 1936, 1945–6, 1963.

Borges, T P Acioli Brazilian champion 1935.

Borisenko, Georgy Konstantinovich *b. 25 May 1922 Zhivet* IMC 1961. GMC 1966. World correspondence championship 1965 2. USSR correspondence champion 1957, 1962 (both joint).

Borisenko, Valentina Mikhailovna (née Belova) *b. 28 Jan 1920 Cherepovets* WIM 1950. WGM 1978. Women's world championship challenger 1949–50. USSR women's champion 1945, 1955, 1957 (joint), 1960 (joint), 1962.

Borthwick, James *b. 3 Mar 1866 Leith d. 4 Aug 1932 Glasgow* Scottish champion 1903.

Botterill, George Steven *8 Jan 1949 Bradford* IM 1978. British champion 1974 (after play-off), 1977. Welsh champion 1973 (joint).

Botvinnik, Mikhail Moiseyevich *b. 17 Aug 1911 Kuokkala* GM 1950. World champion 1948–57, 1958–60, 1961–3. USSR champion 1931, 1933, 1939, 1941, 1944, 1945, 1952 (after play-off). Leningrad champion 1931, 1932. Moscow champion (*hors concours*) 1943–4. Moscow 1936 2. Nottingham 1936 =1. AVRO 1938 3. Moscow 1956 =1.

Boultbee, William H *b. 1832 England d. 5 Nov 1902 Toronto* Canadian champion 1892.

Bourdillon, Dorothea ('Dodie') D.A.H. *b.c. 1918 d. 1968 Kensington* British women's champion = 1st 1958 but lost play-off.

Bourke, Patrick Martin Austin *b. 10 May 1913* Irish champion 1951.

Bourne, Brian Peter *b. 19 Nov 1927 London* Welsh champion 1956.

Boutteville, César *b. 24 Jun 1917 Thin-Hao, Vietnam* French champion 1945, 1950, 1954, 1955, 1959, 1967.

Boyarkov, V A Moscow champion 1902.

Boyd, Frank *b. 16 Sep 1935* IMC 1981. British correspondence champion 1972.

Brandler, Anneliese *b. 4 Mar 1904 Hamburg* German women's champion 1962.

Brekke, Jacob E Norwegian champion 1919, 1920, 1923, 1925.

Breyer, Gyula *b. 30 Apr 1893 Budapest d. 9 Nov 1921 Bratislava* Hungarian champion 1912.

Brinck-Claussen, Bjørn *b. 29 Jan 1942, Copenhagen* Danish champion 1966, 1970 (after play-off), 1977. Nordic champion 1963.

Briscombe, Beryl (now B Jarman) *b. 4 Nov 1931 Rhondda* Welsh women's champion 1975.

Broadbent, Reginald Joseph *b. 3 Aug 1906 Durban, South Africa* British champion 1948, 1950. Equal 1st 1947 but lost play-off.

Brockett, J Scottish women's champion 1925–6, 1926–7, 1939.

Bronstein, David Ionovich *b. 19 Feb 1924 Belaya Tserkov* GM 1950. Challenger 1951. Candidate 1956. Moscow 1959 =1. Teesside 1975 =3. USSR champion 1948, 1949 (both joint). Moscow champion 1946, 1953, 1957, 1961, 1968 (joint), 1982 (joint).

Brown, E British correspondence champion 1951 (joint).

Browne, Walter Shawn *b. 10 Jan 1949 Sydney* IM 1969. GM 1970. USA champion 1974, 1975, 1977, 1980 (joint), 1981, 1983 (joint). Australian champion 1968–9. German champion 1975. Chicago 1982 2. Gjovik 1983 =1. Wijk aan Zee 1983 =3. Naestved 1985 =1.

Bruce, Rowena Mary (née Dew) *b. 15 May 1919 Plymouth* WIM 1951. World junior women's champion 1935. British women's champion 1937 (as Dew), 1950 (after play-off), 1951, 1954, 1959, 1960, 1962, 1963. Joint champion 1955, 1967, 1969. =1st 1946 but lost play-off.

Brunker, Hazel *b. 16 Oct 1932 Bedlinog* Welsh women's champion 1969 (joint), 1970, 1972, 1973, 1982 (joint), 1985.

Brustman, Agnieszka *b. 31 Jul 1962 Warsaw* WIM 1979. WGM 1985. World junior women's champion 1982. European junior women's champion 1980.

Brynhammer, Karl Hilding Nikolaus (né Persson) *b. 26 Jul 1904 Stensele* Swedish correspondence champion 1940, 1944.

Bryntse, Arne *b. 8 Mar 1916* Swedish correspondence champion 1972.

Bryson, Douglas M *b. 12 Mar 1957* British correspondence champion 1983, 1984, 1985.

Budzinski, N Welsh women's champion 1957, 1958 (joint).

Bullen, Honor World junior women's champion 1931, 1932, 1933.

Burchardt-Hoffmann, Brigitte *b. 17 Oct 1954 Weissenfels* WIM 1975.

Burn, Amos *b. 31 Dec 1848 Hull, Yorks d. 25 Nov 1925 Hammersmith, London* British champion =1st 1870 but lost play-off. German champion 1898.

Bykova, Elizavyeta Ivanovna *b. 4 Nov 1911 Bogoliubovo* WIM 1950. WGM 1976. Women's world champion 1953–6, 1958–62. Challenger 1949–50. USSR women's champion 1947, 1948, 1950.

Byrne, Robert Eugene *b. 20 Apr 1928 New York* IM 1952. GM 1964. Candidate 1974. USA champion 1972.

Cabarkapa, Milenko *b. 24 Jul 1938 Krupice* Blind world champion 1966, 1970.

Cabrera, Armando Cuban champion 1956.

Cafferty, Bernard *b. 27 Jun 1934 Blackburn* British correspondence champion 1960.

Cairncross, J British correspondence champion 1947 (joint).

Caldwell, Susan Linda *b. 2 Oct 1958 Weston* British women's champion =1st 1978 but lost play-off.

Calero, Carlos Cuban champion 1955.

Câmara, Hélder *b. 7 Feb 1937 Fortaleza* IM 1972. Brazilian champion 1963, 1968.

Câmara, Ronald *b. 11 Apr 1927 Fortaleza.* Brazilian champion 1960, 1961.

Cameron, Arthur James Aveling *b. 1872 London*

d. 1928 Cape Town South African champion 1920 (joint).

Campora, Daniel Hugo *b. 30 Jun 1957 San Nicolás* IM 1982.

Campos Moreno, Javier Benito *b. 6 Mar 1959 Santiago* IM 1979. Chilean champion 1979, 1980 (both after play-off).

Canal, Estaban *b. 19 Apr 1896 Chiclayo d. 14 Feb 1981 Varese* IM 1950. Emeritus GM 1977. Hungarian champion 1933.

Capablanca, José Raúl *b. 19 Nov 1888 Havana d. 8 Mar 1942 New York* World champion 1921–7. San Sebastián 1911 1. St Petersburg 1914 2. New York 1924 2. New York 1927 1. Berlin 1928 1. Moscow 1936 1. Nottingham 1936 =1. Semmering-Baden 1937 =3.

Cappello, Guido *b. 14 Apr 1933 Pisa* Italian champion 1960.

Carls, Carl Johan Margot *b. 16 Sep 1880 Varel d. 11 Sep 1958 Bremen* IM 1951. German champion 1934.

Carrasco de Budinich, B *b. 19 Dec 1914 Chile* WIM 1954. Women's world championship challenger 1939.

Carvahlo, Flavio de Brazilian champion 1952.

Castaldi, Vincenzo *b. 15 May 1916 Marradi d. 6 Jan 1970 Florence* IM 1950. Italian champion 1936, 1937, 1947 (after play-off), 1948 (after play-off), 1953, 1959 (after play-off).

Castillo Larenas, Mariano *b. 25 Dec 1905 Santiago* Chilean champion 1924, 1926, 1927, 1929, 1934, 1940, 1948, 1949, 1953.

Cebalo, Mišo *b. 6 Feb 1945 Zagreb* IM 1978. GM 1985.

Chaikovskaya, Alla Mikhailovna *b. 21 Jun 1934 Zaporozhe* WIM 1962. USSR women's champion 1968 (joint).

Chambers, John D *b. c.1842 d. June 1930 Cardiff* Scottish champion 1891.

Chandler, Clifford R *b. 18 Jul 1955 Edmonton* British correspondence champion 1982.

Chandler, Murray Graham *b. 4 Apr 1960 Wellington* IM 1977. GM 1983. New Zealand champion 1975–6. Commonwealth champion 1984 (joint). London 1984 =2. London 1986 =2.

Charlick, Henry *b. 8 July 1845 London d. 26 July 1916 Adelaide* Australian champion 1887. =1st 1888 but lost play-off.

Charousek, Rezsö *b. 19 Sep 1873 Prague d. 18 Apr 1900 Nagytétény* Budapest 1896 =1st but second after play-off.

Chaudé de Silans, Chantal *b. 9 Mar 1919 Versailles* WIM 1950. Women's world championship challenger 1949–50.

Chavkin, Alexander *b. 1892 Sagar, Lithuania d. 27 May 1946 Johannesburg* South African champion 1920 (joint), 1924.

Chekhov, Valery Alexandrovich *b. 27 Nov 1955* IM 1975. GM 1984,. World junior champion 1975.

Chekhover, Vitaly Alexandrovich *b. 22 Dec 1908 St Petersburg d. 11 Feb 1965 Leningrad* IM 1950. IMComp 1961. Leningrad champion 1937 (joint), 1949.

Chepurnov, Anatoly Alexeyevich (Tschepurnoff) *b. 19 Oct 1871 Loviisa d. 29 Apr 1942 Helsinki* Finnish champion 1922, 1928.

Cherepkov, Alexander Vasilyevich *b. 30 Oct 1920* IM 1984. Leningrad champion 1967, 1968 (after play-off), 1982 (after play-off).

Chernin, Alexander Mikhailovich *b. 6 Feb 1960* IM 1980. GM 1985. Candidate 1985. USSR champion 1985. European junior champion 1979 – 80.

Chéron, André *b. 25 Sep 1895 Colombes d. 12 Sep 1980 Leysin* IMComp 1959. French champion 1926, 1927, 1929.

Chesters, Graham H *b. c.1944* Welsh champion 1964, 1970 (joint).

Chevaldonnet, François *b. 22 Jul 1950 Reims* French champion 1976.

Chiburdanidze, Maia Grigoryevna *b. 17 Jan 1961 Kutaisi* IM1978. WIM 1974. WGM 1977. Women's world champion 1978 to date. USSR women's champion 1977. Women's Oscar 1984, 1985.

Chigorin, Mikhail Ivanovich *b. 12 Nov 1850 Gatchina d. 25 Jan 1908 Lublin* Challenger 1889, 1892. Russian champion 1899, 1901, 1903. Hastings 1895 2. Budapest 1896 1 (after play-off).

Chistyakov, Alexander Nikolayevich *b. 22 Jan 1914 Moscow* Moscow champion 1950 (joint).

Christensen, Emma Danish women's champion 1955.

Christensen, Inger Danish women's champion 1964.

Christiansen, Larry Mark *b. 27 Jun 1956 Riverside* GM 1981. USA champion 1980, 1983 (both joint). Linares 1981 =1.

Christoffel, Martin *b. 2 Sep 1922 Basel* IM 1952. Swiss champion 1942 (joint), 1943, 1945, 1948, 1952.

Christoffersen, H C Norwegian champion 1926, 1929, 1936.

Christoph, Manfred *b. 28 May 1931 Düsseldorf* West German champion 1969.

Cifuentes, Pilar Spanish women's champion 1953, 1955.

Cifuentes Parada, Roberto *b. 21 Dec 1957 Santiago.* IM 1984. Chilean champion 1982, 1983, 1984, 1985.

Ciocâltea, Victor *b. 16 Jan 1932 Bucharest d. 10 Sep 1983 Manresa* IM 1957. GM 1979. Romanian champion 1952, 1959, 1961, 1969, 1970, 1971, 1975, 1979.

Clarke, Margaret Eileen Elizabeth (née Wood) *b. 29 Oct 1937 Sutton Coldfield* British women's champion (joint) 1966.

Clarke, Peter Hugh *b. 18 Mar 1933 London* IMC 1976. GMC 1980. British correspondence champion 1977.

Cleland, Robert Alexander *b. 1854 d. 6 Jul 1923 Dunedin* New Zealand champion 1898 – 9.

Coast, Peter Scottish champion 1959.

Cobo Arteaga, Eldis *b. 5 Sep 1929* IM 1967. Cuban champion 1950 (joint).

Combe, Robert Forbes *b. 16 Aug 1912 Logie-Buchan d. 12 Feb 1952 Aberdeen* British champion 1946.

Condie, Mark L *b. 12 Feb 1965* IM 1984.

Conquest, Stuart *b. 1 Mar 1967, Ilford* IM 1985. World under-16 champion 1981.

Contedini, Ennio *b. 8 Oct 1934 Milan* Italian champion 1963.

Cooper, John Grantley *b. 14 May 1954 Cardiff* IM 1984. Welsh champion 1976 (joint), 1978 (joint), 1983 – 4, 1984 – 5.

Corrodi, Oswald *d. 1893 Zurich* Swiss champion 1892 (joint).

Corzo y Principe, Juan *b. 24 Jun 1873 Madrid d. 27 Sep 1941 Havana* Cuban champion 1902.

Coull, Alison Jane *b. 20 Mar 1967 St Andrews, Fife* Scottish women's champion 1983.

Court, Roger A *b. 1935* New Zealand champion 1963 – 4.

Cox, Thomas *b. c.1912 d. 1939* Irish champion 1937, 1938.

Crackanthorp, Spencer *b. 17 Feb 1885 Sydney d. 1 Aug 1936 Sydney* Australian champion 1923 – 4, 1925 – 6, 1926, 1927

Cramling, Dan *b. 5 Feb 1959 Stockholm* IM 1982. Swedish champion 1981.

Cramling, Pia A R-D *b. 23 Apr 1963 Stockholm* IM 1983. WGM 1982. Women's Oscar 1983.

Crane, William *b. 14 Apr 1851 Parramatta d. 23 Apr 1920 Sydney* Australian champion 1888 (after play-off), 1897.

Cranston, T G *b. c.1877 Dublin* Irish champion 1922, 1931.

Creevey, James C Irish champion 1933, 1934.

Crépeaux, Robert *b. 24 Oct 1900 Grasse* French champion 1924, 1925, 1941.

Lloyds Bank 1982, and 19-year-old Pia Cramling looks wistful. (John Stone/Lloyds Bank)

Crum, A M Scottish women's champion 1935, 1946, 1948, 1949.

Crum, John *b. 1842 d. 27 Apr 1922 Edinburgh* Scottish champion 1884.

Cruz, Walter Oswaldo *b. 1910 Petrópolis d. 1967 Rio de Janeiro* Brazilian champion 1938, 1940, 1942, 1948, 1949, 1953.

Csom, István *b. 2 Jun 1940 Sátoraljaújhely* IM 1967. GM 1973. Hungarian champion 1972, 1973 (joint).

Cuevas, María Luisa Spanish women's champion 1985.

Cummings, David H *b. 24 Jan 1961* IM 1984.

Cunliffe, Steve D British correspondence champion 1979 (joint).

Cunninghame, A D Smith Scottish women's champion 1908, 1914 – 15.

Curling, Grace (née Ellis) British women's champion 1908 (after play-off).

Curtin, Eugene *b. 3 Apr 1960 Athlone* Irish champion 1984, = 1st 1985.

Curtis, Donald A *b. 16 Oct 1935 Cardiff* Welsh champion 1959.

Cvenkel-Alkalaj, Slavica *b. 6 June 1919 Ljubljana* Yugoslav women's champion 1949 (joint).

Cvitan, Ognjen *b. 10 Oct 1961 Šibenik* IM 1982. World junior champion 1981.

Czerniak, Moshe *b. 3 Feb 1910 Warsaw d. 31 Aug 1984 Tel Aviv* IM 1952. Israeli champion 1936, 1938, 1955.

Daniel, Roger *b. 18 May 1915 Le Havre* French champion 1942.

Danielsson, Gösta Erik Vilhelm *b. 24 Jun 1912 Helenelund d. 17 Oct 1978 Knivsta* Swedish champion 1933 (joint), 1955.

Darga, Klaus Viktor *b. 24 Feb 1934 Pankow* IM 1957. GM 1964. West German champion 1955, 1961. Winnipeg 1967 = 1.

Da Silva, Luis Tavares *b. 13 Apr 1916 Recife* Brazilian champion 1957.

Da Silva Rocha, A Brazilian champion 1941.

Daunke, M (Germany). Women's world championship challenger 1927.

D'Autremont, L (France). Women's world championship challenger 1933.

Davey, S C British correspondence champion 1957, 1961 (joint).

Davie, Alexander Munro *b. 4 Apr 1946 Broughty Ferry, Dundee* Scottish champion 1964, 1966, 1969.

Davies, Arthur William Oswald *b. 1875 UK d. 16 Jan 1928 Auckland* New Zealand champion 1904 – 5, 1908, 1926 – 7, 1927 – 8 (after play-off).

Davies, G H British correspondence champion 1975 (joint).

Davies, Mary Elizabeth *b. 11 Oct 1925 Barry* Welsh women's champion 1974.

Davies, Nigel Rodney *b. 31 Jul 1960 Southport* IM 1982.

Davison, A T Canadian champion 1891, 1894.

De Firmian, Nicholas Ernest *b. 26 Jul 1957 Fresno* IM 1979. GM 1985.

De Freitas, Marcío Elísio *b. 26 Nov 1925 Belo Horizonte* Brazilian champion 1947.

Delaney, John Anthony *b. 27 Jun 1962 Dublin* Irish champion 1982 (on tie-break).

Delaney, Paul *b. 3 Jul 1956 Dublin* Irish champion 1980.

De Lange, Daan *b. 4 Aug 1915* Norwegian champion 1960.

De La Villa, Jesús *b. 30 Aug 1958 Palencia* Spanish champion 1985.

Dely, Péter *b. 5 July 1934 Sárospatak* IM 1982. Hungarian champion 1969.

Denker, Arnold Sheldon *b. 21 Feb 1914 New York* IM 1950. Emeritus GM 1981. USA champion 1944.

Devenney, Ray *b. 1947 Belfast* Irish champion 1977 (joint).

De Vere, Cecil (real name Valentine Brown) *b. 14 Feb 1845 d. 9 Feb 1875 Torquay* British champion 1866. = 1st 1868 and 1872 but lost play-offs.

De Villiers, Charles *b. 25 Mar 1953 Cape Town* South African champion 1975 (joint), 1977 (joint), 1981, 1985 (joint).

Diesen, Mark Carl *b. 16 Sep 1957 Buffalo* IM 1976. World junior champion 1976.

Diez del Corral, Jesús *b. 6 Apr 1933 Saragossa* IM

1967. GM 1974. Spanish champion 1955, 1965.

Dimitrov, Krstiu Krstev b. 6 Feb 1916 Bulgarian champion 1949.

Dlugy, Maxim b. 29 Jan 1966 Moscow IM 1982. World junior champion 1985.

Dobson, Dinah Margaret (later Wright, then Norman) b. 21 Aug 1946 Exeter British women's champion 1968, joint champion 1967, 1969. Grand Prixette (UK) 1976 (as Wright).

Doda, Zbigniew b. 22 Feb 1931 Poznań IM 1964. Polish champion 1964, 1967 (after play-off), 1968.

Dodson, Peter B British correspondence champion 1964.

Dolmatov, Sergei Viktorovich b. 20 Feb 1959 Kiselevsk IM 1978. GM 1982. World junior champion 1978.

Donchev, Dimitar Ivanov b. 21 Jul 1958 Sofia IM 1980. Bulgarian champion 1983 (after play-off).

Donner, Johannes Hendrikus b. 26 July 1927 The Hague IM 1952. GM 1959. Netherlands champion 1954, 1957, 1958.

Donoso Velasco, Pedro H b. 26 Feb 1944 Santiago Chilean champion 1970, 1977, 1978.

Dorfman, Iosif Davidovich b. 1 May 1952 IM 1977. GM 1978. USSR champion 1977 (joint).

Doulton, Joan British women's champion (joint) 1955.

Douthwaite, Brian V Welsh champion 1958.

Doyle, Anthony b. 13 Jul 1949 Dublin Irish champion 1974.

Drewitt, John Arthur James b. 17 Oct 1873 Patching d. 19 Mar 1931 Hastings London champion 1927, 1928, 1929–30.

Dreyer, Kurt b. 31 Jul 1909 Bielefeld d. 29 Sep 1981 Johannesburg South African champion 1937 (after play-off), 1945–6 (joint).

Dreyev, Alexei World under-16 champion 1983, 1984.

Dubinin, Peter Vasilyevich b. 30 Jun 1909 Gorky d. 1983 IM 1950. GMC 1962. World correspondence championship 1962 2. USSR correspondence champion 1957 (joint).

Dückstein, Andreas b. 2 Aug 1927 Budapest Austrian champion 1954, 1956, 1977.

Duhan, H South African champion 1910.

Duhm, Andreas b. 22 Aug 1883 Basel d. 23 Nov 1975 Heidelberg Swiss champion 1900, 1901 (joint), 1913.

Duhm, Dietrich b. c.1880 d. 22 Jul 1954 Gailingen am Hochrhein Swiss champion 1907, 1914 (both joint).

Duhm, Hans Swiss champion 1896 (joint), 1901 (joint).

Duignan, P A Irish champion 1947.

Dünhaupt, Heinz Wilhelm b. 7 May 1912 Bückeberg IMC 1963. GMC 1973. German correspondence champion 1975.

Dunlop, John Boyd b. 10 Oct 1886 Dunedin New Zealand champion 1920–1 (after play-off), 1921–2, 1922–3 (after play-off), 1933–4 (after play-off), 1938–9, 1939–40.

Dünmann, A (aka Delmar) Austrian champion 1924.

Dunne, David b. 27 Feb 1959 Dublin Irish champion 1983, (joint) both 1979 and 1981.

Dunphy, William Richard b. 5 Sep 1929 Australia d. Mar 1985, Hastings Irish champion =1st 1957, lost tie-break.

Duras, Oldřich b. 30 Oct 1882 Prague d. 5 Jan 1957 Prague GM 1950. Czech champion 1905, 1909, 1911. German champion 1912 (joint). St Petersburg 1909 =3.

Dvoretsky, Mark Izraelivich b. 9 Dec 1947 Moscow IM 1975. Moscow champion 1973.

Dzindzikhashvili, Roman Yakovlevich b. 5 May 1944 Tbilisi IM 1970. GM 1977. Israeli champion 1977. USA champion 1983. Geneva 1977 =3. Amsterdam 1978 =3. Tilburg 1978 =3.

Eastman, Charles John George (né Ostman) b. 4 Mar 1903 Stockholm d. 16 May 1975 Detroit Canadian champion =1st 1931 but lost play-off.

Ebbett, D British correspondence champion 1975 (joint).

Edwards, Joseph b. c.1857 d. 25 Jul 1922 Dunedin New Zealand champion 1893–4.

Ehlvest, Jaan b. 14 Oct 1962 IM 1982. European junior champion 1982–3.

Ehrat, Jules b. 1905 Lohn Swiss champion 1942 (joint).

Eidenfeldt, Gunnar b. 1913 d. 29 Apr 1982 Swedish correspondence champion 1952.

Einhorn, Viacheslav Semyenovich b. 23 Nov 1956 IM 1984.

Ek, Hans b. 6 Oct 1928 Jönköping Swedish correspondence champion 1967.

Ekenberg, Bengt August Edvard b. 27 Jun 1912 Göteborg Swedish champion 1943, 1962.

Ekström, Nils Johan Folke b. 12 Oct 1906 Lund IM 1950. IMC 1971. Swedish champion 1947, 1948. Swedish correspondence champion 1941, 1964, 1971.

Elder, Nancy Conchar (née Gordon) b. 25 May 1915 Kirkmabreck, Kirkcudbright d. 4 Mar 1981 Perth Australia Scottish women's champion 1950 (as Gordon), 1956 (jointly), 1957, 1958, 1961, 1962, 1963, 1964, 1966, 1967, 1968, 1970, 1971, 1972, 1973, 1980.

Eley, Brian Ratcliffe b. c.Aug 1946 Don Valley British champion 1972.

Tal

All too briefly world champion, the biggest enemy of physician's son Tal is his health. Perhaps the main cause of his defeat after only one year at the top is a kidney weakness, not helped by alcohol and tobacco. It forced him to retire from the 1962 Candidates tournament but in 1969 a kidney was removed and he has been in better shape since.

Tal shot to the top and seized the admiration of the chess world because of his astonishing tactical creativity. Never had there been a player who combined such imagination and skill. His style of play appeals to the gallery. The top players may be less impressed and indeed Korchnoi said that his attacks are all routine, but when he became the youngest world champion up to then, in 1970, it was a popular outcome. Botvinnik wrote: 'By that time everybody was pretty fed up with me, most of all my fellow grandmasters. For just how long can one occupy the chess throne?'

Tal set another record by losing the title after only a year and five days. Botvinnik had cracked Tal's secret which was to throw the game always into its most complicated line when his unmatched speed of calculation would find resources that escaped his opponent. However, Tal still ranks highly (14 at Jan 1986).

Tal at the 1982 Olympiad. (Stephane Bureau)

Eliskases, Erich Gottlieb *b. 15 Feb 1913 Innsbruck* IM 1950. GM 1952. Austrian champion 1929 (joint). Hungarian champion 1934. German champion 1938, 1939.

Eller, August *b. 1907* Estonian champion 1944 (joint).

Ellis see Curling

Elstner, Rudolf *b. 13 Oct 1893 Berlin d. 12 Aug 1966 Berlin* East German champion 1950.

Emma, Jaime J *b. 17 Jan 1938* IM 1978. Argentine champion 1978.

Endzelins, Lucius *b. 21 May 1909 Tartu d. 27 Oct 1981 Adelaide* GMC 1959. World correspondence championship 1959 =2. Australian champion 1960.

Enevoldsen, Antonina Danish women's champion 1951, 1954, 1968.

Enevoldsen, Harald *b. 27 Jan 1911 Aalborg* Danish champion =1st 1951 but lost play-off.

Enevoldsen, Jens *b. 23 Sep 1907 Copenhagen d. 23 May 1980* Danish champion 1940 (after play-off), 1943, 1947 (after play-off), 1948, 1960. =1st 1939, lost play-off. =1st 1950 lost lottery.

Englisch, Berthold *b. 9 Jul 1851 Holtzenplatz d. 19 Oct 1897 Vienna* German champion 1879.

Ensor, Albert W Canadian champion 1873.

Entefält, see Eszik

Erdelyi, Stefan *b. 17 Nov 1905 Timişoara d. 26 Oct 1968 Resita* IM 1950. Romanian champion 1931, 1934, 1949.

Erichsen, A M Norwegian champion 1922.

Eriksen, John E South African champion 1953.

Ermenkov, Yevgeny Petkov *b. 29 Sep 1949 Sofia* IM 1974. GM 1977. Bulgarian champion 1973, 1975 (after play-off), 1976, 1979 (after play-off), 1984 (joint).

Erskine, John Angus *b. 29 Jan 1873 Invercargill d. 27 Apr 1960 Melbourne* New Zealand champion 1928 – 9, 1934 – 5.

Esling, Frederick Karl *b. 20 Jul 1860 Creswick d. 31 Jul 1955 Melbourne* Australian champion 1885.

Espig, Lutz *b. 5 Jan 1949 Griez* IM 1972. GM 1983. East German champion 1969, 1971.

Estéves Morales, Guillermo *b. 16 Oct 1947* IM 1972. Cuban champion 1975.

Estrin, Yakov Borisovich *b. 21 Apr 1923 Moscow* IM 1975. GM 1984. IMC 1965. GMC 1966. World correspondence champion 1971 3, 1975 1. USSR correspondence champion 1962 (joint).

Eszik, Lajos (now Lars Entefält) *b. 22 Sep 1935 Hungary* Swedish correspondence champion 1985.

Etruk, Rein Toomas *b. 22 Mar 1938* Estonian champion 1965 (after play-off), 1969.

Euwe, Machgielis *b. 20 May 1901 Amsterdam d. 26 Nov 1981 Amsterdam* GM 1950. World champion 1935 – 7. Challenger 1948. Candidate 1953. World amateur champion 1928. Netherlands champion 1921, 1924, 1926, 1929, 1933, 1938, 1939, 1942, 1947, 1948, 1950, 1952, 1955. Nottingham 1936 =3.

Evans, Deborah (later Cooper) *b. 18 Feb 1961 Bangor* Welsh women's champion 1977, 1979.

Evans, Larry Melvyn *b. 22 Mar 1932 New York* IM 1952. GM 1957. USA champion 1951, 1961 – 2, 1968, 1980 (joint).

Fahrni, Hans *b. 1 Oct 1874 Prague d. 28 May 1939 Ostermundingen* Swiss champion 1892 (joint).

Faibisovich, Vadim Zelmanovich *b. 8 May 1944 Perm* Leningrad champion 1965 (after play-off), 1969, 1977.

Fairhurst, William Albert *b. 21 Aug 1903 Alderley Edge d. 13 Mar 1982 Auckland* IM 1951. Scottish champion 1932, 1932 – 3, 1933 – 4, 1935 – 6, 1936 – 7, 1938, 1946, 1947, 1948, 1949, 1962. British champion 1937. Unofficial Commonwealth champion 1950.

Falk, Raphael Alexandrovich *b. Jul 1856 Liepaja d. 27 Apr 1913 Tübingen* Moscow champion 1901 (joint).

Fallone, Michael Scottish champion 1963.

Farago, Clara (Hungary). Women's world championship challenger 1937.

Farago, Ivan *1 Apr 1946 Budapest* IM 1974. GM 1976.

Fatalibekova, Yelena Abramova (née Rubtsova) *b. 4 Oct 1947 Moscow* WIM 1977. WGM 1977. USSR women's champion 1974.

Fatima *b. ?Pakistan* British women's champion 1933.

Fazekas, Stefan *b. 23 Mar 1898 Sátoraljaújhely, Hungary d. 3 May 1967 Buckhurst Hill, Essex* IM 1953. IMC 1964. British champion 1957.

Feigin, Movsa *b. 28 Feb 1908 Daugavpils d. 11 Aug 1950 Buenos Aires* Latvian champion 1932 (after play-off).

Feneridis, Arcadios *b. Russia* New Zealand champion 1956 – 7 (joint).

Fernandez Leon, José Cuban champion 1944, 1976.

Fernández Fernández, Angel *b. 18 Apr 1942 Siones* Spanish champion 1967.

Ferrer Lucas, Pepita *b. 7 May 1938 Barcelona* WIM 1974. Spanish women's champion 1961, 1963, 1969, 1971, 1972, 1973, 1974, 1976.

Fichtl, Jiří *b. 16 Feb 1921* IM 1959. Czech champion 1950 (joint), 1960 (after play-off).

Filip, Miroslav *b. 27 Oct 1928 Prague* IM 1953. GM 1955. Candidate 1956, 1962. Czech champion 1950 (joint), 1952, 1954.

Fine, Reuben b. 11 Oct 1914 New York GM 1950. Nottingham 1936 = 3. Semmering-Baden 1937 2. AVRO 1938 = 1.

Finn, Kate Belinda b. 16 Dec 1870 d. 8 Mar 1932 Kensington, London British women's champion 1904, 1905.

Fischer, Robert James b. 9 Mar 1943 Chicago IM 1957. GM 1958. World champion 1972 – 5. Candidate 1959, 1962. USA champion 1957 – 8, 1958 – 9, 1959 – 60, 1960 – 1, 1962 – 3, 1963 – 4, 1965, 1966. Chess Oscar 1970, 1971, 1972. Bled 1961 2. Santa Monica 1966 2. Palma de Majorca 1970 1. Rovinj-Zagreb 1970 1.

Fišerová, Nelly (Czechoslovakia). Women's world championship challenger 1937.

Fiter, J Blind world correspondence champion 1975 – 6.

Flatau, Leo Hans b. 9 Feb 1934 Aachen German correspondence champion 1967.

Flatow, Alfred b. 28 Aug 1937 Berlin Australian champion 1969 – 70.

Flear, Glenn Curtis b. 12 Feb 1959 Leicester IM 1983. London 1986 1.

Flemming, Richard F Canadian champion 1889 (after play-off).

Flohr, Salomon Mikhailovich b. 21 Nov 1908 Gorodenka d. 18 Jul 1983 Moscow GM 1950. Candidate 1950. Moscow 1936 3. Czech champion 1933 (after play-off), 1936.

Flondor, Tudor b. 11 Jun 1929 Cernauti d. 12 Dec 1952 Bucharest Romanian champion 1951 (joint).

Flores Alvarez, Rodrigo b. 23 Aug 1913 Santiago Chilean champion 1931, 1935, 1941, 1944, 1950, 1952, 1956, 1961, 1965.

Flórián, Tibor (né Feldmann) b. 2 Mar 1919 Budapest IM 1950. Hungarian champion 1945.

Flörow-Bulhak, Barbara (Poland) Women's world championship challenger 1937.

Flum, Gerhard b. 18 Mar 1931 Wildbad German correspondence champion 1964.

Foggie, R P Scottish women's champion 1953, 1955.

Foisor, Ovidiu b. 6 Apr 1959 Iaşi IM 1982. Romanian champion 1982.

Foltys, Jan b. 13 Oct 1908 Svinov d. 11 Mar 1952 Ostrava IM 1950. Czech champion 1940, 1943 (joint).

Footner, J K British correspondence champion 1976.

Forbes, M C Scottish women's champion 1920, 1935 – 6.

Forgács, Léo (né Fleischmann) b. 5 Oct 1881 Budapest d. 17 Aug 1930 Berettyóújfalu Hungarian champion 1907.

Forhaug, G Swedish champion 1933 (joint).

Forintos, Gyözö Victor b. 30 July 1935 Budapest IM 1963. GM 1974. Hungarian champion 1968 – 9.

Forsyth, David b. 16 May 1854 Alness, Scotland d. 30 Dec 1909 Dunedin New Zealand champion 1901.

Forwell, M Scottish women's champion 1976.

Foulds, Fred Alex b. 15 Sep 1932 Auckland New Zealand champion 1955 – 6, 1958 – 9 (joint).

Fox, Maurice b. 14 Jan 1898 London Canadian champion 1927, 1929, 1931 (after play-off), 1932, 1935, 1938, 1940, 1948.

Fraguela Gil, José Miguel b. 7 Dec 1953 Las Palmas IM 1977. Spanish champion 1975.

Fraser, George Brunton b. 1831 d. 1 Dec 1905 Wormit, Fife Scottish champion 1898.

Fred, Jalo Aatos b. 11 Apr 1917 Pori Finnish champion 1946 – 7, 1955 (after play-off).

Fredericia, Louise b. c.1971 Danish women's champion 1984, 1985.

Friedemann, Gunnar b. 1909 d. 1943 Estonian champion 1932 – 3.

Friedgood, David b. 11 Jul 1946 Cape Town South African champion 1967, 1971, 1973.

Frigard, Marie Jeanne (France). Women's world championship challenger 1927.

Ftáčnik, Lubomír b. 30 Oct 1957 Bratislava IM 1977. GM 1980. Czech champion 1981, 1982, 1983, 1985. European junior champion 1976 – 7.

Fuchs, Reinhart b. 28 Sep 1934 Berlin IM 1962. East German champion 1953, 1956.

Fuderer, Andrija b. 13 May 1931 Subotica IM 1952. Yugoslav champion 1953 (joint).

Fuller, John A b. 12 May 1928 British correspondence champion 1954, 1955.

Fuller, Maxwell Leonard b. 28 Jan 1945 Sydney Australian champion 1971 – 2 (joint).

Furman, Semyen Abramovich b. 1 Dec 1920 Moscow d. 17 Mar 1978 Leningrad IM 1954. GM 1966. Leningrad champion 1953, 1957 (joint). Bad Lauterberg 1977 3.

Fuss, Immo b. 1910 Austrian champion 1933.

Füster, Géza b. 19 Feb 1910 Budapest IM 1969. Hungarian champion 1941.

Gadia, Olício b. 2 July 1928 Campinas Brazilian champion 1959, 1962.

Gale, Sydney Eugene b. c.1893 British Guiana d. 23 Sep 1950 Lansing Canadian champion 1920.

Galia, Karl b. 1916 Austrian champion 1948.

Gallego, Julita Spanish women's champion 1979.

Gaprindashvili, Nona Terentievna b. 3 May 1941 Zugdidi IM 1962. GM 1980. WIM 1961. WGM 1976. Women's world champion 1962–78, USSR women's champion 1964, 1973 – 4, 1981 (joint), 1983. Women's Oscar 1982.

Garbett, Paul A b. 18 Dec 1952 New Zealand champion 1974 – 5, 1982 – 3 (joint), 1983 – 4.

García, Nieves b. 23 Jul 1955 Madrid WIM 1978. Spanish women's champion 1975, 1977, 1978, 1981, 1982, 1984.

García, Raimundo b. 27 May 1936 IM 1964. Argentine champion 1963.

García González, Guillermo 9 Dec 1953 Las Villas IM 1974. GM 1976. Cuban champion 1974, 1976, 1983.

García Martínez, Silvino b. 4 Jul 1944 Havana IM 1969. GM 1975. Cuban champion 1968 (after play-off), 1970, 1973, 1979 – 80.

García Padrón, José b. 23 Mar 1958 Las Palmas Spanish champion 1953.

García Padrón, Maria de Pino b. 23 Aug 1961 Arucas Spanish women's champion 1980, 1983.

García Palermo, Carlos H b. 2 Dec 1953 La Plata IM 1981. GM 1985.

Garwell, Jane b. 16 Jun 1961 Solihull British women's champion 1982. Welsh women's champion 1976, 1978, 1980, 1981 (joint), 1983.

Gattie, Walter Montague b. 21 Jul 1854 London d. 17 Nov 1907 Bournemouth British champion (amateur) 1886.

Gauffin, Thorsten b. 2 Jun 1901 Turku d. 28 Nov 1970 Turku Finnish champion 1937.

Gavrikov, Viktor Nikolayevich b. 29 Sep 1957 GM 1984. USSR champion 1985.

Gavrilovic, Mikhail b. Belgrade Welsh champion 1968 (joint), 1969, 1970 (joint).

Geller, Uzi b. 27 Jan 1931 Givat-Chaim Israeli champion 1971 – 2.

Geller, Yefim Petrovich b. 2 Mar 1925 Odessa IM 1951. GM 1952. Candidate 1953, 1956, 1962, 1965, 1968, 1971. USSR champion 1955 (after play-off), 1979. Palma de Majorca 1970 =2. Hilversum 1973 =1. Teesside 1975 1.

Gemzøe, Jacob Erhard Wilhjelm b. 25 Jul 1896 Danish champion 1928. =1st 1932 but lost play-off.

Georgadze, Tamaz Vasilyevich 9 Nov 1947 Tbilisi IM 1975. GM 1979.

Georgiev, Kiril b. 28 Nov 1965 IM 1983. GM 1985. World junior champion 1983. Bulgarian champion 1984 (joint).

Gerber, Woolf b. 1908 Ponovez, Lithuania d. 3 Jun 1967 Johannesburg South African champion 1961.

Gerlecka, Regina (Poland). Women's world championship challenger 1935, 1937.

German, Eugênio Maciel b. 24 Oct 1930 Belo Horizonte IM 1952. Brazilian champion 1951, 1972.

Geshev, Georgy b. 8 Oct 1903 d. 15 Jul 1937 Bulgarian champion 1933 (after play-off), 1934, 1935, 1936.

Gheorghiu, Florin b. 6 Apr 1944 Bucharest IM 1963. GM 1965. World junior champion 1963. Romanian champion 1960, 1962, 1964, 1965, 1966, 1967, 1973, 1977, 1984.

Ghindă, Eugenia b. 26 Nov 1950 Turda Romanian women's champion 1982.

Ghindă, Mihai-Viorel b. 25 Jul 1949 Bucharest IM 1977. Romanian champion 1976, 1978, 1982, 1983.

Ghiţescu, Teodor b. 24 Jan 1934 Bucharest IM 1961. Romanian champion 1963.

Gibaud, Amédée b. 1885 Rochefort sur Mer French champion 1928, 1930, 1935, 1940.

Gibson, William b. May 1873 Wigtown(shire) d. 27 Mar 1932 Giffnock, Renfrewshire Scottish champion 1907, 1912, 1913 – 14, 1921, 1922, 1928 – 9, 1930, 1930 – 1, and, after play-off, 1922 – 3. = 1st 1910 and 1920 but lost play-offs.

Giersing, Johannes Hjalmar b. 18 Nov 1872, Odense d. 11 Nov 1954, Copenhagen Nordic champion 1903. Danish champion 1915.

Giffard, Nicolas b. 4 Oct 1950 La Baule IM 1980. French champion 1978, 1982.

Gilbert, Colin Welsh champion 1967.

Gilchrist, Mary Dinorah b. c.1882 d. 14 Jan 1947 Edinburgh Women's world championship challenger 1933, 1937. British women's champion 1929, 1934. Scottish women's champion 1921, 1922, 1922 – 3, 1938.

Gilfer, Eggert b. 12 Feb 1892 Njarthvik d. 1960 Icelandic champion 1918, 1920, 1925, 1927, 1929, 1935, 1942.

Gipslis, Aivar b. 8 Feb 1937 Riga IM 1963. GM 1967. Latvian champion 1955, 1956, 1957, 1960, 1961, 1963, 1964, 1966. Moscow 1967 =2.

Giulian, Philip Maurice b. 6 Jun 1951 Glasgow Scottish champion =1st 1976 but lost play-off.

Giuroiu, Lidia b. 6 Oct 1929 Bucharest Romanian women's champion 1953, 1954, 1958.

Giustolisi, Alberto Mario b. 17 Mar 1927 Rome IM 1962. Italian champion 1961, 1964, 1966.

Gjørup, Ida Danish women's champion =1st 1936 but lost play-off.

Gladig, Matteo b. c.1880 Trieste d. 1915 Italian champion 1911.

Glass, Eduard Austrian champion 1929 (joint).

Glienke, Manfred b. 19 Aug 1954 Hundshausen West German champion 1982.

Gligorić, Svetozar b. 2 Feb 1923 Belgrade IM 1950. GM 1951. Candidate 1953, 1959, 1968. Yugoslav champion 1947 (joint), 1948 (joint), 1949, 1950, 1956, 1957, 1958 (joint), 1959, 1960, 1962, 1965, 1971. Dallas 1957 =1. Bled 1961 =3. Budva 1967 =2. Lugano 1970 =3. Rovinj-Zagreb 1970 =2. Wijk aan Zee 1971 =2.

Godoy Bugueño, David *b. 15 Jan 1944 Ovalle* Chilean champion 1968.

Goetz, Alphonse (aka A Geoffroy-Dausay). *b. 1865 Strasbourg d. 12 Jul 1934 Chaumont-en-Vexin* French champion 1914.

Goldenberg, Richard *b. 21 Nov 1947 Paris* French champion 1981 (joint).

Goldstein, Maurice Edward *b. 6 Apr 1901 Kingston-upon-Thames d. 12 Oct 1966 Sydney* New Zealand champion 1932–3.

Gollogly, David A New Zealand champion 1982–3 (joint).

Golmayo de la Torriente, Manuel *b. 12 Jun 1883 Havana d. 7 Mar 1973 Madrid* Spanish champion 1902, 1912, 1921.

Golombek, Harry *b. 1 Mar 1911 London* IM 1950. Emeritus GM 1985. British champion 1947 (after play-off), 1949, 1955. =1st 1959 but lost play-off.

Gómez, Mario *b. 5 Feb 1958 Santurce* Spanish champion 1980.

Gómez-Baillo, Jorge H *b. 19 Apr 1959* Argentine champion 1983 (after play-off).

Goncharov, Alexey Fedorovich *b. 16 Jan 1879 Moscow d. 23 Apr 1913 Moscow* Moscow champion 1901 (joint), 1909.

González, Juan *b. 15 Apr 1917 Havana* Cuban champion 1942, 1943, 1951, 1952.

Goodman, David Simon Charles *b. 25 Feb 1958* IM 1983. World under-18 champion 1975.

Gordon see Elder

Gorelov, Sergey Georgyevich *b. 18 Aug 1957 Moscow* Moscow champion 1985.

Gossett, Thorold British correspondence champion 1925.

Gouveia, Carlos Eduardo Brazilian champion 1975.

Grabovietchi, Elena *b. 2 Sep 1922 Brăila* Romanian women's champion 1952.

Graf, Sonja *b. 16 Dec 1914 d. 6 Mar 1965 New York* WIM 1950. Women's world championship challenger 1937, 1939, and match 1937.

Grau, Roberto Gabriel *b. 18 Mar 1900 Buenos Aires d. 12 Apr 1944 Buenos Aires* Argentine champion 1926, 1935, 1936, 1939.

Green, Ewen McGowen *b. 29 Jun 1950 Auckland* New Zealand champion 1979–80 (joint).

Greenfeld, Alon *b. 17 Apr 1964 New York* IM 1983.

Grefe, John Alan *b. 6 Sep 1947 Hoboken* IM 1975. USA champion 1973 (joint).

Gregory, Rita World junior women's champion 1928, 1929, 1930.

Gresser, Gisela Kahn *8 Feb 1906 Detroit* WIM 1950. Women's world championship challenger 1949–50.

Grierson, John Cresswell *b. c.Nov 1856 Altrincham d. 5 Feb 1933 Auckland* New Zealand champion 1902–3, 1912–13 (after play-off).

Griffith, Richard Clewin *b. 22 Jul 1872 London d. 11 Dec 1955 Hendon* British champion 1912.

Griffiths, Arthur S Welsh champion 1955.

Grigoriev, Nikolai Dmitryevich *b. 14 Aug 1895 Moscow d. 10 Nov 1938 Moscow* Moscow champion 1921–2, 1922–3, 1923, 1924, 1929.

Grigoryan, Karen Ashotovich *b. 7 Sep 1947 Moscow* IM 1982. Moscow champion 1975, 1979.

Grinberg, Nir *b. 17 Mar 1959 Petach Tikva* World under-16 champion 1976.

Grob, Henry *b. 4 Jun 1904 Braunau d. 5 Jul 1974 Zurich* Swiss champion 1939, 1951.

Grødde, Lis Danish women's champion 1947.

Gromek, Jozef *b. 20 Apr 1931 Czestocice* Polish champion 1955.

Gromer, Aristide *b. 1909* French champion 1933, 1937, 1938.

Gruenfeld, Yehuda *b. 28 Feb 1956 Zcerdziniov* IM 1978. GM 1980. Israeli champion 1982.

Grünberg, Hans-Ulrich *b. 9 Jan 1956 Schwerin* IM 1981. East German champion 1980.

Grünberg, Sergiu Henric *b. 27 Jul 1947 Bucharest* IM 1985. Romanian champion 1985.

Grünfeld, Ernst *b. 23 Nov 1893 Vienna d. 3 Apr 1962 Vienna* GM 1950. German champion 1923.

Gudmundsson, Gudmundur S Icelandic champion 1954.

Gudmundsson, Jón Icelandic champion 1932, 1936, 1937.

Guest, Anthony Alfred Geoffrey *b. 1856 Staines d. 29 Jan 1925 Lambeth, London* British champion (amateur) 1888.

Guimard, Carlos Enrique *b. 6 Apr 1913 Santiago del Estero* IM 1950. GM 1960. Argentine champion 1937, 1938, 1941.

Gulbrandsen, Andreas Norwegian champion 1931.

Gulbrandsen, Arne Vinje *b. 27 Mar 1943 Moss (?)* IM 1981. Norwegian champion 1965, 1968.

Gulko, Boris Frantsevich *b. 9 Feb 1947 Erfurt* IM 1975. GM 1976. USSR champion 1977 (joint). Moscow champion 1974. Nikšić 1978 =1.

Gundersen, Gunnar *b. 11 Mar 1882 Bordeaux d. 9 Feb 1943 Melbourne* New Zealand champion 1929–30, 1931–2.

Gunnarsson, Gunnar Kristinn *b. 14 Jun 1933* Icelandic champion 1966.

Gunsberg, Isidor Arthur *b. 2 Nov 1854 Budapest*

d. 2 May 1930 London Challenger 1891. German champion 1885.

Gunston, William Hewison *b. 9 Sep 1856 London d. 25 Jan 1941 King's Lynn* British correspondence champion 1924, 1928.

Gurevich, Mikhail N. *b. 22 Feb 1959* IM 1985. USSR champion 1985 (after play-off and tie-break).

Gurieli, Nina Davidovna *b. 7 Dec 1961 USSR* WIM 1979. WGM 1980.

Gutiérrez, María Luisa Spanish women's champion 1957, 1959, 1965, 1967.

Gutman, Lev *b. 26 Sep 1945 Riga* Latvian champion 1972.

Gygli, Fritz *b. 1896 Villnachen d. 27 Apr 1980 Zurich* Swiss champion 1941 – 2.

Gyles, Alfred William *b. 7 Mar 1888 Wellington d. 9 May 1967 Levin* New Zealand champion 1930 – 1 (after play-off).

Haahr, Merete *b. 18 Nov 1924* Danish women's champion 1952, 1958, 1959, 1962, 1966, 1967, 1970 (after play-off), 1975.

Haase, Graham G New Zealand champion 1961 – 2.

Haave, Einar *b. 1908* Norwegian champion 1954.

Habermann, Lidia *b. 6 Oct 1929 Bucharest* Romanian women's champion 1949.

Hafstein, Hannes *d. May 1933* Icelandic champion 1930.

Hage, Poul *b. 16 Mar 1906 Brandelev d. 11 Dec 1984 Naestved* Danish champion 1937, 1938, 1949, 1950. Last two tied, but in 1949 joint winner died before play-off. In 1950 tie decided by lottery. =1st 1939 but lost play-off.

Haik, Aldo *b. 19 Oct 1952 Tunis* IM 1977. French champion 1972, 1983 (after play-off).

Håkanson, Arthur *b. 1889 Kristianstad d. 26 Dec 1947 Kristianstad* Swedish champion 1922.

Halic, Ivan *18 Sep 1910 Arad d. 8 Jul 1978* Romanian champion 1936.

Hallmark, A M British correspondence champion 1952.

Halvorsen, Trygve Norwegian champion 1933, 1934.

Hamann, Svend *b. 28 Oct 1940 Copenhagen* IM 1965. Danish champion 1972.

Hamid, Mrs Rani (née Sayeda Jasimunnessa Khatun) *b. 14 Jul 1944 Synhet, Bangladesh* WIM 1985. British women's champion (joint) 1983.

Hamilton, Douglas Gibson *b. 15 Aug 1941 Melbourne* Australian champion 1964 – 5 (after play-off), 1967, 1981 – 2.

Hammar, Bengt Eric *b. 5 May 1942 Motala* Swedish correspondence champion 1976.

Hamond, Francis Edward *b. 1869 Walsingham*

d. 8 Feb 1932 Eastbourne British correspondence champion 1921.

Hänni, Alfred Swiss champion 1905.

Hansen, Curt *b. 18 Sep 1964 Bov* IM 1982. GM 1985. World junior champion 1984. Danish champion 1983, 1984, 1985 (last two after play-offs). Nordic champion 1983. European junior champion 1981 – 2.

Hansen, H G Norwegian champion 1921, 1927.

Hartoch, Robert Gijsbertus *b. 24 Mar 1947 Amsterdam* IM 1971. European junior champion 1963 – 4.

Hartston, Jana see Miles.

Hartston, William Roland *b. 12 Aug 1947 London* IM 1973. British champion 1973 (after play-off), 1975. =1st 1974 and 1980 but lost play-offs.

Harum, Gisela (Austria) Women's world championship challenger 1927, 1935, 1937. She entered in 1933 but was absent.

Havasi, Kornél *b. 10 Jan 1892 Budapest d. 15 Jan 1945* Hungarian champion 1922.

Hawksworth, John Crofton *b. 6 Dec 1963 England* IM 1986.

Hay, Trevor *b. 17 Oct 1945 Wagga Wagga* Australian champion 1971 – 2 (joint).

Haygarth, Michael John *b. 11 Oct 1934 Leeds* British champion 1964. =1st 1959 and 1974 but lost play-offs.

Heard, Alice Scottish women's champion 1923 – 4.

Heath, Christopher Barclay *b. 1877 Islington, London d. 10 May 1961 Denmark Hill, London* Scottish champion 1923 – 4.

Hebden, Mark L *b. 15 Feb 1958 Leicester* IM 1982. Grand Prix (UK) champion 1981. Petit Prix 1979, 1985.

Hecht, Hans-Joachim *b. 29 Jan 1939 Luckenwalde* IM 1969. GM 1973. IMC 1980. West German champion 1970, 1973.

Heemskerk, Fenny *b. 3 Dec 1919 Amsterdam* Women's world championship challenger 1949 – 50.

Heemsoth, Hermann *b. 21 Dec 1909 Bremen* IMC 1972. German correspondence champion 1954, 1969.

Heesche, Lydia Danish women's champion 1940, 1941, 1942.

Heidenfeld, Wolfgang *b. 29 May 1911, Schöneberg d. 3 Aug 1981, Ulm* Irish champion 1958, 1963, 1964, 1967, 1968, 1972. South African champion 1939, 1945 – 6 (joint), 1947 (joint), 1949, 1951, 1955, 1957, 1959 (joint).

Heim, Sverre *b. 4 Oct 1951* Norwegian champion 1980.

Hellers, Ferdinand *b. 28 Jan 1969 Stockholm* IM 1985. European junior champion 1984 – 5.

Helmers, Knut Jöran *b. 7 Feb 1957 Oslo* IM 1979. Nordic champion 1981. Norwegian champion 1976, 1977.

Henley, Ronald Watson *b. 5 Dec 1956 Houston* IM 1980. GM 1982.

Henneberger, Moriz *b. 16 Oct 1878 Basel d. 7 Apr 1959 Basel* Swiss champion 1899, 1906 (joint), 1909, 1911 (joint).

Henneberger, Walter *b. 19 May 1883 Ennenda d. 15 Jan 1969 Zurich* Swiss champion 1904, 1906 (joint), 1911 (joint), 1912, 1914 (joint).

Henniker-Heaton, Mary Araluen *b. 26 Nov 1904 d. 31 Jan 1972 Bromley* British women's champion =1st 1950 but lost play-off.

Henry, Paul *b. 9 Jan 1951* Irish champion 1970, =1st 1967 but lost tie-break.

Henschel, Walli (Germany) Women's world championship challenger 1930, 1931.

Hermanowa, Róza Maria *b. 16 Jan 1902 Poland* WIM 1950. Women's world championship challenger 1935, 1937, 1949 – 50.

Hermlin, Aarne *b. 6 Jun 1940* Estonian champion 1968.

Hernández, Román *b. 23 Nov 1949 Santiago* IM 1975. GM 1978. Cuban champion 1981 – 2.

Hernod, Bo *b. 18 Jun 1944* IMC 1982. Swedish correspondence champion 1974.

Herring, Frances British women's champion 1906 and, after play-off 1907.

Herzog, Adolf *b. 6 Jun 1953 Vienna* Austrian champion 1979 (after play-off), 1983.

Heuer, Valter *b. 14 Jul 1928* Estonian champion 1976.

Hicks, William Henry *b. 17 Nov 1816 Portsmouth d. 1892 Montreal* Canadian champion 1874.

Hindin, S New Zealand champion 1937 – 8.

Hindle, Kathleen Josephine (née Patterson) *b. 5 Oct 1948 Glasgow* Scottish women's champion 1975 (joint).

Hjartarson, Johann *b. 8 Feb 1963 Reykjavik* IM 1984. GM 1985. Icelandic champion 1980, 1984.

Hjorth, Gregory *b. 14 Jun 1963 Melbourne* IM 1984. Commonwealth champion 1983 (joint).

Hodgson, Julian Michael *b. 25 Jul 1963* IM 1983.

Hoen, Ragnar *b. 5 Oct 1940 Oslo* Nordic champion 1967. Norwegian champion 1963, 1978, 1981 (after play-off).

Hogarth, L M Scottish women's champion 1952, 1954, 1960, and jointly 1969.

Høi, Carsten *b. 16 Jan 1957 Copenhagen* IM 1979. Danish champion 1978. =1st 1985 but lost play-off.

Høiberg, Nina *b. 17 Feb 1956* WIM 1985. Danish women's champion 1974, 1976, 1977, 1978.

Holford, J M South African champion 1945 – 6 (joint).

Hollis, Adrian Swayne *b. 2 Aug 1940 Bristol* IMC 1970. GMC 1976. British correspondence champion 1966 (joint), 1967, 1971.

Holloway, Edith M Women's world championship challenger 1927, 1935, 1937. British women's champion 1919, 1936.

Holm, Sejer *b. 10 Aug 1939* Danish champion 1965. Nordic champion 1975.

Holt, Eric J *b. 20 Apr 1952 Edinburgh* Scottish champion 1971.

Hölzl, Franz *b. 6 Apr 1946 Kufstein* IM 1985. Austrian champion 1975, 1981 (after play-off).

Hooke, Alice E *b. c.1862 d. 28 Dec 1942 Fulham* British women's champion =1st 1930 and 1932 but lost play-offs.

Hookham, Henry *b. 22 Oct 1824 London d. 8 Dec 1898 Christchurch* New Zealand champion 1879 (after play-off), 1890 (joint).

Hooper, David Vincent *b. 31 Aug 1915 Reigate* British correspondence champion 1944. London champion 1948.

Hooper, W A British correspondence champion 1923.

Hopewell, B British correspondence champion 1970.

Hörberg, Bengt-Eric *b. 9 Feb 1922 Karlskrona* Swedish champion 1954.

Horner, Jeffrey *b. 25 Aug 1949 Bolton* Petit Prix (UK) champion 1977, 1982.

Hort, Vlastimil *b. 12 Jan 1944 Kladno* IM 1962. GM 1965. Candidate 1977. Czech champion 1970, 1971, 1972, 1975, 1977, 1984 (joint). Rovinj-Zagreb 1970 =2. Teesside 1975 =3. Wijk aan Zee 1975 2. Ljubljana-Portorož 1977 =2. Tilburg 1977 =3. Amsterdam 1978 =3. Amsterdam 1979 =1. Bad Kissingen 1981 =2. Wijk aan Zee 1982 =3. Wijk aan Zee 1983 =3. Reggio Emilia 1985 =2.

Horváth, Tamás *b. 23 Oct 1951 Zalaegerszeg* IM 1982. Hungarian champion 1982 (joint).

Houlding, Mary Mills *b. May 1850 d. 19 Feb 1940 Newport, Monmouthshire* British women's champion 1910, 1911, 1914. =1st 1907 but lost play-off.

Houston, Lynne (now Morrison). *b. 24 Apr 1957* Scottish women's champion 1977.

Howe, Henry Aspinall *b. 8 Jul 1815 Guildford d. 12 Feb 1900 Montreal* Canadian champion 1877, 1882 – 3 (joint).

Howell, James Christopher *b. 17 May 1967 Brent* IM 1985.

Hromádka, Karel *b. 23 Apr 1887 Gross Weikersdorf d. 16 Jul 1956* Czech champion 1913, 1921 (joint).

Hruskova-Belska, Nina *b. 5 May 1925 Czechoslovakia* WIM 1950. Women's world championship challenger 1949–50.

Hübener, Joachim Ulrich Georg *b. 10 May 1910 Berlin* German correspondence champion 1958.

Hübner, Robert *b. 6 Nov 1948 Cologne* IM 1969. GM 1971. Candidate 1971, 1980, 1983. West German champion 1967 (joint). European junior champion 1964–5 (joint). Palma de Majorca 1970 =2. Teesside 1975 =3. Tilburg 1977 =3. Tilburg 1978 =3. Chicago 1982 1. Tilburg 1984 =2. Linares 1985 = 1. Tilburg 1985 = 1.

Hug, Werner *b. 10 Sep 1952 Feldmeilen* IM 1971. World junior champion 1971. Swiss champion 1975.

Hugot, Claude *b. 16 Feb 1929 Villiers sur Marne d. 1980* French champion 1949.

Hulak, Krunoslav *b. 25 May 1951 Osijek* IM 1974. GM 1976. Yugoslav champion 1976.

Hund, Barbara *b. 10 Oct 1959 Leverkusen* WIM 1979. WGM 1982. German women's champion 1978.

Hund, Irene *b. 14 June 1962* German women's champion 1980.

Hunter, Charles Stanley *b. 8 Oct 1922 d. 5 Jul 1982 Horley* IMC 1967. British correspondence champion 1961 (joint). In *Guinness Book of Records* as world's fastest speaker.

Husák, Karel *b. 23 Jun 1925* IMC 1965. GMC 1968. World correspondence championship 1968 =2.

Huss, Andreas *b. 15 Oct 1950* Swiss champion 1983.

Hutchings, Stuart James *b. 8 May 1951 Barnstaple* Welsh champion 1973 (joint).

Hutchison Stirling, Florence Women's world championship challenger 1927. British women's champion =1st 1913 but lost play-off. Scottish women's champion 1905, 1906, 1907, 1912, 1913.

Hýbl, Jaroslav *b. 11 Mar 1928* IMC 1965. GMC 1968. World correspondence championship 1968 =2.

Ichim, Traian *b. 1905 Iaşi* Romanian champion 1947.

Iliesco, Juan Traian *b. 18 Apr 1898 Brăila d. 2 Feb 1968 Argentina* Argentine champion 1943.

Ilyin-Genevsky, Alexander-Fedorovich *b. 28 Nov 1884 St Petersburg d. 3 Sep 1941 Novaya Ladoga* Leningrad champion 1925 (joint), 1926, 1929.

Inkiov, Vencislav *b. 19 May 1956 Stanke Dimitrov* IM 1977. GM 1982. Bulgarian champion 1982 (after play-off).

Ioseliani, Nana Mikhailovna *b. 12 Feb 1962 Tbilisi* WIM 1979. WGM 1980. European junior women's champion 1978, 1979. USSR women's champion 1981 (joint), 1982.

Iskov, Gert *b. 28 Jul 1948 Copenhagen* IM 1979. Danish champion 1975.

Israel, Harold British correspondence champion 1949 (joint).

Ivanov, Igor Vasilievich *b. 8 Jan 1947 Leningrad* IM 1981. Canadian champion 1981.

Ivanović, Božidar *b. 24 Aug 1946 Cetinje* IM 1976. GM 1977. Yugoslav champion 1973, 1981, 1983 (joint).

Ivkov, Borislav *b. 12 Nov 1933 Belgrade* IM 1954. GM 1955. Candidate 1965. World junior champion 1951. Yugoslav champion 1958 (joint), 1963 (joint), 1972. Belgrade 1964 =2. Zagreb 1965 =1. Wijk aan Zee 1971 =2.

Jackson, George E Canadian champion 1875.

Jackson, Rosemary Ann *b. 8 Aug 1964 Dundee* Scottish women's champion 1979, 1981, 1984.

Jackson, Sheila *b. 11 Nov 1957* WIM 1981. British women's champion 1980, 1981, and, after play-offs, 1975 and 1978. =1st 1977 but lost play-offs. Grand Prixette (UK) 1977, 1978, 1979, 1980, 1981, 1983 (joint), 1984, 1985.

Jacobsen, Bo *b. 12 Dec 1948 Randers* Danish champion 1976.

Jacobsen, Egil *b. 1897 d. 27 Mar 1923 Copenhagen* Danish champion 1917 (joint), 1922.

Jacobsen, Julius Leigh *b. 28 May 1862 Hull d. 1 Jun 1916 Sydney* Australian champion 1897.

Jakobsen, Ole *b. 19 Oct 1942 Copenhagen* IM 1973. Danish champion 1969 (after play-off), 1971, 1980. =1st 1970 and 1984 but lost play-offs. Nordic champion 1969.

James, Gaynor Diane *b. 15 Jun 1964 Rhydfelin* Welsh women's champion 1981 (joint).

James, Stephen Collin *b. 3 Jun 1963 Pontypridd* Welsh champion 1982–3 (joint).

Jamieson, Peter Michael *b. 1 Jul 1946 Glasgow* Scottish champion 1973, joint champion 1965.

Jamieson, Robert Murray *b. 7 July 1952 Cheltenham, Australia* IM 1975. Australian champion 1973–4.

Janaček, B (Czechoslovakia) Women's world championship challenger 1939.

Janetschek, Karl *b. 17 Apr 1940* Austrian champion 1967, 1973.

Janowski, Dawid Markelowicz *b. 7 Jun 1868 Wolkowysk d. 15 Jan 1927 Hyères* Challenger 1910. London 1899 =2. German champion 1902.

Jansa, Vlastimil *b. 27 Nov 1942 Prague* IM 1965. GM 1974. Czech champion 1964, 1974, 1984 (joint).

Petrosyan & Korchnoi

Korchnoi and Petrosyan in happier days. (Reproduced by courtesy of B.T. Batsford)

Never has there been a less popular world champion than Petrosyan. His games bored most players and his dour personality attracted few to him. He could not have been less like the tiger implied in his name 'Tigran'. His opponents thought a better analogy would be a snake, for playing him was like being slowly crushed to death by a python.

Some thought his play negative, but Botvinnik gave a better description of Petrosyan's 'unique chess talent'. He 'created positions in which events developed as if in a slowed-up film. It is hard to attack his pieces: the attacking pieces advance only slowly and they get bogged down in the swamp. If at last you manage to create an attack then either there is little time left or fatigue comes into play . . . note the excellent technique Petrosyan has in the realization of positional advantage.'

If many had little affection for slow, cautious Petrosyan, one man, mercurial, flamboyant

Korchnoi, had a positive hatred. Korchnoi's autobiography *Chess is my Life*, (somewhat confusingly Karpov's autobiography has the same title), outlines the background. Korchnoi's complaint is table shaking. Korchnoi says that when he was considering his move during their 1974 Candidates match, Petrosyan would cause the table to shake. When Korchnoi asked him to stop Petrosyan objected to the controller that Korchnoi was upsetting him by talking.

This incident led to open hostilities between the two. Or rather three, for Petrosyan's pugnacious wife was always there. (She publicly slapped his second after Petrosyan lost to Fischer.) Korchnoi blames this affair for making life impossible for him in the Soviet Union and his consequent defection. Although his hostility to Karpov has had wider publicity, Korchnoi's hatred of Petrosyan was clearly both deeper and more personal.

After Korchnoi's defection he twice again had to face Petrosyan in Candidate's matches. When Korchnoi won the first of these he looked at his enemy and saw 'a whole gamut of emotions: fury, envy, and, perhaps, fear of censure upon his return to the Soviet Union. My instincts did not fail me: soon after arriving home Petrosyan was dismissed from his position as editor-in-chief of the weekly *64*.'

Their final encounter was in 1980. The English veteran Golombek, chief arbiter, gave his account in the *British Chess Magazine*. When the match began to go against him Petrosyan undertook 'a course of action that was a rather satanic blend of invention and savagery . . . for him simply a matter of self-preservation.' He wrote a letter accusing Golombek of searching his room, and helping Korchnoi in various ways. 'I did not lose to Korchnoi, I lost to Golombek', said Petrosyan. 'His main reason for seeking a scapegoat must lie in his desire to avoid being used himself as a scapegoat by the Soviet chess authorities', was Golombek's opinion.

Jansson, Lars Olof Börje *b. 12 Mar 1942 Tierp* Swedish champion 1968, 1970.

Jiménez Zerquera, Eleazor *b. 25 Jun 1928* IM 1963. Cuban champion 1957, 1960, 1963, 1965, 1967 (after play-off).

Jočić, Ljubica *b. 25 Sep 1936 Bukovac* Yugoslav women's champion 1959.

Joffe, Manne *b. 27 Mar 1927* Swedish correspondence champion 1954.

Johannesen, Inger Danish women's champion 1961.

Johannessen, Svein *b. 17 Oct 1937* IM 1961. Nordic champion 1959. Norwegian champion 1959, 1962, 1970, 1973.

Jóhannsson, Ingi Randver *b. 5 Dec 1936* IM 1963. Nordic champion 1961. Icelandic champion 1956, 1958, 1959, 1963.

Johansen, Darryl Keith *b. 4 Feb 1959 Melbourne* IM 1982. Australian champion 1983 – 4 (joint).

Johansson, John Inge Valfrid *b. 8 Oct 1916 Malmö d. 20 Sep 1966 Malmö* Swedish champion 1958.

Johansson, Martin *b. 6 Aug 1918 Vikmanshyttan* Swedish champion 1966. Swedish correspondence champion 1950, 1962.

Johner, Hans *b. 7 Jan 1889 Basel d. 2 Dec 1975 Thalwil* Swiss champion 1908 (joint), 1923, 1928 (joint), 1929, 1931, 1932 (joint), 1934, 1935, 1937, 1938, 1947, 1950.

Johner, Paul F *b. 10 Sep 1887 Zurich d. 25 Oct 1938 Berlin* Swiss champion 1907 (joint), 1908 (joint), 1925, 1928 (joint), 1930, 1932 (joint). Nordic champion 1916.

Johnsen, Eugen Norwegian champion 1932.

Johnsen, Lárus Icelandic champion 1951.

Jónsson, Sigudur Icelandic champion 1924, 1926.

Jones, Arthur O *b. c.1915 d. 1971 Gorseinon* Welsh champion 1962 (joint).

Jones, Iolo Ceredig *b. 2 Aug 1947 Llandysel* Welsh champion 1982 – 3 (joint).

Jones-Bateman, E British champion (amateur) 1892.

Jørgensen, Gyde *b. 18 Feb 1855 Ribe d. 29 Jul 1934 Copenhagen* Danish champion 1911.

Jovanović, Katarina *b. 31 Oct 1943 Belgrade* WIM 1964. Yugoslav women's champion 1961 (joint), 1971 (2), 1974 (joint).

Jovanović, Ružica *b. 29 Apr 1946 Belgrade* WIM 1971. Yugoslav women's champion 1969.

Jovanović, Verica see Nedeljković.

Joyner, Lionel Berry *b. 28 Mar 1932 Montreal* Canadian champion 1961.

Juárez, Carlos Eleodor *b. 29 Jun 1938* Argentine champion 1969.

Juhl J Danish champion 1916.

Junge, Klaus *b. 1 Jan 1924 Concépcion d. 17 Apr 1945 Welle* German champion 1941 (joint).

Kaenel, Hans-Jürgen *b. 16 May 1952* Swiss champion 1976, 1978, 1980.

Kagan, Shimon *b. 6 Apr 1942 Tel Aviv* IM 1969. Israeli champion 1967, 1969 – 70.

Kahn, Victor *b. 1889 Moscow d. 6 Oct 1971 Nice* French champion 1934.

Kaila, Osmo Ilmari *b. 11 May 1916 Helsinki* IM 1952. Nordic champion 1946. Finnish champion 1938 – 9 (after play-off), 1953 – 4.

Kalchbrenner see Maček.

Kan, Ilya Abramovich *b. 4 May 1909 Kuibyshev d. 12 Dec 1978* IM 1950. Moscow champion 1936 (joint).

Kanko, Ilkka Antero *b. 22 Nov 1934 Salo* IMC 1984. Finnish champion 1964.

Kantardzhiev, Mikhail *b. 24 Oct 1910. Bulgarian champion 1937.*

Karaklajić, Nikola *b. 24 Feb 1926* IM 1955. Yugoslav champion 1955.

Karasev, Vladimir Ivanovich *b. 17 Jun 1938* IM 1976. Leningrad champion 1970, 1974.

Karff, Mona May *b. 20 Oct 1914* WIM 1950. (USA). Women's world championship challenger 1937, 1939, 1949 – 50.

Karlsson, Hilmar Stefán *b. 18 Jul 1957* Icelandic champion 1983.

Karlsson, Lars Carl-Gustaf *b. 11 Jul 1955 Stockholm* IM 1979. GM 1982.

Karlsson, L O Danish champion 1918.

Kärner, Hillar *b. 27 Jul 1935 Tallinn* IM 1980. Estonian champion 1975 (joint), 1977.

Karner, Irmgard *b. 20 Feb 1927* German women's champion 1964.

Karpov, Anatoly Yevgeniyevich *b. 23 May 1951 Zlatoust* IM 1969. GM 1970. World champion 1975 – 85. Challenger 1975 (walk-over). USSR champion 1976, 1983. World junior champion 1969, European junior champion 1967 – 8. West German champion 1977. Moscow 1971 =1. Milan 1975 1. Amsterdam 1976 1. Bad Lauterberg 1977 1. Tilburg 1977 1. Bugojno 1978 =1. Montreal 1979 =1. Tilburg 1979 1. Waddinxveen 1979 1. Amsterdam 1980 1. Bad Kissingen 1980 1. Bugojno 1980 1. Tilburg 1980 1, Amsterdam 1981 =2 Linares 1981 =1. Moscow 1981 1. London 1982 =1. Mar del Plata 1982 =3. Tilburg 1982 1. Turin 1982 =1. Linares 1983 =2. Tilburg 1983 1. London 1984 1. Oslo 1984 1. Amsterdam 1985 1. Oscars 1973, 1974, 1975, 1976, 1977, 1979, 1980, 1981, 1984.

Kasparov, Garry Kimovich (né Harry Weinstein)

b. 13 Apr 1963 Baku IM 1979. GM 1980. World champion 1985 to date. Challenger in aborted match 1984–5. World junior champion 1980. USSR champion 1981 (joint). Moscow 1981 =2. Bugojno 1982 1. Nikšić 1983 1. Chess Oscar 1982, 1983, 1985.

Kavalek, Lubomir b. 9 Aug 1943 Prague IM 1965. GM 1965. Czech champion 1962, 1968. West German champion 1981. USA champion 1973 (joint), 1978. Montilla 1974 =2. Montilla 1975 =3. Tilburg 1977 =3.

Kavli-Jørgensen, Olaf Norwegian champion 1938.

Keene, Raymond Dennis b. 29 Jan 1948 London IM 1972. GM 1976. British champion 1971.

Keller, Dieter b. 19 Jul 1936 IM 1961. Swiss champion 1958, 1960, 1961, 1963.

Keller-Herrmann, Edith b. 17 Nov 1921 Dresden WIM 1950. WGM 1977. Women's world championship challenger 1949–50. German women's champion 1947, 1948, 1951, 1952, 1953.

Kelling, Fedor Kuskof b. 22 Apr 1865 Weimea d. 25 Aug 1946 Wellington New Zealand champion 1908–9, 1914–15.

Kelly, T Irish champion 1954.

Kengis, Edvin b. 12 Apr 1959 Cesis Latvian champion 1984.

Kennedy, Patrick Brendan b. 20 Jul 1929 Clarecastle d. 9 Jun 1966 Nottingham Irish champion 1949.

Kenyon, Beryl E F b. c.1936 Welsh women's champion 1955, 1956.

Keogh, Eamonn A b. Dublin Irish champion (joint), both 1975 and 1979.

Keres, Paul b. 7 Jan 1916 Narva d. 5 Jun 1975 Helsinki GM 1950. Challenger 1948. Candidate 1950, 1953, 1956, 1959, 1962, 1965. USSR champion 1947, 1950, 1951. Estonian champion 1934–5 (after play-off), 1942, 1943, 1945, 1953. Semmering-Baden 1937 1. AVRO 1938 =1. Bled 1961 =3. Los Angeles 1963 =1. Winnipeg 1967 =3.

Kern, Manfred b. 28 Feb 1949 Bretten German correspondence champion 1952.

Kernan, Bernard b. 25 Aug 1955 Dublin Irish champion 1976.

Kestler, Hans-Günter b. 12 Dec 1939 Bamberg IM 1976. West German champion 1972.

Khaldikar see Unni.

Khalifman, Alexander b. 18 Jan 1966 USSR IM 1986. European junior champion 1985–6.

Khasanova, Fliura b. 23 Jan 1964 USSR WIM 1984. World junior women's champion 1983.

Kibbermann, Feliks Estonian champion 1941 (joint).

Kieninger, Georg b. 5 Jun 1902 Munich d. 25 Jan 1975 Düsseldorf IM 1950. German champion 1937, 1940, 1947.

Kier, Aage b. 1896 d. 31 Oct 1941 Copenhagen Danish champion 1913, 1924. =1st 1926 but lost play-off.

King, Daniel John b. 28 Aug 1963 Beckenham IM 1982.

Kinnmark, Olof b. 29 Mar 1897 Göteborg d. 18 Feb 1970 Göteborg Swedish champion (tournament) 1925.

Kirby, Kenneth Farquhar b. 1 Nov 1915 Oudtshoorn South African champion 1959 (joint), 1963 (joint).

Kirov Ivanov, Nino b. 9 Sep 1945 Blagoevgrad IM 1971. GM 1975. Bulgarian champion 1978 (after play-off).

Kirpichnikov, Vladimir b. 24 Jul 1948 Riga Latvian champion 1974 (joint).

Klaman, Konstatin Mikhailovich b. 23 Dec 1917 Leningrad d. 1985 Leningrad champion 1962–3.

Klasup, Karlis b. 1 Jul 1922 Latvian champion 1959 (after play-off).

Klavin, Janis b. 27 Apr 1933 Latvian champion 1952.

Klein, Ernst Ludwig b. 1910 Vienna British champion 1951.

Klemmensen, Magda Danish women's champion =1st 1963 but lost play-off.

Klimova-Richtrova, Eliška b. 1 Jul 1959 Prague WIM 1980. WGM 1982.

Klinger, Josef b. 6 Jun 1968 IM 1985. Austrian champion 1985.

Klovan, Janis b. 9 Apr 1935 Ruba IM 1976. IMC 1968. Latvian champion 1954, 1962, 1967, 1968, 1970, 1971, 1975 (joint), 1979.

Knaak, Rainer Fritz Albert b. 16 Mar 1953 Pasewalk IM 1973. GM 1975. East German champion 1974, 1978, 1982, 1983, 1984.

Koblenc, Aleksander b. 3 Sep 1916 Riga Latvian champion 1941, 1946.

Koch, Berthold b. 22 Feb 1899 Berlin IM 1950. IMC 1959. East German champion 1952. German correspondence champion 1959.

Kochiyev, Alexander Vasilyevich 25 Mar 1956 Leningrad IM 1976. GM 1977. European junior champion 1975–6.

Kølvig, Bent b. 28 Apr 1933 Danish champion 1962.

Konarkowska-Sokolov, Henryka b. 14 Dec 1938 Inowroclaw WIM 1961. Yugoslav women's champion 1968, 1971(1).

Kondratiev, Pavel Yeseyevich b. 8 Jan 1924 Moscow Leningrad champion 1956.

Kongshavn, Harry *b. 23 Feb 1899 Hidri* Norwegian champion 1951.

Konstantinopolsky, Alexander Markovich *b. 19 Feb 1910 Zhitomir* IM 1950. GM 1983. IMC 1966. USSR correspondence champion 1951.

Kopec, Danny *b. 28 Feb 1954 Kfar Saba, Israel* IM 1985. Scottish champion 1980, =1st 1981 but lost play-off.

Kopilov, Nikolai Georgiyevich *b. 26 Oct 1919 Novosibirsk* IMC 1969. Leningrad champion 1954 (after play-off).

Korchnoi, Viktor Lvovich *b. 23 Mar 1931 Leningrad* IM 1954. GM 1956. Challenger 1978, 1981. Candidate 1962, 1968, 1971, 1974, 1983, 1985. USSR champion 1960, 1962, 1964–5, 1970. Swiss champion 1982, 1984, 1985. Netherlands champion 1977. Leningrad champion 1955, 1957 (joint), 1964. Belgrade 1964 =2. Yerevan 1965 1. Budva 1967 1. Rovinj-Zagreb 1970 =2. Wijk aan Zee 1971 1. Wijk aan Zee 1978 2. Oude Meester 1979 1. London 1980 =1. Bad Kissingen 1981 1. Chicago 1982 3. Sarajevo 1984 =1. Titograd 1984 =1. Wijk aan Zee 1984 =1. Linares 1985 =3. Tilburg 1985 =1.

Korostenski, Frank *b. 26 Mar 1949 České Budejovice* South African champion 1979.

Kosenkov, Vsevolod Tikhonovich *b. Mar 1930* IMC 1977. GMC 1979. World correspondence championship 1980 3.

Koshnitsky, Gregory Simon *6 Oct 1907 Kishinev* IMC 1972. Australian champion 1932–3, 1938–9.

Kosten, Anthony Cornelius *b. 27 Jul 1958* IM 1984.

Kostić, Boris *b. 24 Feb 1887 Vršac d. 3 Nov 1963 Belgrade* GM 1950. Yugoslav champion 1935 (joint), 1938.

Kostro, Jerzy *b. 25 Jan 1937 Morczydly* IM 1968. Polish champion 1966, 1970.

Kotov, Alexander Alexandrovich *b. 12 Aug 1913 Tula d. 8 Jan 1981 Moscow* GM 1950. Candidate 1950, 1953. USSR champion 1948 (joint). Moscow champion 1941.

Kouatly, Bachar *b. 3 Mar 1958 Damascus* IM 1975. French champion 1979 (joint).

Kowalska, N (Poland). Women's world championship challenger 1935.

Kozlovskaya, Valentina Yakovleva *b. 18 Apr 1938 Stavropol* WIM 1965. WGM 1976. USSR women's champion 1965.

Kozma, Július *b. 1 Jun 1929 d. 24 Apr 1975* IM 1957. Czech champion 1967.

Krantz, Kurt *b. c.1885 Breslau d. 21 Feb 1915 Davos* Swiss champion 1911 (joint).

Kremenetsky, Anatoly Mikhailovich *b. 14 Jan 1939* Moscow champion 1980.

Kristensen, Alfred August *b. 16 Aug 1905 d. 30 Aug 1974* World blind correspondence champion 1963–4 (joint), 1966–8, 1969–70.

Kristensen, Bjarke *b. 9 Apr 1956 Copenhagen* Danish champion =1st 1981 but lost play-off.

Kristiansen, Erling *b. 17 Dec 1936* Norwegian champion 1972.

Kristiansen, Jens *b. 25 May 1952 Copenhagen* IM 1979. Danish champion 1979, 1982 (after play-off).

Kristinsson, Jón *b. 17 Jun 1942* Icelandic champion 1971, 1974.

Kristol, Luba *b. 26 May 1944 Leningrad* WIMC 1976. IMC 1984. World women's correspondence champion 1984.

Krogdahl, Arne S B *b. 1909 Trondheim* Norwegian champion 1937.

Krogius, Nikolay Vladimirovich *b. 22 Jul 1930 Saratov* IM 1963. GM 1964. Sochi 1973 =3.

Krogius, Ragnar *b. 17 Mar 1903 Jääski d. 31 Dec 1980 Stockholm* Finnish champion 1932.

Kroon, Piet *b. 26 Feb 1945 The Hague* South African champion 1965, 1969, 1975 (joint).

Kruse, Johannes *b. 3 Aug 1879 Vester Nebel* Danish champion 1910.

Krylov, S World blind champion 1978, 1982.

Kuijpers, Franciscus Antonius *b. 27 Feb 1941 Breda* IM 1964. Netherlands champion 1963.

Kuligowski, Adam *b. 24 Dec 1955 Warsaw* IM 1979. GM 1980. Polish champion 1978 (on tie-break).

Künert, Franz Austrian champion 1930.

Kunz, K Swiss champion 1907 (joint).

Kupper, Josef *b. 10 Mar 1932 Luzern* IM 1955. Swiss champion 1954, 1957, 1962.

Kurajica, Bojan *b. 15 Nov 1947 Ljubljana* IM 1965. GM 1974. World junior champion 1965. Wijk aan Zee 1976 =3.

Kushnir, Alla Shulimovna *b. 11 Aug 1941 Moscow* WIM 1962. WGM 1976. Women's world championship challenger 1965, 1969, 1972. USSR women's champion 1970 (joint).

Laakmann, Anni *b. 5 Jan 1937 Ossenberg* German women's champion 1970, 1972, 1974, 1976 (after play-off).

Lacko, Pavel *b. 30 Dec 1954 Prague* Swedish correspondence champion 1983.

Laird, Craig *b. 15 Mar 1953* New Zealand champion 1977–8.

Lambert, François-Xavier *b. 6 Feb 1833 St Antoine de Tilly d. 18 Sep 1920 Ottawa* Canadian champion 1884.

Lamford, Paul A *b. 30 Aug 1953 Llanelli* Welsh champion 1982–3 (joint).

Landau, Salo *b. 1 Apr 1903 Bochnia d. 1943 Auschwitz* Netherlands champion 1936.

Langos, Józsa *b. 28 Aug 1911* WIM 1950. Women's world championship challenger 1949 – 50.

Large, Peter Graham *b. 2 Mar 1956 Bromley* Petit Prix (UK) champion 1985.

Larsen, Ingrid *b. 1 Jul 1909* WIM 1950. Women's world championship challenger 1937, 1939, 1949 – 50. Danish women's champion 1936 and 1937 (after play-offs), 1938, 1939, 1943, 1944, 1945, 1946, 1948, 1949, 1953, 1956, 1957, 1960, 1965, 1969, 1983.

Larsen, Jørgen Bent *b. 4 Mar 1935 Tilsted* IM 1955. GM 1956. Candidate 1965, 1968, 1971, 1977. Danish champion 1954, 1955, 1956, 1959, 1963, 1964. Chess Oscar 1967. Nordic champion 1955, 1973. Dallas 1957 =3. Santa Monica 1966 3. Winnipeg 1967 =1. Lugano 1970 1. Palma de Majorca 1970 =2. Manila 1974 3. Manila 1975 =2. Geneva 1977 1. Ljubljana-Portorož 1977 1. Bled-Portorož 1979 =2. Buenos Aires 1980 1. Bugojno 1980 2. Las Palmas 1981 2. Linares 1981 3. Nikšić 1983 2. Naestved 1985 =1.

Larsen, Øjvind *b. 23 Jun 1882 d. 6 Jul 1960 Maribo* Danish champion =1st 1926 but lost play-off.

Larsson, Ernst *b. 1897 d. 1963* Swedish champion 1936.

Lasker, Emanuel *b. 24 Dec 1868 Berlinchen d. 11 Jan 1941 New York* World champion 1894 – 1921. Hastings 1895 3. St Petersburg 1895 – 6 1. London 1899 1. St Petersburg 1909 = 1. St Petersburg 1914 1. New York 1924 1.

Lauberte, Milda *b. 7 Oct 1918 Vildoga* Women's world championship challenger 1937, 1939.

Laurentius, Leho *b. 1904* Estonian champion 1932 (joint)

Laurent-Lund see Thierry.

Lawson see Stevenson.

Lawton, Geoffrey W *b. 4 Apr 1960* IM 1984.

Lazare, Suchowolski Australian champion 1956 – 7 (joint). Emigrated to Israel before tie could be resolved.

Lazarevic see Marković

Leask, M E Scottish women's champion 1974, and jointly 1975.

Lebedev, Peter Alexeyevich *b. 1905* Moscow champion 1932 (joint).

Lebredo, Gerardo *b. 3 Aug 1950 Havana* IM 1977. Cuban champion 1977 (joint).

Lee, Francis Joseph *b. c.1857 London d. 12 Sep 1909 London* South African champion 1903.

Lee, Peter Nicholas *b. 21 Nov 1943 London* British champion 1965.

Lein, Anatoly Yakovlevich *b. 28 Mar 1931 Leningrad* IM 1964. GM 1968. Moscow champion 1971 (after play-off).

Lemachko, Tatiana Mefodyevna *b. 16 Mar 1948 Izmaila* WIM 1971. WGM 1977.

Lemoine, Claude *b. 1932* French champion 1958.

Lenner, Leopold Austrian champion 1947.

Leonhardt, Paul Saladin *b. 13 Nov 1877 Poznań d. 14 Dec 1934 Kaliningrad* Nordic champion 1907.

Lepviikman, Tom *b. 1900 Estonia* New Zealand champion 1945 – 6, 1946 – 7.

Lerner, Konstantin Zaivelyevich *b. 28 Feb 1950 Odessa* IM 1978.

Letelier Martner, René *b. 21 Sep 1915 San Bernardo* IM 1960. Chilean champion 1957, 1959, 1960, 1964, 1973.

Letzelter, Jean-Claude *b. 25 Apr 1940 Sélestat* French champion 1968, 1971 (joint), 1974.

Levald, Gudrun Danish women's champion 1950 and, after play-off, 1963.

Levenfish, Grigory Yakovlevich *b. 9 Mar 1889 Poland d. 9 Feb 1961 Moscow* GM 1950. USSR champion 1934 (joint), 1937. Leningrad champion 1922, 1924, 1925 (joint).

Levitina, Irina Solomonovna *b. 8 Jul 1954 Leningrad* WIM 1972. WGM 1976. Women's world championship challenger 1984. USSR women's champion 1971, 1978 (joint), 1979, 1980 – 1.

Levitsky, Stepan Mikhailovich *b. 25 Apr 1876 Serpukhov d. 21 Mar 1924 Glubokaya* Russian champion 1911.

Levitt, Jonathan *b. 3 Jun 1963 Southwark* IM 1984.

Levy, David Neil Lawrence *b. 14 Mar 1945 London* IM 1969. Scottish champion 1968, joint champion 1975.

Lewi, Jerzy *b. 22 Apr 1949 Wrocław d. 30 Oct 1972 Lund* Polish champion 1969.

Liberzon, Vladimir Mikhailovich *b. 23 Mar 1937 Moscow* IM 1963. GM 1965. Israeli champion 1974.

Ligterink, Henrik Gert *b. 17 Nov 1949* IM 1977. Netherlands champion 1979.

Lilienthal, Andor *b. 5 May 1911 Moscow* GM 1950. Candidate 1950. USSR champion 1940 (joint). Moscow champion 1939 – 40.

Lilja, Josef Norwegian champion 1918.

Lindberg, John B Swedish champion 1935 (joint).

Lipschuetz, Samuel *b. 4 Jul 1863 Ungvar d. 30 Nov 1905 Hamburg* USA champion 1892.

Lisitsin, Georgy Mikhailovich *b. 11 Oct 1909 St Petersburg d. 20 Mar 1972 Leningrad* IM 1950.

Leningrad champion 1933 – 4 (joint), 1939, 1947 (joint).

Litinskaya see Shul.

Littleton, Michael F *b. 5 Mar 1938 County Clare* Irish champion 1965, joint 1962.

Littlewood, Paul Edwin *b. 18 Jan 1956 Skegness* IM 1979. British champion 1981.

Ljiljak-Ankerst, Milka *b. 6 Apr 1942 Maribor* WIM 1967. Yugoslav women's champion 1966.

Ljubojević, Ljubomir *b. 2 Nov 1950 Belgrade* IM 1970. GM 1971. Yugoslav champion 1977 (joint), 1982. Hilversum 1973 3. Manila 1975 1. Milan 1975 =3. Wijk aan Zee 1976 =1. Buenos Aires 1980 3. Puerto Madryn 1980 =1. Bugojno 1982 =2. Tilburg 1983 =2. Linares 1985 =1. Reggio Emilia 1985 – 6 =1. Wijk aan Zee 1986 =2.

Ljungdahl, John Bertil *b. 8 Dec 1935* IMC 1971. Swedish correspondence champion 1963.

Lladó Lumbera, Jaime *b. 16 Aug 1916 Barcelona* Spanish champion 1956, 1961.

Lob, Paulin Swiss champion 1944, 1959 (after play-off).

Lobron, Eric *b. 7 May 1960 Philadelphia* IM 1980. GM 1982. West German champion 1980.

Locock, Charles Dealtry *b. 27 Sep 1862 Brighton d. 13 May 1946 London* British champion (amateur) 1887 after play-off.

Lokvenc, Josef *b. 1 May 1899 Vienna d. 2 Apr 1974 St Pölten* IM 1951. Austrian champion 1951 (after play-off), 1953. German champion 1943.

Loman, Rudolf Johannes *b. 14 Oct 1861 Amsterdam d. 4 Nov 1932 Amsterdam* Netherlands champion 1912.

Lombard, André *b. 19 Sep 1950 Bern* IM 1976. Swiss champion 1969, 1970, 1973, 1974, 1977.

Lombardy, William James *b. 4 Feb 1937 New York* IM 1957. GM 1960. World junior champion 1957.

Lougheed, A (Canada). Women's world championship challenger 1939.

Löwenborg, Knut Otto Reinhold *b. 2 Mar 1888 d. Dec 1969* Swedish champion (match) 1917.

Lputyan, Smbat Gariginovich *b. 14 Feb 1958 Yerevan* IM 1982. GM 1984.

Lucht, Hannelore German women's champion 1963.

Ludgate, Alan Templeton *b. 31 Aug 1945 Belfast* Irish champion 1978, joint both 1975 and 1977.

Luik, Helmuth *b. 19 Feb 1928* Estonian champion 1967.

Lukács, Péter *b. 9 Jul 1950 Budapest* IM 1976. Hungarian champion 1980.

Lukin, Andrey Mikhailovich *b. 28 Aug 1948*

Leningrad IM 1982. Leningrad champion 1972, 1981, 1983.

Lund, Leif F D Norwegian champion 1924.

Lundholm, Stig Gustav *b. 14 Nov 1917 Luleå* IMC 1983. Swedish champion 1944. Swedish correspondence champion 1948.

Lundin, Erik Ruben *b. 2 Jul 1904 Stockholm* IM 1950. Emeritus GM 1983. Swedish champion 1932 (joint), 1934, 1938, 1941, 1942, 1945, 1946, 1960, 1961, 1964. Nordic champion 1936, and (joint) 1939.

Lundqvist, Åke *b. 26 Feb 1913 Stockholm* GMC 1962. World correspondence championship 1962 3. Swedish correspondence champion 1945.

Lutia see Manolescu.

Lynch, David I *b. c. 1910* New Zealand 1950 – 1 champion.

MacDonald, Edmond Scottish champion 1902.

MacDonald, Ronald Cadell *b. 4 Jul 1868 Inverbrothock d. 26 Jan 1942 Inverness* Scottish champion 1901 (after play-off), 1904, 1905, 1906, 1926 – 7, 1927 – 8. =1st 1900, 1922 – 3, 1925 – 6 but lost play-offs. British correspondence champion 1926, 1927, 1930.

Maček, Vlasta (née Kalchbrenner). *b. 27 Jun 1952 Zagreb* WIM 1974. Yugoslav women's champion 1973 (joint), 1980. =1st 1978 but lost on tie break.

MacFarlane, Donald South African champion 1983.

MacKay, William *b. 1863 Melbourne d. 9 Feb 1933 Karori* New Zealand champion 1894 – 5.

MacKenzie, Arthur John *b. early 1871 Birmingham d. 21 Aug 1949 Hastings* Scottish champion 1908, 1909, 1913.

MacKenzie, George Henry *b. 24 Mar 1837 North Kessock d. 14 Apr 1891 New York* Scottish champion 1888. German champion 1887.

MacLean, Maria *d. 1963 Abertillery* Welsh women's champion 1958 (joint), 1961.

MacLeod, Nicholas Menelaus *b. 8 Feb 1870 Quebec d. 27 Sep 1965 Spokane* Canadian champion 1886, 1888 (after play-off).

Maclès, Jacques *b. 8 Jul 1945* French champion 1970.

Maderna, Carlos Hugo *b. 4 Aug 1910 d. 23 Jan 1976 La Plata* Argentine champion 1940, 1950 – 1 (after play-off).

Madl, Idilko *b. 5 Nov 1969 Tapolca* WIM 1984. European women's junior champion 1984.

Maeder, Karl-Heinz Siegfried *b. 17 Oct 1948 Berlin* IMC 1981. European junior champion 1968 – 9 (joint). German correspondence champion 1980(1).

Magnússon, Olafur *b. 15 Nov 1938* Icelandic

Maher, Vincent *b. May 1929 Dublin* Irish champion 1950, 1955. =1st 1953 but lost tie-break.

Mainz, Wilhelm *b. 1902* German correspondence champion 1962.

Makarczyk, Kazimierz *b. 1 Jan 1901 Warsaw d. 27 May 1972 Łódź* IM 1950. Polish champion 1948.

Makarichev, Sergei Yuryevich *b. 17 Nov 1953 Moscow* IM 1974. GM 1976. European junior champion 1973–4. Moscow champion 1976 (joint), 1983 (joint). Oslo 1984 =2.

Mäki, Veijo *b. 7 Dec 1958 Mänttä.* Finnish champion 1982.

Malcolm, S V A Scottish women's champion 1927–8.

Malich, Burkhard Georg Josef *b. 29 Nov 1936 Schweidnitz* IM 1962. GM 1975. East German champion 1957, 1973.

Malmgren, Harald Valdemar *b. 4 May 1904 Avesta d. 15 Feb 1957 Uppsala* GMC 1953. World correspondence championship 1953 =2. Swedish correspondence champion 1942.

Malmgren, Sven Göran *b. 25 Apr 1943* Swedish champion 1971.

Mangini, José Tiago *b. 4 Jan 1920 Rio de Janeiro* Brazilian champion 1950, 1956.

Mann, E Shirley *b. Birmingham* Welsh women's champion 1963, and, as Mills, 1965 (joint).

Manolescu, Rodica (née Lutia) *b. 1911 Cernauti* Romanian women's champion 1936 (as Lutia), 1957.

Marangunić, Srdjan *b. 31 Oct 1943 Zagreb* IM 1971. Yugoslav champion 1977 (joint).

Marchand, Max *b. 24 Nov 1888 Amsterdam d. 26 Apr 1957 Baarn* Netherlands champion 1919.

Marić, Alisa *b. 10 Jan 1970* World under-16 women's champion 1985. Yugoslav women's champion 1986.

Mariotti, Sergio *b. 10 Aug 1946 Florence* IM 1969. GM 1974. Italian champion 1969.

Marjanović, Slavoljub *b. 6 Jan 1955 Lalinac* IM 1977. GM 1978. Yugoslav champion 1985.

Marković, Gordana (née Jovanović) *b. 4 Jan 1951 Belgrade* WIM 1979. Yugoslav women's champion 1974 (joint), 1977 (joint), 1981.

Marković, Milunka (née Lazarević) *b. 1 Dec 1932 Šantarovac* WIM 1954. WGM 1976. Yugoslav women's champion 1952 (joint), 1954, 1956, 1957, 1960, 1962, 1963, 1975, 1976, 1979, 1982 (all as Lazarević).

Markus, Marcel Swiss champion 1964, 1965 (after play-off).

Maróczy, Géza *b. 3 Mar 1870 Szeged d. 29 May 1951 Budapest* GM 1950. London 1899 =2. Hungarian champion 1932.

Marotti, Davide *b. 1 Jan 1881 Naples d. 18 Jul 1940 Naples* Italian champion 1921.

Marshall, Frank James *b. 10 Aug 1877 New York d. 9 Nov 1944 Jersey City.* Challenger 1907. German champion 1906, 1908. USA champion 1909.

Marshall, James *b. c.1866 d. 11 Aug 1926 Edinburgh* Scottish champion 1889.

Martens, Rolf *b. 1942 Oslo* Swedish champion 1967.

Martin, Andrew David *b. 18 May 1957 West Ham* IM 1984.

Martin, Jules *b. c.1873 d. 21 May 1917 Aigle* Swiss champion 1902 (joint).

Martin, Robert Elmer *b. 10 Feb 1910 d. 9 Feb 1978 Toronto* Canadian champion 1933.

Martín González, Angel *b. 3 Jan 1953 Barcelona* IM 1981. Spanish champion 1976, 1984.

Martinolich, Giovanni *b. 22 Jun 1884 Trieste d. 25 Jul 1910 Trieste* Italian champion 1906.

Mason, James *b. 19 Nov 1849 Kilkenny d. 15 Jan 1905 Rochford* Vienna 1882 3.

Mason, John *b. 1880 Hawkes Bay d. 9 Jul 1975 Napier* New Zealand champion 1909–10 (after play-off). =1st 1903–4, 1905–6 but lost play-offs.

Mason, William Edward *b. 1876 d. c.1960* New Zealand champion 1900 (after play-off), 1903–4 (after play-off), 1910–11, 1911–12 (after play-off), 1913–14, 1919–20.

Matanović, Aleksandar *b. 23 May 1930 Belgrade* IM 1951. GM 1955. Yugoslav champion 1962 (joint), 1969, 1978.

Matison, Herman *b. 28 Dec 1894 Riga d. 16 Nov 1932 Riga* World amateur champion 1924. Latvian champion 1924.

Matulović, Milan *b. 10 Jun 1935 Belgrade* IM 1961. GM 1965. Yugoslav champion 1965, 1967.

Matveyeva, Svetlana *b. 4 Jul 1969 Frunze* WIM 1985. USSR women's champion 1984 (joint).

Mazzoni, Guy *b. 29 Aug 1929* French champion 1961, 1965.

McCarthy, Moss Welsh champion 1973 (joint).

McDougall, F Scottish women's champion 1978.

McGrillen, Hugh Irish champion 1973.

McKay, Roderick McIntosh *b. 11 Feb 1952 Glasgow* Scottish champion 1971 (joint), 1974, 1976 after play-off, 1979, 1982. In 1980 =1st but lost play-off. Petit Prix (UK) champion 1976.

M'Kee, James Alexander *b. 9 Mar 1877 Eastmuir, Glasgow d. c.April 1940 Glasgow* Scottish champion 1911 and, after play-off, 1925–6.

Fischer & Spassky

Take a poll as to the greatest chess player and every world champion, and a few others, would get votes. Ask only grandmasters the question and the answer is near enough unanimous — Bobby Fischer. Yet at the last minute he needed pushing to the title by others including President Nixon, the London financier Jim Slater, and Fischer's rival, Boris Spassky.

Contrary to the usual antipathy between players for the championship these two had a respect and liking for each other — indeed still

have, for they keep in touch even now. Spassky is the most enigmatic of champions. Technically he had no weakness in any department of the game. True, he is prone to laziness, but so were Morphy, Capablanca and Smyslov, for example. What makes Spassky different is his brooding introspection. It is no surprise that Dostoyevsky is one of his favourite authors.

At the top there is little technical difference between masters, success depending on judgement and determination. Every world

champion has had exceptional grit and resilience when faced by surprises or even defeat. In Spassky's case that strength also led him into muted dispute with the Soviet authorities.

Bobby Fischer appeared on the scene, gauche and innocent of everything outside chess, in marked contrast to the urbane, cultured Spassky. Once Fischer was hooked on chess nothing else mattered to him. 'What's that got to do with chess?' was a favourite remark of his. He left school early saying that his teachers had nothing to offer him.

His vast intellect, determination and single-minded dedication to chess produced a unique genius, but left him short of social graces and awareness. Being absolutely honest himself he did not see that interviewers were trapping him into statements that would make him look ridiculous and he soon decided to trust nobody. He was wary of chess players who acted as seconds and those who offered him financial help. Most of all he was suspicious of Soviet players. He believed, with some evidence, that they worked in unison to exclude the rest of the world from the summit.

By the time he had shown he was easily the best player outside the USSR he had attracted huge admiration from chess players and the attention of the media because of what they saw as his outrageous behaviour. Chess became news and millions looked at the game for the first time.

All eyes were focused on Reykjavik in 1972 when at last Fischer qualified to play for the title. For many it was an ideological battle between USA and USSR. The press was there in quantity and quality. Spassky arrived on 19 June to acclimatize himself, but the opening ceremony on 1 July passed with no sign of Fischer. Euwe, then FIDE president, decided on a two-day postponement.

The Icelandic Prime Minister got in touch with the White House and Henry Kissinger was told to phone Fischer and put pressure on him. Meanwhile Jim Slater read that Fischer was quibbling about the financial arrangements so he doubled the prize money, asking that it should be put as a challenge to Fischer not to chicken out on another excuse.

Fischer arrived on 4 July and astonished everyone by sending a written apology to his opponent for 'my disrespectful behaviour in not attending the opening ceremony' etc. The Soviet delegation demanded that Fischer forfeit the first game, but Spassky refused to accept it!

Play began and Spassky won the first game. Then Fischer protested about camera noise (he has genuinely sensitive hearing) and did not turn up for the second game. Spassky was given the game by default and Fischer booked an air ticket home. Persuaded to play the third game in a private room until the camera dispute was settled, Fischer remained and scored five wins and three draws in the next eight games. The match was virtually over.

Having achieved his only goal, Fischer never played again. Spassky was disciplined by loss of travel and other privileges and eventually settled in France.

The first day's play of the 1972 world championship match. Spassky, Fischer and chief arbiter Lothar Schmid. (Chester Fox)

McMahon, P J Irish champion =1st 1926 but lost play-off.

McNab, Colin A *b. 3 Feb 1961 Dundee* IM 1984. Scottish champion 1983, =1st 1981 but lost play-off.

Mecking, Henrique da Costa *b. 1952* IM 1967. GM 1972. Candidate 1974, 1977. Brazilian champion 1965, 1967. Manila 1975 =2.

Medina García, Antonio Angel José *b. 2 Oct 1919 Barcelona* IM 1950. Spanish champion 1944, 1945, 1947, 1949, 1952, 1963, 1964.

Meldrum, William *b. 28 Jul 1865 Kamo d. 13 Feb 1964 Burnham* New Zealand champion 1895 – 6.

Mellbye, Elisabeth (Norway). Women's world championship challenger 1937.

Mellgren, Artur *b. 15 Apr 1907* Swedish correspondence champion 1965.

Menchik, Olga *b. c.1908 Moscow d. 26 Jun 1944 London* Women's world championship challenger 1935, 1937.

Menchik, Vera Francevna *b. 16 Feb 1906 Moscow d. 26 Jun 1944 London* Women's world champion 1927 until her death in an air raid. World junior women's champion 1926, 1927.

Menzies, Barry New Zealand champion 1958 – 9.

Mercer, M M Scottish women's champion 1910.

Messa, Roberto *b. 3 Mar 1957 Brescia* Italian champion 1981.

Mestel, Andrew Jonathan *b. 13 Mar 1957 Cambridge* IM 1977. GM 1982. British champion 1976, 1983. =1st 1974 but lost play-off. World under-16 champion 1974.

Metz, Werner Richard *b. 19 Jul 1944 Stuttgart* German correspondence champion 1976.

Meyer, E Swiss champion 1901, 1902 (both joint).

Mezgailis, Voldemar *b. 22 Apr 1912 Lustuze* Latvian champion 1950.

Michael, Abraham *b. Bristol d. 12 Jul 1933* South African champion 1899.

Michel, Walter *b. 26 Nov 1888 Brienz* Swiss champion 1926.

Micheli, Carlo *b. 15 Sep 1946* Italian champion 1972, 1973.

Michell, Edith Mary Ann (née **Tapsell**) *b. c.1872 d. 18 Oct 1951 Battle* Women's world championship challenger 1927, 1933. British women's champion 1932 (after play-off), 1935. Joint champion 1931. =1st 1921 but lost play-off.

Michell, Reginald Price *b. 9 Apr 1873 Penzance d. 20 May 1938 London* British champion (amateur) 1902.

Mikhailov, Alexey I *b. 1936* IMC 1980. GMC 1983. World correspondence champion 1983 =2.

Mikhalchishin, Adrian Bogdanovich *b. 8 Nov 1954 Lvov* IM 1977. GM 1978.

Milan, Slade *b. c.1922 Yugoslavia* British correspondence champion 1959, 1962, 1963, 1965, 1966 (joint), 1969.

Miles, Anthony John *b. 23 Apr 1955 Edgbaston* IM 1974. GM 1976. World junior champion 1974. British champion 1982. Tilburg 1977 2. Tilburg 1978 =3. Wijk aan Zee 1979 =2. London 1980 =1. Puerto Madryn 1980 =1. Vrbas 1980 1. Oslo 1984 =2. Tilburg 1984 1. Portorož-Ljubljana 1985 =1. Tilburg 1985 = 1. Grand Prix (UK) 1974 (joint), 1975, 1982, 1984. Petit Prix 1980.

Miles, Jana (née **Malypetrova**, then **Hartston**) *b. 9 Dec 1947 Prague* WIM 1969. WGM 1982. British women's champion (as Hartston) 1970, 1971, 1972, 1973, 1974, 1976, 1977 (after play-off), (as Miles) 1979. Grand Prixette (UK) 1982, 1983 (joint).

Miletić, Jovan *b. 26 Nov 1962 Yugoslavia*

Milev, Zdravko A *b. 25 Oct 1929 Trgovishte* IM 1952. Bulgarian champion 1952, 1960, 1961.

Milligan, Helen (née **Scott**) *b. 25 Aug 1962* British women's champion 1983 (joint). Scottish women's champion 1982.

Mills, Daniel Yarnton *b. 29 Aug 1849 Stroud (Sudgrove) d. 18 Dec 1904 Hampstead, London* Scottish champion 1885, 1887, 1892, 1895, 1896, 1897, 1899, and, after play-off, 1900. =1st 1901 but lost play-off. British amateur champion 1890.

Mills, E S see Mann

Mills, John Denley *b. 14 Dec 1935 Plymouth* Welsh champion 1961 (joint).

Milos, Gilberto *b. 30 Oct 1963 São Paulo* IM 1984. Brazilian champion 1984, 1985.

Mineur, Hasse *b. 7 Mar 1942* Swedish correspondence champion 1980.

Minev, Nikolai Nikolayev *b. 8 Jan 1931 Ruse* IM 1960. Bulgarian champion 1953 (after play-off), 1965, 1966 (after play-off).

Minić, Dragoljub *b. 5 Mar 1937 Titograd* IM 1964. Yugoslav champion 1962 (joint).

Miranda, Marcío Brazilian champion 1974 (joint).

Model, Abram Yakovlevich *b. 23 Oct 1896 Daugavpils d. 16 Feb 1976 Leningrad* Leningrad champion 1944.

Moe, Mogens *b. 13 Mar 1944* Danish champion =1st 1969 but lost play-off.

Möhring, Günther *b. 25 Nov 1936 Gera* IM·1976. East German champion 1963.

Moles, John L *b. 22 Sep 1949 Belfast* Irish champion 1966, 1971.

Möller, Baldur Nordic champion 1948, 1950.

Icelandic champion 1938, 1941, 1943, 1947, 1948, 1950.

Møller, Jørgen *b. 4 Nov 1873 Otterup d. 20 Nov 1944 Copenhagen* Nordic champion 1899, 1901.

Monticelli, Mario *b. 16 Mar 1902 Venice* IM 1950. Emeritus GM 1985. Italian champion 1929, 1934, 1939.

Moore, Gillian British women's champion 1966 (joint).

Moore, George P *d. 1973 Cardiff* Welsh champion 1963.

Mora, Maria Teresa *b. 15 Oct 1907 Cuba* WIM 1950. Women's world championship challenger 1939, 1949 – 50.

Morcken, Otto B *b. 1910 Bergen* Norwegian champion 1956.

Morgado, Juan Sebastián. *b. 2 Feb 1947 Argentina* IMC 1980. GMC 1983. World correspondence championship 1984 2.

Morovic Fernández, Ivan *b. 24 Mar 1963 Viña del Mar* IM 1980. Chilean champion 1981.

Morphy, Paul Charles *b. 22 Jun 1837 New Orleans d. 10 Jul 1884 New Orleans.*

Morrison, Graham James *b. 10 Nov 1958 Glasgow* Scottish champion 1981 after play-off.

Morrison, John H *b. c.1870 d. 1 Sep 1935* London champion 1930 – 1 (after play-off).

Morrison, John Stuart *b. 7 Dec 1889 Toronto d. 1 Jan 1975 Toronto* Canadian champion 1910, 1913 (after play-off), 1922, 1924, 1926.

Morry, William Ritson *b. 5 Sep 1910* British correspondence champion 1942.

Mortensen, Erling *b. 5 Jun 1955* IM 1980. Danish champion 1981 after play-off.

Moseley, Amabel Nevill (née Jeffreys, finally Sollas) *b. c.1855 d. 28 Apr 1928 Headington* British women's champion 1913 after play-off.

Motwani, Paul Anthony *b. 13 Jun 1962 Glasgow* World under-16 champion 1978 – 9. Scottish champion 1978.

Muffang, André *b. 25 Jul 1897 St Brieuc* IM 1950. French champion 1931.

Mulcahy, Edmond Noel *b. 1929 Cappoquin d. 24 Mar 1968 Irish Sea* Irish champion 1953. = 1st 1955 but lost tie-break.

Muller, Emanuel *b. c.1877 d. 14 Mar 1936 Zurich* Swiss champion 1903.

Mureşan, Margareta (née Juncu) *b. 13 Mar 1950 Cluj-Napoca* WIM 1975. WGM 1982. Romanian women's champion 1983, 1985.

Musgrave, M British women's champion 1938.

Myhre, Erling *b. 11 Jan 1903 Christiana d. 12 Apr 1971* Norwegian champion 1946, 1950, 1955.

Nadj-Radenković, Marija *b. 7 Dec 1924 Veprovac* Yugoslav women's champion 1955.

Naegeli, Oskar *b. 25 Feb 1885 Ermatingen d. 19 Nov 1959 Fribourg* Swiss champion 1910, 1936.

Nagy, Géza *b. 29 Dec 1892 Sátoraljaújhely d. 13 Aug 1953 Kaposvár* IM 1950. Hungarian champion 1924.

Najdorf, Miguel *b. 15 Apr 1910 Warsaw* GM 1950. Candidate 1950, 1953. Argentine champion 1949, 1951, 1955, 1964, 1967, 1975. Los Angeles 1963 =3.

Nakkerud, Ruth Bloch (Norway) Women's world championship challenger 1937, 1939.

Napier, William Ewart *b. 17 Jan 1881 Camberwell, London d. 6 Sep 1952 Washington, DC* British champion 1904 after play-off.

Napolitano, Mario *b. 10 Feb 1910 Acquaviva delle Fonti* GMC 1953. World correspondence championship 1953 =2.

Narraway, James Ephraim *b. 11 Jun 1857 Sackville d. 16 Jun 1947 Ottawa* Canadian champion 1893, 1897, 1898.

Nättorp, Thor *b. 26 Feb 1920* Swedish correspondence champion 1960.

Nedeljković, Verica (née Jovanović) *b. 16 Sep 1924 Čačak* WIM 1954. WGM 1977. Yugoslav women's champion 1950, 1951, 1952 (joint), 1953 (joint) (as Jovanović). 1958, 1965.

Needham, Teresa M *b. 30 Nov 1965* WIM 1984.

Nei, Iivo *b. 31 Oct 1931* IM 1931. Estonian champion 1951, 1952, 1956, 1960, 1961, 1962, 1971, 1974.

Neikirch, Oleg Nikolaev *b. 8 Mar 1914 Tbilisi d. 1985* IM 1957. Bulgarian champion 1943, 1948 (joint), 1957.

Nemet, Ivan *b. 14 Apr 1943 Sombor* IM 1976. GM 1978. Yugoslav champion 1979.

Nenarokov, Vladimir Ivanovich *b. 1880 Moscow d. 13 Dec 1953* IM 1950. Moscow champion 1900, 1908, 1924.

Nestler, Vincenzo *b. 8 Jan 1912 Agrigento* Italian champion 1943, 1954 (after play-off).

Newcombe, W D *b. Pontypridd* Welsh champion 1962 (joint).

Nicolau, Alexandra Ecaterina (later van der Mije) *b. 22 Jul 1940 Bucharest* WIM 1960. WGM 1976. Romanian women's champion 1960, 1961, 1963, 1964, 1965, 1973.

Nield, Adam Edgar New Zealand champion 1948 – 9.

Nielsen, Bjørn *b. 4 Oct 1907 d. 21 May 1949 Herning* Danish champion 1941, 1942, 1944, 1946. =1st 1947 (lost play-off) and 1949 (died without play-off).

Nielsen, Jens Ove Fries *b. 2 Feb 1960 Esbjerg* IM 1984. Danish championship = 1st 1982 but lost play-off.

Nielsen, Johanne Danish women's champion = 1st 1970 but lost play-off.

Niemelä, Aarne Ilmari *b. 16 Sep 1907 Miehikkälä d. 12 Nov 1975 Helsinki* Finnish champion 1947 – 8.

Niklasson, Christer Lennart Oscar *b. 4 Jan 1953 Stockholm* IM 1977. Nordic champion 1979.

Nikolić, Predrag *b. 11 Sep 1960 Bosanski Šamac* IM 1980. GM 1983. Yugoslav champion 1980, 1984. Sochi 1982 2. Novi Sad 1984 1. Wijk aan Zee 1984 3. Wijk aan Zee 1986 = 2.

Nilsson, Allan *b. 18 May 1899 Göteborg d. 4 Sep 1949 Göteborg* Swedish champion (tournament) 1923 (joint), (match) 1924.

Nilsson, Zandor *b. 2 Jul 1913 Stockholm d. 1 Jul 1973 Stockholm* IMC 1961. Swedish champion 1957, 1965.

Nimzowitsch, Aaron *b. 7 Nov 1886 Riga d. 16 Mar 1935 Copenhagen* Russian champion 1914 (joint). San Sebastian 1912 = 2. St Petersburg 1914 3. Berlin 1928 2. Bled 1931 3. Nordic champion 1924, 1934.

Nogeuiras, José de Jesús *b. 17 Jul 1959 Santa Clara* IM 1972. GM 1979. Candidate 1985. Cuban champion 1978, 1984 (joint).

Nokes, Roger I *b. 13 Aug 1958* New Zealand champion 1980 – 1 (joint).

Norby, Peter H *b. 28 Apr 1940* Danish champion = 1st 1970 but lost play-off.

Norcia, Frederico *b. 31 Mar 1904 Lugo* Italian champion 1952.

Nordström, Eric *b. 27 Feb 1924* Swedish correspondence champion 1966, 1975.

Norman-Hansen, Holger *b. 2 Jan 1899 d. 26 Mar 1984 Malta* Danish champion 1939 after play-off. = 1st 1936 but lost play-off.

Norwood, David Robert *b. 3 Oct 1968 Farnworth* IM 1985.

Nowak, Ignacy *b. 12 Jan 1949 Poznań* Polish champion 1985 (after play-off).

Nunn, John Denis Martin *b. 25 Apr 1955 London* IM 1975. GM 1978. British champion 1980 after play-off. = 1st 1979 but lost tie-break. European junior champion 1974 – 5. Baden 1980 3. Wijk aan Zee 1982 = 1. Gjovik 1983 = 1. Amsterdam 1985 3. Wijk aan Zee 1985 = 2. Grand Prix (UK) winner 1979, 1980.

Nutu, Daniela Silvia (later Terescenco) *b. 8 Jun 1957 Timişoara* WIM 1978. WGM 1983. Romanian women's champion 1978, 1979, 1980.

Nyholm, Gustaf *b. 27 Jan 1880 Stockholm d. 12 Sep 1957 Stockholm* Nordic champion 1917.

Swedish champion (match) 1917, 1921, (tournament) 1921 (joint).

Oakley, Peter James *b. 10 Feb 1931* IMC 1982. British correspondence champion 1958.

Ofstad, Per *b. 27 Nov 1934* Norway champion 1961.

Øgaard, Leif *b. 5 Jan 1952* IM 1974. Norwegian champion 1974, 1975, 1979, 1985.

O'Hanlon, John J *b. 1874 Portadown d. 20 Feb 1960 Dublin* Irish champion 1912, 1915, 1925, 1926, 1930, 1932, 1935, 1936, 1940.

Ōim, Tōnu *b. 16 Jun 1941 Tallinn* IMC 1976. GMC 1981. World correspondence champion 1983.

Ojanen, Kaarle Sakari *b. 4 Dec 1916 Hamina* IM 1952. IMC 1981. Finnish champion 1950, 1951, 1951 – 2, 1952 – 3, 1957, 1958, 1959, 1960, 1961, 1962, 1967, 1972, 1983 (after play-off).

O'Kelly de Galway, Albéric *b. 17 May 1911 Brussels d. 3 Oct 1980 Brussels* IM 1950. GM 1956. GMC 1962. World correspondence champion 1962.

Olafsson, Fridrik *b. 26 Jan 1935 Reykjavik* IM 1956. GM 1958. Candidate 1959. Nordic champion 1953, 1971. Icelandic champion 1952, 1953, 1957, 1961, 1962, 1964, 1969. Los Angeles 1963 = 3. Lugano 1970 2. Wijk aan Zee 1971 = 2. Wijk aan Zee 1976 = 1.

Olafsson, Friman Icelandic champion 1923.

Olaffson, Helgi *b. 15 Aug 1956 Reykjavik* IM 1977. GM 1985. Icelandic champion 1978, 1981.

Olafsson, Stefán Icelandic champion 1919, 1921, 1922.

O'Leary, M Irish champion = 1st 1972 but lost play-off.

Oll, Lembit *b. 7 Nov 1964* IM 1983. Estonian champion 1982.

Olland, Adolf Georg *b. 13 Apr 1867 Utrecht d. 22 Jul 1933 Hague* Netherlands champion 1909.

Ollivier, Arthur Morton *d. 20 Oct 1897 Christchurch* New Zealand champion 1888 – 9.

Olson, Anton *b. 1881* Nordic champion 1919 (joint). Swedish champion (match) 1921, (tournament) 1917 (joint), 1919, 1923 (joint).

Olson, Karl *b. 1888* Swedish champion (tournament) 1924.

Omelchenko, Lev Yevgenyevich *b. 6 Jun 1922 Zhaskov* IMC 1977. USSR correspondence champion 1970, 1972.

Opočenský, Karel *b. 7 Feb 1892 Mostě d. 16 Nov 1975* IM 1950. Czech champion 1927, 1929, 1938, 1943 (joint), 1944.

Oren, Menachem (né Chwojnik) *b. 1913 Poland d. Dec 1962 Tel Aviv* Israeli champion 1951.

Orlov, A Moscow champion 1932 (joint).

Ornstein, Axel Otto *b. 24 Apr 1952 Boliden* IM 1975. Swedish champion 1972, 1973, 1975, 1977, 1984.

Orr, Mark J L *b. 9 Nov 1955 Ulster* Irish champion 1985 (joint).

Ortega, Rogelio *b. 28 Mar 1915* Cuban champion 1958, 1966.

Osnos, Viacheslav Vulfovich *b. 24 Jul 1935* IM 1965. Leningrad champion 1971, 1980.

Østenstad, Berge *b. 16 Sep 1974* Norwegian champion 1984.

Ostermeyer, Peter Ulrich Gerd *b. 12 Oct 1943 Bärwalde* IM 1981. West German champion 1974.

Ostojić, Predrag *b. 22 Feb 1938 Kraljevo* IM 1968. GM 1975. Yugoslav champion 1968 (joint), 1971 (joint).

O'Sullivan, Bartholomew *b. 1900 Limerick d. 20 Mar 1978 Dublin* Irish champion 1939, 1946.

O'Sullivan, Donal J *d. Feb 1960 Dublin* Irish champion 1948, 1956, 1957.

Ozols, Karlis *b. 9 Oct 1912 Latvia* IMC 1977. Australian champion 1956 – 7 (joint).

Pachman, Ludek *b. 11 May 1924 Bělá pod Bezděz em* IM 1950. GM 1954. Czech champion 1946, 1953 (after play-off), 1957, 1958, 1961, 1963, 1966. West German champion 1978.

Padevsky, Nikola Bochev *b. 29 May 1933 Plovdiv* IM 1957. GM 1964. Bulgarian champion 1954, 1955, 1962, 1964 (after play-off).

Page, George *b. 27 Oct 1890 Glasgow d. 26 Jun 1953 Edinburgh* Scottish champion 1925.

Paiva, José Pinto *b. 16 Jul 1938 Salvador* Brazilian champion 1966, 1971.

Palacios de la Prida, Ernesto *b. 13 Nov 1943 Alcala de Guadaira* Spanish champion 1970.

Palciauskas, Vytautus Victor *b. 3 Oct 1941 Kaunas* IMC 1978. GMC 1983. World correspondence champion 1984.

Palda, Karl *b. 14 Apr 1947 Vienna* Austrian champion 1931 (joint).

Palme, Rudolf *b. 6 Mar 1910* Austrian champion 1950.

Panno, Oscar Roberto *b. 17 Mar 1935 Buenos Aires* IM 1954. GM 1955. Candidate 1956. World junior champion 1953. Argentine champion 1953, 1985.

Panov, Vasily Nikolayevich *b. 1 Nov 1906 Kozelsk d. Jan 1973* IM 1950. Moscow champion 1929.

Paoli, Enrico *b. 13 Jan 1908 Trieste* IM 1951. Italian champion 1951, 1957, 1968.

Parma, Bruno *b. 30 Dec 1941 Ljubljana* IM 1961. GM 1963. World junior champion 1961.

Parr, Frank *b. 17 Dec 1918 Wandsworth* British

correspondence champion 1948 (joint), 1949 (joint), 1950, 1956.

Partos, Carol *b. 10 Aug 1936 Timişoara* IM 1975. Romanian champion 1972.

Pasman, Mark *b. 16 Mar 1932* Latvian champion 1951.

Patterson, Nicholas James *b. 9 Jun 1947* Irish champion 1969.

Pavey, Max *b. 5 Mar 1918 Boston USA d. 4 Sep 1957 Manhattan* Scottish champion 1939.

Pedersen, Eigil *b. 23 May 1917 Aarhus* Danish champion 1951 (after play-off), 1953, 1961.

Pedersen, Johannes Danish champion 1920.

Peev, Peicho Chanev *b. 2 Apr 1940 Plovdiv* IM 1973. Bulgarian champion 1967 (after play-off).

Penrose, Jonathan *b. 7 Oct 1933 Colchester* IM 1961. IMC 1980. GMC 1983. British champion 1958 (after play-off), 1959 (after play-off), 1960, 1961, 1962, 1963, 1966, 1967, 1968, 1969. London champion 1949.

Peralta Santana, Carlos Chilean champion 1920.

Perevoznic, Margareta (née Covali) *b. 10 Sep 1936 Cernăuti* WIM 1967. Romanian women's champion 1962.

Pérez, Francisco José *b. 8 Sep 1920 Vigo* IM 1959. Spanish champion 1948, 1954, 1960.

Perkins, N Anthony London champion 1936 – 7 (after play-off).

Pestalozzi, Max *b. 1856 d. Jun 1925* Swiss champion 1889, 1890, 1901 (all joint).

Petersen, Finn *b. 28 Apr 1940* Danish champion =1st 1971 but lost play-off.

Petkevic, Juzef *b. 19 Dec 1940 Riga* IM 1980. Latvian champion 1969, 1974, 1985 (all joint).

Petrosyan, Tigran Vartanovich *b. 17 Jun 1929 Tbilisi d. 13 Aug 1984 Moscow* IM 1952. GM 1952. World champion 1963 – 9. Candidate 1953, 1956, 1959, 1971, 1974, 1977, 1980. USSR champion 1959, 1961, 1969 (joint), 1975. Moscow champion 1951, 1956 (joint), 1968 (joint). Bled 1961 =3. Los Angeles 1963 =1. Yerevan 1965 =2. Zagreb 1965 3. Moscow 1966 1. Wijk aan Zee 1971 =2. Manila 1974 2. Milan 1975 =3. Vrbas 1980 =2. Tilburg 1981 2.

Petrov, Peter Stoinev *b. 18 Sep 1930* Bulgarian champion 1946.

Petrov, Vladimir *b. 27 Sep 1907 Riga d. 15 Mar 1945 Smolensk* Latvian champion 1930 – 1, 1935, 1937, 1938 – 9.

Petrović, Marija *b. 29 Aug 1953 Belgrade* WIM 1981. Yugoslav women's champion 1983, 1984. =1st 1978 but lost tie-break.

Pettersson, A H *b. Stockholm?* Nordic champion 1905.

Pettersson, Einar *b. 9 Sep 1901* Swedish champion (tournament) 1929.

Pettersson, Lars-Eric Nordic champion 1977.

Pettersson, Ragnar Willy *b. 29 Mar 1915 Norrköping* Swedish champion 1937. Swedish correspondence champion 1955.

Petursson, Margeir *b. 15 Feb 1960 Reykjavik* IM 1978.

Pfleger, Helmut *b. 6 Aug 1943 Teplice-Šanov* IM 1965. GM 1975. West German champion 1965 (joint). Montilla 1974 =3. Manila 1975 =2. Montilla 1975 =3. Amsterdam 1978 =3.

Philidor, Francois André Danican *b. 7 Sep 1726 Dreux d. 31 Aug 1795 London*.

Phillips, Alan British champion 1954 (joint).

Phillips, J Rodney *b. 1942 d. 1969 England* New Zealand champion 1956–7 (joint), 1957–8, 1964–5.

Piazzini, Luis Roberto *b. 15 May 1905 Buenos Aires d. 24 Feb 1980* Argentine champion 1934.

Pietzsch, Wolfgang Walther *b. 21 Dec 1930 Wittgendorf* IM 1961. GM 1965. East German champion 1949, 1960, 1962, 1967.

Pihajlić, Amalija *b. 4 Jul 1944 Starčevo* WIM 1976. Yugoslav women's champion 1974(1), 1977 (both joint).

Pillsbury, Harry Nelson *b. 5 Dec 1872 Somerville d. 17 Jun 1906 Philadelphia* USA champion 1897, 1898. German champion 1900 (joint). Hastings 1895 1. St Petersburg 1895–6 3. Budapest 1896 3. London 1899 =2.

Pilnik, Herman *b. 8 Jan 1914 Stuttgart d. 12 Nov 1981 Caracas* IM 1950. GM 1952. Candidate 1956. Argentine champion 1945, 1958.

Pintér, József *b. 9 Nov 1953 Budapest* IM 1976. GM 1982. Hungarian champion 1978, 1979.

Pirc, Vasja *b. 19 Dec 1907 Idrija d. 2 Jun 1980 Ljubljana* IM 1950. GM 1953. Yugoslav champion 1935 (joint), 1936, 1937, 1948 (joint), 1953 (joint).

Piskov, Kámen Penev *b. 7 Aug 1909 d. 19 Dec 1972* Bulgarian champion 1947 (joint).

Pizzi Possi, Tulio Chilean champion 1946.

Planté, Jacques French champion 1969.

Plaskett, Harold James *b. 18 Mar 1960 Dkeliha, Cyprus* IM 1981. GM 1985. Grand Prix (UK) champion 1983.

Plater, Kazimierz *b. 3 Mar 1915 Wilno d. 1982* IM 1950. Polish champion 1949, 1956, 1957.

Platt, Josef Austrian champion 1949.

Pleci, Isaías *b. 27 Oct 1907 d. 27 Dec 1979* IM 1965. Argentine champion 1930, 1931.

Podhorzer, David Austrian champion 1934.

Pogorevici see Albulet.

Polgár, Zsuzsa *b. 19 Apr 1969 Budapest* IM 1984. WIM 1982. World under-16 women's champion 1981.

Polihroniade, Elisabeta (née Ionescu) *b. 24 Apr 1935 Bucharest* WIM 1960. WGM 1982. Romanian women's champion 1966, 1970, 1971, 1972, 1975, 1976, 1977.

Pollock, William Henry Krause *b. 21 Feb 1859 Cheltenham d. 5 Oct 1896 Clifton* Irish champion 1885, 1886.

Polovodin, Igor Alexeyevich *b. 23 Mar 1955* Leningrad champion 1979 (after play-off).

Polugayevsky, Lev Abramovich *b. 20 Nov 1934 Mogilev* IM 1961. GM 1962. Candidate 1974, 1977, 1980. USSR champion 1967 (joint), 1968–9 (after play-off), 1969 (joint). Manila 1975 =2. Montilla 1975 =1. Wijk aan Zee 1979 1. Moscow 1981 =2. Bugojno 1982 =2. Mar del Plata 1982 =3. London 1984 =2.

Pomar Salamanca, Arturo *b. 1 Sep 1931 Palma de Majorca* IM 1950. GM 1962. Spanish champion 1946, 1950, 1957, 1958, 1959, 1962, 1966.

Popa, Toma *b.20 Apr 1908 Mihai-Brau d. 25 Feb 1962 Bucharest* Romanian champion 1948.

Pope, Edwin *b. 14 Mar 1843 Kingston, Ont. d. 3 Apr 1936 Quebec* Canadian champion 1879.

Poplawski, Arthur *b. Poland* Swiss champion 1889, 1890 (both joint).

Popoff, M Swiss champion 1893.

Popov, Lyuben Stoyanov *b. 28 Jan 1936 Plovdiv* IM 1965. Bulgarian champion 1970.

Popov, Vladilen Todorov *b. 21 Jul 1935 Sofia* Bulgarian champion 1959.

Popović, Petar *b. 14 Feb 1959 Orlovat* IM 1977. GM 1981. Novi Sad 1984 =2.

Porat, Yosef (né Foerder) *b. 7 Jun 1909 Breslau* IM 1952. Israeli champion 1937, 1940 (after play-off), 1953, 1957, 1959, 1963.

Porreca, Giorgio *b. 30 Aug 1927 Naples* IM 1957. IMC 1975. Italian champion 1950 (after play-off), 1956.

Portisch, Lajos *b. 4 Apr 1937 Zalaegerszeg* IM 1958. GM 1961. Candidate 1968, 1974, 1977, 1980, 1983, 1985. Hungarian champion 1958(1), 1958(2) (after play-off), 1961 (after play-off), 1962 (after play-off), 1964, 1965(2), 1971, 1975, 1981 (on tie-break). Milan 1975 2. Wijk aan Zee 1975 1. Tilburg 1978 1. Wijk aan Zee 1978 1. Tilburg 1979 3. Wijk aan Zee 1979 3. Tilburg 1980 2. Amsterdam 1981 =2. Tilburg 1981 =3. Mar del Plata 1982 2. Nikšić 1983 =3. Tilburg 1983 =2. Titograd 1984 =3. Portorož-Ljubljana 1985 =1. Reggio Emilia 1985 1.

Poschauko, Karl *b. c.1892* Austrian champion 1952.

Post, Alfred M. Erhardt *b. 23 Sep 1881 Cottbus*

d. 1 Aug 1947 Berlin German champion 1921, 1922.

Postovsky, Boris Naumovich *b. 1937 Moscow* USSR correspondence champion 1980.

Poulsen, Christian *b. 16 Aug 1912 Rind Sogn d. 19 Apr 1981* Danish champion 1945, 1952. =1st 1939, 1940, 1951 but lost all play-offs.

Poutiainen, Pertti Kalervo *b. 5 Dec 1952 Helsinki d. 11 Jun 1978 Helsinki* IM 1976. Finnish champion 1974, 1976 (joint).

Povah, Nigel Edward *b. 17 Jul 1952 Wandsworth* IM 1983. IMC 1983.

Powell, Lynda Annette *b. 25 Dec 1968 Newport* Welsh women's champion 1984.

Prameshuber, Alexander *b. 20 Nov 1926 Sterning* Austrian champion 1958 (after play-off).

Prandstetter, Eduard *b. 15 Dec 1948 Prague* IM 1979. Czech champion 1976, 1978.

Price, Edith Charlotte *b. 1872 Mile End, London d. 1956 Edmonton, London* Women's world championship challenger 1927, 1933. British women's champion 1922, 1923, 1924, 1928, 1948. =1st 1920 and 1921 but lost play-offs.

Prins, Lodewijk *b. 27 Jan 1913 Amsterdam* IM 1950. Emeritus GM 1982. Netherlands champion 1965.

Pritchard, Elaine (née Saunders) *b. 7 Jan 1926* WIM 1957. World junior women's champion 1936, 1937. British women's champion 1939, 1946 (after play-off) both as Saunders, 1956, 1965.

Pritchett, Craig William *b. 15 Jan 1949 Glasgow* IM 1976. Scottish champion 1977.

Prokeš, Ladislav *b. 7 Jun 1884 Prague d. 9 Jan 1966 Prague* Czech champion 1921 (joint).

Prokopović, Olivera *b. 26 Dec 1949 Leskovac* WIM 1979. Yugoslav women's champion 1978 on tie-break.

Przepiórka, Dawid *b. 22 Dec 1880 Warsaw d. Apr 1940 Linz?* Polish champion 1926.

Przewoźnik, Jan *b. 16 Sep 1957 Katowice* IM 1985. Polish champion 1979.

Psakhis, Lev Borisovich *b. 29 Nov 1958 Kalinin* IM 1980. GM 1982. USSR champion 1980–1, 1981 (both joint).

Purdy, Cecil John Seddon *7 Mar 1906 Port Said d. 6 Nov 1979 Sydney* IM 1951. GMC 1953. World correspondence champion 1953. New Zealand champion 1924–5, 1935–6. Australian champion 1934–5, 1936–7 (after play-off), 1948–9, 1951.

Purdy, John Spencer *b. 25 Sep 1935 Sydney* Australian champion 1954–5, 1962–3. His father (above) and grandfather (see Crackanthorp) were both Australian champions.

Pytel, Krysztof *b. 15 May 1945 Chelm Lubelski* IM 1975. Polish champion 1972, 1973.

Quinteros, Miguel Angel *b. 28 Dec 1947 Buenos Aires* IM 1970. GM 1973. Argentine champion 1966, 1980.

Rabar, Braslav *b. 27 Sep 1919 Zagreb d. 6 Dec 1973 Zagreb* IM 1950. Yugoslav champion 1951, 1953 (joint).

Rabinovich, Abram Isaakovich *b. 1878 d. 7 Nov 1943* Moscow champion 1926.

Rabinovich, Ilya Leontyevich *b. 1891 St Petersburg d. 1942 Perm* USSR champion 1934 (joint). Leningrad champion 1920, 1925 (joint), 1928, 1940–1.

Raclauskien, E Lithuania. Women's world championship challenger 1939.

Radulov, Ivan *b. 7 Jan 1939 Burgas* IM 1968. GM 1972. Bulgarian champion 1971, 1974, 1977, 1980–1 (last three after play-offs). Montilla 1974 1. Montilla 1975 =1.

Ragozin, Vyacheslav Vasiliyevich *b. 8 Oct 1908 St Petersburg d. 11 Mar 1962 Moscow* GM 1950. GMC 1959. World correspondence champion 1959. Leningrad champion 1936, 1945.

Raizman, Maurice *b. 26 Feb 1905 Bendery d. 1 Apr 1974 Paris* French champion 1932, 1936, 1946, 1947, 1951, 1952.

Rajković, Dušan *b. 17 Jun 1942 Kruševac* IM 1974. GM 1977. Yugoslav champion 1983 (joint).

Randviir, Jüri *b. 28 May 1927*. Estonian champion 1947–8, 1949 (joint), 1950, 1954, 1957 (after play-off).

Rantanen, Yrjö Aukusti *b. 23 Apr 1950 Tampere* IM 1977. GM 1981. Finnish champion 1976 (joint), 1978.

Ranniku, Maaja *b. 1 Mar 1941* WIM 1964. USSR women's champion 1963 (joint), 1967, 1970 (joint).

Rashkovsky, Nukhim Nikolayevich *b. 18 Apr 1946 Sverdlovsk* IM 1976. GM 1980. Moscow champion 1982 (joint).

Rasmusson, Birger Axel *b. 19 Jun 1901 d. 3 May 1964* Finnish champion 1933.

Rath, Ulrik *b. 25 Dec 1946* IM 1983. Danish champion 1974.

Raud, Ilmar *b. Apr 1913 Viljandi d. 13 Jul 1941 Buenos Aires* Estonian champion 1934, 1938–9.

Ravn, Palle *b. 13 Dec 1928* Danish champion 1957.

Rayner, Emmanuel M *b. 11 Jun 1958 London* Welsh champion 1976 (joint).

Razuvayev, Yury Sergeyevich *b. 10 Oct 1945 Moscow* IM 1973. GM 1976.

Reca, Damián M *b. 1894 d. 4 May 1937 Buenos Aires* Argentine champion 1921, 1923, 1924, 1925, 1927, 1928, 1929.

Ree, Hans *b. 15 Nov 1944 Amsterdam* IM 1968. GM 1980. Netherlands champion 1967, 1969,

1971, 1982. European junior champion 1964–5, 1965–6 (both joint).

Reed Valenzuela, Enrique Chilean champion 1932.

Reggio, Arturo *b. 9 Jan 1863 Gorizia d. 17 Jul 1917 Milan* Italian champion 1900, 1901, 1905, 1913, 1916.

Reid, John *b. Moate* Irish champion 1961, 1962 (joint).

Reilly, Brian Patrick *b. 12 Dec 1901 Menton* Irish champion 1959, 1960.

Reischer, Salome *b. 19 Feb 1899 Austria* (Moved to Palestine then USA). WIM 1952. Women's world championship challenger 1937, 1939.

Rellstab, Ludwig Adolf Friedrich Hans *b. 23 Nov 1904 Berlin d. 14 Feb 1983 Wedel* IM 1950. German champion 1942.

Renaud, Georges *b. 8 Jan 1893 Nancy d. 28 Jul 1975 Peille* French champion 1923.

Renman, Nils-Gustav *b. 18 Dec 1950 Umeå* IM 1980. Swedish champion 1978 (joint), 1980.

Renter, Raul *b. 1 Aug 1920 Tallinn* Estonian champion 1946, 1949 (joint).

Reshevsky, Samuel Herman *b. 26 Nov 1911 Ozorkow* GM 1950. Challenger 1948. Candidate 1953, 1968. USA champion 1936, 1938, 1940, 1942, 1946, 1969. Nottingham 1936 =3. Semmering-Baden 1937 =3. Dallas 1957 =1.

Réti, Richard *b. 28 May 1889 Bratislava d. 6 Jun 1929 Prague* Czech champion 1925.

Rey Ardid, Ramón *b. 20 Dec 1903 Saragossa* Spanish champion 1930, 1933, 1935, 1942.

Reynolds, D I W *b. c.1944* Welsh champion 1965.

Rhodes, H G British correspondence champion 1953.

Ribli, Zoltán *b. 6 Sep 1951 Mohács* IM 1970. GM 1973. Candidate 1983, 1985. Hungarian champion 1973 (joint), 1974, 1977 (joint). European junior champion 1968–9 (joint), 1970–1. Amsterdam 1978 2. Bled-Portorož 1979 =2. Wijk aan Zee 1983 2. Bugojno 1984 2. Tilburg 1984 =2. Portorož-Ljubljana 1985 =1.

Richardson, Keith Bevan *b. 2 Feb 1942 Nottingham* IMC 1968. GMC 1975. World correspondence championship 1975 =3, 1984 =3.

Richmond, George W *b. Jun 1877 Manchester d. Nov 1941 London* Scottish champion 1910 after play-off.

Richter, Emil *b. 14 Jan 1894 Kr. Vinohradech d. 16 Mar 1971 Prague* IM 1951. Czech champion 1948 (after play-off).

Richter, Kurt *b. 24 Nov 1900 Berlin d. 29 Dec 1969 Berlin* IM 1950. German champion 1935.

Rinder, Friedl *b. 20 Nov 1905 Schrobenhausen* WIM 1957. Women's world championship

challenger 1939. German women's champion 1949, 1955, 1956, 1959.

Rinne, Paul Estonian champion 1922–3, 1932 (joint).

Ritchie, M M Scottish women's champion 1925.

Rittner, Horst Robert *b. 16 Jul 1930 Breslau* GMC 1961. World correspondence champion 1971. German correspondence champion 1956.

Rivas Pastor, Manuel *b. 13 Jul 1960 Jaen* IM 1980. Spanish champion 1978, 1979, 1981.

Robatsch, Karl *b. 14 Oct 1928 Klagenfurt* IM 1957. GM 1961. Austrian champion 1960.

Roberts, Edward *b. c.1854 d. 4 Sep 1916 Cape Town* South African champion 1892 (joint), 1897.

Rocas, Orlando Brazilian champion 1932, 1933, 1944.

Rocha, Antonio *b. 13 Jun 1944* IM 1979. Brazilian champion 1964, 1969.

Roche, W L British correspondence champion 1936, 1937, 1940.

Rodríguez, Amador *b. 18 Oct 1957 San German, Cuba* IM 1975. GM 1977. Cuban champion 1984 (joint).

Rodríguez González, Jesús *b. 2 Jul 1939* IM 1972. Cuban champion 1969, 1971, 1972.

Rogers, Ian *b. 24 Jun 1960 Hobart* IM 1980. GM 1985. Australian champion 1979–80, 1985–6. Commonwealth champion 1983 (joint).

Röhrl, Karl *b. 11 Jan 1941 Wilhelmsburg* Austrian champion 1969 (after play-off), 1971.

Rojahn, Ernst *b. 13 Aug 1909 Tønsberg* Norwegian champion 1945, 1958.

Rojas Sepulveda, Eduardo *b. 22 Oct 1969* World under-16 champion 1985.

Rolland, Pierre *b. 9 Sep 1926 Aude d. 10 Feb 1967* French champion 1956.

Romanishin, Oleg Mikhailovich *b. 10 Jan 1952 Lvov* IM 1973. GM 1976. European junior champion 1972–3. Leningrad 1977 =1. Tilburg 1979 2. Sochi 1982 =3. Moscow 1985 1. Reggio Emilia 1985–6 =1.

Romanovsky, Peter Arsenyevich *b. 29 Jul 1892 St Petersburg d. 1 Mar 1964 Moscow* IM 1950. USSR champion 1923, 1927 (joint). Leningrad champion 1925 (joint).

Romero, Rosendo Cuban champion 1950 (joint).

Roodzant, Catherine (Netherlands). Women's world championship challenger 1937, 1939.

Roos, Louis *b. 7 Dec 1957 Strasbourg* IM 1982. French champion 1977, 1980.

Roos, Michel *b. 27 Aug 1932 Strasbourg* French champion 1964.

Rosselli del Turco, Stefano *b. 17 Jul 1877 Florence*

d. 18 Aug 1947 Florence Italian champion 1920, 1923, 1931.

Rossetto, Héctor Decio b. 8 Sep 1922 Bahía Blanca IM 1950. GM 1960. Argentine champion 1942, 1944, 1947, 1960, 1972.

Rossolimo, Nicolas b. 28 Feb 1910 Kiev d. 24 Jul 1975 New York IM 1950. GM 1953. French champion 1948.

Rothén, Håkan b. 14 May 1958 Swedish correspondence champion 1984.

Rõtov, Boriss b. 20 Aug 1937 Moscow Estonian champion 1975 (joint).

Rõtova, Merike b. 19 Aug 1936 WIMC 1976. Women's world correspondence championship 1977 3, 1984 2.

Rovner, Dmitry Osipovich b. 8 Jan 1908 Leningrad champion 1937 (joint).

Ruban, Ye b. c.1946 Leningrad champion 1966.

Rubanraut, Serge b. 16 Mar 1948 Shanghai. Australian champion 1975 – 6.

Rubel, Igor Georgyevich b. 1933. d. 4 Apr 1963 Leningrad champion 1958.

Rubinetti, Jorge b. 31 Mar 1945 IM 1969. Argentine champion 1971 – 2, 1982 (after play-off).

Rubinstein, Akiba Kiwelowicz b. 12 Oct 1882 Stawiski. d. 15 Mar 1961 Antwerp GM 1950. Russian champion 1907 – 8, 1912. Polish champion 1927. Austrian champion 1922. German champion 1912 (joint). St Petersburg 1909 =1. San Sebastián 1911 =2. San Sebastián 1912 1.

Rubtsova, Olga Nikolayevna b. 20 Aug 1909 Moscow WIM 1950. WGM 1976. IMC 1973. Women's world champion 1956 – 8. Challenger 1949 – 50. Women's world correspondence champion 1971; in 1977 2nd. USSR women's champion 1927, 1931, 1937.

Rubtsova, Tatiana b. 8 May 1962 USSR WIM 1984.

Rudenko, Lyudmila Vladimirovna b. 27 Jul 1904 Lubni. d. Mar 1986 WIM 1950. WGM 1976. Women's world champion 1950 – 3. Challenger 1956. USSR women's champion 1952.

Rudensky, Nikolai Stepanovich b. 22 Sep 1935. World blind champion 1975.

Ruiz, Sofia Spanish women's champion 1951.

Rumens, David Edward b. 23 Sep 1939 Grand Prix (UK) champion 1976, 1978.

Runström, Harry b. 20 Feb 1917 Swedish correspondence champion 1969.

Rynd, J A Porterfield d. 19 Mar 1917 Dublin Irish champion 1865.

Ryumin, Nikolai Nikolayevich b. 5 Sep 1908 Moscow. d. 1942 Siberia Moscow champion 1931, 1933 – 4, 1935.

Sacconi, Antonio b. 5 Oct 1895 Rome. d. 22 Dec 1968 Rome IM 1951. Italian champion 1935.

Sack, Herman Swiss champion 1897.

Sadomsky, Anatoly Mikhailovich b. 20 Oct 1910 USSR correspondence champion 1960.

Salas Romo, Julio Chilean champion 1937, 1954, 1955, 1962.

Salo, Toivo b. 22 Jan 1909 Helsinki. d. 5 Apr 1981 Helsinki Finnish champion 1938, 1949, 1956 (after play-off).

Salov, Valery b. 26 May 1964 IM 1984. World under-16 champion 1980. European junior champion 1983 – 4.

Salskov, A Danish champion 1914.

Salvioli, Carlo b. 2 Nov 1848 Venice. d. 29 Jan 1930 Mirano Italian champion 1881.

Salwe, Georg Henryk Solomonowicz b. 24 Oct 1862 Warsaw. d. 15 Dec 1920 Łódź Russian champion 1906.

Sämisch, Friedrich b. 20 Sep 1896 Berlin. d. 16 Aug 1975 Berlin GM 1950. Austrian champion 1921.

Sanakoyev, Grigory Konstantinovich b. 17 Apr 1935 Voronezh IMC 1971. GMC 1984. World correspondence championship 1984 =3.

Sanderson, E Canadian champion 1876, 1881 – 2.

Sándor, Béla b. 14 Dec 1919 Budapest. d. 21 Mar 1978 Budapest IM 1964. Hungary champion 1953.

Sanguineti, Raúl C b. 3 Feb 1933 Parana IM 1957. GM 1982. Argentine champion 1956, 1957, 1962, 1965, 1969, 1973, 1974.

Sanz Aguado, José b. 20 Nov 1907 Barcelona. d. 14 Dec 1969 Madrid Spanish champion 1943.

Sanz Alonso, Francisco Javier b. 13 Dec 1952 Avila IM 1977. Spanish champion 1973.

Sarapu, Ortvin b. 22 Jan 1924 Narva IM 1966. New Zealand champion 1951 – 2, 1952 – 3, 1953 – 4, 1954 – 5, 1959 – 60, 1960 – 1, 1965 – 6, 1966 – 7, 1968 – 9 (joint), 1969 – 70, 1972 – 3, 1973 – 4, 1976 – 7, 1978 – 9, 1979 – 80 (joint), 1980 – 81 (joint).

Sarén, Ilkka Juhani b. 16 May 1940 Helsinki Finnish champion 1971.

Sathe, Bhagyashree Vasantrao b. 14 Aug 1961 Sangli, India British women's champion =1st 1984 but lost play-off.

Saunders see Pritchard

Saurén, Jørgen Norwegian champion 1935.

Savon, Vladimir Andreyevich b. 26 Sep 1940 Chernigov IM 1967. GM 1973. USSR champion 1971. Ljubljana-Portorož 1977 =2.

Sawyer, Joseph b. 1 Dec 1874 Three Rivers. d. 1 Mar 1965 Montreal Canadian champion 1908 – 9.

Sax, Gyula *b. 18 Jun 1951 Budapest* IM 1972. GM 1974. Hungarian champion 1976, 1977 (joint). European junior champion 1971–2. Amsterdam 1979 =1.

Schaufelberger, Heinz *b. 19 Nov 1947* Swiss champion 1971, 1972.

Scheffold, Maria *b. 1912. d. 1970 Wangen* German women's champion 1960.

Schlechter, Carl *b. 2 Mar 1874 Vienna. d. 27 Dec 1918 Budapest* Challenger 1910. German champion 1900 (joint), 1904 (joint), 1910.

Schmaus, Adolf *b. 1906* German correspondence champion 1973.

Schmid, Lothar Maximilian Lorenz *b. 10 May 1929 Radebeul* IM 1951. GM 1959. GMC 1959. World correspondence championship 1959 =2. German correspondence champion 1952.

Schmidt, Paul Felix *b. 20 Aug 1916 Narva. d. 11 Aug 1984 Allentown, USA* IM 1950. German champion 1941. Estonian champion 1936, 1937.

Schmidt, Wlodimierz *b. 10 Apr 1943 Poznań* IM 1968. GM 1976. Polish champion 1971, 1974, 1975, 1981 (joint).

Schneider, Attila *b. 14 Apr 1955 Budapest* IM 1984. Hungarian champion 1982 (joint).

Schneider, Lars-Åke *b. 10 Jul 1955 Stockholm* IM 1976. Swedish champion 1979, 1982, 1983.

Schoisswohl, Gertrude Women's world correspondence championship 1972 2.

Scholl, Eduard Cornelis *b. 17 Oct 1944 Leeuwarden* Netherlands champion 1970.

Schöneberg, Manfred *b. 6 Jul 1946 Miltitz* East German champion 1972.

Schönherr, Helmut *b. 24 Jun 1929 Ehrenfriedersdorf* IMC 1975. German correspondence champion 1960.

Schubert, František *b. 27 Apr 1894 Ml. Boleslav* Czech champion 1919.

Schüssler, Harry *b. 24 Jun 1957 Malmö* IM 1977. Swedish champion 1976, 1978 (joint).

Schuster, Mischu Josev *b. Czechoslovakia* Irish champion 1952.

Schutz, Ingemar Swedish correspondence champion 1978.

Schwartzmann, P (France). Women's world championship challenger 1933, 1939.

Schwarzbach, Wilhelm Austrian champion 1963.

Scott, Roland Henry Vaughan *b. 25 Mar 1888 Barnes. d. 10 Jan 1953 Monte Carlo* British champion 1920.

Sefc, Ján *b. 10 Dec 1924* Czech champion 1955.

Segal, Alexandru Sorin *b. 4 Oct 1947 Bucharest* IM 1977. Brazilian champion 1974 (joint), 1978.

Seimeanu, Petre *b. 26 Nov 1917 Bucharest* Romanian champion 1943.

Seirawan, Yasser *b. 24 Mar 1960 Damascus.* IM 1979. GM 1980. Candidate 1985. World junior champion 1979. Bad Kissingen 1981 =2. London 1982 3. Mar del Plata 1982 =3.

Sellos, Didier *b. 20 Feb 1957 Paris* IM 1983. French champion 1979 (joint).

Semyenova, Lydia Konstantinovna *b. 22 Nov 1951* WIM 1976. WGM 1982. USSR women's champion 1978 (joint).

Semyenova, Olga Izmailovna *b. 9 Sep 1911 St Petersburg. d. 1970 Leningrad* USSR women's champion 1934, 1936.

Semyenyuk, Alexander Andreyevich *b. 10 Sep 1952* USSR correspondence champion 1977.

Seni, Pietro *b. 1841 Rome. d. Dec 1909* Italian champion 1875.

Seret, Jean-Luc *b. 14 Sep 1951 Rouen* IM 1982. French champion 1981 (joint), 1984, 1985 (after play-off).

Sergeant, Edward Guthlac *b. 3 Dec 1881 Gateshead. d. 16 Nov 1961 Kingston-on-Thames* London champion 1951.

Sergeyev, Alexander Sergeyevich *b. 1897. d. 1970* Moscow champion 1924–5.

Shannon, A M S (Ireland). Women's world championship challenger 1935, 1937.

Shaw, Joseph William *b. 1834 Huddersfield. d. 25 Feb 1897 Montreal* Canadian champion 1881.

Shaw, Terrey Ian *b. 12 Oct 1946 Sydney* IM 1981. Australian champion 1977–8.

Shephard, Chris C W IMC 1984. British correspondence champion 1978, 1979 (joint).

Shishkin, Vladimir Vasilyevich *b. 29 Jan 1938* Leningrad champion 1960.

Shocron, Rubén *b. 20 Feb 1921 Buenos Aires* Argentine champion 1952.

Short, Nigel David *b. 1 Jun 1965 Leigh* IM 1980. GM 1984. Candidate 1985. British champion 1984. =1st 1979 but lost tie-break. Petit Prix (UK) 1978, 1983. Wijk aan Zee 1986 1. London 1986 =2.

Short, Philip Michael *b. 15 May 1960* Irish champion 1981. Equal 1st 1982 but lost on tie-break.

Short, Robert *b. 14 Apr 1844 Sherbrooke. d. 21 Aug 1927 Huntingdon, Quebec* Canadian champion 1890.

Showalter, Jackson Whipps *b. 5 Feb 1860 Minerva. d. 5 Feb 1935 Lexington* USA champion 1888, 1890, 1891, 1895, 1906.

Shul, Marta Ivanovna *b. 25 Mar 1949 Lvov* WIM 1972. WGM 1976. USSR women's champion 1972.

In January 1985 the first match was played between the current British and USA champions, with Alburt, on home ground, slight favourite. Short (left) won six games, the other two being drawn. (J. Franklin Campbell)

Siedeberg, Franz Vaughan *b. Oct 1869 Otago* New Zealand champion 1891–2, 1892–3.

Siegheim, Bruno Edgar *b. 24 May 1875 Berlin. d. 5 Nov 1952 Johannesburg* South African champion 1906 (after play-off), 1912.

Sigurjónsson, Gudmundur *b. 25 Sep 1947 Reykjavik* IM 1970. GM 1975. Icelandic champion 1965, 1968, 1972.

Sikora, Bozena *b. 18 Apr 1960 Bielsko Biala* WIM 1985. European women's junior champion 1977.

Silberman, H Romanian champion 1935.

Silva Sánchez, Carlos *b. 19 Jun 1944 San Fernando* Chilean champion 1969 (after play-off), 1971, 1974, 1975, 1976.

Simagin, Vladimir Pavlovich *b. 21 Jun 1919 Moscow. d. 25 Sep 1968 Kislovodsk* IM 1950. GM 1962. IMC 1965. USSR correspondence champion 1964. Moscow champion 1947 (after play-off), 1956 (joint), 1959. Moscow 1966 3.

Sirkiä, Mauri Olavi *b. 18 Jul 1947 Kaarina* Finnish champion 1969.

Skarp, Gunnar *b. Jul 1901 Göteborg. d. 6 Jan 1955 Göteborg* Swedish champion 1933 (joint).

Skjönsberg, Catharina (Norway). Women's world champion challenger 1935.

Sklyarov, Fedor Ivanovich *b. 1910. d. 1972* Leningrad champion 1943.

Sköld, Kristian *b. 26 Sep 1911 Stockholm* Swedish champion 1949, 1950, 1959, 1963.

Skrobek, Ryszard *b. 4 Jul 1951 Oleśnica* IM 1977. Polish champion 1977.

Sliwa, Bogdan *b. 4 Feb 1922 Wieliczka* IM 1953. Polish champion 1946, 1951, 1952 (after play-off), 1953, 1954 (after play-off), 1960.

Sloth, Jørn *b. 5 Sep 1944 Sjørring* IMC 1973. GMC 1978. World correspondence champion 1980. European junior champion 1963–4 (joint).

Small, Vernon A *b. 18 Jul 1954 England* New Zealand champion 1979–80 (joint), 1980–1 (joint), 1981–2, 1984–5.

Smejkal, Jan *b. 22 Mar 1946 Lanskroun* IM 1970. GM 1972. Czech champion 1973, 1979. Sochi 1973 =3. Wijk aan Zee 1975 3. Amsterdam 1979 =3.

Smit, Anatolij *b. 2 Sep 1941 Pskov* Latvian champion 1969, 1975 (both joint).

Smith, Magnús Magnússon *b. 10 Sep 1869 Iceland. d. 12 Sep 1934 Titusville* Canadian champion 1899, 1904, 1906.

Smith, Olle *b. 22 Feb 1915* Swedish correspondence champion 1951, 1956.

Smyslov, Vasily Vasiliyevich *b. 24 Mar 1921 Moscow* GM 1950. World champion 1957–8. Challenger 1948, 1954. Candidate 1950, 1959, 1965, 1983, 1985. USSR champion 1949 (joint). Moscow champion 1938 (joint), 1942, 1944–5. Moscow 1956 =1. Moscow 1959 = 1. Moscow 1967 =2. Rovinj-Zagreb 1970 =2. Moscow 1971 3. Teesside 1975 2. Leningrad 1977 2. Moscow 1981 =2.

Sokolov, Andrey Y *b. 20 Mar 1963* IM 1982. GM 1984. Candidate 1985. World junior champion 1982. USSR champion 1984. Moscow champion 1981 (joint). Novi Sad 1984 =2.

Sokolov, Sergei Mironovich *b. 17 Feb 1937 Moscow* IMC 1982. USSR correspondence champion 1968.

Solin, Hugo Ilmari *b. 19 Sep 1905 Reval. d. 20 Jun 1976 Helsinki* Finnish champion 1945.

163

Karpov & Kasparov

Karpov became world champion in an unfortunate way — default — because Fischer did not defend his title. However his unequalled success in his very active career as champion shows how worthy he was. In 33 tournaments he was first 28 times (5 of them shared) and at worst =4th). Of his 405 games in these events he lost only 18.

Karpov defended his title twice against the man who, in a sense, gave it to him in the first place. In the Candidates final, 1974, he defeated Korchnoi by 3 – 2 with 19 draws to become challenger. By 1978 Korchnoi had defected and his hostility to the Soviet regime inspired him during another epic struggle against Karpov which he lost by the odd game (6 – 5 with 21 draws).

After their Candidate's match Karpov lost 4 kilos of his total 52. Their 1978 encounter was even more trying for him, not merely because he only just scraped home, but because of the off-stage antics. Korchnoi said that a hypnotist, Zukhar, had been planted in the audience to influence him and responded by having two members of a religious sect, Ananda Marga, sitting in lotus position near the Soviet delegation. As the pair were on bail charged with attempted murder, this created a touch of panic.

The 1982 match was less tense, partly because Korchnoi was less hostile, and Karpov won 6 – 2 with 10 draws, giving a career record of +19 =54 −13 in his favour. Korchnoi's wife and son were allowed to leave the USSR.

Karpov had been a pupil of Botvinnik and so had his new rival Kasparov. After his only game with Fischer, at the 1962 Olympiad, Botvinnik published an analysis of the endgame showing that a draw was the right result. In his famous book *My 60 Memorable Games*, Fischer took the analysis further to show a win. Botvinnik then gave this analysis to his pupils and 13-year-old Kasparov demonstrated the draw.

Karpov, slim, reserved, ever-polite, once again faced a lively and somewhat indiscreet

Karpov has a nail-biting finish. (Stephane Bureau)

opponent when Kasparov eventually became challenger. What happened was unprecedented. After eight games Karpov had 4 wins to nil and then followed a record series of 17 consecutive draws. Karpov won the next game to need only one more victory, but three months later he still had not clinched it, was on the verge of physical collapse, and Kasparov had won three games.

It may be years before the full truth is known about what happened next. Having become easily the longest title match, it was halted, setting up a third record. The majority of fans thought that, although he still had a two-point advantage, the decision favoured Karpov because he was in the equivalent condition to a boxer on the ropes.

The replay was limited to 24 games. Kasparov's victory left the lifetime score between the two as 8 wins each and 59 draws (including 3 draws from tournaments). By the time this book appears they will have played a return match, and who knows, the loser could be the next challenger!

Larsen, in 1984, toasting the winner of the forthcoming world championship match. (Reproduced by courtesy of B.T. Batsford)

If I pretend he's not there will he go away? Kasparov and Karpov. (Reproduced by courtesy of B.T. Batsford)

Solmanis, Zigfrid *b. 9 Jul 1913 Riga. d. 6 Sep 1984 Jurmala* Latvian champion 1947.

Solomon, Stephen John *b. 24 Jul 1963 Melbourne* Australian champion 1983 – 4 (joint).

Soloviev, Vladimir Alexandrovich *b. 22 Feb 1928* Moscow champion 1954.

Sosonko, Gennadi *b. 18 May 1943 Troitsk* IM 1974. GM 1976. Netherlands champion 1973, 1978 (joint). Geneva 1977 =3. Wijk aan Zee 1979 =2. Amsterdam 1980 3. Wijk aan Zee 1981 =1. Tilburg 1982 =3.

Southall, Zbyzska *b. Poland d. Wales* Welsh women's champion 1964, 1966, 1967, 1968, 1969 (joint), 1971.

Souza Mendes, João de *b. 23 Jul 1892 Portugal. d. Jul 1969 Rio de Janeiro* Brazilian champion 1925, 1928, 1929, 1930, 1943, 1954, 1958.

Spassky, Boris Vasliyevich *b. 30 Jan 1937 Leningrad* IM 1953. GM 1955. World champion 1969 – 72. Challenger 1966. Candidate 1956, 1974, 1977, 1980, 1985. World junior champion 1955. USSR champion 1961, 1973. Leningrad champion 1959, 1961 (joint). Moscow 1959 =1. Belgrade 1964 1. Santa Monica 1966 1. Winnipeg 1967 =3. Leiden 1970 1. Sochi 1973 2. Bugojno 1978 =1. Baden 1980 =1. Linares 1983 1. Nikšić 1983 =3. Chess Oscar 1968, 1969.

Speelman, Jonathan Simon *b. 2 Oct 1956 London* IM 1978. GM 1980. British champion 1978, 1985.

Spens, Walter Cook *b. 1 Feb 1842 Glasgow. d. 15 Jul 1900 Edinburgh* Scottish champion 1894.

Spielmann, Rudolf *b. 5 May 1883 Vienna. d. 20 Aug 1942 Stockholm* Nordic champion 1919. German champion 1927. St Petersburg 1909 =3. San Sebastián 1912 =2. Berlin 1928 3.

Spiridinov, Nikolai *b. 28 Feb 1933* IM 1970. GM 1979. Bulgarian champion 1969 (after play-off).

Spraggett, Kevin Berry *b. 10 Nov 1954 Montreal* IM 1975. GM 1985. Candidate 1985. Commonwealth champion 1984 (joint), 1985 (joint). Canadian champion 1984.

Sprega, Luigi *b. 1829 Rome. d. 2 Feb 1887 Rome* Italian champion 1878.

Štadler, Tereza *b. 28 Sep 1936 Subotica* WIM 1966. WGM 1977. Yugoslav women's champion 1964, 1973 (joint).

Staehelin, Adolf *b. 5 Apr 1901 Basel. d. 30 May 1965 Zurich* Swiss champion 1927.

Ståhlberg, Anders Gideon Tom *b. 26 Jan 1908 Surte. d. 26 May 1967 Leningrad* GM 1950. Candidate 1950, 1953. Swedish champion (match) 1929, (tournament) 1927 (joint), 1932, 1939. Nordic champion 1928, 1938, and (joint) 1939.

Staunton, Howard *b. 1810 Westmorland. d. 22 Jun 1874 London.*

Stean, Michael Frank *b. 4 Sep 1953 London* IM 1975. GM 1977. British champion =1st 1974 but lost play-off.

Steedman, S M Scottish women's champion 1951, 1959, and twice jointly – 1956, 1969.

Stein, Georg *b. 17 Apr 1909* East German champion 1951.

Stein, Leonid Zakharovich *b. 12 Nov 1934 Kamenets-Podolsk. d. 4 Jul 1973 Moscow* IM 1961. GM 1962. USSR champion 1963 (joint), 1965 (joint), 1966 – 7. Yerevan 1965 =2. Moscow 1967 1. Moscow 1971 =1.

Steiner, Herman *b. 15 Apr 1905 Dunajská Streda. d. 25 Nov 1955 Los Angeles* IM 1950. USA champion 1948.

Steiner, Lajos *b. 14 Jun 1903 Oradea. d. 22 Apr 1975 Sydney* IM 1950. Hungarian champion 1931, 1936. Australian champion 1945, 1946, 1946 – 7, 1952 – 3, 1958 – 9, and also 1st 1936 – 7 (*hors concours*).

Steinitz, William *b. 17 May 1836 Prague. d. 12 Aug 1900 New York* World champion 1886 – 94. Challenger 1897. Vienna 1882 =1. London 1883 2. St Petersburg 1895 – 6 2.

Stekel Grunberg, Moisés *b. 1 Oct 1936 Santiago* Chilean champion 1958.

Stenborg Åke *b. 27 Feb 1926 Eskilstuna* Swedish champion 1956.

Sterner, Björn-Olof *b. 29 Sep 1914 Norrköping. d. 30 Sep 1968 Stockholm* Nordic champion 1957.

Stevenson, Agnes (née Lawson) *d. 20 Aug 1935 Poznan* Women's world championship challenger 1927, 1930, 1931. British women's champion 1920 (after play-off), 1925, 1926, 1930 (after play-off). =1st 1908 (as Lawson), 1913 and 1932 but lost play-offs.

Stewart, A M British correspondence champion 1974, 1979 (joint), 1980.

Stibaner, Ottilie Hedwig *b. 17 Apr 1908 Frankfurt. d. 23 May 1972 Frankfurt* German women's champion 1965.

St John, E (England). Women's world championship challenger 1937.

Stöffels, E W (Belgium). Women's world championship challenger 1939.

Stoltz, Gösta *b. 9 May 1904 Stockholm. d. 25 Jul 1963 Stockholm* IM 1950. GM 1954. Swedish champion (tournament) 1927 (joint), 1928, 1951, 1952, 1953. Nordic champion 1947 (joint).

Strachstein, J London champion 1933.

Strautmanis, August *b. 11 Jul 1907.* Latvian champion 1948 (after play-off).

Strehle, Ernst Swiss champion 1946.

Stronach, Bernard Henry Newman *b. c.1880. d. 21 Jul 1962* London champion 1934 (after play-off).

Struner, Philipp *b. c.1934 Kocevje. d. 15 Dec 1966 Vienna* Austrian champion 1965.

Stupica, Janez *b. 11 Mar 1935 Ljubljana* Yugoslav champion 1968 (joint).

Stupina, Yelena *b. 17 Apr 1958 USSR* European women's junior champion 1981.

Şuba, Mihai *b. 1 Jun 1947 Bucharest* IM 1975. GM 1978. Romanian champion 1980, 1981, 1986.

Sully, David John *b. Jun 1947 Cardiff* Welsh champion 1966, 1979 (joint).

Sultan Kahn, Malik *b. 1905 Mittha Tawana, Punjab. d. 25 Apr 1966 Sarggodha, Pakistan* British champion 1929, 1932, 1933.

Sundberg, Bertil *b. 7 Jul 1907 Mariehäll. d. 20 Jul 1979 Stockholm* Swedish correspondence champion 1938, 1943, 1947.

Sunnucks, Patricia Anne *b. 21 Feb 1927* WIM 1954. British women's champion 1957, 1958 (after play-off), 1964. =1st 1975 but lost play-off.

Sunie Neto, Jaime *b. 2 May 1957 Curtiba* IM 1980. Brazilian champion 1976, 1977, 1979, 1980, 1981, 1982.

Suttles, Duncan *b. 21 Dec 1945 San Francisco* IM 1967. GM 1973. GMC 1982. Canadian champion 1969.

Sutton, Richard John *b. 23 Sep 1938* New Zealand champion 1962–3 (after play-off), 1970–1, 1971–2.

Svedenborg, Paul Norwegian champion 1966, 1967.

Svensson, Sven Johan *b. 5 Aug 1838 Brandsta. d. 4 Jan 1906 Ostraby* Nordic champion 1897.

Svenson, Ulf *b. 19 Feb 1940* Swedish correspondence champion 1977.

Sveshnikov, Yevgeny Ellinovich *b. 11 Feb 1950 Cheliabinsk* IM 1975. GM 1977. Moscow champion 1983 (joint). Wijk aan Zee 1981 =3.

Swanson, Stephen Scottish champion 1975 (joint).

Swiderski, Rudolf *b. 28 Jul 1878 Leipzig. d. 12 Aug 1909 Leipzig* German champion 1904 (joint).

Synnewaag, S (Norway). Women's world championship challenger 1927.

Szabó, László *b. 19 Mar 1917 Budapest* GM 1950. Candidate 1950, 1953, 1956. Hungarian champion 1935, 1937, 1946, 1950(2), 1952, 1954, 1959 (after play-off), 1967–8. Dallas 1957 =3. Hilversum 1973 =1.

Szathmary, Iolanda Romanian women's champion 1950.

Szmetan, Jorge C *b. 26 May 1950 Buenos Aires* IM 1976. Argentine champion 1976.

Sznapik, Aleksander *b. 10 Feb 1951 Warsaw* IM 1977. Polish champion 1976, 1980, 1981 (joint), 1983, 1984.

Taimanov, Mark Yevgeniyevich *b. 7 Feb 1926 Kharkov* IM 1950. GM 1952. Candidate 1953, 1971. USSR champion 1956 (after play-off). Leningrad champion 1948, 1950, 1951, 1961 (joint), 1973. Latvian champion 1949. Moscow 1956 3. Wijk aan Zee 1981 =3.

Tal, Mikhail *b. 9 Nov 1936 Riga* GM 1957. World champion 1960–1. Candidate 1962, 1968, 1980, 1985. USSR champion 1957, 1958, 1967 (joint), 1972, 1974 (joint), 1978 (joint). Latvian champion 1953, 1965. Bled 1961 1. Budva 1967 =2. Moscow 1967 =2. Sochi 1973 1. Wijk aan Zee 1976 =3. Leningrad 1977 =1. Montreal 1979 =1. Sochi 1982 1. Titograd 1984 3.

Tan, Hiong Liong *b. 20 Aug 1938* IM 1963. Netherlands champion 1961.

Tarjan, James Edward *b. 22 Feb 1952 Pomona* IM 1974. GM 1976.

Tarnowski, Alfred *b. 3 Mar 1917 Lwów* Polish champion 1961.

Tarrasch, Siegbert *b. 5 Mar 1862 Breslau. d. 17 Feb 1934 Munich* Challenger 1908. German champion 1889, 1892, 1894.

Tartakower, Saviely Grigoryevich *b. 21 Feb 1887 Rostov-on-Don. d. 5 Feb 1956 Paris* GM 1950. Polish champion 1935, 1937. French champion 1953 (after play-off).

Tatai, Stefano *b. 23 Mar 1938 Rome* IM 1966. Italian champion 1962, 1965, 1967, 1970, 1971, 1974, 1977, 1979, 1983.

Taulbut, Shaun Mark *b. 11 Jan 1958 Portsmouth* IM 1977. European junior champion 1977–8.

Taylor, Alice Scottish women's champion 1909, 1911, 1913–14.

Tempone, Marcelo Javier *b. 6 Sep 1962* IM 1980. World under-16 champion 1979.

Teodorescu, Margareta *b. 13 Apr 1932 Bucharest* WIM 1964. Emeritus WGM 1985. Romanian women's champion 1959, 1968, 1974.

Teschner, Rudolf *b. 16 Feb 1922 Potsdam* IM 1957. East German champion 1948. West German champion 1951.

Thiellement, André *b. 1906. d. 20 Feb 1976* French champion 1962, 1963.

Thierry, Hélène (later Laurent-Lund) *b. 15 Oct 1910 Switzerland. d. 20 Nov 1973* Women's world championship challenger 1935. Danish women's champion 1935. =1st 1937 (as Laurent-Lund) but lost play-off.

Thipsay, Praveen M *b. 12 Aug 1959* Commonwealth champion 1985.

Thomas, Sir George Alan *b. 14 Jun 1881 Istanbul.
d. 23 Jul 1972 London* IM 1950. British champion
1923, 1934. London champion 1946.

Thomsen, F Danish champion 1921.

Thomson, Alexander Aird *b. 20 Feb 1917
Glasgow* Scottish champion 1951. His mother
(FFT) and wife (SMT) were both Scottish
champions.

Thomson, Craig S M *b. 27 Aug 1963* Scottish
champion 1984 after play-off.

Thomson, Florence Frankland *b. 1886 Glasgow.
d. 2 Jul 1939 Glasgow* Women's world championship challenger 1937. Scottish women's champion
1928 – 9, 1930, 1932, 1932 – 3, 1933 – 4, 1936 – 7.

Thomson, J F *d. c.Jun 1933* Scottish women's
champion 1930 – 1.

Thomson, Susan Mary *b. 6 Aug 1938* Scottish
women's champion 1965.

Thorbergsson, Freysteinn *b. 12 May 1931* Nordic
champion 1965. Icelandic champion 1960.

Thorsteinsson, Björn *b. 7 Jan 1940* Icelandic
champion 1967, 1975.

Thorvaldsen, Einar Icelandic champion 1928,
1940.

Thrift, W E Irish champion =1st 1926 but seems to
have lost play-off.

Tiemeyer, Horst *b. 1936* German correspondence
champion 1971.

Tiller, Bjørn *b. 16 Jan 1959 Oslo* IM 1982.
Norwegian champion 1983.

Timman, Jan Hendrik *b. 14 Dec 1951
Amsterdam* IM 1971. GM 1974. Candidate 1985.
Netherlands champion 1974, 1975, 1976, 1978
(joint), 1980, 1981, 1983. Bad Lauterberg 1977 2.
Tilburg 1977 =3. Amsterdam 1978 1. Bugojno
1978 3. Nikšić 1978 =1. Tilburg 1978 2. Bled-
Portorož 1979 1. Amsterdam 1980 2. Buenos Aires
1980 2. Bugojno 1980 3. Tilburg 1980 3.
Amsterdam 1981 1. Las Palmas 1981 1. Tilburg
1981 =3. Wijk aan Zee 1981 =1. Mar del Plata
1982 1. Tilburg 1982 2. Bugojno 1984 1. Sarajevo
1984 =1. Amsterdam 1985 2. Reggio Emilia 1985
=2. Wijk aan Zee 1985 1.

Timofejeva, Lidija *b. 1906* Yugoslav women's
champion 1947 – 8, 1948, 1949 (joint).

Timperley, J British correspondence champion
1968.

Todorcević, Miodrag *b. 10 Nov 1940 Belgrade* IM
1977. French champion 1975.

Tolush, Alexander Kazimirovich *b. 1 May 1910
St Petersburg. d. 3 Mar 1969 Leningrad* IM 1950.
GM 1953. IMC 1965. Leningrad champion 1937
(joint), 1938, 1946, 1947 (joint).

Tonini (France). Women's world championship
challenger 1933.

Torán Albero, Román *b. 8 Oct 1931 Gijón* IM
1954. Spanish champion 1951, 1953.

Tordion, Serge Swiss champion 1949.

Torre, Eugenio *b. 4 Nov 1951 Illcilo City* IM
1972. GM 1974. Candidate 1983. Manila 1976 1.
Bugojno 1984 3.

Torre, Vittorio Italian champion 1892.

Toshev, Yury *b. 24 Dec 1907. d. 19 Apr 1974*
Bulgarian champion 1942, 1947 (joint).

Tóth, Béla *b. 19 Apr 1943 Budapest* IM 1974.
IMC 1978. Italian champion 1975, 1976, 1981(1),
1982, 1984.

Tranmer, Eileen Betsy *b. 5 May 1910 Scarborough.
d. 26 Sep 1983 Ticehurst* WIM 1950. Women's
world championship challenger 1949 – 50. British
women's champion 1947, 1949, 1953, 1961.

Trepat, D B (Argentina). Women's world
championship challenger 1939.

Trevelyan, John *b. 13 Mar 1948 Bridgend* Welsh
champion 1973, 1979 (both joint).

Treybal, Karel *b. 2 Feb 1885 Kotopeky. d. 2 Oct
1941 Prague* Czech champion 1907, 1921 (joint).

Trifunović, Petar *b. 31 Aug 1910 Dubrovnik.
d. 8 Dec 1980 Belgrade* IM 1950. GM 1953. Yugoslav champion 1945, 1946, 1947 (joint), 1952,
1961.

Tringov, Georgy Petrov *b. 7 Mar 1937 Plovdiv* IM
1962. GM 1963. Bulgarian champion 1963, 1981,
1985.

Tröger, Paul *b. 28 Jun 1913 Augsburg* West
German champion 1957.

Troianescu, Octav *b. 4 Feb 1916 Cernăuti. d. 8 Oct
1980 Bucharest* IM 1950. Romanian champion
1946, 1954, 1956, 1957, 1968.

Trompowsky, Octavio F *b. 30 Nov 1897 Rio de
Janeiro. d. 26 Mar 1984 Rio de Janeiro* Brazilian
champion 1939.

Tseitlin, Mark Danilovich *b. 23 Sep 1943
Leningrad* IM 1978. Leningrad champion 1975,
1976, 1978.

Tseitlin, Mikhail Semyenovich *b. 16 Jun 1947* IM
1977. Moscow champion 1976 (joint), 1977.

Tseshkovsky, Vitaly Valerianovich *b. 25 Sep 1944
Omsk* IM 1973. GM 1975. USSR champion 1978
(joint).

Tsvetkov, Alexander Kristov *b. 7 Oct 1914* IM
1950. Bulgarian champion 1938, 1940, 1945, 1948
(joint), 1950, 1951.

Tukmakov, Vladimir Borisovich *b. 15 Mar 1946
Odessa* IM 1970. GM 1972. Tilburg 1984 =2.
Moscow 1985 3.

Türn, Johannes *b. 1899* Estonian champion 1941
(joint), 1944 (joint).

Tylor, Sir Theodore Henry *b. 13 Apr 1900*

Bourneville. d. 23 Oct 1968 Oxford British correspondence champion 1932, 1933, 1934.

Tyroler, Alexandru *b. 19 Nov 1891* Romanian champion 1926, 1927, 1929.

Ubilava, Elizbar Elizbarovich *b. 27 Aug 1950 Tbilisi* IM 1978.

Udovčić, Mijo *b. 11 Sep 1920 Stara Jošava* IM 1957. GM 1952. Yugoslav champion 1963.

Uhlmann, Wolfgang *b. 29 Mar 1935 Dresden* IM 1956. GM 1959. Candidate 1971. East German champion 1955, 1958, 1964, 1968, 1975, 1976, 1981, 1985. Zagreb 1965 =1.

Umansky, Mikhail Markovich *b. 21 Jan 1952. Stavropol* USSR correspondence champion 1978.

Unni, Vasanti (née Khaldikar) WIM 1984. British women's champion 1984 (after play-off).

Unzicker, Wolfgang *b. 26 Jun 1925 Pirmasens* IM 1950. GM 1954. West German champion 1948, 1950, 1952, 1959, 1963, 1965 (joint), and the unique East and West championship 1953. Lugano 1970 =3.

Urzică, Aurel *b. 11 Nov 1952 Bucharest* IM 1980. Romanian champion 1974.

Uusi, Gunnar *b. 23 Jun 1931. d. Aug 1981* Estonian champion 1958, 1959, 1963, 1966, 1979.

Vaganyan, Rafael Artemovich *b. 15 Oct 1951 Yerevan* GM 1971. Candidate 1985. Nikšić 1978 3. Moscow 1985 2. Naestved 1985 =1.

Vaiser, Anatoly Volfovich *b. 5 Mar 1949 Alma Ata* IM 1982. GM 1985. Sochi 1982 =3.

Vaitonis, Paul *b. 15 Aug 1911 Uzpailai. d. 23 Apr 1983 Hamilton* IM 1952. Canadian champion 1951, 1957.

Vajda, Arpád *b. 2 May 1896 Rimavská Sobota d. 25 Oct 1967 Budapest* IM 1950. Hungarian champion 1928.

Van den Meyden, C H South African champion 1963 (joint).

Van der Sterren, Paul *b. 17 Mar 1956 Venlo* IM 1979. Netherlands champion 1985.

Van der Wiel, John C *b. 9 Aug 1959 Leiden* IM 1979. GM 1982. Netherlands champion 1984. European junior champion 1978 – 9. Wijk aan Zee 1982 =3. Sarajevo 1984 =3. Wijk aan Zee 1986 =2.

Van Riemsdijk, Herman Claudius *b. 26 Aug 1948 Tiel* IM 1978. Brazilian champion 1970, 1973.

Varjomaa, Taisto *b. 1 Dec 1939* Swedish correspondence champion 1979.

Vasyukov, Yevgeny Andreyevich *b. 5 Mar 1933 Moscow* IM 1958. GM 1961. Moscow champion 1955, 1958, 1960, 1962 (joint), 1972, 1978. Manila 1974 1.

Veingold, Aleksander *b. 10 Oct 1953* IM 1983. Estonian champion 1975 (joint).

Velat, Gloria Spanish women's champion 1950.

Velimirović, Dragoljub *b. 12 May 1942 Valjevo* IM 1972. GM 1973. Yugoslav champion 1970 (joint), 1975. Titograd 1984 =1.

Verlinsky, Boris Markovich *b. 8 Jan 1888 Bakhmut. d. 1950* IM 1950. USSR champion 1929. Moscow champion 1928.

Veröci-Petronic, Zsuzsa *b. 19 Feb 1949 Budapest.* WIM 1969. WGM 1978.

Vestøl, Aage *b. 23 Dec 1922 Areland* Norwegian champion 1949.

Vidmar, Milan *b. 22 Jun 1885 Ljubljana. d. 9 Oct 1962 Ljubljana* GM 1950. Yugoslav champion 1939. Nordic champion 1909. San Sebastián 1911 =2.

Vigil, M A de (Uruguay). Women's world championship challenger 1939.

Vilela, José Luis *b. 19 Mar 1953* IM 1977. Cuban champion 1977 (joint).

Villegas, Benito Higinio *b. 11 Jan 1877 Buenos Aires. d. 27 Apr 1952* Argentine champion 1922.

Viner, William Samuel *b. 5 Dec 1881 East Maitland. d. 27 Mar 1933 Sydney* Australian champion 1906, 1906 – 7, 1912 – 13, 1913, 1924 (after play-off).

Visier Segovia, Fernando *b. 3 Feb 1943 Madrid* Spanish champion 1968, 1972.

Vitolin, Alvis *b. 15 Jun 1946 Ventspils* IM 1984. Latvian champion 1973 (after play-off), 1976, 1977, 1978 , 1982, 1983, 1985 (joint).

Vladimirov, Boris Timofeyevich *b. 17 May 1929* IM 1964. Leningrad champion 1963.

Voellmy, Erwin *b. 9 Sep 1886 Herzogenbuchsee. d. 15 Jan 1951 Basel* Swiss champion 1911 (joint), 1920, 1922.

Vogt, Lothar Helmut *b. 17 Jan 1952 Görlitz* IM 1973. GM 1976. East German champion 1977, 1979.

Voiska, Margarita *3 Apr 1963 Sofia* WGM 1985.

Voitkevic, Aleksandr *b. 15 Jan 1963 Riga* Latvian champion 1981.

Voitsekh, Anatoly Pavlovich *b. 11 Nov 1937* USSR correspondence champion 1975.

Volovich, Anatoly Abramovich *b. 21 Sep 1936 Osipovichi* Moscow champion 1967.

Volpert, Larisa Ilinichna *b. 30 Mar 1926 Leningrad* WIM 1954. WGM 1977. USSR women's champion 1954, 1958 (joint), 1959.

Vukić, Milan *b. 19 Aug 1942 Sanski Most* IM 1967. GM 1975. Yugoslav champion 1970 (joint), 1971 (joint), 1974.

Vyzhmanavin, Alexei B *b. 1960* Moscow champion 1984.

Wade, Robert Graham *b. 10 Apr 1921 Dunedin*

IM 1950. British champion 1952, 1970. New Zealand champion 1943 – 4 (after play-off) 1944 – 5, 1947 – 8.

Wahlbohm, Magnus *b. 15 Apr 1945* Swedish champion 1974.

Wahltuch, Victor Lionel *b. 24 May 1875 Manchester. d. 27 Aug 1953 London* London champion 1935 – 6 (after play-off).

Wainwright, George Edward *b. 2 Nov 1861 Redcar. d. 31 Aug 1933 Keynsham* British champion (amateur) 1889.

Walbrodt, Carl August *b. 28 Nov 1871 Amsterdam. d. 3 Oct 1902 Berlin* German champion 1893 (joint).

Walker, David *b. 11 Sep 1954 Krugersdorp* South African champion 1977 (joint).

Walker, M A British correspondence champion 1973.

Walker, Susan Kathryn (now Arkell) *b. 28 Oct 1965* WIM 1985.

Walker, William Neish *b. c.1849. d. 8 Sep 1927 near Cupar* Scottish champion 1890, 1893.

Wallace, Albert Edward Noble *b. 16 Dec 1872 Antrim. d. 19 Mar 1928 Sydney* Australian champion 1893, 1895, 1896.

Walter, Max *b. 11 Feb 1896 Bratislava* Czech champion 1923.

Wardhaugh, Carrick *b. 1 Jan 1874 Bradford. d. 26 Sep 1930 Glasgow* Scottish champion 1914 – 5.

Wasnetsky, Ursula *b. 9 Oct 1931* German women's champion 1968.

Watson, Charles Gilbert Marriott *b. 22 Oct 1879 Buninyong. d. 5 Mar 1961 Melbourne* Australian champion 1922, 1930 – 1.

Watson, William Nicholas *b. 18 Apr 1962 Baghdad* IM 1982.

Webb, Simon *b. 10 Jun 1949 London* IM 1977. GMC 1983.

Weilbach, Frederik Immanuel *b. 28 Aug 1863 Copenhagen. d. 4 Dec 1937 Snekkersten* Danish champion 1919.

Welin, Mats Erik Thomas *b. 5 Sep 1959 Salö* IM 1984. Swedish correspondence champion 1982.

Wenman, Francis Percival *b. 6 May 1891 Croydon. d. 19 Mar 1972 Cardiff* Scottish champion 1920, (after play-off).

West, J E British correspondence champion 1929.

Westerinen, Heikki Markku Julius *b. 27 Apr 1944 Helsinki* IM 1967. GM 1975. Finnish champion 1965, 1966, 1968, 1970.

Weye Danish champion 1912.

Wexler, Bernardo *b. 1 Apr 1925 Bucharest* IM 1959. Argentine champion 1959.

Watson. (BCF)

Wheatcroft, George Shorrock Ashcombe *b. 29 Oct 1905* British correspondence champion 1935.

Wheelwright, Amy Eleanor *b. 15 Oct 1890. d. 8 Nov 1980 Watford* British women's champion 1931 (joint).

Whicher, W H British correspondence champion 1931.

Whiteley, Andrew John *b. 9 Jun 1947 Birmingham* European junior champion 1965 – 6.

Wibe, Terje Paul *b. 6 Oct 1947 Oslo* IM 1977. IMC 1982. Norwegian champion 1971.

Wikström, Bertil *b. 12 Feb 1912* Swedish correspondence champion 1968, 1970, 1981.

Wikström, Birger *b. 27 Feb 1917* Swedish correspondence champion 1957.

Williams, Arthur Howard *b. 11 Jun 1950 Pontyclun* British champion =1st 1974 but lost play-off. Welsh champion 1968 (joint), 1971, 1972, 1974, 1975, 1977, 1978 (joint), 1979 – 80, 1980 – 1, 1981 – 2, 1982 – 3 (joint), 1986.

Williams, C Beryl Welsh women's champion 1965 (joint).

Winawer, Szymon Abramowicz *b. 5 Mar 1838 Warsaw. d. 12 Jan 1920 Warsaw* German champion 1883. Vienna 1882 = 1.

Winter, William *b. 11 Sep 1898 Medstead. d. 17 Dec 1955 London* IM 1950. British champion 1935, 1936. London champion 1926, 1928 – 9, 1932, 1939, 1947.

Wirthensohn, Heinz *b. 4 May 1951 Basel* IM 1977. Swiss champion 1979, 1981.

Wise, M E Welsh champion 1957 (joint).

Wisker, John *b. 30 May 1846 Hull. d. 18 Jan 1884 Melbourne* British champion 1870, 1872, each time after play-off.

Witkowski, Stefan *b. 27 Sep 1931 Łódź* IM 1977. Polish champion 1959 (after play-off).

Wockenfuss, Klaus Gerd *b. 29 Aug 1951 Ratzeburg* West German champion 1976.

Wolf, Siegfried Reginald *b. 19 Dec 1867 Prague. d. 5 Jan 1951 Haifa* Austrian champion 1925 (joint).

Wolf-Kalmar, Paula *b. Mar 1881 Agram. d. 29 Sep 1931 Vienna* Women's world championship challenger 1927, 1930, 1931.

Wolpe, Clyde *b. 4 May 1961 Johannesburg* South African champion 1985 (joint).

Wolstenholme, J British correspondence champion 1941.

Wood, Baruch Harold *b. 13 Jul 1909 Sheffield* British correspondence champion 1945.

Wood, Gabriel *b. 23 Jun 1903. d. 5 Nov 1983 Dereham* British correspondence champion 1946, 1948 (joint). London champion 1945.

Wood, M E E see Clarke

Woodford, C British correspondence champion 1981.

Wright see Dobson

Yakovleva, Lora Grigoriyevna *b. 21 Apr 1932 Perm.* WIMC 1975. IMC 1977. Women's world correspondence champion 1977. In 1972 3rd, 1984 3rd.

Yanofsky, Daniel Abraham *b. 26 Mar 1925 Brody, Poland* IM 1950. GM 1964. British champion 1953. Canadian champion 1941, 1943, 1945 (joint), 1947, 1953 (joint), 1959, 1963, 1965.

Yates, Frederic Dewhurst *b. 16 Jan 1884 Leeds. d. 11 Nov 1932 London* British champion 1913, 1914 (after tie), 1921, 1926, 1928, 1931. =1st 1911 but lost play-off.

Yerhoff, Frank J *b. 8 May 1918 Regina* Canadian champion 1945 (joint).

Yordansky, Peter Konstantinovich *b. 1891. d. 1937* Moscow champion 1913.

Yrjölä, Jouni *b. 24 Oct 1959 Vilppula* IM 1984. Finnish champion 1985.

Yudasin, Leonid Grigoryevich *b. 8 Aug 1959 Leningrad* IM 1982. Leningrad champion 1984.

Yudovich, Mikhail Mikhailovich *b. 8 Jun 1911 Roslavl.* IM 1950. IMC 1961. GMC 1973. USSR correspondence champion 1966.

Yusupov, Artur Mayakovich *b. 13 Feb 1960 Moscow* IM 1977. GM 1980. Candidate 1985. World junior champion 1977. Vrbas 1980 =2. Sarajevo 1984 =3.

Zagorovsky, Vladimir Pavlovich *b. 29 Jun 1925 Voronezh* IMC 1964. GMC 1966. World correspondence champion 1965. In 1971 2nd, 1975 =3rd, 1980 2nd. Moscow champion 1952.

Zaitsev, Alexander Nikolayevich *b. 15 Jun 1935 Vladivostok. d. 31 Oct 1971 Vladivostok* IM 1965. GM 1967. USSR champion =1st 1968–9 but lost play-off.

Zaitsev, Igor Arkadyevich *b. 27 May 1938 Ramenskoe* IM 1970. GM 1976. Moscow champion 1969.

Zaitseva, Lyudmila Georgyevna *b. 10 Feb 1956 Voroshilov* WIM 1982.

Zannoni, Fermo *b. 10 Aug 1862 Solagna. d. 1 Feb 1896 Rio de Janeiro* Italian champion 1883, 1886.

Zapata Ramirez, Alonso *b. 22 Aug 1958 Colombia* IM 1980. GM 1984.

Zatulovskaya, Tatiana Yakovlevna *b. 8 Dec 1935 Baku* WIM 1961. WGM 1976. USSR women's champion 1960 (joint), 1962, 1963 (joint).

Zdanov, Igor *b. 27 Jul 1920 Cesvaine* Latvian champion 1943.

Zeitler, Hans World blind correspondence champion 1971–2, 1973–4, 1977–8.

Zhuravlev, Valery Ivanovich *b. 11 Dec 1938 Moscow* Latvian champion 1980.

Zichichi, Alvise *b. 4 Jul 1938 Milan* IM 1977. Italian champion 1985.

Zilber, Israel *b. 25 Jun 1933 Riga* Latvian champion 1958 (after play-off).

Zimmermann, Otto *b. 11 Sep 1892 Zurich. d. 24 Jul 1979* Swiss champion 1924.

Zinn, Lothar *b. 19 Mar 1938 Erfurt. d. 29 Feb 1980 Berlin* IM 1965. East German champion 1961, 1965.

Zita, František *b. 29 Nov 1909 Prague. d. 1 Oct 1977 Prague* IM 1950. Czech champion 1943 (joint).

Zobel, Leo *b. 28 Jan 1895 Nitre. d. 24 Apr 1962* Czech champion 1931.

Zóphróniasson, Pétur Icelandic champion 1913, 1914, 1915, 1916, 1917.

Zubarev, Nikolai Mikhailovich *b. 10 Jan 1894. d. 1 Jan 1951 Moscow* Moscow champion 1920–1, 1927, 1930.

Zuidema, Coenraad *b. 29 Aug 1942* IM 1964. Netherlands champion 1972. European junior champion 1962–3.

Zukertort, Johannes Hermann *b. 27 Sep 1842 Lublin. d. 20 Jun 1888 London* Challenger 1886. London 1883 1.

Zvorykina, Kira Alexeyevna *b. 29 Sep 1919 Nikolayev* WIM 1952. WGM 1977. Women's world championship challenger 1960. USSR women's champion 1951, 1953, 1956, 1957 (joint), 1958 (joint).

Zwaig, Arne *b. 6 Feb 1947 Oslo* IM 1975. Norwegian champion 1964, 1969.

Index

Results of events featured in this book are not indexed here but are summarized under individual names in the section on The Players, pages 128-171. Picture index begins on page 175.

abbreviations 6, 128
Adams 123
Albin, Adolf 125
Alekhine 9, 11, 100, 109, 120, 123, 125
Allgaier, Johann Baptist 8
all-play-all 6
Anderssen 8, 9, 11, 26, 36, 53
Andersson 80
Argentina 87+
Asian Cities 84
Asian team 84
Atwood, George 8
Australia 88
Austria 88+

Balkaniad 84
Barden 123
BCF 8, 90, 93
Belyavsky 80
Bilek 125
Bláthy 125
blindfold chess 125
Bogoljubow 11
Botvinnik 10, 11, 80, 120, 123, 124, 137, 145, 164
Bourdonnais 8, 11, 21, 26, 36
Brazil 89
Breyer 126
briefest world champion 123
British championship 89+
British Chess Problem Society (BCPS) 8
British correspondence chess 93
BCCA (British Correspondence Chess Association) 93
British Chess Federation (BCF) 8, 90, 93
British Postal Chess Federation (BPCF) 93
Bronstein 11, 120
Bruce, Ronald Mackay 125

Buckle 8
Bulgaria 94

cable match 84
Canada 95
candidate 6, 15+, 128
Canute 126
Capablanca 9, 11, 100, 152
Carew 124
Caze 8
challenger 6, 128
Chandler 80
checks 125
Chéron 125
Chigorin 11, 125
Chile 96
City championships 87
Clare Benedict 84
Commonwealth 82+
Composition 125
Cuba 96
Czechoslovakia 96+

Dadian 125
Dawson 125
De Moivre 7
Denmark 97+
Deschapelles 8
De Wendene 126
Djordjević, Radovan 124
Dostoyevsky 152

East Anglian CU 10
East Germany 101+
EEC team 81
Elo rating 6, 126, 128
Estonia 98
European cup 81
European junior 10, 82
European junior women 82
European team 10, 81
Euwe 9, 11, 109, 153

Fennelly 125
FIDE 6, 9, 10, 34, 109, 128, 153

fifty-move rule 6, 124
Filipowicz, Andrzej Zygmunt 124
Finland 98+
Fischer 10, 11, 80, 124, 145, 152+, 164
France 99
Fulk 125

Gaige 4, 37
Geller 80
Germany 99
Gligorić 80
Golombek 145
glossary 6
Grand Prix (UK) 94
Gunsberg 11

Harrwitz 36
Hoffer 53
Hort 80
Hübner 80
Hungary 102
Huon 126

ICCA (International Correspondence Chess Assoc) 34
ICCF 34
Iceland 102+
IFSB 9
International Correspondence Chess Federation 34
international tournaments 37+
Ireland 103+
Israel 104
Italy 104
Ivkov 80

Janowski 11

Karpov 10, 11, 80, 124, 145, 164
Kasparov 10, 11, 67, 80, 123, 164

Keeble   124
Keres   11, 80, 120, 125
Kissinger   153
knock-out   6
Knoppert   125
Kolisch   9
Koltanowski   9, 125
Korchnoi   11, 67, 80, 124,
   137, 145, 164
Kovacevic, Slobodan   124

Larsen, Bent   80
Larsen, Ingrid   123
Lasker   9, 11, 67, 123
Latvia   104+
Leningrad   105
Ljubojević   80
London   105+
London Chess League   8
longest game   124
longest problem   125
longest world champion   123
Löwenthal   36
Lucena   7

MacKenzie   125
marathon   125
Marshall   11, 67
Mashian   124
Mason   125
Matulović   80
McDonnell   8, 21, 26, 36
Menchik   125
Midland Counties CU   8
Miles   80, 124
milestones   7+
Mitropa Cup   84
mobility   125
Mongredien   125
Moreau   125
Morphy   8, 9, 11, 26+, 36+,
   53, 152
Moscow   106
most losses   125
most national
   championships   123
most titles at once   123
most wins   125
most world championships
   123
moves by one piece   125
Murshed   123

Najdorf   80

National championships
   87+
Netherlands   107
Neumann   125
New Zealand   108
Nimzowitsch   100
Nixon   152
Nordic Championship   83
Northern Counties CU   8
Norway   108, 110
Nunn   80
Nykopp   124

Olafsson   80
Oldest national champion
   123
Oldest world champion   123
Olympiads   9, 10, 29+, 123
Oscar   10, 35

Panno   124
Petrosyan   11, 80, 124, 145
Petrović, Nenad   125
Philidor, François-André
   Danican   7, 8, 11
Poland   110
Pollmächer, Herrmann   125
Polugayevsky   80
Portisch   80
Price   123
Prince John   126
problems   35, 125+

Rall   126
ranking   126+
rating   6, 126+
Razuvayev   80
Reichhelm   125
repetition   6
Reshevsky   11, 80, 120
Réti   125
Retrograde analysis   125
Reuben, Stewart   124
Ribli   80
Ristoja   124
Romania   110+
Romanishin   80
Rubinstein   100

Saint Amant   8, 26
Sämisch   125
Santos   124
Sarapu   123
Sarratt, Jacob Henry   8
Schlechter, Carl   11

Scotland   111+
Scottish Chess Association   9
Schürig, Richard   115
Seirawan   80
shortest game   124
Slater, James   152+
slowest move   124
Smederevac, Petar   124
Smyslov   11, 80, 120, 152
Sokolov   80
South Africa   114
Southern Counties CU   8
Spain   114+
Spassky   10, 11, 80, 152+
Stamma, Phillip   7
Staunton   8, 11, 26+, 36
Stein   80
Steinitz   9, 11, 53, 67, 123,
   125
Stepak   124
Sweden   115
Swiss system   6
Switzerland   116

Taimanov   80
Tal   11, 80, 123, 137
Tarrasch   9, 11, 67
telex Olympiad   10, 34
time   125
Timman   80
Tjing-tjin-joe   123
Torre   80
Trois   124
Troitsky   125
Tukmakov   80
Turk   7

Uhlmann   80
Ulf   126
USA   117
USSR   117+
USSR v Rest of World   80

Vaganyan   80
Van Gool   125
Verdoni   8
Vinje   125

Wales   121
Walker, George   21
Walker, William
   Greenwood   21
Watkinson   124
Welsh CU   10
Westerinen   125

West Germany   101
West of England CU   8, 123
women's Olympiad   10, 32
women's world
  championship   22+
world amateur
  championship   28
world championship   9, 11,
  12+
world championships for the
  blind   34
world chess composition   35
world computer
  championship   35

world correspondence
  championship   10, 34
world junior championship
  10, 25
world junior women's
  championship   10, 28
world problem solving
  championship   35
world team championship
  10, 28
world under-16
  championship   10, 28
world under-16 women's
  championship   28

world youth team
  championship   10, 34

youngest national champion
  123
youngest Olympiad player
  123
youngest world champion
  123
Yugoslavia   121+
Yusupov   80

Zukertort   9, 11, 53, 67
Zukhar   164

Illustrations

The colour pages are not numbered.

Adams   123, colour
Adorján   64, 75
Akhmilovskaya   129
Alburt   163
Alekhine   109
Anderssen   9
Andersson   81
Anderton   32

Bellin   colour
Belyavsky   65, 73, 80, 119
Bilek   83, 102
Bird   37
Blackburne   37
Bobotsov   49
Boleslavsky   118
Botvinnik   120
Browne   56

Capablanca   100
Chandler   32, 78
Chernin   82
Chiburdanidze   25
Chigorin   12
Cramling   135
Cruikshank cartoon   10

Damiano title page   48
Dlugy   25
Donner   107
Duncan Lawrie trophies
   colour

Englisch   37
Euwe   109

Fine   117
Fischer   152-3
Flear   79
Fox Talbot historical item   8

Gaprindashvili   24
Geller   17
Georgiev   95
Golombek   91
Grant   32
Gunsberg   37

Hamid   93
Hartston   92
Hebden   colour
Hort   50, 97
Hübner   81

Ioseliani   82
Ivanov   95
Ivkov   46

Jackson   colour

Karpov   14, 57, 80, 119, 164,
   165
Kasparov   20, 80, 119, 165,
   colour
Kavalek   54
Keene   83
Keres   118
Klinger   89
Kolisch   37
Korchnoi   19, 66, 81, 119,
   145, colour

Larsen   81, 165
Lasker   67
Ljubojević   55, 62, 81

Macdonnell   37
Mackenzie   37
Mason   37
Matanović   83
McNab   113, colour
Mestel   32, 93
Miles   60, 81
Morphy   36
Morse   83, 135
Motwani   113
Murshed   123

Nikolić   73
Nunn   32, 81, 83, 92

Olafsson   44

Paulsen   37
Penrose   91

Petrosyan   118, 145
Philidor   7
Pillsbury   39
Plaskett   94, colour
Polgar   87
Polugayevsky   18, 80
Portisch   75
Potter   37

Quinteros   83

Razuvayev   80, 83
Reshevsky   29
Reuben   93
Ribli   59, 81
Rivière   37
Rogers   88
Rojas   28
Romanishin   62, 80
Rosenthal   37

Sax   55
Schallopp   37
Schlechter   42
Schmid   152-3
Seirawan   71, 81
Short   32, 163
Smyslov   45, 63, 80, 120
Smyslov's father   63
Sokolov   80
Sosonko   57
Spassky   152-3
Speelman   32, 74, colour
Staunton   27
Steiner   117
Steinitz   37

Taimanov   118, 119
Tal   57, 78, 80, 137
Tarjan   83
Taulbut   colour
Timman   81
Torre   81
Tukmakov   80

Uhlmann   58

Vaganyan   76, 80
Van der Wiel   68, 73

Watson   170
Winawer   37

Yusupov   20, 70, 80, colour

Zukertort   37